Anti-Atlas

FRINGE

Series Editors
Uta Staiger, UCL European Institute, and
Peter Zusi, UCL School of Slavonic and
East European Studies

The FRINGE series explores the roles that complexity, ambivalence and immeasurability play in social and cultural phenomena. A cross-disciplinary initiative bringing together researchers from the humanities, social sciences and area studies, the series examines how seemingly opposed notions such as centrality and marginality, clarity and ambiguity, can shift and converge when embedded in everyday practices.

Uta Staiger is Associate Professor of European Studies and Director of the UCL European Institute.

Peter Zusi is Associate Professor of Czech and Comparative Literature at the UCL School of Slavonic and East European Studies.

Anti-Atlas

*Critical area studies from the
East of the West*

Edited by Tim Beasley-Murray,
Wendy Bracewell
and Michał Murawski

First published in 2025 by
UCL Press
University College London
Gower Street
London WC1E 6BT

Available to download free: www.uclpress.co.uk

Collection © Editors, 2025
Text © Contributors, 2025
Images © Contributors and copyright holders named in captions, 2025

Cover image: Jan Dziaczkowski, *Piccadilly Circus, London*, from the series *Keine Grenze*, 2008, collage, 123 × 148mm. © Aleksandra Bujnowska, Monika Klonowska, Julian Klonowski.

The authors have asserted their rights under the Copyright, Designs and Patents Act 1988 to be identified as the authors of this work.

A CIP catalogue record for this book is available from The British Library.

Any third-party material in this book is not covered by the book's Creative Commons licence. Details of the copyright ownership and permitted use of third-party material is given in the image (or extract) credit lines. Every effort has been made to identify and contact copyright holders and any omission or error will be corrected if notification is made to the publisher. If you would like to reuse any third-party material not covered by the book's Creative Commons licence, you will need to obtain permission directly from the copyright owner.

This book is published under a Creative Commons Attribution-NonCommercial 4.0 International licence (CC BY-NC 4.0), https://creativecommons.org/licenses/by-nc/4.0/. This licence allows you to share and adapt the work for non-commercial use providing attribution is made to the author and publisher (but not in any way that suggests that they endorse you or your use of the work) and any changes are indicated. Attribution should include the following information:

Beasley-Murray, T., Bracewell, W. and Murawski, M. (eds). 2025. *Anti-Atlas: Critical area studies from the East of the West*. London: UCL Press. https://doi.org/10.14324/111.9781800087811

Further details about Creative Commons licences are available at https://creativecommons.org/licenses/

ISBN: 978-1-80008-779-8 (Hbk)
ISBN: 978-1-80008-780-4 (Pbk)
ISBN: 978-1-80008-781-1 (PDF)
ISBN: 978-1-80008-782-8 (epub)
DOI: https://doi.org/10.14324/111.9781800087811

This book is dedicated to the memory of our dear colleague Philippa Hetherington (1984–2022), who contributed so much to our work.

Contents

List of figures — xi
List of contributors — xiii
Series editors' preface — xvii

Anti-Atlas: an introduction — 1
Tim Beasley-Murray, Wendy Bracewell and Michał Murawski

Part I: Continents and terrains — 27

1. Balkan Balkanologies (and their shifting cartographies) — 29
   Diana Mishkova

2. (Global) chaos — 35
   Joanna Kusiak

3. The children's republic — 39
   Diana Georgescu

4. The countryside – a matter of ruling class — 47
   Alexandra Urdea

5. Digital Eastern Europe? — 53
   Maciej Maryl

6. Dreamland (and its queer map) — 59
   Čarna Brković

7. The early modern Republic of Letters — 65
   Wendy Bracewell

8. Vadim Tsymburskiĭ's Great Limitrophe — 71
   Dimitrii Sidorov

9. *Greater Europe*: a travel guide — 79
   Nóra Veszprémi

10. Low earth orbit: a speculative ethnographer's guide — 87
    Victor Buchli

11	Flying a new flag: how Moscow hippies created a world without time and a land without borders *Juliane Fürst*	95
12	Nation-states of mind: radical geopolitical imagination *Ksenya Gurshtein*	103
13	*Oraşul viitorului*: beyond the Siliconisation of postsocialist Cluj *Erin McElroy*	113
14	Planet ppparadise: decondensing the social in the condition of wild capitalism *Michał Murawski*	121
15	Peripheristan *Francisco Martínez*	131
16	The plus one dimension *Katalin Cseh-Varga*	137
17	The Red Adriatic: the Global East in Trieste *Chiara Bonfiglioli*	147
18	The Second World: building (for) emancipatory futures *Daria Bocharnikova*	153
19	*Sharovarshchyna*: sonic contestations of Ukrainian wildness *Maria Sonevytsky*	161
20	Extracting the future: the socialist Anthropocene through artists' eyes *Maja Fowkes and Reuben Fowkes*	167
21	The stalked zone: late capitalist logics and state socialist models *Jonathan Bach*	173
22	Supercontinents and superdeep boreholes: area studies in three dimensions *Douglas Rogers*	179
23	When Yugoslavia was the Wild West *Natalie Koch*	187
24	*Zwischeneuropa*: mapmaking as image-making *Katarzyna Murawska-Muthesius*	197

Part II: Wandering critics   205

25   The accidental transnationalist: an autobiographical manifesto   207
Choi Chatterjee

26   Crni Srbi and Ron Holsey   213
Catherine Baker

27   Arthur Griffith and Hubert Butler: the rhetoric and inspection of historical parallels between Ireland and Central Europe   219
Aidan O'Malley

28   Krystyna Gryczełowska maps a moving Poland   225
Eliza Rose

29   The engineer as indispensable critic   231
Jelena Prokopljević

30   Il'f and Petrov   239
Lisa A. Kirschenbaum

31   *Komunistki*: Polish communist women   245
Agnieszka Mrozik

32   *Kosmopolitka*: an orphaned subject between home and abroad   251
Karolina Follis

33   The *Kraeved(ka)*: a portrait of the Soviet citizen scientist   257
Sofia Gavrilova

34   The 'last heroes' of perestroika (and their legacy in metamodernist Russia)   265
Maria Engström

35   Mediator sanitar   273
Charlotte Kühlbrandt and Mihai Surdu

36   The migration broker   281
Philippa Hetherington

37   Olga Brookman's everyday eyes: the Russian mail-order bride as ethnographer   287
Emily Curtin

38	Ovid in Tomis and the unreal space of literature *Tim Beasley-Murray*	295
39	Polish architects in the world socialist system *Łukasz Stanek*	301
40	Projectarians *Kuba Szreder*	309
41	Raja: the not-quite critical subject of Sarajevo irony *Stef Jansen and Nebojša Šavija-Valha*	315
42	Sherlock Holmes and his doppelganger: for an anti-atlas of world literature *Antonija Primorac*	321
43	Cartographies of Soviet childhood *Nataliya Tchermalykh*	329
44	TINA and Natasha: mapping exploitation after history's end *Jennifer Suchland*	341
45	Yardsticks and shillelaghs: Croatian migrants to Ireland *Rory Archer*	345
Index		351

List of figures

For ease of reading figures with small type, readers of the print edition can download the free ePDF from the UCL Press website and enlarge the view.

3.1	International child participants in distinctive folk garb or organisation uniforms posing at the international pioneer camp, Năvodari, Romania.	40
3.2	Page from a quiz meant to encourage children from various delegations to know each other better. Brochure used during the Camp of Nations, Danbury Park, Essex, August 1970.	44
8.1	Vadim L. Tsymburskiĭ at a conference in Moscow, 28 March 2008.	72
8.2	Tsymburskiĭ's Great Limitrophe: key areas.	73
9.1	Société Réaliste (Ferenc Gróf and Jean-Baptiste Naudy), *Greater Europe*, 2008–9.	81
9.2	Société Réaliste (Ferenc Gróf and Jean-Baptiste Naudy), *Superimposition of political frontiers at the turn of each century between year 0 and year 2000 on the European peninsula and its surroundings*, 2009.	83
9.3	Société Réaliste (Ferenc Gróf and Jean-Baptiste Naudy), *Spectral Aerosion*, 2011.	84
11.1	A reconstruction of the flag, by Debra Marlin, as exhibited by the Wende Museum, Los Angeles.	96
11.2	Ofelia installing the artworks by Volosy.	97
11.3	Volosy on the steps of the House of Culture.	98
12.1–2	Vitaly Komar and Alexander Melamid, *TransState*, 1977.	105–6
12.3	Yuri Albert, *Signpost I*, 1997, site-specific installation in Cetinje, Montenegro.	108
12.4	IRWIN, Passport of the NSK *State in Time*, issued to the author in 2014.	109
14.1	Selfies in Zaryadye, 2017.	125
14.2	Selfies on Hudson Yards, 2019.	126
14.3	Asocial meditation on The Tide, 2019.	127
16.1a–b	The first edition of the *Dimensionist Manifesto*, 1936.	138–9
16.2	Károly Tamkó Sirató after his return to Budapest in 1936.	141

16.3	Károly Tamkó Sirató: *Paris*, 1936. Electric poem (Dim. I.).	143
18.1	Haus der Statistik, view from the Otto-Braun Strasse and Karl-Marx-Allee intersection.	154
18.2	'Beat the Whites with the Red Wedge' (Klinom krasnym beĭ belykh!), a 1919 lithographic Soviet propaganda poster by El Lissitzky.	156
22.1	Palaeogeographic map of Earth ca. 260 million years ago, showing the supercontinent Pangaea during the Permian period of the Palaeozoic era.	181
22.2	*Pangaea Politica* by Massimo Pietrobon, 2012. An artist's arrangement of the countries of the twenty-first-century world into the approximate shape of the ancient supercontinent Pangaea.	184
23.1	The author, exercising her scepticism from an early age, and her brother in Tucson, Arizona (1989).	188
23.2	Screenshot from *The Treasure of Silver Lake*.	189
23.3	Screenshot from *The Treasure of Silver Lake*.	189
23.4	Screenshot from *The Treasure of Silver Lake*.	190
23.5	Screenshot from *The Treasure of Silver Lake*.	190
23.6	Rocks in Paklenica, Croatia.	191
23.7	Rocks in Monument Valley, Arizona.	191
23.8	Gojko Mitić as Chief Tokei-ihto in *The Sons of Great Bear*.	193
23.9	Winnetou and Old Shatterhand in *Winnetou – Part 1*.	194
24.1	Pawel Josef Šafářik, 'Slovanský zeměvid', in *Slovanský Národopis*.	199
24.2	R. W. Seton-Watson, 'The New Europe on a basis of Nationality', in *German, Slav and Magyar: A study in the origins of the Great War*.	200
39.1	Patterns of geographic deployment of members of the Association of Polish Architects during the Cold War.	304
43.1	Political map of the USSR with national costumes and flags of Soviet republics.	331
43.2	Viktoria Lomasko with banner: 'Imperial education leads to war', at a demonstration against the war between Russia and Ukraine, Moscow, 21 September 2014.	332
43.3	'Imperial education leads to war', banner by Viktoria Lomasko.	333
43.4	*Our Post-Soviet Land*, wall drawing by Viktoria Lomasko.	335
43.5	Viktoria Lomasko in front of her wall drawing *Our Post-Soviet Land*, in the exhibition *Die Neunte Kunst: Unwanted Stories*.	338

List of contributors

Rory Archer is Researcher at the Research Center for the History of Transformations, Vienna.

Jonathan Bach is Professor of Global Studies at The New School, in New York.

Catherine Baker is Reader in Twentieth-Century History at the University of Hull.

Tim Beasley-Murray is Associate Professor of European Thought and Culture at UCL.

Daria Bocharnikova is Visiting Scholar of Modernity and Society 1800–2000 at KU Leuven.

Chiara Bonfiglioli is Associate Professor in Contemporary History in the Department of Humanities at Ca' Foscari University, Venice.

Wendy Bracewell is Emeritus Professor at UCL, in the School of Slavonic and East European Studies.

Čarna Brković is Professor of Cultural Anthropology and European Ethnology at the University of Mainz.

Victor Buchli is Professor of Material Culture at UCL, in the Department of Anthropology.

Choi Chatterjee is Professor of History at California State University, Los Angeles.

Katalin Cseh-Varga is Hertha Firnberg Fellow at the Academy of Fine Arts, Vienna.

Emily Curtin is Teaching Assistant Professor in the Department of Anthropology at the University of North Carolina at Chapel Hill.

Maria Engström is Professor of Russian in the Department of Modern Languages at Uppsala University.

Karolina Follis is Senior Lecturer in Politics, Philosophy and Religion at Lancaster University.

Maja Fowkes is Co-founder of the Translocal Institute for Contemporary Art and Co-director of the Postsocialist Art Centre at the Institute of Advanced Studies, UCL.

Reuben Fowkes is Co-founder of the Translocal Institute for Contemporary Art and Co-director of the Postsocialist Art Centre at the Institute of Advanced Studies, UCL.

Juliane Fürst is Co-Head of the Department of the Leibniz Centre for Contemporary History at ZZF Potsdam.

Sofia Gavrilova is Senior Researcher in the Department of Cartography and Visual Communication at the Leibniz Institute for Regional Geography.

Diana Georgescu is Lecturer in Transnational/Comparative South-east European Studies at UCL School of Slavonic and East European Studies.

Ksenya Gurshtein is Curator of Modern and Contemporary Art at the Ulrich Museum of Art, Wichita State University, Kansas.

Philippa Hetherington (1984–2022) was Lecturer in Modern Eurasian History at UCL, in the School of Slavonic and East European Studies.

Stef Jansen is Professor of Social Anthropology at the University of Sarajevo, Bosnia and Herzegovina.

Lisa A. Kirschenbaum is Professor of History at West Chester University.

Natalie Koch is Professor of Geography and the Environment at Syracuse University, New York.

Charlotte Kühlbrandt is Research Associate in the Department of Population Health Sciences, King's College London.

Joanna Kusiak is Research Fellow in Urban Studies at King's College, Cambridge.

Francisco Martínez is a researcher on the WasteMatters ERC project at Tampere University.

Maciej Maryl is Assistant Professor at the Institute of Literary Research of the Polish Academy of Sciences.

Erin McElroy is Assistant Professor of Geography at the University of Washington.

Diana Mishkova is Professor of History and Director of the Centre for Advanced Study in Sofia, Bulgaria.

Agnieszka Mrozik is Associate Professor at the Institute of Literary Research of the Polish Academy of Sciences.

Katarzyna Murawska-Muthesius is Honorary Research Fellow at the School of Historical Studies, Birkbeck, University of London.

Michał Murawski is Associate Professor in Critical Area Studies at UCL, in the School of Slavonic and East European Studies.

Aidan O'Malley is Associate Professor in the Department of English Studies at the University of Rijeka, Croatia.

Antonija Primorac is Associate Professor in the Department of English Studies at the University of Rijeka, Croatia.

Jelena Prokopljević is Professor of Urban History at the Barcelona Architecture Center.

Douglas Rogers is Professor of Anthropology at Yale University.

Eliza Rose is Assistant Professor and Laszlo Birinyi Senior Fellow of Central European Studies at the University of North Carolina at Chapel Hill.

Nebojša Šavija-Valha is Program Development Manager and Researcher at the Nansen Dialogue Center in Sarajevo, Bosnia and Herzegovina.

Dimitrii Sidorov is Associate Professor of Geography at California State University, Long Beach.

Maria Sonevytsky is Associate Professor of Anthropology and Music, Bard College, New York.

Łukasz Stanek is Professor of Architectural History at the University of Michigan in Ann Arbor.

Jennifer Suchland is Associate Professor of Women's, Gender and Sexuality Studies at Ohio State University.

Mihai Surdu is Visiting Researcher in Science and Technology Studies at the University of Freiburg.

Kuba Szreder is Associate Professor at the Academy of Fine Arts in Warsaw, in the Department for Artistic Research and Curatorial Studies.

Nataliya Tchermalykh is Research and Teaching Fellow at the Centre for Children's Rights Studies at the University of Geneva.

Alexandra Urdea is an independent researcher.

Nóra Veszprémi is Honorary Research Fellow at the University of Birmingham and at Masaryk University, Brno.

Editorial Note

Transliteration of Cyrillic script follows the Library of Congress system.

Series editors' preface

The UCL Press FRINGE series presents work related to the themes of the UCL FRINGE Centre for the Study of Social and Cultural Complexity.

The FRINGE series is a platform for cross-disciplinary analysis and the development of 'area studies without borders'. 'FRINGE' is an acronym standing for Fluidity, Resistance, Invisibility, Neutrality, Grey zones, and Elusiveness – categories fundamental to the themes that the Centre supports. The oxymoron in the notion of a 'FRINGE *centre*' expresses our interest in (1) the tensions between 'area studies' and more traditional academic disciplines; and (2) social, political, and cultural trajectories from 'centres to fringes' and inversely from 'fringes to centres'.

The Anti-Atlas confronts one of the central questions underlying the FRINGE series: how to understand and practise a critical area studies. It represents a major intervention into current efforts to reconceive area studies by reflecting on the limitations of traditional cartographic logics and by revealing more fluid, flexible, or metaphorical understandings of what constitutes an 'area'. In doing so, the Anti-Atlas is aware that how one defines an 'area' brings with it a range of presuppositions about histories, identities, and power relations that – rather than being naturalised through neatly demarcated maps – need to be subject to critical questioning. Such questioning does not deny regional realities and difference in the name of an easy relativism. Rather, it explores the formative role that the observer brings to the identification and construction of 'region' – and that multiple such constructions are always possible. But the book is singularly attentive not just to the *what* but to the *how*. Deliberately and enjoyably 'undisciplined', its critical, creative, at times even playful engagement with area studies is also about reassessing – possibly disrupting – the very tone and mode of academic writing. Formally and substantively, then, the Anti-Atlas supports the aim of the FRINGE Centre to explore how the particularities of embedded knowledge can yield cognitive insights that are transferable to other contexts.

Uta Staiger and Peter Zusi

Anti-Atlas: an introduction
Tim Beasley-Murray, Wendy Bracewell
and Michał Murawski

This Anti-Atlas is an intervention into the scholarly and pedagogical field of area studies, a field that for too long has had a bad name. For scholars who think critically, questioning the basis of units of study, area studies has taken too much for granted. Area studies, according to these views, freezes the globe into artificially bounded regions that it sees as more or less self-evident. And, institutionally and through the notion of area-specific expertise, it polices their frontiers, usually from a position outside the region it studies. Area studies, it is argued, is an anachronistic, rigid and essentialist framework, unsuited to the realities of a fluid, pulsating, twenty-first-century world. In this scenario, practitioners of area studies function as the handmaidens of power, propping up a conception of the world that is divided into convenient blocks reflecting historical and geopolitical hierarchies, the legacies of orientalist, imperial and Cold-War imaginations and practice. Wittingly or unwittingly, area scholars supposedly spend their lives endowing national and supranational political, military or corporate projects with legitimacy and expertise.

Conceptions of area and operations of power often do form a mutually reinforcing nexus. This is clearly evident in the current war of aggression that Russia is waging in Ukraine. Behind all the arguments, that Putin and his ideologues make for their invasion of another sovereign state, lies an understanding of the way that the world is, or ought to be, divided. A critical approach to area studies can show that this war is, in part, an example of a national entity, which is at once *still*-imperial/*still*-colonial (non-decolonised) *and* (semi-)peripheral, uncritically projecting its understanding of its own area planetarily, in the guise of *Russkiĭ mir* (the Russian world). *Russkiĭ mir*, misunderstood as coterminous with the (also fraught and contested) notion of the 'post-Soviet space', is one of many imagined imperial Russias, Russia's desired backyard or sphere of influence. Accordingly, Ukraine, the whole territory from the Donbas to its western borders, is – according to the fascist logic of the *Russkiĭ mir* – an integral part of the world that was, is and always should be Russian, in a broad but immutable sense. For the logic of the Russian state, this conception of area is not simply to be policed in a metaphorical sense, but to be reclaimed and imposed with dreadful, indeed genocidal violence.

If power uses an understanding of area for its own violent purposes, as something that is not to be interfered with and that has a reality outside change, then area studies, in its traditional guise, plays a part in developing and legitimating these understandings. And in turn, area studies – through government, higher education policy, funding schemes and so on – is legitimated and supported by institutional power, with particular areas rising and falling in perceived importance relative to the political demands of the day. Partners in an uncomfortable, but mutually beneficial dance, power and area collude in more fundamental and deep-rooted ways than area studies practitioners are always happy to admit.

So what is to be done? Our goal is to disassociate area studies from the yoke of imperial visions and claims, Cold War securitisation, corporate consultancy and of course the legitimation of violence. We wish to show that area studies has longer, more varied, and more heterogenous histories than either its critics or its uncritical proponents claim. And we wish to indicate that it has a number of possible futures, whose direction has yet to be fully defined and put into practice. In all of these future practices – some of which may well be understood as decolonising or decolonial – scholars and institutions will need to take into account heterogeneity, plurality, the mutability of hierarchies, the perspectives not only of power but also and especially of resistance to power.

Hence our book. Taking 'our' region – centred on Central and Eastern Europe but also encompassing those parts of the state-socialist world located beyond the boundaries of Europe – as a starting point, it aims to show the plural, porous, contested and diverse nature of 'area'. As an 'Anti-Atlas', it subverts the form and politics of the conventional atlas, with its assumptions about knowledge and power, its hierarchies of value, its simplifications, abstractions and evasions. In so doing, it aims to rethink and reclaim area studies in ways that reveal and run against the operations of hegemonic power and that signpost new ways of working together.

We are realistic about this rethinking and reclaiming of area studies and modest about its likely impact. It is not through our counter-concept of critical area studies that Russia is going to be expelled from the Ukrainian territory that it has occupied, for instance. In the dance of power and academic formulations, we the editors know that we are not the lead partners. Still, what we attempt in this volume is a necessary, if not sufficient condition for a more liberated and reflexive way of understanding the world and its variety.

Atlas and Anti-Atlas: perspectives and methods

Let us look at what the Atlas does, at what occurs when the historical, physical and social world that we inhabit is translated onto its pages. And let us look at what the Anti-Atlas does by contrast.[1]

The conventional atlas presents a single god-like view with no apparent standpoint. What might the world look like, viewed from perspectives that acknowledge that they are perspectives? Might it be possible, through a shattering into multiplicity, to know the world not as a flat projection, but in the round?

In 1988, literature historian Zhang Longxi published an essay about Western mythologisations and otherings of China, opening with a reference to what was already a too-often-cited passage from the preface to Foucault's *The Order of Things.* There, Foucault tells us that the idea for his book arose on coming across a description of a 'certain Chinese encyclopedia', in a story by Borges. In this anti-encyclopedia (pointedly opposed to the Enlightenment project of Diderot and his *encyclopédistes*, for whom the entire world can be grasped from Paris), 'animals are divided into: (a) belonging to the Emperor, (b) embalmed, (c) tame, (d) suckling pigs, (e) sirens, (f) fabulous, (g) stray dogs, (h) included in the present classification, (i) frenzied, (j) innumerable, (k) drawn with a very fine camelhair brush, (l) et cetera, (m) having just broken the water pitcher, (n) that from a long way off look like flies'. In this encounter, Foucault burst into 'laughter that shattered … all the familiar landmarks of [his] thought – our thought that bears the stamp of our age and our geography – breaking up all the ordered surfaces and all the planes with which we are accustomed to tame the wild profusion of existing things'. However, as Zhang Longxi shows, Foucault's laughter was neither innocent, well-informed nor particularly well-intentioned. 'Significantly, Foucault does not give so much of a hint to suggest that the hilarious passage from the "Chinese encyclopedia" may have been made up to represent a Western fantasy of the Other'.

Indeed, the 'Chinese' anti-encyclopedia is nothing of the sort. It is the fictional invention of an Argentinian librarian who, despite his location in the Southern hemisphere, is steeped in a canon that is resolutely Western and Eurocentric – a fantasy that goes on to mis-inspire a thinker who, despite his sojourns in Poland, Algeria and elsewhere, remains wedded to a Western tradition of thought and an irrepressible Western will-to-other. As a result, 'its exotic charm' remains exactly that: the chimerical and aesthetic appeal of another system of thought that is, in actuality, a mere fantasy of otherness, forever locked into that which it is called upon to disrupt, like a distorting mirror in a fairground attraction.

Our Anti-Atlas is not Borges's (and especially not Foucault's) 'Chinese' anti-encyclopedia. Most of our content is not fictional, but is grounded in various kinds of archival, ethnographic or other research. Our Anti-Atlas seeks to root itself in systems of thought, practices and historical experiences that actually *are* from elsewhere (an East that actually exists), and it swerves clear of the orientalising fantasies of Borges or Foucault. Our sources of alternative knowledge and taxonomies are the embedded practices and experiences of local history experts, deracinated poets and intellectuals, cosmonauts, mail-order brides and counter-factual dreamers. And we draw on them neither for their exoticism nor for their charm but for their uncanny power, if not to shatter, then to cause fissures and complexities in what is too often taken for granted.

There is laughter in our Anti-Atlas. But this is not the Parisian intellectual's amusement at the invention of the Argentinian librarian, nor the exasperated eye-roll of the Chinese historian. Instead this is a more diverse humour that comes from the ironies of life under socialism, from the sarcastic practices of Sarajevo *kafanas*, and from comic fantasies of alternate and impossible worlds, earthly and cosmic. Still, as the reader will see, the entries in our Anti-Atlas explore a range of modes, genres and forms (fictional as well as non-fictional) that encompasses satire, irony, sarcasm and exuberance. These modes run against the scholarly seriousness that one is accustomed to in academic writing and against the measured and sensible distance of a traditional atlas.

Laughter does contradictory things. On the one hand, it colludes with power and violence, as, for example, the condemnatory mocking of the Stalinist show-trial, or the brutal, sneering absurdities of a speech by Sergeï Lavrov, Minister of Foreign Affairs of the Russian Federation, at the United Nations Security Council. On the other hand, it can act as a critical weapon of liberation. As Bakhtin (a thinker whose ideas are testament to the stubborn power of laughter in the darkness) suggests, as carnival, laughter has the capacity to up-end hierarchies and to turn the world upside down. There is something of the carnivalesque gesture in this volume's cartographic practice. And yet, our practice is not mere reductive topsy-turviness. The Anti-Atlas draws less on carnivalesque reversal of hierarchies (simply swapping one privileged term for another) than on Bakhtin's allied concept of the 'sideways glance', always ironising, always relativising, with a smile more than a belly laugh, unserious in a more subtle and less easy-to-pin-down way. Thus, this volume is based not so much on turning the world upside down as on turning it onto its side. We replace the vertical poles of North and South with the sideways relations of East and West. And we choose to cast our eyes in oblique directions from the standpoint of the East, or rather *an* East, one that is always shifting (because the East is always elsewhere, is always further East …).

Atlas and Anti-Atlas: hierarchy and plurality

An Atlas in its traditional incarnation is a collection of maps that takes continental, imperial, national or urban units as its structuring elements and sets them out, according to a unified scale, in hierarchical dispositions: large to small, West to East, North to South, A to Z. Centring its pages on predefined cartographic spaces, privileging contents rather than borders, centres rather than margins, the Atlas presents a world that has been subjected to a process of knowing, of classifying and of ordering that is simultaneously a process of ranking, of privileging and of subordinating as well as, in its pedagogical function, of disciplining.

An Anti-Atlas takes its cartographic units as permanently to be decided. Indeed, it admits that it makes them up, often as it goes along – or rather that human beings make them up as they go along, whether as state actors, migrants, tourists or dreamers. In this way, an Anti-Atlas makes space for the ways in which order is disrupted, classifications are complicated and blurred, where knowledge is made ambiguous, and where hierarchies are reshuffled. The result is a world that is, on the one hand, *less* knowable and less controllable in simple outline. (So, for example, in an Anti-Atlas, relations of centre and margins are disturbed, not simply by the exchange of one set of centres for another, but rather by a continual kaleidoscopic shifting.) But, on the other hand, the world becomes also *more* accurately knowable in its disorienting plurality and more potent in its capacity for resistance to power.

Atlas and Anti-Atlas: verticals, horizontals, and time

The traditional atlas makes a distinction between a political and a physical map: the physical map gives us heights and depths, twinkling peaks, verdant steppes and arid deserts, but its picture of an untouched natural world – where whales, reindeer and wildebeest migrate with bestial insouciance – gives us little sense that these heights and depths can be plumbed and scaled by human beings.

The political map is different: here the world is presented as an organisation of states, defined by borders: thick lines that contain single colours (mauve for Sudan, green for Brazil, ochre for France). This map presents a world that has been flattened in a variety of ways. It encompasses two dimensions only: no verticals (no mountains, no plains) and no time (the historically contested border between France and Germany, say, is forever fixed, wiped clean of its blood; the imperial cigar ash of the Congress of Berlin has blown off the straight lines that carve up Africa).

What is the Anti-Atlas, by contrast? On the one hand, the Anti-Atlas rejects false verticals (the view from nowhere, from eternity, from above, and above all the view from *those* above) and inscribes new horizontals (the view from the ground, the view from women and men on the streets and in the factories, cafes, galleries and stadiums of a real and ever-moving social and historical world). And, on the other hand, it rejects false horizontals (the homogeneity of, say, all Poles or all Congolese) and inscribes new verticals, whether these be more nuanced and local social relations and hierarchies, or the far-below of tectonic plates and the far-above of outer space.

Thus, the Anti-Atlas reinserts time and speed into a drawing of the world. The Anti-Atlas recognises that to travel through space is also to travel through time: that to travel to the high-tech cityscape of Shanghai or to the environmental and human catastrophe of the mines of Katanga is to journey to competing versions of the future, just as to travel to the Disneyfied husk of historic Dubrovnik or the post-industrial cities of the North American Rust Belt is to travel to competing visions of the past. Similarly, the Anti-Atlas pays attention to technologies of travel, transportation and the circulation of ideas. It allows itself to be held up by closed borders, immigration controls and visa regimes; and it speeds ahead, by the miracles of the imagination and of space travel, to places that the traditional atlas can never map.

Atlas and Anti-Atlas: worlds without, and with, human beings

Perhaps all our points so far come down to this one: the atlas conjures a world without human beings, or rather a world in which human beings have been subject to abstraction as demographic, indeed, biopolitical units. The traditional atlas transforms people into the dots and squares of towns and cities of its political maps and into the greys and browns of urban sprawl of its physical ones. In both cases, human beings, in their boisterous differentiation, slip through the atlas's cracks, fall off the edges of its pages, are swallowed up by the indifference of its coloured spaces.

The Anti-Atlas puts human beings back in the frame: human beings in the fortune and tragedy of their individuation at a particular time and in a particular place; human beings who traverse time and space, whether as migrant, tourist, trader or conqueror; human beings who flee, who explore, who wander, who invade; human beings who depart in hope, despair or boredom and who arrive exhausted or exultant; or indeed, human beings who stay where they are, rooted or trapped, by inertia or by forces beyond their control; human beings who destroy the natural environment or who enhance its beauty; human beings who are the products and creators of history; human beings who make and remake the world.

In short, this Anti-Atlas aims to bring to the fore the elusive, shifting and multifarious character of 'area' and to explore the human trajectories and spaces of contact that get swallowed up in the gutters between the pages of the conventional printed atlas, and conventional area studies.

Critical area studies

This Anti-Atlas is a product of, and contribution to, what we call 'critical area studies' (CAS). Our project did not invent this terminology, though it attempts to put it into wider circulation.[2] The impetus to critique and revise the ways in which academic scholarship weaves nets to catch the world has come from within many disciplines, particularly in social science, with its persistent tension between deep contextual knowledge on the one hand and theory- and method-driven research on the other. Different solutions have been mooted, from 'transnational' or 'transregional' studies, with their focus on border-crossing connections and interactions between societies, to calls for cross-regional contextualised comparisons of areas understood as separate and distinct units.[3] Initiatives such as these and, even more, the anxieties that have driven them, have been surveyed in a number of recent works that assess the past, current state and future of area studies, all with their own paths of travel.[4] Much of this debate has emerged within the specific circumstances of Western universities, in response both to intellectual and – no less influentially – funding challenges. It has been marked by an assumption that the solutions found will be generally applicable beyond those environments. But it is important to recognise that critiques and calls for rethinking have also come from within those regions that are more often thought of as objects of Western study, rather than as producers of generalisable knowledge. The paradigmatic example is that of Edward Said's *Orientalism* (1978), both in its genesis as the product of situated knowledge and in its reception, which was considerably assisted by Said's position in Western academe.

Said's line of argument inspired critiques of Western area studies from an Eastern-European perspective, notably Maria Todorova's influential *Imagining the Balkans* (1997), by a Bulgarian historian working in the United States. Todorova's book both built on and amplified the pre-existing work of scholars in the Balkans, then inspiring further discussions by Balkan scholars of the construction of 'area' through the interaction of local and exogenous discourses, often with deep historical roots, Diana Mishkova's *Beyond Balkanism* (2019) being an excellent example. Similar patterns could be multiplied elsewhere in the lively debates on the origins and utility (or not) of the concepts of Eastern Europe or Central Europe, with antecedents in the political and disciplinary debates of the 1930s and 1940s in the region itself.[5] These discussions, published in English or other languages of international circulation in Western academic centres, have been rightfully influential, though sometimes seen as not only *about* the production of space in generalisable terms but also as tied *to* a specific place, and thus not necessarily able to travel across geographical borders. And this is even more the case for work published in the region and in local vernaculars: the problem of 'knowledge production at the semiperiphery', as Marina Blagojević's trenchant analysis has it.[6] 'Semiperipheral' scholars are all too aware that to enter into a global conversation they must publish in its koine, however much this may impoverish local discussions.

While our approach draws on all these critiques, this Anti-Atlas goes beyond previous works that have tackled the problems of area studies in several ways. First, by showcasing the potential of critical area studies in practice, as well as through abstract theorising. Second, by positioning its contribution through knowledge produced *in* rather than merely *about* the regions which area studies surveys. Third, in its embrace of an explicitly political, institution- and field-building agenda. And, finally, in its insistence that position and perspective are of crucial importance in world-making.

But what precisely do we mean by 'critical area studies'? Here are some coordinates that show the principles that we have attempted to put into action in compiling this volume. They also serve as a manifesto for the future.

Critical area studies is critical

How can an approach to area be 'critical'? All of the essays in this volume engage this question in one way or other, and they put forward numerous implicit and explicit definitions of critique and criticality. From Paul Ricoeur to Bruno Latour and Rita Felski, there is a substantial body of philosophy and literary criticism devoted to the critique of critique. These writers point out that the 'critical' attitude is endlessly fixated on excavating the disavowed or obfuscated *true* or *real* nature of things (whether that truth or reality be psychosexual or political economic, or spiritual, or whatever); and of 'unmasking' the false consciousnesses and/or pathologies which conceal that truth or reality from view. We ought, the critics of critique say, stop being so critical and instead adopt a more humble, less judgemental, more *horizontal* and less *vertical* approach to life and knowledge and thought. Of course, by saying this the critics of critique are implying that they have an even better god's-eye view than the critics do – one which allows them to unmask the critics' own critical false-consciousness.

Critical area studies is incredulous of god's-eye views, whether acknowledged or disavowed. So, while we aspire to be critical, our criticality has a crucial connection to area. We aspire towards developing a more catholic (or heterodox) and more area-informed 'vernacular' or 'emic' understanding and practice of critique. What modes of criticism (or of irony or mimicry) are practised by the interlocutors and writers we draw on? What modes of critique, in particular, have the 'Global East' or 'Second World' or the 'trans-socialist' sections of the world developed, honed and deployed?

There are many answers to that last question, and many of these critics are already well-known or canonical enough. There is Bakhtin and Luxemburg and Lenin – although, to be honest, how much Bakhtin, Luxemburg or Lenin do students of today read, compared to Foucault,

Baudrillard or even Spivak? And there are also Nestor Makhno and Alla Horska, Alexandra Kollontai and Mustafa Dzhemilev, Mieczysław Porębski and Merab Mamardashvili, Dubravka Ugrešić and György Lukács, Radomir Konstantinović and Nasreddin Hodja, Keti Chukhrov and Timur Mutsuraev – and milieus upon schools upon factions of other thinkers, activists, scholars, philosophers, psychologists, strategists, pedagogues and artists profiled, glorified (and critiqued) within (and without) the pages of this atlas. They do not form any kind of comprehensive canon, but they do make for a cast of characters that should be recognised as serious contenders in the practice of critique.

Beyond these academicians and notables, however, we also emphasise that the critical gaze and the critical faculty is not restricted to professional practitioners. In the pages that follow, the reader will meet such vernacular critics as Olga Brookman, the provincial *kraevedka* and the Roma *mediator sanitar*. They all possess the eloquence and influence to rebuild our images and cartographies of the world. And they extend the traction of critique by making it not just the property of academic institutions and public intellectuals, but by connecting it to vernacular knowledge. Note, though, that critique rooted in such vernacular knowledge is not always emancipatory: it can viciously exclude ethnic, racial or sexual 'others' or (often as the flip side of such disdain) fall prey to the seductiveness of the image of a White, Christian, powerful 'West'. Thus, this Anti-Atlas also introduces negative figures, 'dark critics' such as 'migration brokers' or ambivalent ones such as komunistki – those who exploit their knowledge of the world's divisions for profit or for power – as well as including figures whose academic formulations serve to build or reinforce ethnic and racial hierarchies.

Critical area studies seeks to reveal the interests and machinations that stand behind the big constructs of area, but it also aims to produce new ones. This is part of an approach to spatial and political thinking that rejects the viewpoint of state power (or supra-state blocks like the Warsaw Pact, the European Union, the First World) as setting the sole units of analysis. Instead, just as it recognises critics from the famous to the vernacular, critical area studies proposes a variety of spatial scales: units that could be more minute (a city, a district, a region) or much larger (outer space, the so-called Second World). Indeed, it seeks to redraw the categories of classification more fundamentally: neither continents, nor states, nor empires, nor conventional supra-state blocks, but fluid, shifting, contested areas: always provisional, but no less actually real, for all their contingency.

Critical area studies is undisciplined

Critical area studies is committed to dismantling the walls that divide disciplines from each other. At the same time, we are aware that academic expertise – methodological and theoretical – is nothing to be sniffed at. The three authors of this introduction and editors of this volume are an anthropologist, a historian and a literature scholar. And while some of our colleagues might occasionally sniff at us for not being properly orderly, we are all very aware of, marked by and not necessarily averse to the disciplinary cocoons from which we emerge. But, in the final instance, we believe that we will all become more stupid if we do not engage in serious and constant conversations with our colleagues. Therefore, we are not only trans-, inter-, post-, and multidisciplinary; we are programmatically and institutionally undisciplined – disobedient, opportunist and, we hope, fleet-footed. This stance recognises that advances in knowledge often come from unexpected and unplanned encounters and the insights that they confer. 'Area' is a ground upon which the disciplines can meet and recognise what they have in common. It is a means of maximising transformative serendipity. CAS also recognises that academic departments and disciplinary journals are not the only places where knowledge is produced, and seeks to break down the barriers between academic institutions and other settings, from artists' studios and planners' offices, to streets, marketplaces and front lines. This desired de-academisation of knowledge production takes seriously theories and interpretations based on multiple different experiences of the world.

Critical area studies is collaborative

Recognising the many spaces in which knowledge about the world is produced also implies a mission to level the playing fields of knowledge, to make more space for a diversity of voices and standpoints to be heard. Accordingly, this Anti-Atlas has been crowdsourced from as wide a set of communities as possible, crossing continents, disciplines and academic hierarchies: more Wikipedia than *Encyclopaedia Britannica*. Still, it has to be recognised that this Anti-Atlas has been curated, so to speak, from a particular position, with the power to define criteria and select the entries. Power often wishes to be invisible or present itself as anonymous in its drawing of area, but the practitioners of CAS know that they too are part of the picture and don't try to hide the fact. As a result, we are not a faceless collective; rather we try to recognise our own location and perspective – and the limitations of that perspective.

The editors of this volume come from very different places, including disciplinary and 'area' ones, but they are all privileged, not least by having permanent academic positions in an elite Western university. This does not mean that they are entitled to make conservative claims about 'expertise' or about the time they have invested in the study of languages, places or people. Instead, this confers a certain responsibility when it comes to collaborative work. For instance, what does it mean to make space for different voices, but then to impose on them the constraints of standard academic English-language writing? Recognising that this style of English is necessary to be heard and understood in academic settings, we have played the role of editorial activists, collaborating with the Anti-Atlas contributors on their texts, whether in mentoring student writers and early career authors in their modes of presentation, or editing for language. And in turn, we have had some of our assumptions about what might work challenged productively. This sort of collaboration is costly in terms of time and efficiency, but worth doing in terms of real inclusivity. (Efficiency excludes!) Not all allies and collaborators have the luxury of making such an investment, but making this necessary labour visible is the first step to making it more sustainable in a university sector that is already overburdened by workplace demands.

Critical area studies is a view from somewhere

Critical area studies is, by definition, related to and dependent on *a place* and *an area*, but, in line with its criticality, it is not rooted in it. And while place is important, CAS studies problems *in* places – not abstract problems or places that are intrinsically interesting because of their uniqueness. Still, critical area studies must be related to a particular somewhere, a somewhere that it takes seriously, without fetishisation.

For us and for the contributors to this volume, writing and thinking from somewhere is a complicated business, but in all cases this somewhere has something to do with that place that we call 'Eastern Europe' (though treating the term with reserve and, sometimes, inverted commas, given its problematic past).[7] This somewhere – that could in fact be located anywhere – is *our* somewhere, from which and on which this volume has been constructed. But, as scholars of *critical* area studies, we recognise that this term, 'Eastern Europe', is a flag of convenience, not a transhistorical organism or a geopolitical destiny, and can be changed at will and according to circumstances and tactical needs.

Centring this Anti-Atlas on the east of Europe is less an example of the omphalos syndrome, whereby geographers place their own societies at the centre of the world, and more an attempt to denaturalise area studies through (grounded) reorientation. Some of the concepts discussed here will be familiar to Western audiences (such as the Republic of Letters, the Balkans, the Second World, Europe) but appear here from a different, perhaps disorienting perspective. While recent critiques of area studies condemn the conventional divisions of the world as projections of Western power, imposed on others, we show instead the ways such divisions have been locally generated, contested, used and abused. We also explore terrains and concepts of space that are or have been meaningful to local actors, with an eye to what they can tell us about cartographical imaginaries, transnational processes and entanglements, or unexpected origins. The point here is not to be comprehensive in cataloguing the myriad cartographies employed in the east of Europe (an impossible task), still less to shift the prime meridian eastwards. Instead, the multiple, overlapping categories introduced here are meant to be both provocative and revealing.

Still, smuggling in 'Eastern Europe' to stand for the subject of critical area studies writ large may look self-aggrandising, coming as it does from a group of people who work on and in the area. (But isn't this what area studies has always done tacitly, hiding a Euro-Atlantic standpoint under that god-like position from above?) Nonetheless, there are distinct advantages to using this fluid, contested, changing unit as a starting point. Explicitly acknowledging the specific, messy and contingent position from which we conceptualise area studies is just the beginning. Some revisions of area studies have begun by inverting a global North–South polarity. But this tends to replicate some problematic assumptions, in particular the overriding importance of binary divisions, and shapes the resulting insights (an acceptance of the existence of radical alterities, for instance, often answered by celebrating 'hybridity'). In this view, the South is everywhere ('Global'), but also always the 'Other' to an essentialised North. Thinking in terms of Eastern Europe complicates this paradigm in helpful ways, not just because it is at once simultaneously 'North' (or to put it in more familiar postcolonial terms, 'Europe') and Other: never fully or unproblematically European. States in the region have been simultaneously colonised and colonisers; both racialising and racialised ('White, but not quite'); economically backwards but culturally and politically developed; either doubly peripheral to West *and* East or a so-called 'imperial subaltern' in the case of Russia.[8] East and West are not opposed categories (*pace* Kipling); rather they are constantly shifting, depending on perspective and trajectory. These complexities prevent the easy application of theories and vocabularies developed elsewhere, and force engagement with the specificity of local histories, circumstances and perceptions (and necessitate understanding in local vernaculars and languages of cross-cultural communication). This in turn makes it harder to think in terms of easy binaries and instead focuses attention on complex formulations of difference, and the strategic uses to which they are put.

The useful, problematic Global East

It is not just the east of Europe which forces such rethinking. We want to consider a case for the 'Global East' as a tool to this end, but without essentialising it, even strategically. There have been various attempts to define a Global East, which has been proffered as a device for plugging the postsocialist world (not just the European part) into a 'planetary conversation' ordinarily dominated by the (unequal) binary between the 'Global South' and 'Global North'.[9] If the former of the two spheres is made up, by and large, of decolonised or decolonising state entities and the latter of colonising or post-imperial ones, where does that leave the countries of the former socialist bloc, which did not fit neatly into either camp? Usually ignored.

Attempts to redress this state of affairs, however, have paradoxically aimed to fix the Global East to a specific time and place, in much the same way that a potentially contingent 'Eastern Europe' often tends to be used as a restrictive (and Eurocentric) synonym for the broader postsocialist, post-Soviet world and even still-officially-socialist world. Furthermore, an uncritical adoption of the idea of the 'Global East' also naturalises the reductivism of 'Global North' and 'Global South', sidestepping the broad rejection of the latter term by decolonial scholars and activists. We face, therefore, the conundrum of how to enter either an 'East European' or a 'postsocialist' critical area studies into such a planetary conversation without reducing the region to Euro- or Russo-centric fixations on the one hand, and, on the other, without reproducing the epistemic violence written into reductive geopolitical umbrella terms.

This Anti-Atlas therefore takes the 'Global East' in the same way as it adopts 'Eastern Europe' – as a problematic but nonetheless useful term. It is both multiple and relational: it is not 'the East', but rather east *of something*, unlike the fixed 'polar' oppositions of North and South. Indeed, go far enough and any 'East' becomes west of something. Hence the self-deprecating North (sic) Macedonian joke: 'pity the country for which Albania is the West'. But the Global East – or Easts – cannot be taken as a free-floating, 'globalised' set of connections either. Place and history matter (and their weight and specifics vary according to time and location, too).

It is true that definitions of the 'East' as in-between are often derived from the eye of an outsider. If Eastern Europe is often the Global North's 'semi-Other', it is also very frequently the Global South's 'demi-Other': similar enough to show a family resemblance, but different enough to be set apart. *Self*-definitions as 'eastern' can also be traced to the practice of looking through other eyes, particularly when these perspectives are self- or anti-orientalising. But focusing *only* on the view from outside reduces our subject to nothing more than an epiphenomenon of others' desires or anxieties. There are other ways of defining 'easternness' as something in-between, for instance through specific material conditions and relationships: 'semi-periphery' is still a useful concept for some purposes. But world-system theory, which divides the world into core, semi-periphery and periphery, has its disadvantages and blind spots, as well. The Global East can play the role of intellectual vanguard, for example, while nonetheless remaining in a semi-peripheral position economically.

So the Global East is here conceived as relational, provisional and heuristic. The concept is not primarily a project of definition but of tool-building and analysis. The question is not 'where is it?' but 'what is it useful for?' and 'for whom?'. This approach to tool-building makes the Global East useful for fruitful comparisons; for testing 'universals' or indeed any theory generated elsewhere; and for theorising.

Is critical area studies decolonial?

The 'decolonial turn' has been a focus of attention in western academic discourse for some time, where it has highlighted the persistence of colonial power relations but has also involved challenging the universalist claims of 'Western' knowledge and its role in perpetuating inequalities. Decolonisation thus not only encompasses movements for political self-determination and independence, but also demands for the revaluation of indigenous forms of knowledge. This can sometimes take the form of a romantic search for autochthonous identity, a rejection of modernity, a suspicion of cultural appropriation, and an embrace of victimhood-as-innocence.[10] More positively, decolonisation can be understood as the process of identifying unequal global structures, relationships and imaginaries, often taken as 'common sense' or as universal truths, placing such cultural perceptions and power relations in historical context, and working to challenge their hegemony. In this sense, CAS, with its scepticism towards universal truths, its focus on local histories and its collaborative ethos, is happy to claim the badge of 'decolonial'. But decolonisation is not the primary aim of this Anti-Atlas, although it is a good starting point for thinking about what it might take to achieve.[11]

As far as Eastern Europe goes, the decolonial agenda takes two forms. The first has to do with its political potential. This Anti-Atlas is alert to the partial, problematic and chauvinist positions from which postcolonial and decolonial theories are sometimes hijacked for political purposes, not least by scholars and cynics from the Global East itself. The Polish-American theorist Ewa Thompson, for example, produced an important dissection of imperialist tropes in nineteenth-century Russian literature. Both in the text of her analysis and in the author's subsequent activism, however, this dissection was enthusiastically mobilised in the service of Polish victimhood, exceptionalism and Roman Catholic chauvinism. Today, Russian diplomats trawl the United Nations headquarters and the capitals of Africa, Latin America and Asia, seeking allies in their call to engender a new 'multipolar' world, united against the threat of Western 'colonial' hegemony. In doing so, they are enacting the 'decolonial' and 'multipolar' theories of Aleksandr Dugin, a Russian theorist of Eurasianism who, for several decades, has actively called for the destruction of Ukraine and the eradication of its inhabitants, and peppers his genocidal hyperbole with explicit references to decolonial thought and practice.[12]

But at the same time, scholars, critics and practitioners – vernacular or otherwise – in the many parts of the world formerly affected by Russian and/or Soviet colonial violence, from Helsinki to Bishkek, have become energised by the clarion call to decolonise. But the slogans of decolonisation have also received considerable impetus in response to aspects of Western intervention in the region (particularly EU enlargement and NATO expansion) – and have contributed to trenchant critiques, for example, of the EU's neocolonial transformation of the post-Yugoslav Balkans into a dependent semi-periphery.[13] Thus decolonisation, understood as an actionable ideology with immediate cultural, aesthetic, political and military application, currently has a great deal of political traction – not always to emancipatory ends.

But the second aspect of the decolonial agenda is concerned with the politics of knowledge production in the academy – and here is where it is most relevant to CAS. Critiques of the idea of decoloniality – most prominently formulated by post-Marxist political and legal philosopher Olúfẹ́mi O. Táíwò – reject an uncritical insistence on 'indigenous forms of knowledge' as an alternative to the so-called 'Western' ideas of reason, progress, humanism and radical universalism.[14] (The embrace of 'indigenous ontologies' implies assumptions of radical alterity, whereas the Global East does not exist outside global processes of capitalism, industrialisation, urbanisation, secularisation and so on). But at the same time, non-Western scholars complain, with reason, that it is difficult for their voices to be heard and their contributions to knowledge to be recognised in global academia. Decolonising area studies thus means noting and finding means to redress inequalities in the global distribution of academic capital. Furthermore, CAS recognises that work in the fields of Russian and/or East European studies can produce, reproduce and consolidate existing hierarchies of cultural value – for instance, those dispositions that see literary creativity in *some* linguistic or geographical positions (English, Russian) as 'Literature' and others as *merely* 'Croatian' or 'Congolese' literature.

Our particular somewhere: UCL's School of Slavonic and East European Studies

Area definitions are often slippery, shifting and overlapping; the institutions set up to study these areas are often, on the contrary, all too solid, unchanging and fenced off. The disadvantage of this is that the framework and assumptions of area studies research can lag behind or even ignore developments in the field. But a degree of institutionalisation is also a virtue, for it contributes to a critical mass of scholars and scholarship focused on units above and below the nation-state, highlighting patterns that might otherwise fall out of sight. In the best cases it enables conversations that cross disciplinary boundaries as well as linguistic or national ones. It also provides formal conduits for collaboration not just between disciplines but perhaps more importantly, between area 'insiders' and 'outsiders'.

All three editors are associated with UCL's School of Slavonic and East European Studies. The history of SSEES exemplifies the points in the paragraph above, while also putting into question some of the familiar criticisms of area studies institutions: that they are in hock to state interests, theoretically and methodologically naive, reducing knowledge to a subject/object relationship, and converting that knowledge into power. SSEES was founded at the end of the First World War to advance the interests of the 'small nations' of Europe amid collapsing empires and has always been staffed by scholars from the region alongside Western experts. It evolved within the context of post-Second World War ideological conflict and the Cold War, while notoriously serving as a recruiting base for both sides. The school subsequently found a *raison d'être* in the post-Soviet era of 'transition' and ethnic conflict, though usually at odds with UK government policy. The ebb and flow of 'relevance' has meant that, at least in this case, area studies has not had the luxury of unreflexive self-confidence, but has been forced to look hard at its own methods and assumptions (including this project of an Anti-Atlas). If 'Eastern Europe' is a good starting point for reconsidering the shape and scope of area studies, SSEES is an equally good springboard for the effort. Indeed, perhaps it is a 'critical continent' of its own, straddling conventional frontiers.

Anti-Atlas organisation: continents and terrains, and wandering or indigenous critics

As argued above, the conventional atlas can obscure other meaningful terrains and territories. Borderlands, crossroads and networks provide obvious examples: tracing these doesn't just smudge the outlines of taken-for-granted areas, but more importantly shows how people's lives can be shaped by maps that don't necessarily coincide with the nation-state or historical region. Questioning the flat, two-dimensional projections of the conventional atlas calls attention to claims made to territories beyond the Earth's atmosphere, or beneath its surface, and the ways these claims are legitimated by tying them to specific territories. It is high time for area studies to discover new continents and terrains, and to rip apart, reassess, or redraw the old ones. Some of these continents and terrains form the subject of the first part of our Anti-Atlas.

All continents and terrains are known, inhabited, traversed and transgressed by people whose paths reveal or deny boundaries. These are – despite (or thanks to) their lack of academic credentials – de facto critics, the vanguard scholars of critical area studies. They are the subject of the second part of our Anti-Atlas. The continents and terrains discussed above come into focus through the trajectories – and sometimes also the critical voices – of such figures. These contributions raise questions about gender and sexual normativity, racial hierarchies, or East European 'whiteness', as well as about global hierarchies of centre and periphery, the direction of transnational flows, the multiple, overlapping categories of inclusion and exclusion. But here too the choice of figures is selective, focusing primarily on examples that unveil both the political and economic logic of state and regional frontiers, and the ways in which individuals and groups may operate according to a very different logic.

This introduction is meant as a map to the paths traced in the individual entries of this Anti-Atlas. Each entry also begins with a brief editorial comment that further serves as an orientation device – a textual compass rose – that helps to place these contributions in relation to the wider themes raised here.

Lacunae, future directions and an invitation

To be critical necessarily means to be self-critical, to work in the mode of the monastic-socialist practice of *samokritika*. It may seem odd to draw attention to lacunae in this project, given that the criteria for inclusion in this Anti-Atlas are selective and to some extent arbitrary. But lacunae and blind spots can be just as revealing as tables of contents.

One striking gap in the coverage here has to do with the academic disciplines and approaches of the contributors. Anthropology, history, art and architectural history, literary and cultural studies are all well represented here; political science, sociology, geography(!) and especially economics, scarcely at all. The imbalance between humanities and social-science approaches is not due to editorial blinkers. Approaches in the humanities generally take for granted the importance of 'area', though often labelled according to other spatial units (especially national), and they habitually approach their problems through the specific, the individual and the contextual, so that the shape of this Anti-Atlas is immediately comprehensible in disciplinary terms. By contrast, while many of those working in the social sciences have incorporated qualitative methods into their research, others still rely on theorising that can minimise the importance of local cultural, historical and contextual factors – in a word, 'area'. But quantitative and comparative methods have much to contribute to a reassessment of the relevance of area specificities. This allows the opportunity to interrogate social-scientific assertions of universal knowledge, and to show how a critical approach to 'area' can trouble the normative approaches and fundamental assumptions of academic disciplines.

A second set of lacunae has to do with the demographics of the editors and contributors. While the genres of the contributions may vary from straightforward analysis to playful parody, we are almost all academics, speaking to academics. Widening the scope of contributors to include vernacular practitioners and critics of area – artists, citizens' groups, border guards, politicians – would more forcefully have made the point that critical area studies is not limited to the academy but is an everyday life practice. There is an overrepresentation of those working in North Atlantic institutions and in the region, though we have done better on this account than many other 'rethinking area studies' collections, in flattening the implicit hierarchies of academic life, and of observer/observed. The interests of the contributors mean that neither the 'continents' discovered here, nor the 'critics' who wander through them, are evenly distributed across our specific terrain. This may be a function of comparative densities of scholarship, but is not intended to suggest that this specific selection exhausts the revelatory potential of the Czech lands, say, as compared to Russia or Poland. At the same time, the contributors reflect the overall character of the professional field, including their preponderant whiteness. Their perspectives could have been enriched by seeking out more contributors from area studies institutions outside these circles. What differences or similarities does area studies research coming from London and Chicago show in comparison with that from Beijing or Hokkaido, all of which have institutes focusing on eastern Europe? And how does 'Europe' look to Iraqis or Libyans or Ugandans growing up among the Cold War architectural projects of the socialist bloc, or to those countries in Asia and Africa that sent generations of students to study in the Soviet Union or Yugoslavia? Such questions are gradually but steadily beginning to be asked. As a result, the contributors to this Anti-Atlas – for all their criticality – mirror with remarkable precision the traditional geographic and disciplinary terrain of the imperial husk that is East European Studies.

However, this Anti-Atlas is not intended to serve as a summary and assessment of the state of such studies. If it were, we would devote more space in this list of lacunae to the ways Eastern Europe is so often narrowly drawn, excluding the Caucasus and Central Asia on the one hand and the German or Greek lands on the other; to the disproportionate interest in relations with 'the West' and the Global North, at the expense of entanglements with Latin America, Africa and Asia; to the relative absence of attention to race and racialised discourse in analysing social stratification, beyond studies on Roma and Jews; to the relative failure of such studies to generate theory, and not just adopt and adapt insights and methods developed elsewhere.

Instead, this Anti-Atlas is meant to prompt a critical assessment of area studies more generally. This list of gaps, biases and drawbacks is thus a start at specifying the reach, rather than the universal validity, of critical area studies in general, not just for the east of Europe. It is only in this way that the knowledge gained from the exercise can be defended as precise, and can serve as a basis for new insights and theoretical innovations that can better capture the complexity of the world.

So deliberately grounding a critical area studies in a provisionally defined Eastern Europe is not (just) a rude gesture in the direction of an area studies that has long been tacitly associated with 'Western' interests, asserting instead forms of knowledge rooted in more slippery and ambiguous positions. In part, we want to highlight and advertise work done in this area that may escape the view of those in more 'central' fields, as well as those elsewhere who may find parallels with their own positions and preoccupations. Beyond the benefits of unexpected comparisons, we hope that the methods and approaches explored here are, at least in part, exportable. The emphasis here on the primacy of the problem or question, not the area label or definition, should help ensure that the issues explored have wider resonance, and that our methods can be translated and adapted in other contexts. More broadly, the approaches advocated here push in the direction of a critical engagement with the construction of knowledge, admitting the influence of positionality, but also asking whose knowledge ultimately counts, where and for what purposes? Thinking on these lines provides a means of arguing for new collaborations, different funding priorities, and even a path to change.

Above all, in relation to what is missing here and what is needed next, an Anti-Atlas never claims the encyclopedic completeness of a traditional atlas, bound between gilded boards. Indeed, we would do better to speak of the process of Anti-Atlas making than of an Anti-Atlas. By definition, an Anti-Atlas always has blank pages for new cartographic practices, always invites palimpsestic overwriting and redrawing, always invites new, overlooked producers of knowledge to the party. Above all, this Anti-Atlas, aware of its limitations and its incompleteness, is an invitation to collaboration and to conversation.

A provisionally final word

It is always hubristic to claim a final word: time and the world moves on and someone else comes along to say something new. As editors, we are desperately aware of the extent to which our project, too, has been subject to time in a world that moves on in ways we hadn't necessarily predicted. This Anti-Atlas was conceived, and the bulk of its contributions written, before Russia's full-scale invasion of Ukraine in February 2022. It would be dishonest to say that this world – a world of *before*

February 2022 – was an age of innocence, like the world of before August 1914, for example, that Joseph Roth mythologises in his *Radetzky March*. The imperial violence of Russia was already at its dreadful work and there to see, whether historically (as the Russian Empire or the Soviet Union) or in the present with, at the very least, the initial invasion of Ukraine in 2014. And we should have seen this and taken it more fully into account. This world, of before February 2022, was less an age of innocence than an age of naivety and blindness on our part as editors. It makes little difference that we shared this naivety and blindness with a huge number of other, largely Western scholars of our region – many of whom are now belatedly waking up to things as they are, reassessing so much of what they thought they knew about Russia and about those societies unfortunate enough to have been shaped by Russian violence, unlearning old ways to think and learning new ways to see.

In this world *after* February 2022, we have sought to address this situation: here, in our editors' introduction, in the editorial glosses that appear before each contribution to the volume, and, in some cases, in final decisions on the content of contributions and, indeed, their inclusion or exclusion. Still, traces of this volume's genesis in an age of partial blindness and naivety may well remain; readers may – as do we – have the sense, at times, that our volume is something of a photographic album, containing snapshots of a disappeared past, evoking – as snapshots so often do – an uneasy mixture of naive nostalgia, guilt and incompleteness. In particular, we regret the relative paucity of contributions that take Ukrainian topics and perspectives as their starting point (as well as Central Asian and Caucasian ones). What we have not done, however, is excise all contributions that take Russia, in its various guises, as a starting point. In many spheres, curators, cultural programmers, translators and others are seeking to turn their backs on Russia and Russian culture, in rejection of imperialist and colonialist violence, and perhaps rightly so. In the sphere that is academia, however, we feel the obligation to continue to throw some light, at least, on Russian world-making and its impact on the world, to attempt to understand it critically, all the better to understand its pernicious actions in the present. At the same time, we leave Russia overrepresented in the content of the Atlas in part not to whitewash or elide the extent of its overrepresentation among scholarship in our region. The table of contents of this book is an artefact of a time immediately preceding an epistemic rupture, sparked by a brutal war. Had we put it together now, this table of contents would have looked different. But we did not, and we leave it here as it was.

But a final provisional word on tone, on laughter and on seriousness. Towards the beginning of this introduction, we spoke of laughter (a phenomenon closely allied to play) and, by extension, of the positive role of play – defamiliarising, decentring, giddy and disruptive – in this project, as well as of laughter's ambivalence. There is no doubt that this volume emerged, in part, from a spirit of laughter and play: from the coming together of three friends and colleagues and from our laughter and joy in working together. And, indeed, we shared a sense that ludic freedom might precisely be the best way to challenge the pieties and orthodoxies of area studies and to rethink the all-too-serious world.

As the prophet says: 'to every thing there is a season and a time to every purpose under heaven … A time to weep, and a time to laugh'. If in the world before February 2022, a playful approach seemed apt, perhaps, in the world after February 2022, this is less the case. If our volume retains, in part or in whole, a gesture of playfulness, then we now recognise that life in our region has revealed itself, for so many, to be altogether more serious, as a place where the consequences of what this volume sometimes treats with the lightness of play are all too real. In short: we fear that sometimes the laughter may now ring hollow. Still, we stand by the importance of academia as a place to think with the power and freedom of play, even in dark times. And we fervently pray for, and work towards, a future world where it will be once again a time to laugh – and, within it, a future Ukraine where, as the author of the Book of Revelation says: 'God shall wipe away all tears from their eyes and there shall be no more death, neither sorrow, nor crying, neither shall there be any more pain'.

Notes

1 For the avoidance of doubt, in this book the term 'Anti-Atlas' does not at any point refer to the Anti-Atlas mountain range in Morocco. Our choice of the term 'Anti-Atlas' to characterise this collection draws inspiration from kindred projects. These include the 'antiAtlas of borders' project, a group of researchers and artists exploring the mutations of twenty-first-century borders (https://www.antiatlas.net/antiatlas-of-borders/. Accessed 21 July 2024); as well as *This is Not an Atlas*, a collection of forty activist counter-cartographies (https://notanatlas.org/book/. Accessed 21 July 2024); and *The Baltic Atlas*, a publication emerging from the three Baltic states' attempt at non-national, collective representation at the 2016 Venice Biennale of Architecture. Other kindred volumes include *Former West: Art and the contemporary after 1989* (Maria Hlavajova and Simon Sheikh, eds, 2016); the three volumes of the *Global Encyclopaedia of Informality* (Alena Ledeneva, ed., 2016); and the recent *Decoloniality in Eastern Europe: A lexicon of reorientation* (Ana Vilenica, ed., 2023).
2 See, for example, Koch, 2016, for one (rather sceptical) genealogy of the term within the discipline of geography, or Jackson, 2019, writing from within anthropology, with a perspective closer to that of this Anti-Atlas.

3   See, for these examples, Middell and Naumann, 2010; Ahram et al., 2018.
4   For example, Szanton, 2004; Clowes and Bromberg, 2015; Mielke and Hornidge, 2017; Milutinović, 2019.
5   For example, Murawska-Muthesius, 2021; Zarycki, 2014; Mishkova and Trencsényi, 2017.
6   Blagojević, 2009: a text that has not had the attention it deserves, thus exemplifying one part of her argument.
7   As editors, recognising its tactical and contextual provisionality, we have not imposed 'Eastern Europe' on our authors. Terms like 'Central-East Europe' or 'Eurasia' have their usefulness and their histories. Other possible terms include 'trans-socialism' (as opposed to postsocialism), a concept that continues to recognise the imprint of the state socialist century (or half-century) on our (planetary) present-day – and which does not imply that socialism is necessarily a 'former' state, nor reduces our understanding of socialist space to the Warsaw Pact. Another productive term is that of the 'former west', introduced by Boris Buden and his collaborators (https://archiv.hkw.de/en/programm/projekte/2013/former_west/start_former_west.php. Accessed 21 July 2024). Others are floated in this Anti-Atlas: Bocharnikova's 'Second World' or Stanek's 'World Socialist System', for example.
8   It is significant to note, given our discussion here of the hijacking of 'critical' and 'decolonial' discourses by reactionary agendas, that Viacheslav Morozov, Professor of International Political Theory at the University of Tartu and proponent of the idea of Russia as a 'subaltern empire', was arrested by Estonian authorities in January 2024 and accused of spying for Russia. In June 2024, Morozov pleaded guilty and was sentenced to six years in prison.
9   For example, Müller, 2020; more recently, and with a useful emphasis on the multiplicity of possible Global Easts, Müller and Trubina, 2020.
10 See Kassymbekova and Laruelle, 2022.
11 For an attempt to adapt 'decoloniality' as a field of enquiry in Eastern Europe that has something in common with this Anti-Atlas, though with a more enthusiastic embrace of decolonial discourse, see Vilenica, 2023.
12 See Ivakhiv, 2022. For a critique of the pseudo-leftist ideology of 'multi-polarity', see Krishnan, 2023.
13 Štiks and Horvat, 2015; Rexhepi, 2022.
14 Táíwò, 2022.

Bibliography

Ahram, Ariel Ira, Patrick Köllner and Rudra Sil, eds. *Comparative Area Studies: Methodological rationales and cross-regional applications*. Oxford: Oxford University Press, 2018.

Blagojević, Marina. *Knowledge Production at the Semiperiphery: A gender perspective*. Belgrade: Institut za kriminološka i sociološka istraživanja, 2009.

Clowes, Edith W. and Shelly Jarrett Bromberg, eds. *Area Studies in the Global Age: Community, place, identity*. DeKalb: Northern Illinois University Press, 2015.

Ivakhiv, Adrian. 'Decolonialism and the invasion of Ukraine', *e-flux Notes*, 23 March 2022. Accessed 21 July 2024. https://www.e-flux.com/notes/457576/decolonialism-and-the-invasion-of-ukraine.

Jackson, Peter. 'South East Asian area studies beyond Anglo-America: Geopolitical transitions, the neoliberal academy and spatialized regimes of knowledge', *South East Asia Research* 27(1) (2019): 49–73.

Kassymbekova, Botakov and Marlene Laruelle. 'The end of Russia's imperial innocence', *Russia.Post*, 25 May 2022. Accessed 21 July 2024. https://russiapost.info/politics/the_end_of_russias_imperial_innocence.

Koch, Natalie. 'Is a "critical" area studies possible?', *Environment and Planning D: Society and Space* 34(5) (2016): 807–14.

Krishnan, Kavita. 'Multipolarity, the mantra of authoritarianism', *The India Forum*, 20 December 2022. Accessed 21 July 2024. https://www.theindiaforum.in/politics/multipolarity-mantra-authoritarianism.

Middell, Matthias and Katja Naumann. 'Global history and the spatial turn: From the impact of area studies to the study of critical junctures of globalization', *Journal of Global History* 5(1) (2010):149–70.

Mielke, Katja and Anna-Katharina Hornidge, eds. *Area Studies at the Crossroads: Knowledge production after the mobility turn*. Basingstoke: Palgrave Macmillan, 2017.

Milutinović, Zoran, ed. *Rebirth of Area Studies: Challenges for history, politics and international relations in the 21st century*. London: I. B. Tauris, 2019.

Mishkova, Diana and Balázs Trencsényi, eds. *European Regions and Boundaries: A conceptual history*. New York: Berghahn Books, 2017.

Müller, Martin. 'In search of the Global East: Thinking between North and South', *Geopolitics* 25 (2020): 734–55.

Müller, Martin and Elena Trubina. 'The Global Easts in global urbanism: Views from beyond North and South', *Eurasian Geography and Economics* 61(6) (2020): 627–35.

Murawska-Muthesius, Katarzyna. *Imaging and Mapping Eastern Europe: Sarmatia Europea to post-communist bloc*. Abingdon: Routledge, 2021.

Rexhepi, Piro. *White Enclosures: Racial capitalism and coloniality along the Balkan route*. Durham, NC: Duke University Press, 2022.

Štiks, Igor and Srećko Horvat, eds. *Welcome to the Desert of Post-Socialism: Radical politics after Yugoslavia*. London: Verso, 2015.

Szanton, David, ed. *The Politics of Knowledge: Area studies and the disciplines*. Berkeley: University of California Press, 2004.

Táíwò, Olúfémi. *Against Decolonisation: Taking African agency seriously*. London: Hurst, 2022.

Vilenica, Ana, ed. *Decoloniality in Eastern Europe: A lexicon of reorientation*. Novi Sad: New Media Center, 2023.

Zarycki, Tomasz. *Ideologies of Eastness in Central and Eastern Europe*. London: Routledge, 2014.

Part I
Continents and terrains

There are more areas to study than the seven continents we think we know, and the linguistically-defined 'families' or post-imperial husks after which we name our departments and institutes. It is time to recognise the existence of other spaces, mapped according to different principles. Some of the entries below deal with territories that have a distinct place in time (the Second World; Il'f and Petrov's *Amerika*), other conceptual framings are reformed and reborn in new conditions (Eurasia; *Zwischeneuropa*), others exist as projects or imaginary spaces (the Children's Republic; Dreamland; Yugoslavia's Wild West). Still others are virtual spaces shaped by technology (the Republic of Letters; the Digital East), while some force us to reassess our preconceptions (Red Adriatic; the Zone; the order of Chaos). They operate on scales from the micro (the Moscow House of Culture) through the meso (the Balkans) to the macro and the meta (the Anthropocene or low earth orbit). This selection of territories is not intended to add up to a new synthesis that area studies must take into account (a reconceived Eastern Europe, say, or a static, reified Global East). Far from it. While we aim to deconstruct global projections centred on Paris or New York City, we do not advocate replacing these with a single, definitive world map centred on, say, Tirana or Tbilisi (and certainly not on Moscow). Rather than replace one set of standardised maps with a new set, we argue for multiple, overlapping categories that can allow us to grasp the widely varying patterns, practices and aspirations that shape human lives across the planet. The key point here is not only that 'areas' can be mapped in different ways; rather, we need to recognise that our scholarly maps don't need to be those that are pre-given. They can most profitably be generated by the questions that we want to answer.

1
Balkan Balkanologies (and their shifting cartographies)
Diana Mishkova

'Area studies' is not just something inflicted on people and places by 'experts' outside the region in question, for purposes of acquiring or exerting power through producing knowledge. Diana Mishkova dissects the history of Balkan studies in South-eastern Europe, and in so doing shows how its transnational academic conceptual and institutional frameworks developed in a creative tension with other entities and ideas, whether neighbouring nations, regional geopolitical threats, or broad discourses of civilisation and backwardness. An awareness of the changing contingencies shaping Balkan Balkanologies serves as a warning against over-essentialising spatial categories of analysis anywhere; the political ends of such Balkanologies is an equally pertinent reminder that local, regional or transnational categories are not inherently methodologically (or morally) superior to national ones – indeed, they are often inseparable from them.

The history of regional categories like 'the Balkans' and 'South-eastern Europe' date back to the nineteenth century, when they emerged as economic, political or romantic identity projects, simultaneously with the European nation-states. The imperial frameworks that survived well into the modern era, and the subsequent political problems that this inherited cultural diversity sustained, provided the distinctive context where local social sciences took shape, as well as incentives to go beyond national borders. A region notoriously associated with militant and irreconcilable nationalisms engendered, around the turn of the twentieth century, methodologies constructing a sort of Balkan or South-east-European unit of analysis. By the 1930s the theoretical and methodological groundwork for regionalist South-east European studies was already in place. At the same time, the belated processes of nation-formation in the region also meant that creating national disciplinary canons to prop up nation-state building remained on the agenda well into the twentieth century. The tension between the presence of transnational frameworks and the drive to nationalisation continues to shape the academic cultures of these countries to this day.

Methodologically, as well as geopolitically, one can distinguish four periods of academic regionalisation of 'the Balkans'. The late nineteenth and early twentieth century, characterised by radicalisation of national discourses, also saw the construction, for the first time, of an encompassing Balkan/South-east-European unit of analysis. Significantly, the same disciplines that played a leading role in the construction of national peculiarities and borders – linguistics, ethnography, literary studies and history – also proved to be the first areas in which the idea of a Balkan historical commonality was seriously deliberated. That was a time marked by prevalence of the comparatist method and concerned primarily with exchange and interaction between nations. The construction of the nation went hand in hand – and was compatible with – the construction of an overarching regional unity.

The period between the two world wars saw the rise of new paradigms promoting ontological, cultural-morphological models for explaining spatial similarities and differences. They were less concerned with comparativism than with devising shared origins and structures for these societies. That was the aim of the new science of Balkanology, backed by an impressive number of scholars across the region, who furnished the first comprehensive statement of Balkan studies. The concept of the Balkans that emerged challenged the nation-state as the primary organising principle of research and was deployed as an anti-paradigm privileging cross-national histories of peoples, ideas and material cultures. A veritable blueprint for what would come to be called 'area studies' after World War II, combining the humanities and the social sciences, originated in the 1930s in the region itself.

On the symbolic level the shift produced by this transnational, multidisciplinary agenda was spectacular. Precisely at the time when the Western discourse of Balkanism peaked, in the local regional context the term 'Balkans' – and being Balkan – witnessed systematic rehabilitation and veritable thriving as both a political and cultural concept. The movement toward a 'Balkan Conference' and 'Balkan Pact', the founding of 'Balkan institutes' to conduct 'Balkan research' on the 'Balkan patrimony' and the 'Balkan man' (and woman), the appeals for a 'Balkan fatherland', 'Balkan consciousness' and 'Balkan patriotism' converged in the slogan 'the Balkans for the Balkan peoples' as a new political concept.

The meaning of 'Balkanism' was recast within a discourse through which intellectuals and scholars envisaged an alternative Balkanism flying in the face of the Western Balkanist discourse, a focal point of collective self-identification, and a powerful frame of reference. Interwar academic Balkanism thus vied to supply the conceptual toolkit and the scholarly basis to construct a Balkan identity. In the process the Balkans gelled into a discrete civilisational sphere, occasionally underpinned by overt racism and couched in moralising oratory or cosmic, metaphysical, even mystic references.

After World War II the Balkans as a political notion all but disappeared, nor was it considered a discrete economic region such as Eastern or Western Europe. It survived as a cultural-historical space ploughed by a cluster of historically-oriented human sciences and as a terrain for exercising the soft power of scholarly diplomacy. In postwar conceptualisations of Balkan studies, cultural politics, geopolitics and national propaganda were closely entwined, and the unprecedented expansion of state-sponsored institutional infrastructure came with a new wave of politicisation of Balkanist research. International congresses and conferences served as venues for showcasing the latest developments in validating the fundamental assumptions on which the 'national sciences' were built. The 'historical Balkans' came to be understood as a mosaic of national spaces, where the agents of interaction and exchange were taken to be firmly established and, in essence, immutable ethnic or national communities fully conscious of their distinct character. Unsurprisingly, such a regional approach did not affect the writing of national history, which remained a self-contained, didactic and parochial field.

The post-1989 period has been characterised by a theoretical chasm among scholars of the Balkans. Some, mainly in literary and cultural studies, conceive the Balkans not as a product of geography, history or culture, but as a 'place' in a 'discourse-geography' – a mental construct and a chain of metaphors used to define self and other in highly politicised discursive situations. Accordingly, a great deal of research after the mid 1990s centred around the nature of this discourse, how it had been established, its characteristics and its critique. But there are also those who have continued the search for the 'historical reality' of the Balkans, variously defined in terms of a cluster of historical-structural and cultural characteristics or historical legacies. The theoretical discussions this schism gave rise to placed the Balkans in the centre of the debates on the meaning of regions and the mechanisms for the production of space that have led to interrogating definitions, traits and boundaries.

What, then, does the long tradition of Balkan academic regionalisation tell us that could be of use when thinking about the promises and pitfalls inherent in transnational regional research? And how can it contribute or serve as a warning to the project of critical area studies?

Overall, the story of Balkan regionalisations invites us to question the seeming naturalness and self-evidence of regional constructs and reveals the inherent ambiguities of most geographical notions. Awareness of historical contingency and the mechanisms of inclusion and exclusion underpinning spatial terminology prevents us from thinking of regions as objectified units functioning as quasi-national entities with fixed boundaries and clear-cut lines between insiders and outsiders, but rather as flexible and historically changing frameworks for interpreting certain phenomena. It thus serves as a warning against falling into the trap of essentialising the spatial units of our research. Tailoring academic research to established spatial categories tends to predetermine its conclusions. The endless debates about the boundaries of the Balkans have been the result not only of differing political agendas or geographical determinism, but of the scholarly fallacy of projecting a spatial category coined at a particular time and for particular purposes backwards and forwards in time, where it sits uneasily with very different political realities.

Historicising our regional notions also helps us interrogate the underlying assumptions concerning the relationship between nationalism and regionalism (transnationalism). Balkan transnationalisms came to be construed in dialogue with national autarchy and nation-centred scholarly paradigms. The outcome was patently ambivalent: the supranational region could at one time erode and, at another, buttress national differences, serve to bolster a nationalist project or 'extrapolate' a national geopolitical framework. Typically, the drive for transnationalisation originated from essentially national concerns and was meant to safeguard the nation. Present-day champions of transnationalism seem to believe that intrinsic to it is a virtuous quality, a superior vision that offers a way 'to overcome the narrow framework of national narratives'. Historically this has not been the case. There has been no sharp separation of national and regional perspectives, but interconnectedness on many levels, no clear-cut difference but a complex relationship, often interpenetration, between national and transnational representations.

Regional narratives were often exposed to political contingencies, were sometimes unabashedly ideological, and could stand for diametrically opposed value systems. When we talk about the challenge to the national framework, we are often made to believe that we refer to politically 'progressive' projects. While certain representations of the regional 'specifics' vindicate such a view, others epitomised far more ambiguous political stances, sometimes blatantly antiliberal. Consequently, the Balkans could be referred to as the root of European civilisation or envisaged as the driver of an alternative, anti-European value system; it could signify a younger Europe which would resuscitate the old one or represent a stigmatising notion denoting deficiency in civilisational terms, to be overcome by efforts at Europeanisation.

The 'Balkan' example also induces us to rethink the relationship between 'Western' and 'peripheral' regionalisations. The extra-regional tendency to treat the Balkan states en bloc had, as a rule, political and economic incentives. Yet academic interest in this region often reflected political debates back home: the pressure of the 'nationality question' in Austria-Hungary, disputes over the British approach to international relations and the consequences of industrialisation, or debates on Russian identity and relations to 'the West'. One should also add the hidden or more explicit agendas of the German *Südostforschung*. The relationship between imperialism and academic engagement, however, was not necessarily a straightforward one. Italian imperialist pursuits in the region in the interwar period failed to engender academic interest, whereas Russian imperial cartography operated with various configurations: the Slavic world, the Balkans or a satellite Eastern Europe.

Nor did internal and external regionalisations necessarily converge. The local insistence on 'the Balkans' as a cultural and political concept in the 1930s was aimed at counteracting extra-regional geopolitical reconfigurations, the German notion of South-eastern Europe from Slovakia to Ukraine, in particular. As powerful as the post-Enlightenment 'Western discourse' (or rather different national Western discourses) of the European east and south-east might have been, it was neither the sole nor, at all times, the dominant agent of regionalisation. Instead, parallel, external and internal processes of constructing regional discourses could connect to or polemicise with each other. The transfer of regional concepts and semantics, however, was not a unidirectional, West to East, traffic, but a two-way flow, overriding on occasion preoccupations with the Balkan margins' asymmetric conceptualisation and enforcing alternative definitions and classifications.

Finally, historical conceptualisations of the Balkans highlight the intimate relationship between processes of spatialisation and identity formation on a national and transnational scale. Regionalisation in this sense can be described as the lexicalised expression of processes of self-reflection and self-description condensed into spatial terminology, and regions as broad spatial metaphors, semantic markers and ideologemes related to domestic and international agendas. The attraction of the 'Balkan idea' ultimately resided in the symbolic resources that it provided for posing questions about modernity and negotiating the nation's relationship to transnational cultural, social and economic processes. Again, historicising the different layers of discourse created by different actors teaches us how basic notions of modernity are intimately linked to spatial categories. And the other way round: these spatial categories are themselves indicative of the coexistence and competition of different layers and visions of modernity.

The recent pan-European and global opening of academic discussion has rightly proved antagonistic to the self-contained nature of traditional area studies. Yet actual research suggests that the connection of the local to the global is, more often than not, mediated by the regional. As the itinerary of 'the Balkans' indicates, sustaining the relevance of regions as a terrain of action and an object of study entails shifting the focus of discussion to the social, political and intellectual mechanisms effecting the materialisation of regions, and to human agency. Recognising the social processual nature of space – the actual linkages, policies and imaginations that shape space – means appreciating the changeability, fuzziness and open-endedness of our units of analysis.[1]

Note

[1] The author's approach to the scholarly conceptualisations of the Balkans along such lines is expounded in Mishkova, 2018.

Bibliography

Mishkova, Diana. *Beyond Balkanism: The scholarly politics of region making*. Abingdon: Routledge, 2018.

2
(Global) chaos
Joanna Kusiak

This entry explores the concept and reality of 'chaos': on the one hand, as a word that gives voice to human beings' inability to make sense of the complexity of global capitalism, and hence a political stumbling block that needs to be overcome; and, on the other hand, as the sign of attempts by the globe's dispossessed to survive in a hostile economic and political environment. Investing this phenomenon with geopolitical specificity – since, for the West, where else does chaos originate but in the Global East and Global South? – Kusiak suggests that, in this second sense, chaos itself might be the source of revolutionary potential.

> *Today, world order is increasingly chaotic. Power relations are less clear.*
> UN Secretary-General António Guterres at United Nations General Assembly, 26 September 2018

The so-called 'global order' seems to be beset by chaos. The notion of 'chaos' is increasingly present in the media reports on the state of the world. From the Eastern European, or Global Southern, perspective this talk about chaos is nothing new. What is new, however, is its geographical scope. For a long time, the political keyword 'chaos' had a clear vector: it pointed from the West towards those ostensible aberrations of the East and the South. In this vein, there exists a vast literature on 'post-socialist', 'post-Soviet' or even 'post-Maoist' chaos, as well as on the shanty-metropolitan chaos of the Global South. Occasionally, the West would use the word 'chaos' to label its own subaltern worlds, especially whenever the latter would try to enter the mainstream of political attention. The suburban rioters of London and Paris, or the Syrian refugees travelling across Europe, were all accused of bringing in chaos. Yet only recently, and with some fright, chaos has been discovered in the alleged headquarters of the global order. Not only does the everyday 'muddling through' of the street-seller in Lagos now count as 'chaos', so, too, do the diplomatic actions of United States's President Donald Trump, or Great Britain's unplanned five-year plan of Brexit. So, what are we speaking about when we speak of 'chaos' in (geo)politics?

To start with, 'chaos' is a political keyword and not an analytical or critical notion. While the latter are rational abstractions that isolate specific aspects of reality, 'chaos' is a generalisation that fuses many different phenomena into one. The implied reference to chaos theory embellishes the word with a scientific halo, yet 'chaos' in politics concerns neither the absolute randomness nor the deterministic chaos of dynamic systems. Instead of an analysis, however, 'chaos' operates very successfully as a complaint.[1] This is not to underestimate its role. Especially in Eastern Europe, complaint is a long-acknowledged mode of epistemological access to the status quo. Indeed, true complaint always reaches beyond its immediate meaning, towards the entirety of a subject's condition. Similarly, kvetching about chaos always goes beyond naming fragmented problems, whether Trump, Brexit or global warming: it hints that there is something seriously wrong with the way in which the world is organised. In a postmodern public sphere that obsessively avoids totalising statements, the keyword 'chaos' serves as a rhetorical picklock that makes it possible to address the totality of the political system.

Consequently, more than to the ontological condition of the world, 'chaos' refers to our need to grasp the complex reality of global capitalism – and to our epistemological inability to do so. We are constantly affected by what Fredric Jameson calls 'absent causes', namely phenomena that influence our lives and yet remain invisible to us, as they operate on a different geographical scale or in different temporalities.[2] Taken merely as a metaphor with a scientific aura, 'chaos' can indeed be seen to hit on something important: the proverbial flapping of the wings of a financial adviser in California in 2005 brought about the tornado in the life of a 33-year-old teacher in Budapest that, in 2009, left him unable to afford his mortgage; and the poor households in rural Poland that burn tires to generate warmth in winter may ultimately ruin the Arctic. Nonetheless, if made only at a general level, such statements remain both true and trivial. The infinity of potential connections to be made causes a numbness enabling us to watch the multifarious televised pictures of global suffering without making any connections at all. To overcome such numbness, Jameson puts forward a pedagogy of cognitive mapping: a programmatically impossible and yet politically crucial endeavour aimed at approaching the totality of relations that determine a subject's position in global capitalism. In other words, to defeat what we perceive as 'chaos', we need to focus on the orders organising it.

And yet, as a political keyword, 'chaos' works against the emancipatory efforts of such mapping. If in early capitalism the appearance of a centralised order concealed messy political processes, in late capitalism '(global) chaos' becomes a mask for the structured orders responsible for the systematic monopolisation of power and resources. With its scientific aura and systemic references, talk about 'chaos' functions as a sort of conspiracy theory, yet one with a more sophisticated aesthetics. While vulgar conspiracy theories reduce the complexity of a political situation to a single cause (most often the workings of a designated other), 'chaos' postulates absolute randomness, or fetishises the complexity of interrelated causes to the point at which any cognition seems impossible. As an ersatz analysis, 'chaos' exempts us from the labour of cognitive mapping and alleviates symptoms of cognitive discomfort. The temporary relief is, however, often followed by fear. For 'chaos' represents the threatening totality of the system without giving any rational access to it. Middle classes especially tend to identify 'chaos' with the danger of losing ground. One response is the retreat into the private which gives the illusion of preserving a pocket of order in the illegible world of chaos. But equally often the fear of 'chaos' – despite the term's liberal, quasi-scientific elegance – devolves into the usual conspiracy-theory style of othering. 'Chaos is not only the oldest brouhaha of the world' – wrote a political refugee from Nazi Germany, Joachim Schumacher, in his forgotten treatise from 1936, titled *The Fear of Chaos: About the false apocalypse of the bourgeoisie* – 'it is also the oldest argument for the suppression of the weak ... To understand what anarchy is, when not a revolution, we need to understand capitalism in its mode of turning into fascism.'[3]

'The antithesis to chaos', continues Schumacher, 'is not the authoritarian state – which too often actually produces and masks real chaos – but the organization of freedom'.[4] Indeed, the question of organisation remains the most pressing one for contemporary progressive politics. From this perspective, it's also worth noting that the keyword 'chaos' also relates to a set of organisational skills. Especially in its classical geographical directionality – in accounts about Eastern Europe and the Global South – the keyword 'chaos' is used to describe the ability of the dispossessed to survive despite the unfavourable systemic conditions, as well as act resourcefully in under-resourced environments, using both legal and illegal means. Viewed from the West, the acknowledgement of such transgressive 'chaos' is often tainted with the naive romanticisation of the 'creativity' of dispossession. One classic example here is Rem Koolhaas, a starchitect who, travelling the world from Kinshasa to Shenzhen, remains in constant awe that things actually work, while repeatedly overlooking the human price of the human-infrastructural ensembles that he admires. And yet, because the dispossession brought about by late capitalism is manifest not only in the material impoverishment of the masses, but also as the impoverishment of political ideals, the question arises if the skills of 'chaos' can be actually transferred from the domain of infrastructure into the domain of politics. Can we make progressive politics work, if the repository of revolutionary ideas has been plundered? It might be that only after the global chaos's actually existing orders are exposed can we approximate and redeem the other, revolutionary art of chaos: the one that, according to Nietzsche, one must still have in oneself to be able to give birth to a dancing star.[5]

Notes

1   Kusiak, 2017.
2   Jameson, 2005, 413.
3   Schumacher, 1978, dust jacket.
4   Schumacher, 1978, dust jacket.
5   Nietzsche, 2006, 9.

Bibliography

Jameson, Fredric. *Postmodernism: Or, the cultural logic of late capitalism*. Durham, NC: Duke University Press, 2005.

Kusiak, Joanna. *Chaos Warszawa: Porządki przestrzenne polskiego kapitalizmu* [Chaos Warsaw: Spatial orders of Polish capitalism]. Warsaw: Bęc Zmiana, 2017.

Nietzsche, Friedrich. *Thus Spoke Zarathustra*, edited by Adrian del Caro and Robert Pippin. Cambridge: Cambridge University Press, 2006.

Schumacher, Joachim. *Die Angst vor dem Chaos: Über die falsche Apokalypse des Bürgertums* [Fear of Chaos: The false apocalypse of the bourgeoisie]. Frankfurt am Main: Syndikat Verlag, 1978.

3
The children's republic
Diana Georgescu

While a 'children's republic' now sounds like a theme park where parents pay to have their offspring learn the principles of capitalism and neoliberalism, by acting them out behind shop counters and in uniforms, in the period after the Second World War it embodied an ideal of a self-governing children's community that could overcome national, cultural and geopolitical boundaries, while, at least as far as the Soviet bloc was concerned, creating the socialist citizens of the future (and to that extent foreshadowing today's theme parks). Like many such internationalist experiments, in practice such children's camps had unintended and sometimes paradoxical outcomes, often reinforcing borders and differences while hoping to erase them. But if the network of exchanges, pioneer camps and more rustic campsites did not trace a children's continent, drawing up a map of their similarities and differences, tensions and solidarities, it does complicate the picture of a Europe divided East and West in the twentieth century.

Following the Second World War, the widespread practice of youth exchanges often served to forge new geopolitical alliances and revive old ones. International camps organised as children's republics became a staple in state socialist countries, where they facilitated the cohesion of the emerging Soviet bloc, and among left-wing youth movements associated with social democrat, socialist and labour parties in western, central and northern Europe, where they resuscitated prewar socialist collaboration (Figure 3.1). The Soviet policy of opening to the West in the wake of Stalin's death, as well as the atmosphere of détente of the 1970s, ensured that children acting as cultural ambassadors also increasingly crossed the Iron Curtain to attend youth camps during the late Cold War.

Figure 3.1 International child participants in distinctive folk garb or organisation uniforms posing at the international pioneer camp, Năvodari, Romania. *Cutezatorii*, May 1974.

UCL Special Collections, IOE Archives, London.

Although set within specific national and geopolitical boundaries, children's republics promised to transgress them by creating internationalist, multicultural and egalitarian communities of child-citizens from around the world, whether the Soviet bloc, Western Europe or the Global South. Despite the presumed universality of childhood and seemingly shared ideals of democracy and internationalism, children's republics were shaped by diplomatic tensions, ideological disagreements and divergent leftist pedagogies. Thus, even as they sought to transgress national or Cold War boundaries (between East and West, socialism and capitalism), left-wing youth camps often reinforced them. Here I explore the children's republic as a category of practice, that is, an ideological and pedagogical concept invested with universalist connotations by historical actors throughout the twentieth century, and deploy it as a category of analysis to rethink the geopolitical divisions of the Cold War and the older East–West dichotomy on which they were based.

Cold War children's republics continued a prewar Soviet and more broadly European pedagogical tradition of raising children as socialist citizens by training them in the practice of self-government and self-management. As befits an ideal with internationalist pretensions, this pedagogy emerged across the imaginary East–West divide in Europe through analogous responses to profound change and the cross-pollination of progressive educational ideas after the Russian Revolution and the First World War. The most radical pedagogies developed in post-revolutionary Russia in the attempts to remake society by breaking with the authoritarianism of tsarist schools and addressing the social consequences of war. In pedagogical experiments like Moiseĭ Pistrak's Lepeshinskiĭ School Commune or Anton Makarenko's Gorky Colony, utopianism met the challenge of millions of homeless, orphaned street children by creating labour communes.[1] Because these communes invested children with autonomy, placing the child collective as a self-sustaining and self-governing unit at the heart of education, they appealed to pedagogues in the New Education movement and socialists and social democrats in Europe and the United States.

The innovative climate of the New Education movement, with its emphasis on child autonomy, play and anti-authoritarianism, inspired Austrian and German social democrats to experiment with children's republics, as opportunities to give working-class children a political apprenticeship in democracy and comradeship, at the turn of the twentieth century. Through the Falcon youth movements (now IFM-SEI), their ideas spread to central Europe, France and Britain throughout the 1920s and 1930s. European socialists drew on Soviet child psychology on the inherently social and political character of children and on the Soviet pedagogies of Nadezhda Krupskaia and Moiseĭ Pistrak on the role of the collective in the child's socio-political and moral development.[2] In these 'toy republics', meant to lay the ground for a larger social and political transformation, children learned by doing, experiencing direct democracy and self-government (electing representatives, making decisions), self-management (cooking, cleaning, and so on) and the camaraderie of communal life.

Envisioning children as social and political actors, but also as malleable and free of prejudice, the prewar pedagogy of children's republics lent itself easily to the postwar goal of socialist internationalism, friendship and peace. If interwar children's republics sought to raise the citizens of a future socialist society, international children's camps aimed for a world that could overcome national, cultural and geopolitical borders, creating a unified socialist front in the Soviet bloc and building bridges with progressive allies across the Iron Curtain. Although state socialist Pioneers and leftist youth in the West did not speak the same language, the shared vocabulary of socialist internationalism obscured their different practices and pedagogies.

Among state socialist regimes, the model of the international children's republic was set by the flagship Soviet camp at Artek in the Crimean Peninsula, a model learned through the annual system of 'mutual youth exchanges'. By the 1960s, international pioneer camps offered a predictable programme of political activities, sports competitions and festivals of folk dance and music that culminated with 'National Day' celebrations. These activities marked a shift from the original educational goal of children's republics to a primarily diplomatic mission: showcasing socialist achievement. While pioneer camps were still advertised as experiments in self-management and self-government, they were monitored by adult leaders, mediated by translators and administered by specialised staff. Camps also mobilised significant state resources, offering modern facilities and specialist personnel. Featuring diverse youth dancing together in folk garb, marching against imperialist aggression in Vietnam, or daring each other in sports, children's republics fulfilled their twin goals: the performance of cultural diversity and its transgressing through practices of internationalism, thus creating the impression that Eastern Europe formed a united socialist front.

In practice, diplomatic tensions and competing agendas ensured that international camps were rarely the idealised communities conjured by the organisers. The Soviet model itself was fraught with ambiguity, projecting a vision of internationalism as 'Soviet suprematism' and 'cultural imperialism'.[3] Hosting 40,000 children from around the world by the 1960s, Artek became a central site in the diplomatic efforts of the Soviet Union to articulate a morally superior alternative to Western capitalism that could function as a model for the rest of the world. Camp dynamics reflected this hegemonic view and the emerging cracks in the barely consolidated Eastern 'bloc' and broader socialist world. When Romanian child delegations arrived at Artek following Nicolae Ceaușescu's proclamations of 'independent socialism' during the Sino-Soviet split, they were welcomed by 'insinuating questions' during 'friendly meetings': 'Do Romanian pioneers still wear scarves? Do they still celebrate the Great October Socialist Revolution? Why does Romania maintain a neutral position on China's cultural revolution? How does it view its participation in the Warsaw Pact?'[4] The universalist pretensions of socialist internationalism gave Romanians discursive room to contest the Soviet model. Positioning themselves as defenders of authentic internationalism, they critiqued the dogmatism, militarism and suprematism attributed to the Soviet (or Soviet-style) model, while Soviet organisers excluded Romanian teams from camp-wide competitions, German Democratic Republic (GDR) interpreters monitored the Romanian team relentlessly, and Hungarian hosts imposed mandatory military drills, ignoring the children's tender age.

If children's republics did not engender the idealised Soviet vision of socialist internationalism as cross-cultural friendship, they nevertheless contributed to cultural exchanges within the socialist world. Socialist organisations continued to participate in youth exchanges, making international children's camps one of those shared institutions and experiences that gradually gave the Second World an air of family resemblance.[5] Even at the height of diplomatic tensions, Romanian guests were still awed by Artek's worldwide delegations, modern facilities and natural beauty. Despite their critique of hegemonic Soviet internationalism, Romanians embraced this model, aspiring to exert a similar influence on the world stage and expanding their relations to include organisations from the Global South and Western Europe from the 1960s.

When they crossed the Iron Curtain to participate in children's republics in places like France, Germany, Austria or the United Kingdom, Romanian pioneers were looking for progressive allies against Soviet hegemony and diplomatic venues to popularise Romania's national culture and independent foreign policy. Here, their paths intersected with alternative pedagogies of collective life, seeking to cultivate youthful internationalism through practices of child autonomy, self-management and self-government. Following the student protests of 1968, these traditions were also revisited by a radical New Left that provided many of the young monitors volunteering to run camps, resulting in a renewed focus on anti-authoritarian, laissez-faire pedagogies.

If the abstract language of socialist internationalism brought diverse youth organisations together, it could not always solve the actual tensions emerging from distinctive pedagogies. While some Romanian delegations enjoyed the elective, informal and play-centred character of Western camps, others objected to the lack of discipline and ideological substance. By both choice and necessity, many Western camps were small and, being organised on camping grounds, required communal work and the practice of direct democracy in the very process of living, working and playing together. Familiar with Soviet-style camps, some Romanian delegations came unprepared for rough life and daily chores, an attitude that struck their British hosts, for example, as lack of solidarity and internationalist spirit: '[Romanians] flatly refused to participate at all [in their allocated rotas] (except when they thought that they would be able to steal food). We all got the opinion that they were making a mockery of the whole of our organisation'.[6] Similar points of contention emerged when Westerners visited pioneer camps and complained about the rigidity, formality and competitive character of camp activities.

Athletic competition, they opined, discouraged participation. Similarly, the large scale of pioneer camps, compounded by the formal, ritualistic nature of delegation meetings, made it impossible to cultivate genuine friendships.

Where state socialist organisations like the Romanian Pioneers and left-wing movements found common ground was in the performance of cultural/national diversity. Following the Soviet model, the Romanians saw international camps as opportunities to perform their national

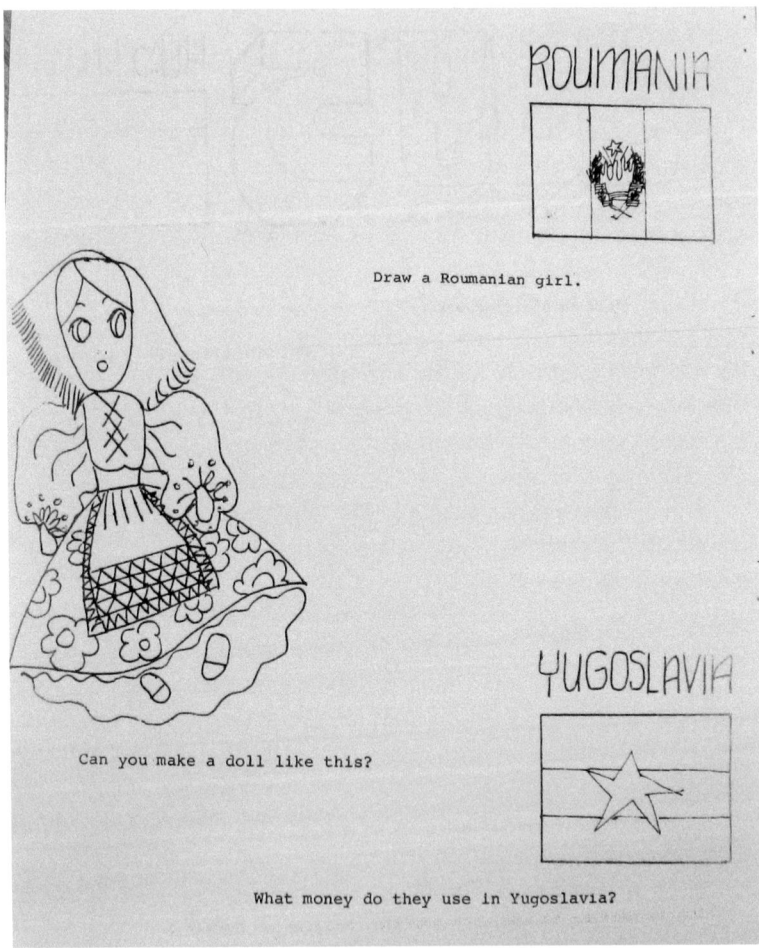

Figure 3.2 Page from a quiz meant to encourage children from various delegations to know each other better. Brochure used during the Camp of Nations, Danbury Park, Essex, August 1970.

UCL Special Collections, IOE Archives, London.

specificity – embodied in folk song and dance – on an international stage. For their part, many leftist Western organisations aimed at cultivating youth's multicultural sensibility, a sensibility they saw as a prerequisite for mutual understanding and internationalism and even a strategy to overcome 'cultural imperialism'. To facilitate cultural understanding, organisers included country-specific quizzes or activities that, like the performances of folk traditions, essentialised national identities as 'cultural traditions' even as they sought to transgress them (Figure 3.2).

Exploring the Cold War through internationalist spaces like children's republics allows us to rethink the monolithic nature of geopolitical 'blocs' and explore the porous nature of the 'Iron Curtain'. Children's republics illustrate how historical actors – whether the Soviet Pioneers or seemingly marginal organisations like the Romanian Pioneers – deployed the universalist language of internationalism to give ideological cohesion to emerging political and economic alliances in the socialist world. But they also reveal the cracks in this world, the diplomatic tensions, ideological divisions and alternative paths among fraternal regimes that did not march in unison. If the socialist 'bloc' cohered into a space distinct from both the First and the Third World, it was less because its members transgressed national and cultural differences, and more because shared institutions and experiences emerged through cultural encounters.

Not least because institutions like the children's republics had a longer European history that involved ideological dialogue across the East–West divide since the beginning of the twentieth century, they also speak to transsystemic exchanges during the Cold War. International camps enabled state socialist and left-wing organisations to build bridges with fellow travellers in Europe. In spite of these organisations' shared vocabulary of internationalism, however, their encounters reinforced as much as transgressed cultural, ideological and geopolitical borders.

Notes

1 Fitzpatrick, 1970, 50; on Makarenko see Kharkhordin, 1999, 9–102.
2 Downs, 2002, 213–25.
3 Kelly, 2008, 735.
4 Archive of Romanian Pioneers, file 7/1967, 'Informare', Elena Popard, 166–7, and file 24/1974, 'Informare: Tabăra internaţională Artek, URSS', 98–9.
5 On the Second World as a set of 'similar institutions, blueprints, and experiences', see Babiracki and Jersild, 2016.
6 Davis, 'Report', Youth Movement Archive/Woodcraft Folk, FH42.

Bibliography

Archive of Romanian Pioneers, National Children's Palace, Bucharest, Romania.

Babiracki, Patryk and Austin Jersild. 'Introduction'. In *Socialist Internationalism in the Cold War: Exploring the Second World*, edited by Patryk Babiracki and Austin Jersild, 1–16. London: Palgrave Macmillan, 2016.

Davis, Violet. 'Report of visit of Roumanian Pioneers to Crayheath District and to International Camp, Malvern, 1979', Youth Movement Archive/Woodcraft Folk, FH42. LSE Library Archives and Special Collections, London.

Downs, Laura. *Childhood in the Promised Land: Working-class movements and the colonies de vacances in France, 1880–1960*. Durham, NC: Duke University Press, 2002.

Fitzpatrick, Sheila. *The Commissariat of Enlightenment: Soviet organization of education and the arts under Lunacharsky, October 1917–1921*. London: Cambridge University Press, 1970.

Kelly, Catriona. 'Defending children's rights, "In Defense of Peace": Children and Soviet cultural diplomacy', *Kritika: Explorations in Russian and Eurasian History* 9 (2008): 711–46.

Kharkhordin, Oleg. *The Collective and the Individual in Russia: A study of practices*. Berkeley: University of California Press, 1999.

4
The countryside – a matter of ruling class
Alexandra Urdea

Urdea proposes the countryside, particularly the East European one, as a continent of the imagination – as well as the location of contemporary lives – and teases out the functions this category can be made to serve, particularly for domestic and foreign elites. Her interpretation of a critical area studies points to unexpected similarities – between England and Transylvania, castles and countryside, or prince and peasant – to show how, in each case, claims of 'authenticity' assert imaginative value while concealing functional obsolescence.

Not so long ago, images of Prince Charles, among the rolling hills of Transylvania, dancing in a circle dance (*hora*) alongside people in pristine white folk attire, were a common occurrence in the Romanian and British media, drawing attention to the Romanian countryside as an example of nature and culture in need of protection.[1] For the Romanian press, Prince Charles's visits were proof of the value of the countryside – alas, one that Romanian elites do not capitalise on as successfully as foreigners. The countryside of eastern Europe, richly decorated in folk motifs, has a fruitful history in the imagination of both Western and Eastern European artists, politicians and travellers. And while these visitors to the countryside have created lasting images and tropes of the countryside at different points in history, their endeavour was also to fashion themselves in very specific images – according to what the times required: as either nationalists, modernisers of the country or defenders of the culture and nature.

Theorists of nationalism, such as Hobsbawm, argued that a recurring image of the countryside – as populated for centuries by the same communities, with their enduring culture and beliefs – emerged with the creation and consolidation of nation-states by nineteenth-century elites in Eastern Europe, and elsewhere.[2] Nationalism's territorial claims assumes an enduring connection between land, people and culture. In the ethnically mixed areas of Eastern Europe, nationalisms often dressed in peasant garb, to legitimise the regimes and rulers of the newly created nation-states as being 'of the people'. In Romania, from the turn of the twentieth century and up to the Second World War, the royal family (imported from a German noble family) and the local elite, posed in folk attire and endorsed the production of folk-inspired art. 'Folklore' proved a useful ideological tool in drawing cultural and physical borders to delimit national territories, and this trope is still present today, visible in every corner of Romanian public culture.

But nationalism was not the only ideology that generated meaning around East European rurality. Around the turn of the twentieth century, artists and travellers from across Europe roamed the East European countryside, avidly recording vernacular cultures and taking inspiration from them, rushing to preserve fragments of what they perceived to be dying cultures. Modern artists drew on vernacular motifs to disrupt Western artistic conventions, or to paint a picture of a world disrupted by modernity, or to imagine rural alternatives to the menacing effects of industrialism and capitalism. Long before the need to protect biodiversity became stringent, the countryside emerged as a particular kind of alterity to the industrialised modern world, valued as much for the 'nature' as for the local culture dubbed 'authentic' – to mean untouched by modernity, inspired by and in communion with nature. Like the colonial space of 'the native', the countryside was and often still is thought to be a place 'without a history', as opposed to the urban centres, which drive change and historical progress.[3] A wealth of other oppositions ensue: modern (high) culture versus folklore; a class-based society as opposed to a homogeneous class of peasants; an atomised society as opposed to tight-knit communities; progress as opposed to tradition.

The Prince of Wales's discourse about the Transylvanian countryside fits nicely into this narrative of the rural as an alternative to the modern. 'Here, globalisation has not reached', says the Prince's associate and manager of his estate, Hungarian aristocrat Tibor Kálnoky.[4] Prince Charles owns properties in remote areas of Transylvania, where he strives to protect biodiversity and historical patrimony by refurbishing old houses and endorsing sustainability projects through eco-tourism. Since traditional, unindustrialised agriculture, such as the one practised in these areas of Romania in the past, is far from sustainable, the solution is to transform 'the local' into a brand which brings together the landscape, its people, their culture and their work practices, to be marketed to those hungry for such things. Scything may not be agriculturally efficient, but it preserves biodiversity, and it certainly looks dramatic. 'You can get an idea of what Britain was like some 700–800 years ago. The patterns of farming, everything would have been almost identical', Prince Charles tells us.[5] In this view the countryside illustrates premodern history, and feeds the modern nostalgia for lost traditional communities living in harmony with the land. Another common image of the countryside is that of a place in need of protection from globalisation; meanwhile, like in the case of many UNESCO sites, heritagisation of the countryside is imagined as an economic solution. By making property purchases, the Prince exerts some control over the preservation of heritage and landscape.

According to Raymond Williams, in England too the discourse of nostalgia and the need to safeguard the countryside are recurrent tropes in literature and art, which can also work to conceal the social history of these places. Myths about the closely bound countryside communities of the past are common to both England and Romania, even though their histories of property and social relations could not be more different. The history of the English countryside is marked by the enclosure of common land by large landowners, leaving the majority of those working the land as tenants, with few land rights and largely at the mercy of landowners. Although it accelerated by the eighteenth century, the process lasted over centuries – a history which could be regarded as 'continuous from the long process of conquest and seizure, the land gained by killing, by repression, by political bargains'.[6] This was no harmonious, unchanging 'community of peasants'. Crucially, capitalism changed social relations between the workers and the owners of land. The English lords who, today, find themselves owners of land let to tenants, are subject to very different cultural and economic constraints than their forefathers, and it is very difficult to speak of continuation. Williams's commentary on the cultural meanings of English stately homes helps us question the narrative around these places we now visit as tourists, where the story presented tells us so little of the social history, of those who worked or profited from the land owned by the lords.

In Romania, the image of secluded peasant communities is highly prevalent and narrated in folklore museums across the country, among other cultural places. Yet this narrative of a timeless countryside sits at odds with school-taught history, of a peasantry mired in poverty throughout the eighteenth and nineteenth centuries, working as serfs on the boyars' estates, their violent uprisings and even worse aftermaths.

In Transylvania ethnic and social groups often overlapped, and ethnicity is, and was throughout modern history, politically charged. A large part of the Romanian rural population was under direct feudal control by Magyar nobility, which meant that at the turn of the twentieth century national and social emancipation overlapped. After the First World War, the creation of an independent Great Romania came with a large-scale social reform, whereby peasants were given land – if they could prove they were ethnically Romanian. A social order based on the cohabitation of different ethnicities was overturned, and in some parts ethnic heterogeneity remains problematic, after a tumultuous history of land collectivisation (in the socialist period) and restitution (in postsocialism). After the Second World War, the socialist party invested a great deal in 'folklore', as a homogenised version of national culture through which communist modernity (to mean collectivisation of land in all but mountainous areas) was legitimised and where ethnic minorities were further marginalised.

By the time peasants were receiving the land after World War I, 'folklore' was already being assiduously collected, to be rescued from imminent disappearance. Today the folklore museums of Romania, while displaying the world of the 'rural', with its colourful seasonal rituals, make little reference to its history. The disappearance of 'folk' objects from the countryside is mourned – 'the real peasant is long dead', declared the head of the Romanian Peasant Museum in the 1990s. And yet what this fails to show is that almost half of Romania's population still lives in rural areas – and so do their possessions, beliefs and practices, all of which are constantly changing. Naturally, some of the old objects used by rural populations have indeed been discarded, either because they fell out of fashion, or because they have become redundant. Heritagisation and the reintroduction of certain items and practices is itself a process of social change – like the interest in traditional attire in some parts of the country. Donning a certain kind of folk attire does not mean bringing the past back – to the contrary, it is about interpreting the past, and selecting what is considered valuable.

From the large-scale agriculture of multinational companies to depopulation or transnational migration, to the replacement of traditional material culture with modern items, globalisation is considered a threat to the countryside, leading to a homogenised global culture, against local ways of living off the land. But what are Prince Charles's actions in Transylvania if not global? No different than the UNESCO heritage list, or other organisations with a global reach, aiming to protect the local. Inevitably, his travels to Transylvania and his role there had an effect not only on those places, but also helped to reinvent his image and place HRH into contemporary global movements. Meanwhile, Prince Charles was hardly the only one travelling the world trying to refashion himself. Many of those from the Transylvanian villages where he owns property do it too, as migrants in search of a better life.

One striking characteristic of the properties that Prince Charles owns in rural Transylvania is just how simply and tastefully they have been decorated, as if consciously avoiding vulgarity – for both country people and aristocrats are prone to being judged as vulgar. Romanian country folk who aspire to have modern or fashionable houses, cars, clothes, might be described as 'inauthentic'. Meanwhile many of the English aristocrats' homes have now become part of national heritage, and obvious displays of wealth have, for a while now, been considered 'non-U'. The Prince's room in his house in Szeklerland can be rented, and tourists are always struck by its simplicity. The Transylvanian countryside is 'a spiritual resource as much as anything else, it's part of the country's heritage. Romania is a very rural country. We have our great castles and cathedrals, they have their countryside and crafts', explains John Akeroyd, botanist working with the Prince of Wales.[7] There is a rhetoric of equivalence between the two types of heritage, English castles and Romanian countryside. Like any *lieu de mémoire*, both reveal some aspects of the past and present, while concealing others.

Notes

1 This entry was written before King Charles's accession to the throne in 2022.
2 Hobsbawm, 1990.
3 Wolf, 1982; Williams, 1975.
4 'Royal special: Prince Charles on the future of rural communities', BBC Radio 4, 2015.
5 'Royal special: Prince Charles on the future of rural communities', BBC Radio 4, 2015.
6 Williams, 1975, 97.
7 'Royal special: Prince Charles on biodiversity', BBC Radio 4, 2015.

Bibliography

Hobsbawm, Eric J. *Nations and Nationalism since 1780: Programme, myth, reality*. Cambridge: Cambridge University Press, 1990.
Mediafax. 'Profilul consumatorului rural: 46% au mașină, 63% au smartphone, 70% au cont bancar' [Profile of rural consumers], Departmentul Economic. Accessed 11 November 2017. https://www.mediafax.ro/economic/romania-rurala-profilul-consumatorului-rural-46-au-masina-63-au-smartphone-70-au-cont-bancar-16833564.
'Royal special: Prince Charles on biodiversity', *On Your Farm*, BBC Radio 4, 9 August 2015. Accessed 30 July 2024. https://www.bbc.co.uk/programmes/b064x6w0.

'Royal special: Prince Charles on the future of rural communities', *On Your Farm*, BBC Radio 4, 16 August 2015. Accessed 30 July 2024. https://www.bbc.co.uk/programmes/b065rv5r.

Tsing, Anna. *Friction: An ethnography of global connection*. Princeton, NJ: Princeton University Press, 2004.

Williams, Raymond. *The Country and the City*. New York: Oxford University Press, 1975.

Wolf, Eric. *Europe and the People without History*. Berkeley: University of California Press, 1982.

5
Digital Eastern Europe?
Maciej Maryl

What holds an 'area' together? How do regional and vernacular commonalities find a place in global processes? Here we find that a taken-for-granted area is not enough to support an initiative in digital humanities, despite shared assumptions, methods and sense of identity: 'Eastern Europe' contains too many cross-cutting divisions (linguistic, historical, or even geographical) to unite potential participants. Mere cultural proximity is not (always) enough, as a binding force. The digital humanities experiences described here gesture towards the potential of research questions defining the area, rather than the area setting the boundaries of research.

At the first attempt to conceptualise an area, we failed to grasp it or even to name it. However, there seemed to be a shared, genuine need to establish a common scholarly space in digital humanities (DH), aligned with the geographical relationships of Eastern Europe. But does this space exist? And if so, why is it so hard to delineate it?[1]

It all started in Budapest, where a 'text analysis across disciplines' workshop took place in May 2017, organised by Jessie Labov, Marcell Sebők and Tamás Kiss, from the Digital Humanities Initiative at Central European University (CEU), back in those ancient times when not only could people travel freely without the risk of being quarantined but also when CEU was still flourishing, before being forced out of Hungary. The meeting featured presentations of digital humanities (DH) projects by guests from Austria, Czechia, Estonia, Hungary, Poland and Romania, followed by a 'closed-door meeting about Hungarian DH and regional network'. The discussion points for that session included the question of whether it would be valuable to have a regional DH network, 'and, if so, why?' The organisers suggested we might need such cooperation to establish a training network, run collaborative projects or share resources (multilingual projects, shared geographic areas). Participants seemed to like the idea of a regional network (in the sense of area-framed digital humanities). In a way, participants shared a notion resembling the 'ideology of Eastness', that is to say, a perception of a regional bond produced by a clear opposition between the region and the more advanced digital networks of Western Europe.[2] This idea of regional (digital) uniqueness is neatly unpacked by McElroy writing on *oraşul viitorului* (in this volume), where 'Siliconisation' means a complex interplay between global processes and the affordances of the vernacular culture. Our perception of a regional common ground might also have been reinforced by shared methodological traditions in the region, formalism, semiotics and structuralism, for instance, as well as bilateral cultural transfers between the countries involved. Hence, this feeling of joint purpose went beyond a simple exchange of tools and good practices (which could be achieved with countries outside the region as well). Then we started to look for a name, as the banner of this initiative, and this is where the problems started.

'Let's call it DH East', someone said, but this was quickly opposed by participants citing associations with Far East and Middle East – areas clearly not covered by the participants. 'So, maybe Central-East DH', another person proposed. However, what about the Baltic countries, which are technically North-East? North-East-Central was also not an option, as the Balkans are clearly in the South. So, we left with nothing. It was somewhat symbolic that although the common interest lay not only in shared methods and tools but also in regional identity, we failed to find a way to frame the region, perhaps not just because of the connotations of geographical indicators, but also because of the complexity of relationships between the countries involved and the lack of a stronger foothold in existing projects.

A similar meeting took place later that year in Budapest, at Eötvös Loránd University (ELTE).[3] This time the setting was different, as ELTE's Gábor Palkó organised the event in the framework of DARIAH, the Digital Research Infrastructure for the Arts and Humanities, and the focus was on the Visegrád Group countries, as the participants came from Austria, Czechia, Hungary, Poland and Slovakia. This shift in geographical scope made the regional aspect a bit less problematic; however, as we shall see, it failed to remove all the obstacles encountered at CEU in May. During this meeting, the DARIAH Central-European Hub (CEH) was founded, which focuses on three kinds of collaboration: 'establishing a regional repository of digital humanities research, aligning teaching activities by sharing knowledge and developing/ using common eLearning materials and fostering the usage of multilingual computational language tools in the humanities and the social sciences'. Although we know what CEH plans to achieve, what is the rationale for cooperation between those particular countries? A little detour through the concept of the global digital humanities may be particularly helpful here.

Digital humanities is not a discipline but rather a set of approaches or methods feeding into other, already well-established disciplines. Although few would challenge the claim that the global version of DH evolved around an English-speaking centre, creating and spreading to wider peripheries, more recent scholarship aims at reclaiming the local specificity of DH.[4] We cannot, of course, forget that in many countries, especially in Eastern Europe, DH developed when the global centre was already established. Yet DH, like non-digital humanities, is by no means a uniform, globally standardised methodology but rather, a research approach heavily influenced by the local context, and by a variety of research questions and methodological traditions. Institutional frameworks and funding regimes also influence the directions in which vernacular digital humanities projects expand.[5]

This tension between the local and the global is visible in various mapping efforts, like the Global Outlook::Digital Humanities project, which aimed at presenting the diversity of approaches around the globe. The resulting map, *Around DH in 80 Days*, gives an impression of totality, striving to represent diversity, yet obviously omitting many projects or initiatives which were not selected by the editors.[6] Based on her experience as a contributor to this project, Roopika Risam proposed to view the difference between the global and the local through the theory of accent, which she claims, 'recognises both local specificity and global coherence in DH'.[7] The concept of DH accent is built upon Global English and its variations.[8] However, the notion of the accent may be just as totalising as the concept of the centre and periphery, as it presumes that there is one common root or even one 'proper' version of DH and its regional variations. Risam's notion of the accent seems to describe a specific local preference for tools or methods, rather than to reflect local specificity, which would depend on the general position of humanities inquiry in a given setting, or culturally-specific methodological preferences.

However, something is troubling about the geography of DH scholarship in general. Recent discussions on the importance of establishing institutionalised networks of DH scholars and institutions in various regions of Europe prompt us to consider whether applying geographical categories to this particular field is useful and productive. Here I am not referring to digital area studies (digitally enabled or supported area studies),[9] but rather something we might call area digital humanities, with an underlying assumption that various fields and approaches can be bound together by the sole means of digital methodology and geographical or cultural proximity.

It seems to work at least for some communities. The Alliance of Digital Humanities Organizations (ADHO) encompasses continental (Europe, Australia, Southern Africa), as well as several national organisations being members of ADHO or continental branches (including USA, Canada, Czechia, Italy, Japan, Russia, Taiwan). There are also some cross-national associations, such as the Australasian Association for Digital Humanities Inc (aaDH, established 2011), Red de Humanidades Digitales (RedHD, established 2011), Humanidades Digitales Hispánicas (HDH, established 2011), Digital Humanities im deutschsprachigen Raum (DHd,[10] established 2013), Digital Humanities in the Nordic and Baltic countries (DHNB,[11] established 2015) and L'association francophone des humanités digitales (Humanistica,[12] established 2014). They seem to flourish because they share a certain level of cultural transfer among participating nations, as well as language in most of the cases. So in these cases cultural proximity (shared methodological traditions, cultural transfer, and so on) enables area digital humanities, that is, a level of commonality allowing for fruitful research exchange in a regional context.

Why doesn't it work in Eastern Europe? First of all, there is language. We could, for instance, think about the cooperation of Slavic countries in this respect. And indeed there is a Slavic-DH group at ASEEES (Association for Slavic, East European and Eurasian Studies),[13] which aims 'to support the teaching, scholarship, curation and preservation of digitally-rendered work in Slavic (as well as East European and Eurasian) Studies'. The group comprises those members of the association who are eager to incorporate the digital into their workflows or simply try to take advantage of the digitised sources vital for their work. Yet the umbrella here is largely institutional, with a strong leaning towards national literatures in practice, and does not have much to do with actual areas.

For us, regional DH practitioners gathered in Budapest in 2017, a disciplinary-driven focus would not have made much sense, due to profound linguistic differences between Slavic countries, the lack of shared cultural space and also the fact that strong DH players in the region (Austria, Romania, Hungary) are non-Slavic. During the first meeting in Budapest, we felt we had something in common, but we did not know what it was exactly. Admittedly, it was not the language, since we brought together Slavic languages, a Romance one (Romanian), Finnic and Finno-Ugric.

One may also notice a difference in approach. Whereas it was scholars who formed these regional DH associations through bottom-up processes, Central-European Hub, to use the second example, was the result of a top-down process initiated in the framework of the DARIAH grant 'Humanities at Scale'. The region has some shared experiences relevant to DH inquiry, but these are mostly due to similar academic regimes or practices. For instance, there are many similar documentation practices in the field of bibliographies, biographies, lexicons, dictionaries, which now become fuel for DH projects, and enable possible cooperation in cross-mapping resources. A quick look at recent DH initiatives in the region seems to support this claim: establishing the COURAGE digital registry[14] of collections pertinent to dissident legacies, creating the European Literary Text Collection (ELTeC) in a Distant Reading[15] COST Action, or surveying the digital needs of historians of dissent by the NEP4DISSENT[16] COST Action.

So, it seems that the local potential for area digital humanities lies not so much in geographical affordances, but in the actual research questions pertinent to, and shared by, scholars in the region, such as the legacy of dissent in the former Soviet bloc. And this inevitably brings us back to digital area studies, topic-driven and digitally-informed research into particular problems in a geographical framework. Hence the creation of the imagined regional community of Central-European Hub is important for political reasons, to position the scattered, emerging local initiatives on the field of global DH and foster cooperation among the less-advanced late adopters. The CEH members applied to the Visegrád funding scheme, under the lead of Katalin Bella from ELTE. In the application we claimed that what brought the partners together is:

> scarce national funding of the humanities; a paradigm change in scholarly research that was followed by the Central European researchers and research policy makers later than by Western European countries; rigid organizational structure of academic institutions and study curricula. A Central European collaboration will help us nominate stronger teams into the international grant competition and provide reliable partners for international cooperations.

These are all arguments based on institutional and political matters, hence, it seems that the cooperation is so far of a somewhat strategic, if not tactical, nature. Perhaps it will prepare the ground for more topic-driven joint initiatives, and the possibility of a digital area studies in the future.

Notes

1. This work was partly supported by the COST Action New Exploratory Phase in Research on East European Cultures of Dissent (NEP4DISSENT; CA16213) and EC grant: 'Shaping Interdisciplinary Practices in Europe' (SHAPE-ID; #822705). The author thanks Jessie Labov and Wendy Bracewell for comments on the earlier draft of this paper.
2. Zarycki, 2014.
3. ELTE-DH, 2020.
4. See Schreibman, 2012.
5. O'Sullivan, Murphy and Day, 2015.
6. Global Outlook::DH, 2020.
7. Risam, 2017, 378.
8. Risam, 2017, 380.
9. See Pitman, 2015. Accessed 19 August 2024.
10. https://dig-hum.de/. Accessed 19 August 2024.
11. https://dhnb.eu/. Accessed 19 August 2024.
12. https://www.humanisti.ca/. Accessed 19 August 2024.
13. https://aseees.org. Accessed 19 August 2024.
14. http://cultural-opposition.eu/. Accessed 19 August 2024.
15. https://www.distant-reading.net/. Accessed 19 August 2024.
16. https://nep4dissent.eu/. Accessed 19 August 2024.

Bibliography

ELTE.DH. 'DARIAH CEH'. Accessed 31 July 2024. https://elte-dh.hu/dariah-ceh/.
Global Outlook::Digital Humanities. 'Around DH in 80 days'. Accessed 16 March 2020. https://arounddh.elotroalex.com/journey/.
O'Sullivan, James, Órla Murphy and Shawn Day. 'The emergence of the digital humanities in Ireland', *Breac: A Digital Journal of Irish Studies* October (2015). Accessed 31 July 2024. https://breac.nd.edu/articles/the-emergence-of-the-digital-humanities-in-ireland/.
Pitman, Lesley. *Supporting Research in Area Studies: A guide for academic libraries*. Oxford: Chandos Publishing, 2015.
Risam, Roopika. 'Other worlds, other DHs: Notes towards a DH accent', *Digital Scholarship in the Humanities* 32(2) (2017): 377–84.
Schreibman, Susan. 'Digital humanities: Centres and peripheries', *Historical Social Research/Historische Sozialforschung* 37(3) (2012): 46–58.
Zarycki, Tomasz. *Ideologies of Eastness in Central and Eastern Europe*. London: Routledge, 2014.

6
Dreamland (and its queer map)
Čarna Brković

Is Dreamland an 'area'? Guides to interpreting dreams, widely published and read in the Balkans since the nineteenth century, reproduce particular visions of the world. Their maps of Dreamland trace a shared set of expectations and understandings, so they might indeed be understood as mapping a specific area, one that smudges nationalism's sharp boundaries in the post-Yugoslav space. 'Queering' the classical dreambook, and thus transforming social relations and categories, constitutes an intervention into those maps of the world. But this intervention usefully shifts the coordinates of study: not so much Dreamland as area, rather mapping Dreamland as a social and political project.

What do dreams mean? How can we think about various dreamscapes? In what way do dreams shape social relations – and vice versa? These questions led a group of scholars, activists and artists from former Yugoslavia to map the topography of Dreamland in a queer manner. The queer map of Dreamland emerged out of their friendship, mischievous fascination with Balkan heritage, and political commitment to imagining the world otherwise. The result of this work was published as *The Queer Dreambook* – a book that offers a map of the terrain of dreams, alternative not just to the Western dream dictionaries, but also to the classic dreambooks of the Balkan region, called *sanovnik* or *sanjarica*.

English language dream dictionaries aim to offer a map of the unconscious parts of the mind. Their purpose is to help a person discover how they really think and feel, deep down, hidden from the judging eye of the conscious self. These dictionaries are grounded in a Freudian belief that dreams are an expression of the unconscious. While dreams may appear random and nonsensical when taken literally, interpreting them 'is the royal road to a knowledge of the unconscious activities of the mind'.[1]

A classic *sanovnik* approaches dreams differently: it aims to provide a map to the future, rather than a key to the inner and hidden parts of self. Here, dreams are prophecies of what shall come to pass. The main purpose of the *sanovnik* is to help a dreamer to decipher what the dreams say about the forthcoming course of events. Classic dreambooks are compilations of traditional and folk knowledge from the Balkans concerning the meanings of dreams. They have been used in the former Yugoslav countries since the mid nineteenth century and they continue to live today: the classic dreambooks are found in many households, libraries and bookstores, as well as online, on websites dedicated to fortune telling.

The *Queer Dreambook* (or *Kvir sanovnik*) provides yet another kind of a map through the land of dreams: it is a key to understanding and reinterpreting social relations. This queer map of Dreamland does not revolve around a subject – what dreams may say about my subconscious mind and about me as a person is irrelevant. The truth value of dreams – the cornerstone of classic dreambooks – is also irrelevant. The important thing from the perspective of the *Kvir sanovnik* is how dreams can help to understand and reshape social relations, particularly those that emerge through love, sexuality and kinship. Briefly, the *Kvir sanovnik* is grounded in an assumption that a dreambook – just like any other kind of map – is a socially effective artefact that helps us to imagine a particular kind of world and a particular kind of relations within this world. *Kvir sanovnik* presents an intervention into classic dream-maps so as to offer an alternative, linguistically promiscuous and politically fairer map through Dreamland. Let me explain this further.

A map of dreams: *sanovnik*

While the *sanovnik*, in its different editions, is widely read and used throughout the former Yugoslav countries, it is not equally widely believed in. Some readers take an ironic stance and consult the *sanovnik*, although they do not believe in it. Others say that you can never know – occasionally dreams do come true. Yet others understand the *sanovnik* as one approach among many to interpreting dreams.

The fact that the *sanovnik* is so widely present in everyday life makes it socially effective. As discussed in the introduction to the

Queer Dreambook, the classic *sanovnik* shapes, to some extent, people's understanding of relations between certain concepts.[2] Some of the links codified by the classic dream-map are innovative: for instance, to dream of a watermelon indicates jealousy when awake. Some are archaic, since they reflect nineteenth-century everyday life – this period was when the *sanovnik* was first created as a form of knowledge and a genre of writing. For example, to dream of a duvet or a mattress indicates lordship and being well-off when awake; this conceptual link made sense back in an age when having a duvet was a sign of material prosperity. Some links may be funny or subtly sexual – for instance, to dream of firefighters indicates that your wishes will be fulfilled.

However, many conceptual links offered by the classic *sanovnik* are clearly heterosexist, patriarchal, racist and/or nationalist.

According to the *sanovnik*, dreaming of beating your wife suggests that she is cheating on you. Similarly, engaging in a physical argument with your wife suggests a forthcoming fight in the home. In copy and pasting such entries from one edition to the next, dreambooks have reproduced conceptual links between fidelity and gender violence diachronically. In so doing, they have helped normalise the idea that love, fidelity or infidelity has something to do with violence. Furthermore, the *sanovnik* suggests that dreaming of Roma travelling home is a sign of a possible robbery, while dreaming of the fez is a sign of 'scarcity and sorrow'.

All of this suggests that dreambooks are neither politically naive nor innocent. As playfully imaginative and interesting as they may be, these dream-maps codify certain expectations and ideas about men and women, sexuality, love, nationality, race, religion, class and so forth.

A queer map of Dreamland

The *Queer Dreambook* was created as an attempt to retain the imaginative and intellectually provocative frames of knowledge offered by classic dreambooks, while erasing or transforming their politically problematic elements. It was made through the joint efforts of a group of scholars, artists and activists from Montenegro, Bosnia and Herzegovina, Croatia and Serbia – some of the countries where dreambooks are widely used in everyday life, reprinted and published.

Generally speaking, the guiding principle behind the creation of the queer map of Dreamland was to follow the logic and the language of classic dreambooks, so that their problematic elements would be transformed, without the transformation being overt. Let me now explain the kinds of interventions made in the *Queer Dreambook*, through several examples.

Classic dreambooks often offer an interpretation of what it means to dream of 'watching a rape', or of 'raping', but not of surviving it. While sexual violence is codified as a concept and as a word in many classic dreambooks, consensual sexual relationships are hidden behind the phrase 'love experience' and only explicitly mentioned when talking of 'losing one's virginity', or of 'giving yourself to someone' (classic dreambooks suggest that dreaming this signifies 'a great shame', and that 'only danger awaits you for making such a mistake', respectively). In the *Queer Dreambook*, all of the entries referring to rape were deleted, because the authors found it completely unacceptable to codify a brutal crime with a singular meaning. Rape is not only a criminal act, but also an incredibly traumatic event, after which every survivor searches in their own way to attribute meanings to and understand their traumatic experiences. The entries referring to 'wife beating' were also deleted. Additionally, entries such as 'losing one's virginity' and 'giving yourself to someone' were transformed, because no consensual sexual act – the first, the thousand and first, lesbian, gay, straight, marital or not, between two or more people, with a long-term partner or someone you have just met – should be considered a shameful act, whether in the *Queer Dreambook* or beyond it.

Classic maps of dreams codify not just sex and sexual violence, but also kinship relations. For instance, dreaming of an uncle signifies 'a sudden celebration', while dreaming of an aunt signifies 'a family fight'. Here, an uncle, as a male consanguine relative, is linked with something nice. On the other hand, an aunt, as an affinal female relative, symbolises a fight. This is supposedly a reflection of the household economy of the extended family which was present in the nineteenth- and twentieth-century Balkans, where married women were seen as 'entering' a new, relatively foreign family – and thus carrying the potential to usurp it or even to break it down.[3] This interpretation was transformed in the *Queer Dreambook*, because animosity between women presents one of the key mechanisms for reproducing patriarchy. In the *Queer Dreambook*, an aunt is not a symbol of a fight, but of gifts – the ultimate way to acknowledge and reproduce intangible social relationships in everyday life.

Besides transforming misogynous entries, the authors also included several new terms in order to make non-heterosexual relations more visible. In the *Queer Dreambook* you can read about what dreaming of something related to a *muželožnik* or *adžuvan* (archaic terms for a gay man) might signify, and as well as the meanings associated with dreaming of a *ženeložnica* (a lesbian) or *džuvljarka* (a lesbian in the Roma language). One of the authors, Jasmina Čaušević, helped to forge a new term for bisexual persons: *suguboložnik/suguboložnica* (*sugubo* means 'bi', or 'both' in the Old Church Slavonic language). There are also entries explaining what it means to dream of indulging in a *rukoblud* (an archaic term for masturbation). In addition, registered life partnerships and romantic relationships have been added to the entries mentioning marriage, break-ups and separations have been added to those referring to divorce, and so forth.

In working to intervene in the classic dreambooks – the *Queer Dreambook* follows their linguistic codes. Therefore, just as in a classic dreambook, the phrase 'love experience' (*ljubavni doživljaj*) in the *Queer Dreambook* refers to sex, while 'love fire' (*ljubavna ognjica*) is another term for passion.

Some of the ethno-national and racial categories were deleted, while others were kept, in accordance with the different ideas of different authors. Some of the entries which were clearly stereotypes have been kept (such as an 'Eskimo', or 'a Black person'), since this minimises the impression that everyday life in the former Yugoslav countries is necessarily White.

What orientation in the world does this queer map allow? What picture of the East emerges from it? This map of Dreamland indicates that critical area studies could approach the Global East with a queer eye, focusing on relationships and practices, rather than on subjects and identities.

In line with the absence of interest in subjects and identities, the *Queer Dreambook* is linguistically promiscuous. The dream interpretations were written in Montenegrin, Bosnian, Croatian and Serbian. The choice of which author worked on which letter was made randomly and the authors' interventions generally followed the language norms in which they usually speak and write. This makes it impossible to state clearly 'whose' cultural heritage the *Queer Dreambook* reinterprets, in ethno-national terms. This queer map of dreams also suggests that 'cultural heritage' and 'traditional knowledge' in South-east Europe are not frozen categories, but segments of everyday practice that allow various interventions, inscriptions and alterations.

Furthermore, in the *Queer Dreambook*, dreams do not speak about subconsciousness, or the future, of the dreamer. Here, dreams provide a relative location of its reader – this map suggests that existing paths through the land of dreams can be changed, new paths can be found, and that dreamers can have a say in how to interpret their location, especially when they act in concert, interweaving friendship with politics and pleasure. This map suggests that 'wonder' needs to remain a part of 'wandering', through Dreamland and elsewhere. *Queer Dreambook* as a map helps its readers to (re)interpret relations between dreams and wakefulness, so as to make room for different experiences and unequally valued practices. It approaches dreams as devices for understanding and reshaping love, kinship and sexual relations – those that affect the reader, as well as those that affect the wider social framework in which dreambooks are read.

Notes

1   Freud, 2010, 604.
2   Parts of this text were published in the 'Introduction' to the *Queer Dreambook*.
3   See also Denich, 1974.

Bibliography

Čarna Brković, ed. *Veliki vječiti kvir sanovnik* [The great eternal queer dreambook]. Podgorica: Queer Montenegro and Aquamarine Press, 2016. Accessed 9 October 2024: https://aquamarinepress.com/kvir%20sanovnik_eng.html.
Denich, Bette. 'Sex and power in the Balkans'. In *Woman, Culture, and Society*, edited by Michelle Rosaldo and Louise Lamphere, 243–62. Stanford, CA: Stanford University Press, 1974.
Freud, Sigmund. *The Interpretation of Dreams*. New York: Basic Books, 2010.

7
The early modern Republic of Letters
Wendy Bracewell

The Republic of Letters offers an example of the different ways in which a critical area studies might investigate (and learn from) the contours of an imagined space. Attempts to map the early modern world of learning digitally have so far relied on the quantitative collation of 'hard' evidence: correspondence, publishing houses, or translated editions, for instance. This gives us a picture of a hierarchically organised space that, naturally, has both capitals and peripheries. Shifting attention to more qualitative indicators – debates and embedded ideas – shakes up this map, giving us instead a much more complex cartography, one that is far less determined by economic power or cultural gradients.

How does area studies map a virtual space? The early modern Republic of Letters, imagined as a long-distance community held together by a commitment to learning, poses this conundrum.

Emerging in an age of monarchies and rigid social hierarchies, the term 'republic' gestured to egalitarianism: here standing derived from intellectual merit, not status, and membership was theoretically open to all who contributed to the pursuit of knowledge. Sixteenth-century humanists carrying out classical and biblical scholarship cooperated through correspondence – the Republic's 'letters' had an apt double meaning. Seventeenth- and eighteenth-century print culture reduced the importance of personal contact. Books and, even more, the new institution of the learned journal, circulating in French and other languages of international communication, both broadened the social reach and accelerated the spread of new knowledge, with an increasing focus on natural science and philosophy. Many regard this community of learning as having disintegrated in the nineteenth century, with scholarly specialisation. However, the term 'Republic of Letters' survived as a metaphor for literary production (a 'belletristic republic'?), and even as a programme for a literary cosmopolitanism that would counter the inward-looking character of national literatures. Interdisciplinary efforts at building bridges between different branches of knowledge have drawn on the model of an egalitarian republic, but the most striking current version is associated with the infrastructure of the internet and the ethos of the knowledge commons: a digital Republic of Letters.[1]

The early modern Republic of Letters was a virtual space. Its physical settings (studies, coffee houses, learned societies or bookshops) may have defined a local milieu, but its long-distance communications gave it a reach that was imagined as having no frontiers. Early modern erudites made this explicit by referring to it as a 'world' as well as a republic. In practice, their learned exchanges fell short of this planetary ideal, tracing more circumscribed networks. Nonetheless, the Republic's imagined frontierlessness underwrote a cosmopolitan ethos, elevating dialogue and exchange over religious and political differences.

How can one chart the contours of what Anthony Grafton has called a continent 'without maps, without administrative officials, without borders'?[2] A great deal of effort has gone into mapping this Republic through digital humanities projects.[3] Some pin it down to a physical geography by tracing exchanges of letters, the circulation of journals or patterns of translation. As executed, this approach suffers from problems – the focus on canonical authors such as Voltaire inevitably reproduces a Paris-centred version of the Republic, though it can also throw up surprising findings (the cosmopolitan Voltaire exchanged letters overwhelmingly with French correspondents; he sent very few letters beyond Europe; the intensity of his exchanges with English correspondents is low).[4] Shifting the focus to less familiar figures might be more revealing: for instance, mapping the autograph albums compiled during the peregrinations of Transylvanian students would show the Europe-wide reach of their networks, while also demonstrating whether their exchanges replicated the multiconfessional character of their homeland.[5] Broadening the source base beyond famous men of learning (and their easily digitised editions of letters) could show us what the Republic looked like beyond its metropolitan hubs.

Other forms of cartographic mapping highlight the density or otherwise of the Republic's physical infrastructure: academies, salons, libraries, universities, publishing houses. It's no surprise that cities were its forcing-houses – the metropolises of Rome, Paris and London, of course, but also urban centres with more specialised profiles: merchant Amsterdam, imperial Prague or academic Göttingen, for instance. These were the Republic's great capitals. But interstices and border zones had their own advantages, allowing intellectual autonomy, the cross-fertilisation brought about by refugee colonies, or a means of evading censorship (Prussian-ruled Neuchâtel for publishing in French; Vienna for diaspora Greek periodicals). Often such places had a role disproportionate to the wealth of their urban resources. Other mappings are needed to perceive these. For instance, superimposing the itineraries of travellers – particularly beyond the conventional British Grand Tour of France and Italy – throws up some surprising discoveries: Bucharest in the 1760s–80s, for instance, played host to an extraordinarily cosmopolitan array of erudite figures, from the German mathematician Carsten Niebuhr, returning from his exploration of Arabia, to the English philosopher Jeremy Bentham heading for Russia; from the Italian archaeologist Domenico Sestini to the Ragusan historian Stefan Raicevich, not to mention a parade of learned diplomats. (Bentham's experiences there prompted the first recorded use of the term 'Europeanised' in English; the role of Bucharest as a space of eighteenth-century European encounter still awaits close analysis.) Different types of nodes in a web of contacts and exchanges might better characterise the Republic of Letters than a map of its capitals and, by implication, its provinces and peripheries.

But *could* this Republic have peripheries? If membership in this community was based on intellectual merit, and was potentially planetary in scope, how could it be ordered by cultural or spatial hierarchies? Such power relations are difficult to derive from a series of digital data points. An adequate answer requires a qualitative, rather than a quantitative approach.

One approach is to analyse the public polemics that constituted the lifeblood of the Republic – far more so than its polite exchanges. By the eighteenth century, disputes over theology or natural philosophy were being joined by heated debates concerning the varieties of mankind. Was it climate, political organisation or stage of historical development that led to differences among nations? Were their characteristics innate and immutable, or were they subject to change? Philosophical travellers contributed empirical evidence to this debate, assessing societies within Europe as well as beyond. What was at stake was the present and future place of nations on the map of civilisation: how far were manners and customs relative to historical circumstance, and to what degree was a nation capable of improvement?

The travellers' intended audience rarely included those that they described – but the ever-intensifying circulation of print meant that Europe's 'travellees' – those whom travellers met in their travels and described in their writings – frequently read these accounts. Infuriated by their superficial observations, by the implications of the foreign travellers' conclusions, and by the spread of misleading characterisations in print, a substantial cross-section of such readers published rebuttals. Russians, Swiss, Spanish and Greeks disputed with French travellers; Welsh, Scottish and Irish authors rebuked English disparagement; Italians engaged with French and British writers; polemicists as far apart as Dalmatia and Sweden took issue with Italian characterisations; Icelanders defended their nation against Germans: all addressing their complaints to the Republic of Letters in languages of international circulation, taking their arguments beyond a domestic audience. Not only did many travellers reply to these challenges, but others piled in as well, often from well beyond the original sites of controversy: a Breton commenting on a Swedish-Italian polemic, for instance, a Pole taking the side of Sicilians against Anglo-Irish insults, or a Ragusan defending Moldavians and Wallachians against French and German disparagement.[6]

As this sketch suggests, these polemics cannot easily be interpreted in terms of the relations between a hegemonic cultural 'core' and its peripheries – although such a relationship was very frequently implied in certain travellers' texts, in the form of 'civilisation meditating on barbarism', and claims about a European gradient that determined where knowledge about mankind was produced or consumed. Thus the French traveller in Moldavia and Wallachia, Jean-Louis Carra: 'it is not for these barbaric, ignorant peoples to know us; ... in the end it is for us to know these peoples, before these peoples may learn to know themselves'.[7] It was such arrogance, as much as anything, that outraged travellee-polemicists.

Belonging to a traduced nation licensed the travellee to write in response, insofar as a native was more competent than an outsider to understand and explain local manners and customs. But it was from a self-confident position as equal members of the Republic of Letters that these native ethnographers addressed a multinational audience, rejecting any imputation of alterity, assuming the right to represent their own communities as men of learning, and demanding to have their evidence assessed on a rational basis, not as a function of their origins. When challenged, philosophical travellers could not easily dismiss such counterclaims. A surprisingly frequent strategy was to imply that their travellee-opponents lacked the necessary civilisational standing to argue on an equal basis: equating linguistic or cultural difference with social hierarchies, belittling one's disputant as 'impertinent', or simply disqualifying him as a 'barbarian'. The Republic of Letters, in these calculations, was equated with the social and cultural conventions of a subset of the European nations.

In turn, travellee-polemicists laughed at the notion of social and intellectual peripheries to the Republic of Letters: such claims were rooted in the misconceptions of travellers who knew only their own cultures (and thus betrayed their own provincial limitations, regardless of where they came from). The cosmopolitan critics of such centre–periphery assumptions knew that culture is relative to place and circumstance, but intellectual authority is not. This did not mean, however, that reason or even empirical evidence was the ultimate arbiter in these disputes. Whose version of the character of a nation *counted* (whose works were cited and recirculated, for instance) often came down to affinity or proximity: shared nation or religion, or membership in the same academic network.

A dismissive reception of travellee arguments in self-designated centres of the Republic of Letters did much to teach societies at Europe's geographical margins a lesson about their intellectual and cultural peripherality. One reaction was an appeal to a shared European identity, often in solidarity with other similarly misrepresented regions. Listen to the Ragusan Raicevich criticising travel accounts of those nations 'called barbarous' by travellers like J. L. Carra, and going on to align his fellow 'Illyrians' and other Slavs with the unjustly maligned Romanians: 'Wallachia, Moldavia, Illyria, and even Russia itself are less known than America, and yet they are in Europe'.[8] This was less a restatement of an egalitarian Republic of Letters than a claim to equal membership in a European geo-cultural community. These philosophical travellees rejected any essential difference between their own cultures and those of their critics by essentialising a boundary between Europeans and *their* others: here in contrast to America, while others rebut charges of barbarity by insisting on their distance from 'Hottentots' or Tierra del Fuegians. Claims to Europeanness came at the expense of a wider community, however much these peripheral polemicists stood to benefit from the Republic of Letters' universalism. In the end this Republic, even for these citizens, was a continent, and not a world.

This exercise in mapping the virtual Republic of Letters shows a polycentric space, shaped as much by translocal, cross-cultural negotiations of authority as by its correspondence networks or the distribution of cultural resources. It does not easily break down into familiar binaries, whether the 'West and the Rest' or a learned Europe revolving on an elliptical orbit around Paris and London, though it may have something to tell us about the development of Europe's cultural hierarchies and the ex-centric origins of a European sense of identity. The patterns sketched here call for the discussion of comparisons as well as connections between the Republic of Letters' different spaces, using qualitative as well as quantitative sources. The Republic of Letters also suggests that early modern Europe does not map neatly onto concepts of East and West, or Global North and South. The 'provincial cosmopolitans' of the Republic of Letters occupy a position that is acted upon, but has its own agency. They are equipped to mount a critique as well as a defence of European ideas of cosmopolitanism and universalism. Whether in Wallachia, Spain or Sweden, they are all potential citizens of a putative 'Global East' as well as the Republic of Letters.

Notes

1. Bots and Waquet, 1997.
2. Grafton, 2008.
3. For example, www.republicofletters.net and www.culturesofknowledge.org. Accessed 22 July 2024.
4. Mapping the Republic of Letters, 2013.
5. For examples see, Inscriptiones Alborum Amicorum, n.d.
6. For details see Bracewell, 2015.
7. Carra, 1777.
8. Raicevich, 1788, 4.

Bibliography

Bots, Hans and Françoise Waquet. *La République des Lettres* [The Republic of Letters]. Paris: Belin, 1997.

Bracewell, Wendy. 'The travellee's eye: Reading European travel writing, 1750–1850'. In *New Directions in Travel Writing Studies*, edited by Julia Kuehn and Paul Smethurst, 215–27. London: Palgrave Macmillan, 2015.

Carra, Jean-Louis. *Histoire de la Moldavie et de la Valachie* [History of Moldavia and Wallachia]. Jassy: Aux dépens de la Société typographique des Deux-Ponts, 1777.

Grafton, Anthony. 'A sketch map of a lost continent: The Republic of Letters'. *Republics of Letters* 1(1) (2008). Accessed 26 July 2024. https://shc.stanford.edu/arcade/publications/rofl/issues/volume-1-issue-1/sketch-map-lost-continent-republic-letters.

Inscriptiones Alborum Amicorum. 'Main page'. Accessed 22 July 2024. http://iaa.bibl.u-szeged.hu/index.php?page=home.

Mapping the Republic of Letters. 'Voltaire and the Enlightenment'. Accessed 22 July 2024. https://republicofletters.stanford.edu/casestudies/voltaire.html.

Raicevich, Stefan. *Osservazioni storiche, naturali, e politiche intorno la Valachia e Moldavia* [Historical, Natural and Political Observations on Wallachia and Moldavia]. Napoli: Presso Gaetano Raimondi, 1788.

8
Vadim Tsymburskiĭ's Great Limitrophe
Dimitrii Sidorov

Often continents arise in the mind of only one person, but then replicate themselves as political circumstances render them useful. This entry deals with one such continent, the Great Limitrophe, dreamt up by Vadim Tsymburskiĭ. It maps a self-avowedly heterodox vision of Eurasia, that pivots the world around Russia, but also separates Russia from the world. For all of its apparent ex-centricity, this limitrophic vision of an isolated irredentist macrostate has been actualised with uncanny precision in the decades following its demarcation. It now appears as an aspect of current Russian 'world making', aspects of which have been implemented with genocidal intent following Russia's invasion of Ukraine in 2014 and its launch of full-scale war in February 2022.

Vadim Tsymburskiĭ (1957–2009, Figure 8.1) is arguably the least known outside of Russia but its most original geopolitical theorist of the post-Soviet period. Born in Lviv (Lvov), a borderland city in western Ukraine, with mixed Polish and Austro-Hungarian heritage, he grew up in eastern Ukraine and Belarus, and eventually moved to study at Moscow State University, in the Philology Department. Upon graduation, he worked at several academic institutions in Moscow. His early research interests in the ethnolinguistic history of the classical Mediterranean area and political discourse studies evolved in the 1990s into the history and theory of geo- and chrono-politics as well as the civilisational structuring of the post-Soviet, post-Cold War space of Eurasia.

Despite the unmatched originality, depth and relevance of Tsymburskiĭ's writings, none of his work so far has been translated into English, including one early essay that is now considered a classic in

Figure 8.1 Vadim L. Tsymburskiĭ at a conference in Moscow, 28 March 2008.
© D. Sidorov.

Russia: 'Island Russia'.[1] Published the same year as Samuel Huntington's globally famous essay, 'The clash of civilizations?', it independently and simultaneously proposed a new analytical paradigm for predicting the contours of post-Cold War international systems, that of civilisational geopolitics.[2] Challenging the dominant discourses of globalisation, the post-ideological end-of-history, and the like, this paradigm highlighted the growing geopolitical importance of regional cultural (or civilisational) differences.

Tsymburskiĭ's geopolitics challenges the very core of the clash-of-civilisations thesis that made Samuel Huntington a household name among post-Cold War intellectuals. In direct opposition to what is arguably the weakest part of the clash-of-civilisations thesis, the rigid conceptualisation of the so-called 'fault lines' between civilisations, Tsymburskiĭ, the 'Russian Huntington', highlighted instead an intercontinental geopolitical belt of so-called 'strait-territories' that in the 1990s he elaborated into a dynamic concept – the Great Limitrophe (Figure 8.2) (the term itself was suggested by Stanislav Khatuntsev).[3]

For Tsymburskiĭ, the Great Limitrophe is:

> a geocultural belt that stretches across Euro-Asia from Finland to Korea and includes Eastern Europe, the Caucasus, as well as

Figure 8.2 Tsymburskii's Great Limitrophe: key areas.
Rendering © D. Sidorov.

the 'new' (post-Soviet) and the 'old' (Mongol-Tibetan-Xinjiang) Central Asia. This belt is formed by peripheries of civilizations of the Old World. It is a field separating Russia from reference areas of the Roman-Germanic Western Europe, Arabic-Iranian Middle and Near East, India and China.[4]

Tsymburskiĭ's Great Limitrophe is Eurasia-centric and differs from other intermediate regional or pan-Eurasian geopolitical borderland predecessor concepts such as Fairgrieve's 'crush zone', Curzon's 'buffer zone', Spykman's 'rimland' or Cohen's 'shatterbelt', with their focus on geostrategic themes of separation, containment, control or conflict. Evolved in the post-Cold War, postimperial period, Tsymburskiĭ's geopolitical construct is decidedly rooted in *civilisations*, their systems and interactions over their borderlands (the Great Limitrophe). As such, it is both a *meta*-civilisational and *inter*-civilisational theory, even if Russia-centric: Tsymburskiĭ saw the Great Limitrophe acquiring its 'structural limitrophe role' only with the emergence of Russia several centuries ago.[5] For Stanislav Khatuntsev, 'it is not clear why specifically Russia and not, say, Europe or, for instance, India received the "distinction" of being surrounded by the Great Limitrophe'.[6] Khatuntsev's own independently developed conceptualisation of the Great Limitrophe is a more universalist and precise classification, both geographically and historically, yet its appeal is more limited compared to that of Tsymburskiĭ's Russia-centric theory.

As a manifesto of isolationism, Tsymburskiĭ's 'Island Russia' (1993) perhaps was a reaction to both the failed Soviet messianic globalist effort and the universalist socialist cultural project. For him, postsocialist Russia's self-isolation (or retreat to its core civilisational platform, to the 'island') is a positive move allowing Russia to finally focus on developing its inner regions and securing its historical sustainability. He even promoted movement of the capital into Russia's interior, closer to the area of the Urals and Siberia.[7] Paradoxically, the reduction of Russia's political territory and re-*Orient*ation to the East could allow the country to remain a subject of geopolitics as one of its major poles after the end of the bipolar Cold War world (perhaps a core of an emergent Global East, although that was not a term he used). According to Mezhuev:

> Tsymbursky believed it was irrational and disadvantageous for Russia to destroy what he called a 'one-and-a-half-polar world', in which the United States occupied a dominant position, but where it had to reckon with regional centers of power … a manifestation

of Tsymbursky's 'civilizational realism': Russia should uphold its position as a regional center with a concrete gravitational orbit, but not seek to achieve a final fragmentation of the entire 'one-and-a-half-polar world' system.[8]

It is in this context that the Great Limitrophe is of prime importance for Tsymburskiĭ: not only does it serve as a protective civilisational buffer for the newly 'islandic' (self-isolated) Russia but it also becomes Russia's major new geopolitical partner/competitor, a belt of most important future geopolitical developments. As evident in the 2008 war in Georgia, eastern Ukrainian separatism (since 2014) and the emergence of quasi-states from Transnistria to Abkhazia, Tsymburskiĭ's focus on the limitrophic spaces has arguably been better in predicting these conflictual cases in Eurasia than have Huntington's constructs. In the new epoch, the interaction between civilisations' cores and peripheries for Tsymburskiĭ are more (or equally) important and geopolitically insightful than the relatively rare cases of unmediated clash of civilisations prophesied by Huntington.

Tsymburskiĭ's isolationism is not a one-way process; interaction with 'the main civilizations' (especially the West) remains of utmost importance yet it has certain dynamics, cycles and rhythms. Tsymburskiĭ's conceptualisation is both geopolitical and chrono-political: his geopolitics is exceptionally dynamic and focuses on partnership/competition among satellite civilisations. Unlike Huntington's 'fault lines', the Great Limitrophe is instead a dynamic borderland between Eurasia's main 'civilisational platforms' (such as 'Island Russia') that has been (and still is) affected by the chrono-geopolitical cycles of Russia's engagement with/departure from Europe (conceptualised as periods of Russia's 'abduction by Europe' followed by its reorientation to the East). I would suggest calling this dynamic a kind of choreographic geopolitics – it is arguably characteristic of Eurasia and not of the more stable, ocean-bounded civilisation of the Global West. The emergent Global East versus Global West/Global North versus Global South 'quadchotomy' should be viewed through the context of the classical geopolitical binary opposition of continental versus oceanic powers. Although the Great Limitrophe's dynamic structuration is most relevant to our age of mobility and hybridity, it may remain largely confined to Eurasia – the largest continental landmass, the centre of Mackinder's World Island, with the greatest number of inter-civilisational borderlands.[9]

In Russia, Tsymburskiĭ's writings are most respected in conservative intellectual circles, perhaps for providing an uncommonly hopeful interpretation of the painful dismemberment of the Soviet Union and the associated reduction of the Russian imperial realm. Often labelled as an early manifesto of neo-isolationism, his works perhaps deserve wider exposure and analysis in the period of post-globalisation isolationist tendencies around the world.[10] Tsymburskiĭ was visionary in his focus on geopolitical isolationism well before the era of Brexit and Trumpism. The Great Limitrophe concept arguably advances the critical area studies agenda in several aspects. It challenges the normativity of regions and areas by focusing on very different 'units' and analysing them in a fluid, dynamic fashion. The porous, transitional, unstable, dynamic characteristics of the Great Limitrophe are too often neglected in the traditional area studies paradigm as well as in the cultural-civilisational rhetoric of Samuel Huntington. This is even more typical in the post-Cold War research agenda that focuses on universalising themes (for example development, democracy) at the expense of considerations of regional diversity. Tsymburskiĭ's scholarship (the Great Limitrophe is only one of his several innovative concepts) belongs perhaps to the trans-area studies trend, with its focus on transregional, transnational and transcontinental phenomena.[11] In Tsymburskiĭ's words, Russia is a 'trans-regional power' corresponding to the specifically transregional structuration of the Limitrophe-in-Eurasia.[12] The Great Limitrophe becomes of central importance for the new Global East – serving as its dynamic borderland/spine, both separating and uniting civilisations.

Notes

1. Tsymburskiĭ, 1993.
2. Huntington, 1993.
3. Tsymburskiĭ, 1993; Tsymburskiĭ, 2000, 13.
4. Tsymburskiĭ, 2000, 3, 13.
5. Tsymburskiĭ, 2000, 15.
6. Khatuntsev, 2011.
7. Tsymburskiĭ, 2000, 107–15.
8. Mezhuev, 2017.
9. Mackinder, 1904, 421–37.
10. Tsymburskiĭ, 2000, 9.
11. Sidorov, 2006.
12. Tsymburskiĭ, 2000, 15.

Bibliography

Huntington, Samuel. 'The clash of civilizations?', *Foreign Affairs* 72(3) (1993): 22–49.
Khatuntsev, Stanislav. 'Limitrofy: Mezhtsivilizatsionnye prostranstva starogo i novogo sveta' [Limitrophes: The inter-civilizational spaces of the old and new worlds], *Polis* 2 (2011): 86–98.

Mackinder, H. J. 'The geographical pivot of history', *Geographical Journal* 23(4) (April 1904): 421–37.
Mezhuev, Boris. '"Island Russia" and Russia's identity politics', *Russia in Global Affairs*, 2 June 2017. Accessed 1 August 2024. https://eng.globalaffairs.ru/number/island-russia-and-russias-identity-politics-18757.
Sidorov, Dimitrii. 'Post-imperial third Romes: Resurrections of a Russian Orthodox geopolitical metaphor', *Geopolitics* 11 (2006): 317–47.
Tsymburskiĭ, Vadim. 'Ostrov Rossiia: Perspektivy rossiiskoĭ geopolitiki' [Island Russia: Perspectives of Russian Geopolitics], *Polis* 5 (1993): 11–17.
Tsymburskiĭ, Vadim. *Rossiia – Zemlia za Velikim Limitrofom: Tsivilizatsiia i eë geopolitika* [Russia – Land Beyond the Great Limitrophe: Civilization and its geopolitics]. Moscow: Editorial URSS, 2000.

9
Greater Europe: a travel guide
Nóra Veszprémi

In Civilization and its Discontents, *as an illustration of how the unconscious mind works, Freud summons up a phantasy-image of the city of Rome in which 'nothing that has once come into existence will have passed away and all the earlier phases of development continue to exist alongside the latest one'. Here, 'on the Piazza of the Pantheon we should find not only the Pantheon of to-day, as it was bequeathed to us by Hadrian, but, on the same site, the original edifice erected by Agrippa; indeed, the same piece of ground would be supporting the church of Santa Maria sopra Minerva and the ancient temple over which it was built', and here 'the observer would perhaps only have to change the direction of his glance or his position in order to call up the one view or the other'. Such a vision is at the heart of the artwork,* Greater Europe, *that this piece presents to us: a Europe of impossible coexistence, the dream-image of our collective and individual desires and of their (disquieting) reconciliation.*

Have you travelled across Europe in all directions? Do you feel like you have seen everything? Does the easy accessibility of Airbnb bore you? Do you miss the excitement of passing through militarised border controls? Then *Greater Europe* is the place for you. In *Greater Europe*, borders are strictly enforced. But there is no need to worry: it is the continent of peace. All nations have been allocated all the territories they have ever laid claim to, so they have no reason to fight … What do you mean by overlaps? There might be overlaps in the Europe you know, but not in *Greater Europe*. Here, if an area is claimed by more than one nation, it is simply replicated as many times as needed. You say the continent looks a bit bloated? We say it is packed with fun, excitement and adventure.

Greater Europe is a fictional continent – but who is to say that makes it less real? It was created in 2008–9 by the artists Ferenc Gróf and Jean-Baptiste Naudy, who formed the collective Société Réaliste. It was part of a larger project called *Culture States: Exposition des arts et techniques appliquées à la vie moderne*, which was inspired by the 1937 Paris World's Fair. At an event like that fair, national culture is constituted as definable and homogenous, and its boundaries are equated with the boundaries of the nation state. This is the vision offered by *Greater Europe* (Figure 9.1). Its culture states exist in splendid isolation, separated by large patches of no-man's land.

What? You find this bleak? Come on. Don't tell me it is not what you wanted. Let me take you for a tour to change your mind. Where would you like to start? Lviv? You mean Lvov? You mean Lwów? You mean Lemberg? Well, to see all four you will have to travel about 2,000 miles (it is hard to judge distance here), but I assure you it is worth it. And you end up in Greater Austria, which is a treat in itself. The coffee houses, the waltz, the *Gemütlichkeit*! All the ethnic groups, wearing their picturesque costumes, speaking so many strange languages, and yet all of them Austrian – none of them would ever doubt it. You can still see them in human zoos now and then.

Don't miss all the Rococo revival theatre buildings in Austrian Budapest! In Hungarian Budapest they tore them all down. They have even banned Sacher cakes! Unforgivable. But there is a lot to like there still. You do know Hungary's Budapest is renowned for its musical culture. You can listen to concerts of the highest calibre, whole marathons of Bartók – minus the modernism, of course. If you travel north to Kassa, you will be able to observe the effects of Magyarisation: all those people with Slovak and German names chatting away in Hungarian as soon as they notice you watching! You would like to hear Slovak? No worries. If you manage to cross the border (it can get a bit dangerous here) to nearby Košice, you will find your friends again, this time speaking exclusively Slovak. Kaschau? It is in Austria, naturally. You say that just because Kaschauer burghers spoke German, they were not necessarily Austrians? Well, you really are impossible to please.

You know what? Let us visit the Balkans. Just take a walk in one of the many Sarajevos and tell me *Greater Europe* hasn't brought peace. And look, having several copies of beautiful Mostar can only enrich a continent. The same can be said about the beaches. Oh, the beaches of *Greater Europe*! Whether you go to Split or Spalato, Dubrovnik or Ragusa, you are bound to have a wonderful time.

Figure 9.1 Société Réaliste (Ferenc Gróf and Jean-Baptiste Naudy), *Greater Europe*, 2008–9. Digital print mounted on Dibond, 200 × 120 cm. Image courtesy of the artists and acb gallery, Budapest.

You prefer a colder climate? Let us fly to Iceland. I adore this country: Rejkjavík with its colourful corrugated iron buildings, its sophisticated cultural offerings, and then to think about the vast, empty land that surrounds it! Nowhere else in Europe will you find such large areas of undisturbed nature. Did you know that, in the year 1000, Icelanders voted to collectively convert to Christianity because they had had enough of religious quarrels? Take our Golden Circle tour and you can visit Þingvellir National Park, the stunning site of that ancient parliament, as well as the monumental Gullfoss waterfall and my favourites, the geysers of the Geysir Geothermal Area. It's such a shame we only have one of this amazing island. Denmark must have forgotten to register its claim – we must remind them.

Greater Europe is always in flux. In 2008 there seemed to be no need for another Scotland, but we are working on it as we speak. We do already have two Irelands though. And, as you are probably aware, the United Kingdom has always been ambivalent about belonging to *Greater Europe*. The time has now come to draw up its separatist version. You will find it floating like a majestic lost vessel, somewhere in the ocean, out of the frame.

You tell me to imagine there are no borders? Channelling John Lennon there, aren't you? You think you are clever, but what you really mean is administrative borders – everyone knows those can be changed. You can even create a union where borders are barely noticeable, at least inside. You don't need to remind me that borders have shifted throughout history. Société Réaliste have another map for you that visualises exactly this: *Superimposition of political frontiers at the turn of each century between year 0 and year 2000 on the European peninsula and its surroundings* (Figure 9.2). The title speaks for itself. Here is the same image engraved on Necurite (a form of recycled polyurethane): *Spectral Aerosion* (Figure 9.3). Hauntingly beautiful, isn't it? The lines are entangled and blurred, almost unrecognisably. It is possible to imagine anything based on this. Anything and its opposite.

You see, imagination is not the solution – it is part of the problem. All those borders in *Greater Europe* are imagined by people. All those visions of monolithic, culturally homogeneous nation states. They might not be real. But throughout the twentieth century, people have been displaced, persecuted and killed in the name of these visions. Imagined borders are much more enduring than those drawn up by politicians and peace treaties. You need to make something of this uncomfortable truth.

Visions of pure 'culture states' conflate geography with culture, and both of those with political entities. You can scoff at them, but in the end, doesn't your precious concept of Central Europe operate in

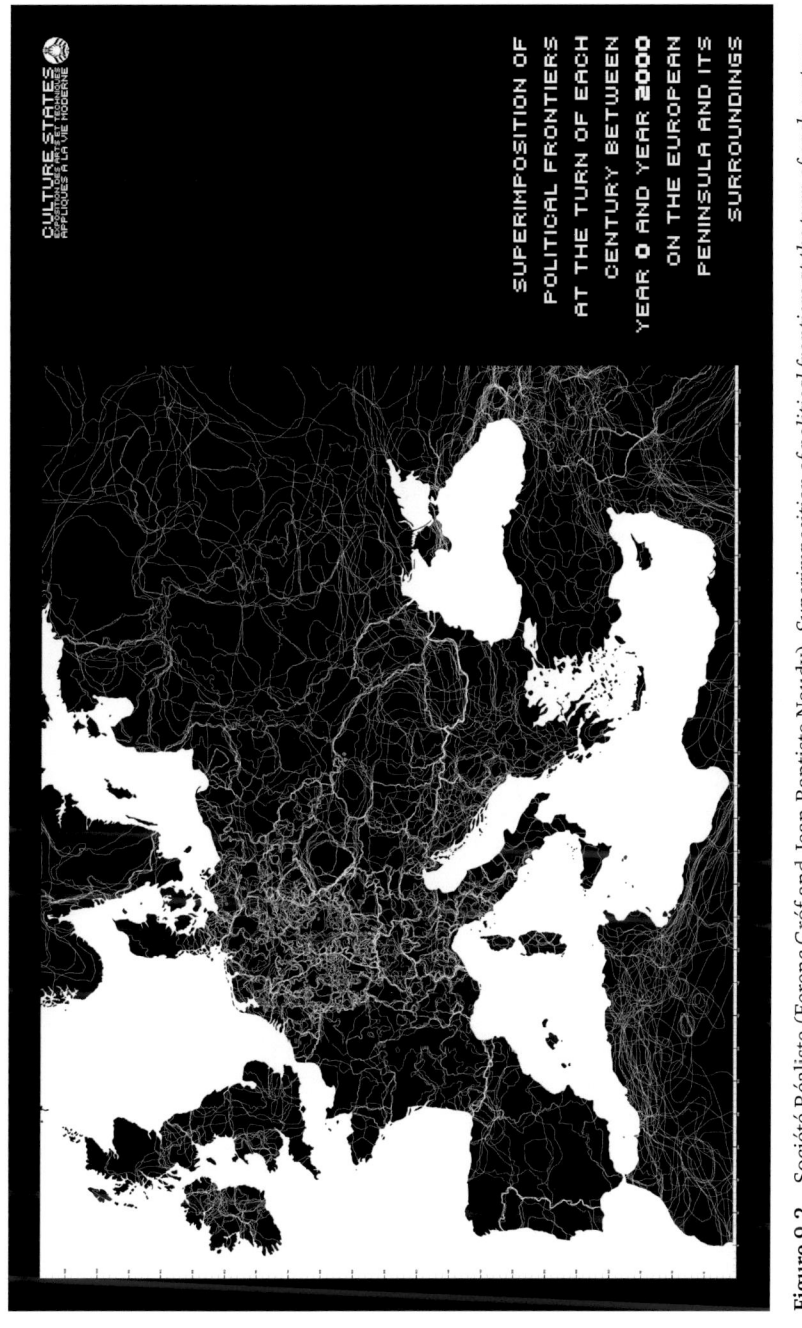

Figure 9.2 Société Réaliste (Ferenc Gróf and Jean-Baptiste Naudy), *Superimposition of political frontiers at the turn of each century between year 0 and year 2000 on the European peninsula and its surroundings*, 2009. Digital print mounted on Dibond, 200 × 120 cm.

Image courtesy of the artists and acb gallery, Budapest.

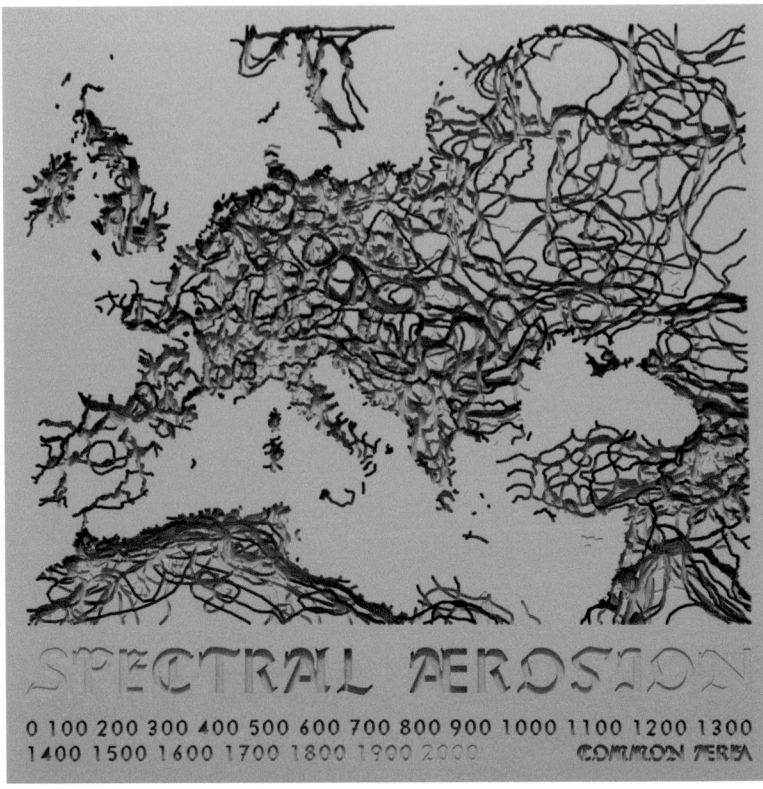

Figure 9.3 Société Réaliste (Ferenc Gróf and Jean-Baptiste Naudy), *Spectral Aerosion*, 2011. Engraved Necurite, 75 × 75 × 5 cm.

Image courtesy of the artists and acb gallery, Budapest.

a similar way? You either define it by drawing up your own imagined borders, or you simply equate it with the lands of the Habsburg Empire, which is a little bit lazy, to be honest. And your careful references to the 'historical Kingdom of Hungary', intended as politically correct – don't they equate a country with a cultural space? Of course, we all need reference points; we need concepts to grasp what we are talking about, otherwise we would not be talking at all. You employ these concepts because you want to recognise the multiethnicity, the multicultural character of the region, as well as the shifting borders – fair enough. But can you recognise the workings of your imagination, the workings of other people's imagination, the entangled borders you have all collectively dreamed up: can you see through them, can you set them aside while simultaneously acknowledging their crucial power in shaping minds? Can you see them as both real and unreal?

When we began our tour, you were right to mention overlaps. There are no overlaps in *Greater Europe*, but that is because *Greater Europe* is actually about the overlaps. It reminds us of them by getting rid of them. I see it has touched you; and now you say the way forward is to replace visions of purity with an understanding of culture as a wondrous, ever-changing mix. That if we cannot get rid of imaginary borders, then at least we should accept, explore and cherish their intersections, so that they finally connect us, instead of pushing us apart. You know what? I like your thinking. And I'm sure there is a reality like that somewhere. Good luck! I hope you find your continent.

As for me, I'm stuck here. It's my job. Don't worry, it's not as bad as it looks. When I'm off duty, I spend my time in the grey areas between the culture states. Those are the places where anything can happen. Where there are no expectations, norms and stereotypes. Where nobody forces you to choose.

Note

This article is part of a project that has received funding from the European Research Council (ERC) under the European Union's Horizon 2020 research and innovation programme (grant agreement no. 786314).

Bibliography

Freud, Sigmund. *Civilization and its Discontents*. London: Hogarth, 1951.
Hornyik, Sándor. 'A térképész tekintete: Kultúrakritikai geográfia ma Magyarországon' [The cartographer's gaze: Cultural critique and geography in Hungary today], *Régi-új Magyar Építőművészet* 6 (2011): 34–6.
Mélyi, József. 'The imagined map: cartographic references in the works of Société Réaliste'. In *Société Réaliste: Empire, state, building,* edited by József Mélyi, Olivier Schefer and Giovanna Zapperi, 199–229. Budapest: Ludwig Museum, 2011.
Société Réaliste. Web portfolio selection. Accessed 26 July 2024. http://www.ferencgrof.com/sr_web_portfolio_selection.pdf.
Somzé, Catherine. 'Société Réaliste: Dealing with politics, history and social commitment', *Artpulse Magazine* (2011). Accessed 31 July 2024. https://artpulsemagazine.com/societe-realiste-dealing-with-politics-history-and-social-commitment.

10
Low earth orbit: a speculative ethnographer's guide
Victor Buchli

Outer space constitutes just as much a legitimate terrain for (critical) area studies as do more grounded territories of our planet. From Gagarin onwards, the great majority of earthlings' extraterrestrial energies and adventures (and the greater part of the debris that they have tossed into the ether) have, however, rarely extended beyond low earth orbit (LEO) – that part of space below an altitude of ca. 2,000 kilometres from the surface of Earth. Buchli's text makes sense of the competing and complementary cultures of cosmic exploration – Soviet, American and otherwise – that have impacted not only the LEO itself, but – even more markedly – the grounded realities of life on Earth.

Since Gagarin's 1961 flight into orbit around the Earth, low earth orbit (LEO) has constituted a new part of the Earth poorly understood by anthropologists. This entry will attempt a speculative ethnographic approach to a part of Earth which does not conform to traditional geographic understandings of territoriality. With numerous satellites, telescopes and space debris orbiting Earth, LEO has also been continuously inhabited by the International Space Station (ISS), orbiting ca. 400 kilometres above the surface of the planet, for the past 20 years at the time of writing. Yet this new part of Earth is more accessible than some of the most remote regions of our planet and is the closest human settlement to the even more remote Point Nemo (the oceanic pole of inaccessibility) in the South Pacific, where space-borne debris from LEO is brought down into its ocean depths. Further, each and every human with a smartphone is linked live to LEO 24/7 through various social media, in addition to the multiple terrestrial mission controls that are coterminous within this expanding nexus of habitation. Our inhabitation of LEO continuously upsets our pre-Copernican and post-Copernican understandings of the world, along with our conventional, gravity-based orientations of the body and the environment.[1] This entry will consider the peculiar intimate geographies and nexuses that are produced within this context. In particular, it will address mainly Russian understandings of this part of the world, its mapping, and its configuration. Specifically I want to focus on the use of the dead to claim and occupy this space, and the enduring traditions of Russian Cosmism which underpin Russian histories of outer space and Cosmism's particular focus on the extraterrestrial resurrection of the dead.

The ISS in LEO is intimately part of a nexus between terrestrial and extraterrestrial sites that includes a global network of mission controls from Houston, Munich and Moscow to Tsukuba. Each entity that inhabits and works on the ISS has its own discrete mission control – from those attached to various national space agencies, to the individual commercial concerns that have a presence there. Even the Russian Orthodox Church has what can only be called its own makeshift mission control, where the Patriarch himself can periodically communicate directly with the cosmonauts of the ISS and attend to their spiritual needs – literally – in the heavens.[2] And, arguably, every human being with a smartphone passively participates in (rather than actively manages) aspects of life on the ISS through polymedia.[3] This global participation and earthly inhabitation of, and expansion into, LEO was first heralded by the Soviet Union's 1957 launch of *Sputnik*, whose first beeps were designed to be picked up by amateur radio enthusiasts on Earth (especially American ones).[4] Thus, every radio ham actively participates in and inhabits LEO.

The Soviet Union's first occupation of LEO must be understood within the wider tradition of Russian nineteenth-century Cosmist thought regarding the inhabitation of the Cosmos. I want to argue that this is the spiritual origin of the Russian and Soviet space programmes, constituting LEO as a Cosmist site.[5] This represents a particular Slavic strain of thought that also resonates to some degree with Singularitarians in the US who similarly imagine humanity's evolution into a new collective consciousness and life beyond our mortal bodies.[6] It is the nineteenth-century Russian Orthodox mystic and philosopher Nikolai Fedorov and his obscure yet highly influential writings, namely *Filosofiia obshchego dela* ('The Philosophy of the Common Task'),[7] that are the spiritual foundation of Russian and Soviet space exploration. In terms of his secular influence, Fedorov was the mentor of Tsiolkovski, the rocket scientist and father of the Soviet and Russian space programme.

Fedorov argued for the necessity of space travel and exploration, so that humans as a species might inhabit new worlds where all of our ancestors will be reincarnated; the cycles of life and death would end, and a new era of immortality would arise. In this new era, all the resurrected ancestors of the past would inhabit new worlds made possible by space travel – hence our collective purpose and need to leave Earth.

Broadly put, and at the risk of overemphasising nuanced distinctions to produce an unwieldy binary that obscures certain common strains of thought, the American space programme ostensibly reprises the settler narratives of individualism and frontier expansion,[8] while the Russian/Soviet narratives tend to emphasise new forms of collectivity, human life, habitation and evolution. Historically the Soviet space programme emphasised habitation and occupation over exploration, and the constitution of a new Soviet extraterrestrial Person – a continuation of the social engineering of Homo Sovieticus – the first substantively realised specimen of which was Yuri Gagarin himself.[9] The primacy of the consolidation of space with terrestrial territory, power and occupation – and the survival of these narratives and practices today – cannot be more eloquently demonstrated than in the contemporary imagery of the 2018 FIFA World Cup. The Russian logo for the event was launched simultaneously by cosmonauts on the ISS in LEO and, on Earth, projected onto the façade of the Bolshoi Theatre in Moscow. Here, terrestrial and extraterrestrial realms at the heart of these Russian utopian narratives are merged. The logo, through its complex polysemy, at once evokes the Romanov Tercentenary Fabergé egg, commemorating the expansion of the Russian State from 1613 to 1913, merged with images of cosmonauts, the stars and the legacy of twentieth and twenty-first century space exploration. Football – in the context of the 2018 World Cup – took on a distinctly Russian, expansionist and Cosmist accent.

As Stacia Zabusky observes through her ethnography of the ESA satellite programme in LEO, the European Space Agency actively facilitates European integration, reiterating European notions of collaboration and European space more generally on Earth, in LEO and beyond.[10] The inhabitation of LEO, both terrestrially and extra-terrestrially, is also part of a larger and well-established project of the Western and primarily anglophone 'overview effect' as described by White – a visual and political aesthetic of the gaze focused on the apprehension of Earth from space that would produce a new universal consciousness and politics.[11] European Space, with its new ex-Soviet postsocialist accession states, is as distinct from ex-Soviet/Russian Space as it is from American Space and the legacy of NASA.

It is the historical legacy of utopian habitation at the heart of the Soviet space programme which is the foundation of the first space habitations launched by the Soviet Union: the *Salyut* stations followed by the American's own *Skylab* and subsequent Soviet/Russian *Mir* stations.[12] The first *Zarya* module of the ISS was built by the Russian space programme on the basis of earlier Soviet era modules and design, and it is the core of the ISS into which other spacefaring nations attach their subsequent modules.

It is worthwhile considering two very different imperial understandings of geographic space in relation to Susan Buck-Morss's characterisation of Soviet space-time at the beginning of the foundation of the Soviet Union, apropos her discussion of Lenin's policies in the wake of the Brest-Litovsk treaty.[13] Buck-Morss argues that it was expedient for the early Bolshevik state to concede national capitalist terrestrial space in order to conquer revolutionary time, and thereby human social evolution. Here, as regards the current Russian occupation of LEO, one might update Buck-Morss's observation in terms of conceding exploration and expansion in order to conquer space and time and human evolution – a very different imperial legacy tending to privilege occupation over exploration.

In this respect it is worthwhile considering two phenomena related to the Russian occupation of LEO and the historical Cosmist legacy which has underpinned it. The chatbot Spotti can be seen as an inherently Cosmist phenomenon: an AI digital avatar produces a resurrected consciousness that merges with others, albeit a companion animal/nonhuman person similar to Laika and other dogs used in Soviet space missions. Laika, the celebrated canine in space, is here a nonhuman person resurrected off-world as 'Spotti'. Originally conceived to be launched on the ISS, Spotti has two modes of existence. It is a chatbot that is virtual in cyberspace in the Russian-language social media platform VKontakte. And it simultaneously exists physically, as a proposed floating spherical console with a cutaway screen (reminiscent of Gagarin's own reentry module) displaying the Spotti avatar, to eventually float and operate in the ISS. As of 11 July 2018, Spotti has 13,000 followers in its virtual mode of existence, and the console has not yet been launched.

Similarly, one can refer to the recent rituals associated with the contemporary post-Soviet movement of the Immortal Regiment of World War II, honouring the ancestral dead of the Second World War, a memorialising technology not pursued by other national space agencies but one that is distinctly post-Soviet and Russian in this particular context.[14] Julie Fedor argues that the wider Immortal Regiment movement is a manifestation of Russian *passionarnost'* (roughly translated as vitality or drive) echoing the Eurasianist evolutionary anthropology of Lev Gumilev. The questions of transcendence, immortality and kinship at the heart of Cosmism find new purchase here in the Immortal Regiment movement in LEO. This state sponsored event revives Russian *passionarnost'* to reconsolidate lost Soviet terrestrial space, while cosmonauts participate in the Immortal Regiment movement and resurrect their dead ancestors in LEO on the ISS. They position their ancestor's portraits, floating in microgravity, along with various icons onboard the ISS in the Russian module.[15] Thus they realise in ever closer terms the Fedorovan ideal of claiming and settling space to resurrect all of our dead ancestors.[16] Here, icon-like, the images of ancestors presented in a quasi-secularised fashion are immortalised, and the two earthly and transcendent realms are merged and simultaneously projected momentarily through these icons onto heavenly realms in this emergent Fedorovan cosmist space.

Space may not have other alien life forms (yet), but both the European and American space programmes express their various forms of colonial expansion and occupation without the burden of indigenes, terrestrial and extraterrestrial, to colonise and oppress. This is the case despite the erasure and continued oppression of historically oppressed peoples on Earth. But the Fedorovan legacy reminds us that many of our dead occupy these new expanded zones of the Earth and LEO. This has not been ignored in comparable, but considerably muted, American rituals regarding immortality and kinship, when NASA 'flew' flags on the ISS to commemorate the victims of 9/11.[17] The dead have always been the traditional markers of occupation and control and wider nation-building projects – where one's ancestors are buried and commemorated is one's territory and the dead most emphatically are used here to colonise and lay claim to these expanding notions in LEO. Here the Russian dead are clearly being placed in attenuated forms both traditional (through the occupation of space and time as represented through the ancient Byzantine space-time consolidating technology of the icon) and contemporary.[18]

Such neo-evolutionary perspectives are not absent in American examples. Silicon Valley cyberneticists, AI theorists, space scientists and enthusiasts conceive of the 'singularity' where a new unitary, transcendent, disembodied and immortal collective consciousness emerges, as Americanist space exploration heralds this next step in human evolution.[19] This chimes with the Fedorovan strains of the Soviet and Russian space programmes and is similarly positioned at the heart of its programmes, albeit more discretely.[20] American expansionist and individualist frontier narratives may claim territories and resources for neoliberal commercial interests, but Russian Cosmist claims, like those attributed to Lenin in the wake of Brest-Litovsk, have their sights not just on the conquering of revolutionary time but of eternity itself.

Notes

1. Oliver, 2015.
2. Radio Free Europe/Radio Liberty, 2018.
3. Madianou and Miller, 2012; Jakubowski, 2016.
4. Miller, 1991, 17.
5. See Siddiqi, 2010; Young, 2012.
6. See Harrison, 2013.
7. Fedorov, 1928.
8. See Olson, 2018; Valentine, 2012; Valentine, Olson and Battaglia, 2012; Messeri, 2016; Battaglia, Valentine and Olson, 2015.
9. See Siddiqi, 2010; Young, 2012.
10. Zabusky, 1995.
11. White, 2014.
12. Siddiqi, 2010.
13. Buck-Morss, 2002.
14. See Fedor, 2017.
15. See Salmond, Walsh and Gorman, 2020.
16. Fedor, 2017; Roscosmosofficial, 2017.
17. Catchpole, 2008.
18. See Mondzain, 2004; Salmond, Walsh and Gorman, 2020.
19. Valentin, 2012.
20. See Harrison, 2013.

Bibliography

Battaglia, Debbora, David Valentine and Valerie Olson. 'Relational space: An earthly installation', *Cultural Anthropology* 30(2) (2015): 245–56.

Buck-Morss, Susan. *Dream Worlds and Catastrophe: The passing of mass utopia in East and West.* Cambridge, MA: MIT Press, 2002.

Catchpole, John E. *The International Space Station: Building for the future.* Chichester: Springer Praxis Books, 2008.

Fedor, Julie. 'Memory, kinship and the mobilization of the dead: The Russian state and the "Immortal Regiment" movement'. In *War and Memory in Russia, Ukraine and Belarus,* edited by Julie Fedor, Markku Kangaspuro, Jussi Lassila and Tatiana Zhurzhenko, 307–45. London: Palgrave Macmillan, 2017.

Fedorov, Nikolai F. *Filosofiia obshchego dela* [The Philosophy of the Common Task]. Harbin: n.p., 1928.

Harrison, Albert A. 'Russian and American cosmism: Religion, national psyche, and spaceflight', *Astropolitics* 11(1) (2013): 25–44.

Jakubowski, Dariusz. 'Expandable Space Aesthetics: International Space Station social media as an expandable democratic surround'. PhD dissertation, UCL, 2016.

Madianou, Mirca and Daniel Miller. *Migration and New Media: Transnational families and polymedia.* London: Routledge, 2012.

Messeri, Lisa. *Placing Outer Space: An earthly ethnography of other worlds (experimental futures).* Durham, NC: Duke University Press, 2016.

Miller, Jay, ed. *Soviet Space: An exhibition in the city of Fort Worth*. Fort Worth, TX: The Fort Worth Museum of Science and History Association, 1991.

Mondzain, Marie-José. *Image, Icon, Economy: The Byzantine origins of the contemporary imaginary*. Palo Alto, CA: Stanford University Press, 2004.

Oliver, Kelly. *Earth and World: Philosophy after the Apollo missions*. New York: Columbia University Press, 2015.

Olson, Valerie. *Into the Extreme: U.S. environmental systems and politics beyond Earth*. Minneapolis: University of Minnesota Press, 2018.

Radio Free Europe/Radio Liberty. 'Putin hails "eternal Christian values" amid Orthodox Christmas celebrations', 7 January 2018. Accessed 1 August 2024. https://www.rferl.org/a/putin-christmas-russia-belarus-georgia-kazakhstan-macedonia-moldova-serbia-ukraine-armenia/28959952.html.

Roscosmosofficial. 'Kosmonavt Oleg Novitskiĭ (@novitsky_iss), kotoryĭ seĭchas rabotaet na Mezhdunarodnoĭ kosmicheskoĭ stantsii, prisoediniaetsia k aktsii #Bessmertnoĭ Polk' [Cosmonaut Oleg Novitsky (@novitskiy_iss), who is currently working on the International Space Station, joins the #ImmortalRegiment campaign], Instagram photo, 9 May 2017. Accessed 2 August 2024. https://www.instagram.com/p/BT3j9T6DWWs/?igshid=b39buxee20vm.

Salmond, Wendy, Justin Walsh and Alice Gorman. 'Eternity in low earth orbit: Icons on the International Space Station', *Religions* 11(11) (2020): 611.

Siddiqi, Asif A. *The Red Rocket's Glare: Spaceflight and the Soviet imagination 1857–1957*. Cambridge: Cambridge University Press, 2010.

Valentine, David. 'Exit strategy: Profit, cosmology and the future of humans in space', *Anthropological Quarterly* 85(4) (2012): 1045–67.

Valentine, David, Valerie Olson and Debbora Battaglia. 'Extreme: Limits and horizons in the once and future cosmos', *Anthropological Quarterly* 85(4) (2012): 1007–26.

White, Frank. *The Overview Effect: Space exploration and human evolution*. Reston: American Institute of Aeronautics and Astronautics Inc., 2014.

Young, George. *The Russian Cosmists*. Oxford: Oxford University Press, 2012.

Zabusky, Stacia E. *Launching Europe*. Princeton, NJ: Princeton University Press, 1995.

11
Flying a new flag: how Moscow hippies created a world without time and a land without borders

Juliane Fürst

If official maps projected a vision of the diverse, ordered and powerful Soviet Union, then Soviet hippie counterculture traced a quite different one: ostensibly borderless, time-defying, internationalist and even global in its aspirations. The two cartographies are not as different as might at first appear: not only did they share concrete physical spaces, both were animated by utopian ideals. But the hippie map analysed below suggests the importance of alternative cartographies for a critical area studies, not least for the way it prompts a fresh look at Soviet and more distant Cold War borders, divisions and solidarities.

In September 1975 a red flag was hung in the House of Culture at the Exhibition of Achievements of National Economy (VDNKh) complex in Moscow. Like any flag it was representative of an imagined community (Figure 11.1). Its insignia and symbols depicted a defined identity. Yet this flag was not reaffirming borders but denying them. It did not claim territory but disputed the very idea of nations as geographical entities. It stood for a land that existed only in the minds and souls of those who believed in it. It was a Soviet, yet more importantly, it was a global banner. It was man-made, but all its symbols referred to the ever-replenishing power of nature: hair, flowers, butterflies – and time. It was a flag representing the Soviet hippie-land: an extraterritorial piece of counterculture behind the Iron Curtain, endowed with utopian hopes and rooted in the soil of Soviet reality.

The flag was the centrepiece of the Volosy art collective's contribution to an exhibition of nonconformist art organised by Oscar Rabin, grudgingly sanctioned by the Moscow authorities. It was no coincidence that the flag was red. Red communism, or better, 'actually existing

Figure 11.1 A reconstruction of the flag, by Debra Marlin, as exhibited by the Wende Museum, Los Angeles.

Photo © J. Fürst.

socialism', was the background to Soviet hippie life. It was the canvas on which Soviet hippie ideology was painted, stitched and patchworked. This ideology was represented on the flag by pieces of American jeans and textiles depicting a guitar, a poppy, a dissolved Dali-type clock, a butterfly and a border post that had been crossed out. The most prominent items of the text, including its central proclamation 'Make Hair Everywhere', affirmed a commitment to global hippie symbols and were written in the lingua franca of 1960s youth culture: English. The Russian inscriptions in the corners of the flag referred to the specific Soviet situation of the flag's creators. Alongside a nod to the border-crossing quality of sound ('Open your ears') and the fragility of Soviet hippies ('Long live butterflies'), its most controversial words were: 'Our Life – Day without End' (*Nasha zhizn' – Den' bez kontsa*) and 'Country without Borders' (*Strana bez granits*). It was the latter – not the reference to opium represented by the poppy – that caused the wrath of the inspecting Moscow official Mikhail Sergeevich Shkodin. 'There will always be borders', he angrily exclaimed during the preopening inspection. 'But comrade, you are a communist, surely under communism there will be no more borders', the artists countered.

'Even under communism there will always be borders', Shkodin insisted.[1] The flag was confiscated. Volosy was charged with tailoring a new flag. The second flag was smuggled like contraband into the building, around which the Moscow authorities had established security cordons and restricted entry regimes (Figure 11.2). The exhibition opened. Borders were crossed in the form of foreign journalists, gathered for the unveiling of the flag. Twenty minutes of borderless chaos reigned. Pictures were taken. Officials ran in and out of the room. Then the authorities fought back. The entire building was closed down under the pretext of a broken pipe. The second flag was confiscated. The artists went on strike in protest. The group Volosy sat under the empty space on the wall, where once their flag had hung.

This little-known episode of the 1970s Soviet culture wars neatly demonstrates the importance of physical and mental geographies in the conversation between regime and late socialist subjects. It indicates how the well-known topography of official Moscow was constantly overlayered by alternative maps drawn by people at odds with the regime. It showcases how Soviet borders were frequently challenged and often subverted. And it gives Moscow a different gloss of internationalism – not as a Cold War headquarters but as a site of global counterculture. It is

Figure 11.2 Ofelia installing the artworks by Volosy.
Photo © Igor Palmin.

worthwhile to untangle the different narratives inherent in the incident and read them with an eye to the spatial meta-story that is embedded in the microhistory of a few turbulent days.

Strictly speaking, the story starts in the 1930s with the construction of the VDNKh, designed by Stalin to showcase Soviet economic power, and the contemporaneous introduction of the doctrine of socialist realism. The established order was then turned on its head in 1975, when two nonconformist art exhibitions were allowed to exhibit in the VDNKh pavilions. These exhibitions drew thousands of people who patiently queued for hours, unwittingly mirroring and challenging the image of the queue forming around the Lenin mausoleum a few kilometres south. The exhibitions diluted the carefully constructed Stalinist map of Moscow. Rather than a beacon of Soviet achievement, the VDNKh briefly became a hotbed of cultural (and inevitably also political) nonconformism. One of the most subversive images from the September exhibition is a picture taken by the photographer Igor Palmin, who captured the hippie artists lounging on the stairs of the baroque House of Culture in their ornamental hippie finery with two rather helpless policemen in their uniforms watching them from the back (Figure 11.3). The hippies had the Moscow City Council's permission and Western journalists ready for their defence. The Soviet policemen were helpless. Stalinist architecture witnessed a reversal of power relations.

Figure 11.3 Volosy on the steps of the House of Culture.
Photo © Igor Palmin.

The representatives of the system felt this subtle shift in the hierarchical topography yet lacked both authority and intellect to articulate their unease. Shkodin was undoubtedly right to smell subversion, in the flag in general and in the pronouncement of a borderless world in particular. Ever since Stalin had confronted Trotsky's internationalism with the concept of 'socialism in one country', national borders had played a significant role in Soviet life and ideology. Moreover, Soviet control mechanisms were mostly spatial. Soviet citizens had to register at their place of living. They were controlled through their place of work. The dissolution of borders as propagated by the flag was an affront against the whole Soviet order. Indeed, it went even further, since its concomitant demand for timelessness challenged the entire modern conception of how life was to be ordered, both spatially and in temporal terms. Yet the order of time was of much less importance to a Soviet official than that of space. At best the dissolution of time would have struck him as silly, while the dissolution of space was subversive.

What Shkodin did not know was that the flag was not only a utopian rallying cry, but an expression of a world that already existed in Shkodin's very own Moscow. The flag itself was tailored in several hippie *flety* – apartments used as assembly spots, often decorated with psychedelic frescos, furnished only with mattresses, darkened against the outside world. Ofelia lived on University Boulevard, in a building for people employed by the military secret service GRU (her mother was an English teacher at the military training academy). It was thus in the very heart of the Soviet secret state that the flag was produced. There were many other apartments in the centre that became quasi hippie salons. Opposite the restaurant Praga, favoured by Party officials, Ofelia's ex-boyfriend Shekspir had had his 'pad' before emigrating to Israel. Budding hippie Sergeĭ Moskalev lived next to him. Down the Arbat, a girl, later famous under her hippie moniker Masha Arbatova, assembled hippies almost nightly. The most notable salon was the apartment of the daughter of the Lenin Museum's main curator. Sveta Markova and her husband Sasha had transformed the two-bedroom apartment near Prospekt Mira into their 'experiment in living'. They painted the hallway yellow, their bedroom blue with red dots, and adorned it with a stolen garden fence. Sveta's mother, a high-ranking apparatchik in the food ministry, lived in the remaining, non-hippie bedroom. Sveta and Sasha fervently believed in free love without jealousy, fashioned Moscow's hippest clothes, and hosted dozens of people every evening who discussed everything that could not be discussed elsewhere.

They escaped time and place via music, drugs and creativity, touching base with existing late socialism only to fulfil their work obligations. Soviet reality existed for them as a background onto which they pasted their own, more colourful life. To make their rejection of the socialist system clear, Moscow hippies chose a name straight from the socialist world. They called themselves the 'sistema' – the system. As Ofelia said: 'We are more than a culture or an art form, we are a system'. The implication was clear – their system was to overtake and overpower the corrupt system of late socialism and replace it with a world that was better than the one they lived in.

From the very beginning the sistema was busy constructing an alternative topography: first in Moscow and then across the Soviet Union. The hippie map of Moscow was seemingly anchored around the same landmarks as tourist maps, yet it generated very different messages. Hippies too walked on Gorky Street, hung around the Bolshoi Theatre, looked at Pushkin's statue on the eponymous square, and made use of the modern facilities on Kalinin Prospekt. But for them Gorky Street was the *strit*. The statues of Mayakovky and Pushkin and their surrounding squares were, for the hippies, meeting places, not because of their cultural connotations but because there were benches to sit on and a metro station nearby. The 'psichodrom' was the insider name of the courtyard in front of the old Moscow State University building, site of many hippie gatherings including their ill-fated demonstration in 1971, when around 600 young people were arrested. In the early years of the Soviet hippie community, the second floor of Café Sever was the reserve of the inner circle around Solntse (Sunny), Moscow's best-known hippie and creator of the concept of sistema. The Café Aromat, nicknamed 'Babylon', on the Garden Ring became the hang-out for the so-called second sistema. The reference to the famous multilingual biblical city confirmed the hippies' rejection of borders, not geographically but spiritually. The Babylonian hippies experimented with whatever drug the Soviet Union could muster, explored Eastern spirituality, and considered their life a constant, uncompromising expression of existentialism. The Soviet hippie world could indeed at times seem like a space of eternal youth and endless possibilities.

Those who craved a more physical manifestation of uninhibited space took to the road. Hitchhiking became a defining hippie practice. Within a few years the sistema spread widely across the Soviet Union – all the way west to Lviv and all the way east to Tashkent and Samarkand, where they linked with local hippie communities in a relentless extension of the alternative Soviet map. The pull was indeed dual. To the West, where life seemed freer (especially Tallinn, which was known for its tolerance of youth cultures and vibrant music scene). And to the East, because of a fascination with Russian and oriental spiritualism as found in Siberia and the Altai, and the supply of drugs in Central Asia. It is tempting to detect here an alternative kind of globality in the making – one that arose out of the special geography of the Soviet Union. But while the Soviet hippies created a truly Soviet internationalism in their sistema, with Balts, Russians, Ukrainians and Jews befriending each other across borders and religions, their case also shows the limitations of this internationalism. The Soviet hippies looked West. Even their fascination with the East was derived from the West. They learned about Buddhism and Hinduism from books translated from English or German or written by Russian émigrés to the West, such as Nicholas Roerich. Most of those who reached Central Asia found the locals bewildering or outright dangerous. Few if any Soviet Muslims became part of the sistema. Soviet hippies did not create a global East. They wanted to be part of the global West.

When the borders did indeed disappear in 1991, it became apparent that the hippies' allegiance to the West was built on very Soviet ideas. The allegiance to and veneration of all things Western had been part of a collective enchantment, saying more about the enchanted and less about what they were enchanted by. In post-Soviet times the community of sistema soon fell apart as new borders replaced the old ones. The Soviet sistema was now divided by visa regulations and by political outlook. Even more importantly, the reality of the West disappointed those who for decades had fought to have access to it. It became apparent that the West also had borders, just different ones. And love, peace and time were in short supply under capitalism. Suddenly it seemed that only in the Soviet past could one live 'days without end' and move in a 'world without borders'. The collapse of time in a society widely perceived as stagnant, and the anarchy of a place ruled by myriad informal practices now seemed like the perfect playground for a counterculture thriving in, and on, the forbidden, marginal, adventurous and borderless. At a second look, the Soviet hippies emerge less as an outlier of a Western phenomenon and more a product of their time and place – a time and place that paradoxically allowed them to exist in a liminal space between reality and utopia, while at the same time providing strict borders to cement their identity.

Note

1 Rabin, 2010.

Bibliography

Rabin, O. 'Nasha zhizn' budet polna sobytiiami' [Our life will be full of events]. In *Eti strannye semidesiat'ie ili poteriia nevinnosti*, edited by Georgii Kizeval'ter, 236–37. Moscow: NLO, 2010.

12
Nation-states of mind: radical geopolitical imagination
Ksenya Gurshtein

What might compel artists to think like a new kind of state – to invert the logic of existing geopolitical power structures and imagine a world in which the rights of stateless people, refugees, exiles and diasporas would be at the centre rather than the margins of our conception of the world? Personal experience with powerlessness and marginality in relation to global realpolitik seems to help, not just in reimagining the world on utopian terms, but also in recognising the limits of such imaginings. In what follows, Ksenya Gurshtein discusses artists from Eastern Europe who have taken such personal experiences and transformed them into works that rethink the boundaries of the 'areas' we study.

During their twenty-odd year collaboration, the Soviet/Russian/Jewish artist duo of Vitaly Komar and Alexander Melamid excelled at making personal histories central to their artistic projects. Born in 1943 and 1945 respectively, both were teens in 1956 when, thanks to Nikita Khrushchev's 'secret speech', much of what they were taught by Stalinist propaganda was declared to be untrue.[1] Years later, in the early 1970s, Komar and Melamid were shown a place where a large bust of Stalin had allegedly been buried during de-Stalinisation.[2] According to the art critic Carter Ratcliff, 'The knowledge that Stalin's effigies lurked in the very earth of Russia awoke Komar and Melamid to his persistence deep in their own memories'.[3] Having come of age during Khrushchev's Thaw, when Russia fully lived up to its reputation as a country with an unpredictable past, the artists henceforth experienced the grand narratives of national history as deeply personal stories.

This is evident in *TransState*, a work that Komar and Melamid created in 1977, while awaiting emigration visas to Israel. The piece was the culmination of several others created between 1975 and 1978 which manipulated the accoutrements of state authority, including the Soviet Constitution, passport and other forms of state-issued ID. In 1976 the artists submitted their emigration applications, which led to them to be branded 'anti-Soviet' and denied access to jobs and professional benefits. At the time they invented *TransState*, Komar and Melamid had already received one rejection of their emigration applications and were stuck in a refusenik limbo.[4] Under these circumstances, *TransState*, which from the start was created in idiosyncratic English, was a deeply personal attempt to grapple with a crisis of faith in the world as it was and to point to a world as it ought to be. It was also a conceptual work of art par excellence, especially fitting for artists who were smuggling their work out of the country – here was an *idea* of nationhood and citizenship envisioned on a truly grand scale to 'constitute a more perfect social structure [and] to insure [sic] the independence and autonomy of the personality against encroachments by the Powers of Darkness'.[5]

The main part of the work's physical form consists of four texts: the *Provisional Constitution of TransState*; the *Declaration of Independence of TransState*; the *Address of the Government of TransState to the Heads of the Great Powers* (China, France, the USSR, the UK and USA – the permanent members of the United Nations Security Council); and the *Address of the Consuls of TransState to the United Nations*. The focus on addressing the 'great powers' and the United Nations is another telling reference to the artists' biographical circumstances. Komar and Melamid's eventual 1978 departure from the Soviet Union, first to Israel and then to the United States, was significantly aided by the 1975 Helsinki Accords, a set of principles agreed on by NATO and Warsaw Pact countries to de-escalate Cold War tensions. Seen by Soviet authorities as a diplomatic victory, the accords also opened up a loophole in the Iron Curtain that allowed people like Komar and Melamid to slip out,[6] surely making the artists sensitive to the power that can reside in international diplomacy's circumlocutions.

The founding documents of *TransState* elaborate in a pointedly official manner its premise for a radically new form of global governance – 'a federation of free and independent state-individuals – "I-States" – with the right of self-government and autonomy, even including secession'. *TransState* citizenship could be extended to any person who 'in his own opinion falls outside the structure of functioning state systems', provided this person does not seek the violent overturn of existing systems and does no bodily harm to other I-States. The punishment for the latter would be expulsion from *TransState* to the jurisdiction of regular countries.

The existence of other countries was not an impediment to *TransState* since it consists of 'the total area of the body surface of all members … freely existing in and transiting through spacc'. The I-States should be free to move anywhere and everywhere, which makes *TransState* a state of mind that one can be in while located anywhere in space, as the road marker that the duo built indicates (see Figure 12.1). All one has to do to be in *TransState* (a homophone for 'trance state') is believe in its existence and be treated as if everyone believes in it, too. To give such faith material form, Komar and Melamid designed *TransState* passports and money (see Figure 12.2).

These mocked-up accoutrements of sovereignty expose the way in which ineffable faith and trust underpin *all* nations, which are, on

Figure 12.1 Vitaly Komar and Alexander Melamid, *TransState*, 1977, mixed media. Collection of Le Centre Pompidou.

Image courtesy of the artists and Ronald Feldman Fine Arts, New York. Photo by D. James Dee.

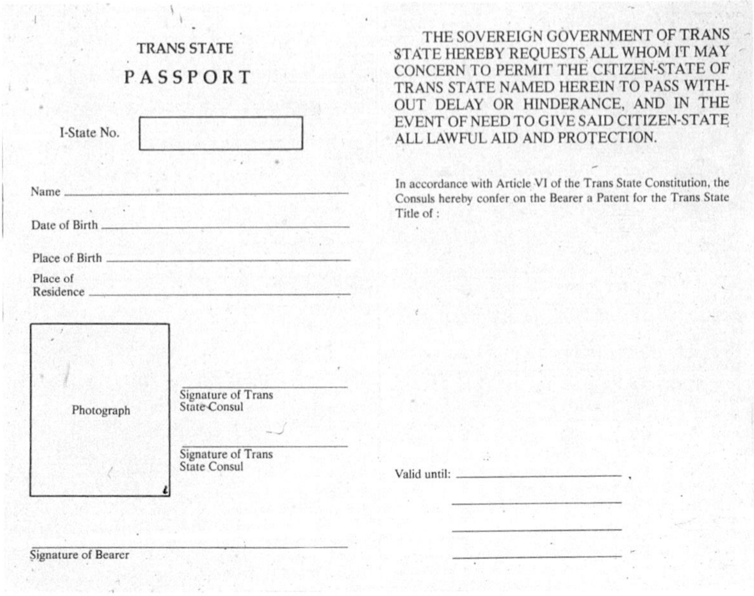

TRANS STATE

PASSPORT

I-State No.

Name

Date of Birth

Place of Birth

Place of Residence

Photograph

Signature of Trans State Consul

Signature of Trans State Consul

Signature of Bearer

THE SOVEREIGN GOVERNMENT OF TRANS STATE HEREBY REQUESTS ALL WHOM IT MAY CONCERN TO PERMIT THE CITIZEN-STATE OF TRANS STATE NAMED HEREIN TO PASS WITHOUT DELAY OR HINDERANCE, AND IN THE EVENT OF NEED TO GIVE SAID CITIZEN-STATE ALL LAWFUL AID AND PROTECTION.

In accordance with Article VI of the Trans State Constitution, the Consuls hereby confer on the Bearer a Patent for the Trans State Title of :

Valid until:

Figure 12.2 Vitaly Komar and Alexander Melamid, *TransState*, 1977, mixed media. Collection of Le Centre Pompidou.

Image courtesy of the artists and Ronald Feldman Fine Arts, New York.

a most fundamental level, *imagined* communities. Ever historically-minded, Komar and Melamid drew inspiration from flipping on its head an authoritarian claim made by the monarch who, more than anyone, promoted the emergence of modern nation statehood. Louis XIV's 'L'État c'est moi', in Komar and Melamid's interpretation, becomes available to any individual as her own motto.

The *TransState* founding documents are not a practical guide to the future. Instead, the work reminds citizens about the *possibility* of denying the legitimacy (if not the authority) of political systems they do not believe in and the option of forming new ones. That the artists locate their political discontent in the world of visual art suggests an important parallel between the two spheres. Both art and political participation are, for Komar and Melamid, creative acts – a view resonant with the vision of civil society that Václav Havel outlined a year later in *The Power of the Powerless*. In that key text of Soviet bloc dissent, Havel described the 'independent life of society' as one in which 'living within the truth becomes articulate and materialises in a visible way'.[7] As artists, Komar and Melamid follow the impulse to visualise what 'living within the truth' might look like for those caught in the transnational inequities of modern geopolitics. Unable to make *TransState* a reality or leave the USSR on their own terms, they could convert the territory of Ronald Feldman Fine Arts, the New York gallery where the work was originally shown in May 1977, into a heterotopia where citizenship and artistic practice did come together, and the artists could imagine themselves as citizens of the world while acknowledging their specific roots.

The 1990s, a decade when over two dozen new nation states emerged in Eastern Europe and Eurasia, were fruitful for Eastern European artists who carried on Komar and Melamid's legacy of critique of borders and geopolitical divisions. In 1997, Yuri Albert, a far more pragmatic member of the Moscow Conceptualist scene than Komar and Melamid, installed his own version of a signpost, both echoing the post that his teachers created for *TransState* and negating its utopian optimism. Albert's *Signpost I* (Figure 12.3) was installed in the small Montenegrin town of Cetinje during the 1997 edition of the *Cetinje Biennial*.[8]

Each of the arrows on the post shows the direction and distance to one of the world's major art museums. Great art, the signpost indicates, is not here in Cetinje; it is elsewhere. While the work addresses Albert's long-standing interest in demarcating the boundary between 'real' and 'contemporary' art, it also (literally) points to the way postsocialist reality continued to replicate the geographic hierarchies in which 'the West' (almost all the museums to which the markers point are in Western Europe) is seen as the home of culture and the object of yearning for its peripheral Eastern neighbours.[9]

Komar and Melamid's truest heirs, though, were the artists of the Slovene collective IRWIN, who, without knowing about the existence of *TransState*, arrived at a closely related idea – namely, that nationality should coincide with one's state of mind rather than be determined by geographic and temporal accidents of birth. Working as part of the Neue Slowenische Kunst (NSK) movement, in 1991 IRWIN invented the NSK *State in Time* – an entity for which IRWIN has since then issued passports, established temporary embassies, held meetings of its citizens, and even created temporary displays of military power (see Figure 12.4).

Like *TransState*, the NSK *State in Time* has no physical territory and, instead, 'confers the status of a state not upon territory but upon the mind, whose borders are in a state of flux, in accordance with the movements and changes of its symbolic and physical collective body'.[10] According to Inke Arns, the *State in Time* was a response to the artists' feelings of disillusionment with the wave of nationalism and ensuing bloody conflicts that led to the collapse of Yugoslavia.[11]

Figure 12.3 Yuri Albert, *Signpost I*, 1997, site-specific installation in Cetinje, Montenegro.

Image courtesy of the artist.

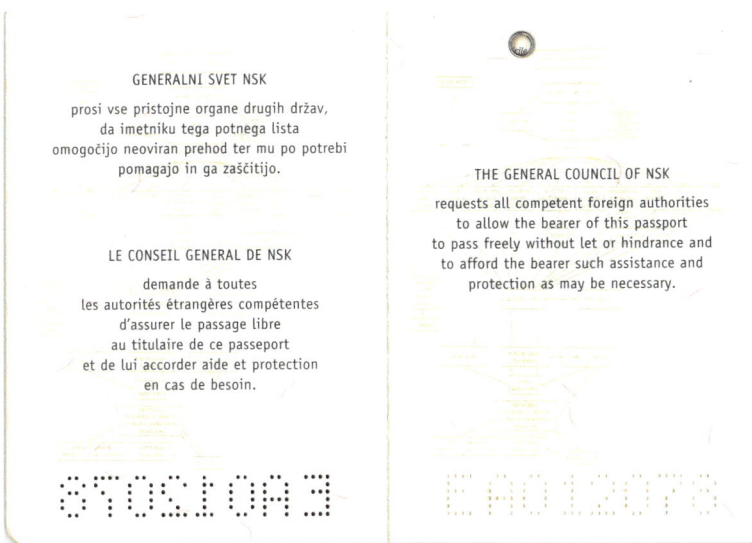

Figure 12.4 IRWIN, Passport of the NSK *State in Time*, issued to the author in 2014.

Image by permission of the artists.

Arns has observed that IRWIN created the *State in Time* as an 'escape vehicle' that gave the artists opportunities to leave mentally and, occasionally, physically, the space of the nationalist rhetoric they found so limiting. Following a 2010 visit to Lagos, alongside Miran Mohar and Borut Vogelnik, two of IRWIN's four members, Arns also noted that the meaning of *State in Time*'s citizenship had been reconfigured by citizens of Nigeria. For them, an NSK passport held the opposite symbolic potential – rather than responding primarily to a desire for escape from an undesirable place, it was an 'entry vehicle' to a place of greater material wellbeing and safety. Indeed, the reason for the trip to Nigeria was the artists' concern that unauthorised migrants would try to use NSK passports as actual official entry documents into Europe.

The mismatch between Second World and Third World problems led IRWIN to behave very differently when explaining *State in Time* in Lagos. The State's founders, 'who had always thought of the state as an abstract concept and an intellectual tool', Arns writes, 'were suddenly confronted with a position that no longer maintained a "safe" ironic distance from the promise made by the NSK passport … Ambivalence and irony did not prove helpful when the genuine fear was that the promise made by a document … would soon prove to be empty'.[12]

This encounter with people who had far fewer rights and possibilities to leave a difficult situation than IRWIN members, who possess the benefits of EU citizenship, clearly highlighted the conceptual limits and the potential practical pitfalls of the artists' utopian vision. Yet it also created a rare opportunity for empathy and solidarity across national, racial and class lines – a chance to acknowledge global inequality in a personal way and, for IRWIN, to do what Eastern Europeans do all too rarely – examine their own complicated and shifting place of both marginality *and* privilege in the existing global system.

Perhaps it should go without saying that artistic feats of imagination, no matter how artfully conceived or well-intentioned, were never going to be an equal counterbalance to the complexities, injustices and uneven distribution of power in the world outside museum and gallery walls. Yet for all their practical impossibility and their tangled mix of cynicism and hope, the works described above remain vitally relevant in the discussions of the 'real world' struggles surrounding the meaning of human rights, citizenship and national sovereignty that, with the Cold War in the rearview mirror, show no sign of being resolved in the observable future.

Notes

1. An earlier version of this text was published in German in the exhibition catalogue that accompanied the travelling exhibition *Verführung Freiheit: Kunst in Europa seit 1945* [The Desire for Freedom: Art in Europe since 1945], which originated at the Deutsches Historisches Museum in Berlin. See Flacke, 2012.
2. Frazier, 1986, 35.
3. Ratcliff, Komar and Melamid, 1988, 17.
4. Komar, 2005.
5. The *TransState* documents can be found in their entirety in Ratcliff, Komar and Melamid, 1988, 198–204. All the quotes from those documents cited here are drawn from this source.
6. United States Department of State, 2017. According to John Lewis Gaddis, Brezhnev had looked forward to the 'publicity he would gain … when the Soviet public learned of the final settlement of the postwar boundaries for which they had sacrificed so much … [instead, the Helsinki Accords] gradually became a manifesto of the dissident and liberal movement … [that made it possible to] claim official permission to say what they thought'. Gaddis, 2006, xxvi.
7. Havel, 2018.
8. Two similar signposts were subsequently installed in Russia, in Moscow (2005) and Perm (2008).
9. See Albert's comments on this work (in Russian), Albert, 2018.
10. Čufer and IRWIN, 1994.
11. Arns, 2012.
12. Arns, 2012.

Bibliography

Albert, Yuri. 'V sovremennom iskusstve nepominanie ne menee vazhno, chem ponimanie' [In modern art, misunderstanding is just as important as understanding], *sredaobuchenia.ru*, 21 February 2018. Accessed 2 August 2024. https://sredaobuchenia.ru/albertlecture.

Arns, Inke. 'The Nigerian connection: On NSK passports as escape and entry vehicles', *e-flux Journal* 34 (2012). Accessed 2 August 2024. https://www.e-flux.com/journal/34/68336/the-nigerian-connection-on-nsk-passports-as-escape-and-entry-vehicles/.

Čufer, Eda and Irwin. 'NSK *State in Time*'. In *Irwin: Zemljopis Vremena/Geography of Time*, edited by Eda Čufer and Irwin. Umag: Galerija Dante Marino Cettina, 1994.

Flacke, Monika, ed. *Verführung Freiheit: Kunst in Europa seit 1945* [The Desire for Freedom: Art in Europe since 1945]. Dresden: Sandstein Verlag, 2012.

Frazier, Ian. 'Profiles: Partners', *New Yorker*, 29 December 1986.

Gaddis, John Lewis. *The Cold War: A new history*. London: Penguin, 2006.

Havel, Vaclav. 'The power of the powerless, translated from Czech by Paul Wilson', *East European Politics and Societies* 32(2) (2018): 353–408. https://journals.sagepub.com/doi/abs/10.1177/0888325418766625.

Komar, Vitaly. Komar and Melamid: Chronology. Accessed 12 November 2024. http://www.komarandmelamid.org/chronology.html.

Ratcliff, Carter, Vitaly Komar and Alexander Melamid. *Komar and Melamid.* New York: Abbeville Press, 1988.

United States Department of State. 'Milestones: 1969–1976'. Office of the Historian. Accessed 9 May 2017. https://history.state.gov/milestones/1969-1976/helsinki.

13
Oraşul viitorului: beyond the Siliconisation of postsocialist Cluj
Erin McElroy

The label of 'the Silicon Valley of Europe', for a Romanian city, implies a wholesale transplant of technologies and practices that the slogan's authors want us to believe will turn Cluj into 'the city of the future' – a future conceived on Western, technocapitalist lines. In this essay, however, we discover the highly specific socialist and postsocialist histories and entanglements that have underpinned Cluj's recent development, as well as the costs that are being exacted. McElroy shows us critical incredulity emerging from comparisons, between here and there, then and now. But must this process always be only one-way? What insights would emerge were we to think of Black, working-class East Palo Alto, say, with its history of segregation, redlining and predatory lending, now subject to aggressive gentrification from an influx of young, well-paid tech professionals from across the globe, as 'the Cluj of the West'?

In 2018, Cluj's mayor Emil Boc announced the introduction of a public robot named Antonia, as part of Cluj, Romania's newfound status as 'the Silicon Valley of Europe'.[1] Although Antonia proved only to be a computer algorithm, lacking the robotic stock-image body displayed in the press, she, as the first 'public robot mayoral servant', was nevertheless conjured as part of a widespread techno-futurist vision reflected in Romanian infrastructure and imaginaries alike. One only has to momentarily peruse Cluj's Mărăşti neighbourhood to breathe in new construction particles and observe fibre optic cabling sticking out of buildings like alien tentacles, waiting to be connected. New condos and co-working spaces materialise overnight, while former industrial socialist factories are transformed into office spaces for Western firms such as NTT Data, Bosch and iQuest. Sitting in the front yard of a local anarchist, feminist social centre, A-casă, where I have attended meetings, workshops and skill shares over the years, the overgrown fruit trees and vegetables growing around me, not to mention the centre's aging dog, feel out-of-joint juxtaposed to the newly erected development closing in on the centre. But nevertheless, I am there with a handful of comrades and members of the housing justice group, Cași Sociale ACUM! (Social Housing NOW!), mapping out new anti-eviction efforts in the rapidly gentrifying city. Yet our conversations get interrupted by the sounds of construction nearby, as NTT Data flashes its astrofuturist sign above the Siliconising horizon.

As we have observed, across Mărăşti, rents have risen, and evictions too. Numerous Roma residents are being squeezed out, sometimes ending up homeless, sometimes banished to uninhabitable 'social housing' at the city's waste site, Pata Rât. Just blocks away from NTT, on Anton Pann Street, a Roma family who had been living there for twenty-two years was recently evicted. And today, on a sunny spring day in 2018, we ran into a Roma couple living between the new residential complex, City Casa and the German iQuest, who will be displaced later this month. 'All of the space around here is becoming too valuable', they lamented. While socialist urbanisation provided housing and jobs to Roma, many of whom had been living precariously before, postsocialist techno-urbanisation results in the opposite, restoring former privatisation regimes.[2] While there are undoubtedly racialising and gentrifying processes that Siliconisation induces, sitting upon the threshold of *oraşul viitorului* (city of the future), we find ourselves growing suspect of a form of comparativity that sees Cluj as Silicon Valley, rather than a city with its own non-fungible technoscapes. By Siliconisation, I refer to practices of becoming Silicon Valley, in which local imaginaries and materialities alike are co-opted by Silicon Valley's imperial structures of desire. As I suggest, Siliconisation does inhere new forms of technocapitalism, inciting contexts of gentrification, but at the same time, by simply understanding urban processes as such, unique techno-urban histories are torn from the palimpsest that is postsocialist Cluj.

Still sitting there in A-casă's front yard, we are peering at the surrounding 'chic modernist' development springing up in Mărăşti. While it appears flashy and new, in fact it builds upon former industrial and residential spaces. The German iQuest sits upon the ruins of the Flacara textile factory on Someșului Street, adjacent to where another German multinational, Bosch, is developing a new campus. The former factory's canteen now houses firms bearing techno-esoteric names such as Doc.Essensis and CCSCC. One block down, the old Napochim plastics factory (known as 'The Red Flag' when it first opened in 1947) and the former Arbator butchery are being transformed into a new apartment block and the 'Oxygen Mall' respectively. 'See, it's not greenwashing of postsocialism – it's oxygen-washing!' we laugh. Today, the top floor of the nearby Central Commercial Centre, established as a centre of commerce in the 1970s, has been transformed into ClujHub, a co-working space with daily talks in which successful Westerners attempt local entrepreneurial inculcation. It also houses Uber, much to the chagrin of local taxi drivers, many of whom have been engaged in protests against the California-based startup. There, the futurism of the socialist project during which industrialisation, urbanisation and also informatics were made central priorities, poke out through the veneer of Siliconisation despite the newness that it espouses.

Here I want to pause and offer that, despite the imperiality of Silicon Valley and its fantasies of replication, perhaps more generative understandings of local techno-urbanism might emerge through analytic decentralisation. What other worlds might emerge if Silicon Valley ceased being the zero point in contemporary analysis and if we read history as accumulative rather than as repetitive? After all, the Siliconisation of Cluj does not simply reproduce technocultural dynamics upon a *tablă ștearsă* (tabula rasa). On the contrary, it lands upon the infrastructure of former plants, most of which were part of socialist modernity's own project of techno-urbanism – a project conceived of to implement class equality, national autonomy and urbanisation. Siliconisation also entangles with other post-1989 infrastructural processes of property restitution and privatisation, which have been cumulatively restoring presocialist property to the heirs of former owners through the anti-communist rhetoric of 'transitional justice'.[3] Due to a long history of racism in Romania, few Roma were presocialist property owners. Not only did many Roma workers lose industrial employment post-1989, but many also lost their homes. Siliconisation, while framed as futuristic, in fact incentivises the restoration of presocialist racist private-property topographies while nevertheless co-opting socialist-era infrastructure. In writing about the impossible dreams of becoming California's Silicon Valley, locally and globally, it suggests that 'Silicon Valley was always a promise, never a place'.[4] *Orașul viitorului* too is always a promise, one today layered by a thick palimpsest of various futurisms – not only that of socialism and transition, but also that of presocialism. Presocialism, plagued by antisemitic and anti-Roma eugenic technoscientific visions, was also the era in which Bucharest aspired to become 'the Little Paris of the East' – a different yet connected *orașul viitorului*.

While seeking to restore presocialist private-property regimes in the name of *oraşul viitorului*, by co-opting socialist-era infrastructure, Siliconisation preys upon the technological and linguistic prowess of Romanian workers as well. As I have repeatedly heard, the only real requirement for IT employment is English fluency, as most jobs are simply communications outsourcing. As a German CEO of a smaller Cluj startup explained, Romania's interstitial geography provides the cheap labour costs of 'further East and South' locales, but also a sense of Europeanness harder to obtain elsewhere. Meanwhile, Romanian software developers, often praised for 'being so damn good at programming', are only paid a fraction of their Western contemporaries, a friend working for a small Seattle-based startup grumbled. But why is it that there is such technological and linguistic prowess in Romania to begin with?

In Cluj, IT is the largest professional sector, driven by global capital and outsourcing, and fed by public universities offering a wealth of courses in programming.[5] Yet it is not simply global capital nor universities responsible for expertise. Unbeknown to many promulgators of Siliconisation, socialist Romania excelled in hardware production. This was partly due to the country's own maverick status in the Soviet-led satellite state trade agreement, Comecon. Though Romania was slated to specialise in agriculture, the Communist Party dreamt of other futures, ones involving industrialisation, urbanisation and informatics. As Vasile Baltac, who had been a key researcher in the state's first computer projects, recounted to me in the same Bucharest office in which he worked during socialism (and in which he now leads a software company), socialist Romania invested heavily in computer production. Soon it produced more third-generation computers than any other Eastern bloc state, selling machines to China and the Middle East. Meanwhile, university informatics, physics and cybernetics research centres became highly valorised. By the end of socialism, Romania had produced more than 25 computer models, from the FELIX in Bucharest to the TMS in Timișoara. As a programmer in Cluj recollected to me one day over beers, in the 1980s the national radio station even broadcast raw code after midnight on Thursdays, so that emergent programmers could record and then decode it on their computers. Most of these computers were replicas of Western models, either developed in state factories (which cloned models such as the British Spectrum or French IRIS) or assembled in apartments and university computer labs. In fact, more models were built underground than in factories, a practice that continued after socialism ended in 1989 and austerity plagued the country.[6]

After 1989, the land that factories (computer and otherwise) sat upon was bought by real estate speculators, divided into joint-stock trades, and sold. Western firms such as IBM swept in, absorbing former workers. In Cluj, the production of HC386 computers was halted, and 'everything just shut down', Bogdan Tirziu, a self-taught programmer and retrocomputing enthusiast, explained. There are only four HC386s left in the country today. Bogdan is trying to implement a local computer museum in Cluj, but he has received no funding support from the City Hall. Official computer memory, it seems, has become devoured by what Liviu Chelcea and Oana Druța describe as 'zombie socialism', the anti-communist discourse that in valorising neoliberal futurity pathologises socialism as a dark aberration to be overcome through the ongoing project of transition.[7]

But Bogdan offers another insight, useful for theorising the entwining of Siliconisation and zombie socialism in Cluj: 'Contrary to what people think, the tech boom is not being led by firms, but by a particular generation of people, now in their mid thirties'. This 'Xennial' generation, occupying that interstitial space between Gen X and Millennials, correlates with what Bogdan describes as the 'X86 Generation', a reference to Intel's x86 microprocessor architecture. Conceived of in Cold War-era Silicon Valley the x86 microprocessor has since embodied numerous iterations, and still dominates desktop and mobile technology. In the West, Xennials are defined as being born pre-digital, but easily adapting to digitisation in the 1990s. But in post-socialist Romania, most Xennials were not able to afford Silicon Valley technology, despite its growing prevalence. Instead, this generation learnt how to create its own hardware and infrastructure, often by adapting and hacking existing models. By reading computer magazines and socialising in internet cafes, Bogdan learned how to create his own internet network, and soon connected twenty-four people in his block. It's really people in this generation that are creating all of the software and systems that the West desires, he tells me. This underground techno-culture was one that many characterised as șmecherie, a Romanian word with Romani roots inferring cunning, or a street-smart cleverness.[8] It was șmecherie cyber deviancy rather than official computing culture that Bogdan understands as having established the bedrock for Siliconisation. 'Our language skills are related to this too', he explains, offering a history of how, after socialism, Western undubbed programming flooded the channels with English. 'Now schools teach English to all the kids, but we learned from the Cartoon Network.' It is the perfect combination of socialist informatics, socialist and postsocialist austerity, and Xennial temporality that created the foundation for Cluj's Siliconisation.

Gentrification is not the fault of this generation, and while intricately connected to phenomena ranging from the Cartoon Network to socialist computer development and șmecherie computer cloning, is reducible to none. Rather, perhaps it can be understood as a complex process in which Western firms capitalise upon a unique layering of presocialist, socialist and transitional technological histories, which, through zombie socialism, seek to replace presocialist versions of *orașul viitorului* with that of Siliconisation. Critical area studies is a useful tool in understanding the spatiotemporal entanglements of this conjuncture in which the installation of Siliconised public mayoral robots is all but a fantasy, yet in which the materialities of Siliconisation still bear material and often racially dispossessive effects. Perhaps writing *orașul viitorului* requires crafting a new 'field language' committed to what Gayatri Chakravorty Spivak describes as the 'irreducible work of translation'.[9] Such a language bears its own interstitial geography, neither part of nor fully absorbed by any cardinal direction.

Like Intel's x86 microprocessor, area studies emerged under the auspices of Cold War knowledge production. While Intel's technology was hacked, modified and altered to bypass Western technocapitalism's paywall, critical area studies too has sought to creatively avert Cold War disciplinarity.[10] Spivak has suggested that by entwining comparative literature with area studies, a new 'planetary' path can be forged to facilitate cultural translation beyond post-Cold War globalisation and its necessary erasures.[11] Such a translational approach avoids the pitfalls of comparative methods which, as Lisa Lowe warns, too often are used to universalise Western rationality and ideals, upon which everything else gets compared.[12] Yet at the same time, by focusing on connections and entanglements, rather than only comparisons, enduring imperial geographies and their connected digital transits of global capital come into focus.[13] As an 'imperial formation',[14] Silicon Valley thus needs to be studied both in terms of its own global desires, but also through local critiques of its universal and often anti-communist aspirations. Spivak writes: 'Just as socialism at its best would persistently and repeatedly wrench capital away from capitalism, so must the new comparative literature persistently and repeatedly undermine and undo the definitive tendency of the dominant to appropriate the emergent'.[15] Not writing for a new comparative literature but rather for a connected and translational approach to mapping the entanglements, connections and frictions of Siliconisation alongside other technological futures past and present beyond its reach, *orașul viitorului* has much to offer.

Notes

1. This text was based upon the book, *Silicon Valley Imperialism: Techno fantasies and frictions in postsocialist times* (McElroy, 2024).
2. Vincze, 2017, 29–54.
3. Popovici, 2020, 97–111.
4. Schrock, 2020.
5. Petrovici, 2014.
6. Fiscutean, 2017.
7. Chelcea and Druță, 2016.
8. McElroy, 2024.
9. Spivak, 2003, 13.
10. Koch, 2016.
11. Spivak, 2013, 15–16.
12. Lowe, 2005, 409–14.
13. By entanglements, connections and frictions, here I draw upon Karen Barad's (2007) *Meeting the Universe Halfway: Quantum physics and the entanglement of matter and meaning*, as well as Anna Tsing's (2004) *Friction: An ethnography of global connection*.
14. Stoler, 2008.
15. Spivak, 2003, 100.

Bibliography

Barad, Karen. *Meeting the Universe Halfway: Quantum physics and the entanglement of matter and meaning*. Durham, NC: Duke University Press, 2007.

Chelcea, Liviu and Oana Druță. 'Zombie socialism and the rise of neoliberalism in post-socialist Central and Eastern Europe', *Eurasian Geography and Economics* 57 (2016): 521–44.

Fiscutean, Andrada. 'The underground story of Cobra, the 1980s' illicit handmade computer', *Ars Technica*, 1 November 2017. Accessed 3 August 2024. https://arstechnica.com/gadgets/2017/11/the-underground-story-of-cobra-the-1980s-illicit-handmade-computer/.

Koch, Natalie. 'Is a "critical" area studies possible?', *Environment and Planning D: Society and Space* 34(5) (2016): 807–14.

Lowe, Lisa. 'Insufficient difference', *Ethnicities* 5(3) (2005): 409–14.

McElroy, Erin. *Silicon Valley Imperialism: Techno fantasies and frictions in postsocialist times*. Durham, NC: Duke University Press, 2024.

Petrovici, Norbert. 'Personal development and flexible contracts: Depoliticized class struggles between highly skilled workers and manual workers in Cluj'. Vienna: ERSTE Foundation, 2014.

Popovici, Veda. 'Residences, restitutions and resistance: A radical housing movement's understanding of post-socialist property redistribution', *City* 24(1–2) (2020): 97–111.

Schrock, Andrew. 'Silicon Valley is not a place', *Public Books*, 9 April 2020. Accessed 3 August 2024. https://www.publicbooks.org/silicon-valley-is-not-a-place/.

Spivak, Gayatri Chakravorty. *Death of a Discipline*. New York. Columbia University Press, 2003.

Stoler, Ann Laura. 'Imperial debris: Reflections on ruins and ruination', *Cultural Anthropology* 23(2) (2008): 191–219.

Tsing, Anna. *Friction: An ethnography of global connection*. Princeton, NJ: Princeton University Press, 2004.

Vincze, Eniko. 'The ideology of economic liberalism and the politics of housing in Romania', *Studia Universitatis Babes-Bolyai, Europaea* 62 (2017): 29–54.

14
Planet ppparadise: decondensing the social in the condition of wild capitalism

Michał Murawski

What happens when a concept from the Soviet 1920s in architecture and urban planning, aiming to bring citizens together in public space and intensify the possibilities of collective, revolutionary energies, is put into practice in the post-industrial cityscapes of late capitalist modernity? Murawski traces the transplantation of the avant-garde notion of public space as 'social condenser' and its perversion as atomising social decondenser in the public-private spaces of New York's High Line, London's ersatz High Line and the Zaryadye Park in Moscow. An object lesson in critical area studies, this piece globalises a concept that emerged in the Soviet experiment and brings it back home to Moscow with a trenchant critique of fauxparadisiacal political ecologies of Putinism.

The 'social condenser' – formulated in the Soviet Union during the late 1920s – is one of the most influential architectural concepts of the last century. During the past several decades, it has been soundly 'unanchored' from the geographical, historical and political-economic context of its conception; mutated in a bewildering and perverse variety of ways, and, more recently, misappropriated and deployed as the design inspiration for a dubious new breed of multifunctional, self-avowedly 'paradisiacal' parks and public spaces (many, but not all, of them quasi-publicly, downright privately or private-publicly owned): starting in the 1980s and 1990s with Paris's Parc de la Villette and Promenade Plantée; and culminating in the second decade of the twenty-first century with Manhattan's High Line, Singapore's Gardens by the Bay, Moscow's Zaryadye Park, Salesforce Park in San Francisco; as well as projects closer to home, among them Greenwich Peninsula's 'The Tide' (a particularly dystopian ersatz High Line, also designed by Diller, Scofidio + Renfro) and the failed Garden Bridge project. These new quasi-social condensers, crucially, have an odd tendency to advertise themselves as projects devoid of infrastructure: these are self-avowedly infrastructureless or post-infrastructural terrains, which claim to function exclusively on the superstructural level of emotion, spectacle and 'wow effect'.

The parameters of this ideology of 'victory over infrastructure' were expressed with particularly earnest lucidity by Timur Bashkaev (speaking at a 2017 public discussion devoted to architecture and power, which I organised during my field research in Moscow), one of the local Russian architects working on the Zaryadye project together with Diller Scofidio: '[The High Line] triggers emotions … and that's it, there's nothing else there … no communication, no transport, no nothing … And so Zaryadye, its main task, yes … [is to] trigger enormous positive emotions … colossal "wow effects"'.

In this chapter, I trace – across time and space – the fortunes of some of these planetarily-proliferating post-infrastructural private-public paradises – ppparadises for short. Ppparadise, I argue here (and at greater length elsewhere),[1] constitutes an emergent hegemonic template for (stealthily) extractive public space in the condition of literally-existing 'wild capitalism' – a type of obfuscatory primitive accumulation wherein enclosure and extractivism masquerade as commons and ecologism.[2]

A note on '(self-)criticality'. By virtue of the comparisons, juxtapositions and critiques provided, this chapter constitutes an exercise in critical area studies. On the other hand, it might be seen to engage in a self-critique *of* critical area studies, insofar as it provides an example of one of its core commandments – that of unanchoring concepts and practices from their origin-points in the 'East' and deploying them globally – gone awry. In doing so, however, it provides a foil to commonplace understandings of Western-derived concepts being dumbly imported to or superficially mimicked in the East (or South). In the course of its migration to (or expropriation by) the wild capitalist West from the state socialist East, the social condenser becomes *de-*condenser; in its ppparadisiacal Western incarnation (and, subsequently, in its reimported ppputinist variant) the social condenser is reduced, in other words, to 'form without substance', a decontextualised, infrastructureless perversion of the 'real' thing.[3]

Public-private ppputinist potpourri

As proposed by the Soviet Constructivists, the social condenser conceives architecture, the city and public space as coalescing into an integrated machine for bringing people into close proximity with each other; and – like a condenser or transformer in an electrical circuit – increasing the 'voltage' or intensity of their interactions. The effect of this act of social condensation, for Moiseĭ Ginzburg and others, would be to transform people from functioning as alienated, isolated bourgeois subjects to self- and mutually-fulfilled members of a collectively-oriented, radical new society.[4]

Rediscovered by French Marxist scholars like Anatole Kopp and Henri Lefebvre in the 1960s, the social condenser was then picked up by the most influential young architects and theorists of the time, among them Rem Koolhaas, Elia Zenghelis, Bernard Tschumi and Zaha Hadid; it was incorporated into the language of an emerging new ideology of architecture and public space, but – in the process – it was stripped of its radical content. This ideology – and practice – of public space advocated bringing bodies together in a close, sensuously, haptically, somatically intense type of interaction; but it now lost its connotations of radical, transformative social change. Somatic communism (in Paul Preciado's phrase) realised as somatic capitalism.[5]

This concept became a key source of inspiration for theories of the design of new types of parks and public spaces. Koolhaas explicitly deployed this concept in his design for the Parc de la Villette in Paris (1982); and even mock-'patented' the idea of the condenser he developed for La Villette, in his book *Content* (2004), defined (in classic late twentieth-century architect gibberish) as 'programmatic layering upon vacant terrain to encourage dynamic coexistence of activities and to generate, through their interference, unprecedented events'.

Koolhaas did not win the competition, but Tschumi's realised concept incorporated many of the same inspirations and ideas as Koolhaas's. La Villette became the blueprint for a new typology of multifunctional, high-intensity public-private paradisiacal 'post-park' (ppppparadise), which – via projects such as Chicago's Millennium Park (2004) and Paris's Promenade Plantée (1993) – saw its most celebrated realisation in New York's High Line (2009). In the words of landscape architect James Corner – who worked on the High Line together with the practice Diller, Scofidio + Renfro – 'the visitor becomes as much a performer as a viewer, more deeply engaged in participating in the theatricality of urban life – the promenade as an elevated catwalk, urban stage and social condenser'. In this new type of urban 'parkscape' the stroll becomes much more than a stroll. It is conceived as a multilevel, multisensorial, intersubjective, even artistic and theatrical, experience of 'social condensation'. Intense on every level, but utterly depoliticised.

A similar understanding of sensorial intensity underlies the use ideology of Zaryadye Park, opened by Vladimir Putin in September 2017, in the shadow of Moscow's Kremlin. As the park's first director, Pavel Trehleb, told me, Zaryadye consists of 'an incredible potpourri of unlimited, diverse types of services'. These services, said Trehleb, allow visitors to complete a 'unique pathway' (*unikalnyĭ marshrut* – marching route) and 'experience a series of awesome emotions in an average time of just 2–3 hours!' This two- to three-hour *marshrut* is not the only one available, he qualified. There are, in fact, a series of visiting 'cycles', which have been 'programmed into' the park, lasting 'from a minimum of one and a half hours … all the way up to an entire day'. This kind of intricate visitor programming is necessary and essential, Trehleb insisted, because 'for the brain it is very important that you find yourself constantly within some sort of external impulses which constantly nourish our emotional system'.

Without knowing it, Trehleb gave very literal expression to this mutated understanding of Zaryadye as a 'social condenser', an intensifier of electrical currents. He did so by making use of the fact that the name Zaryadye, itself taken from the old trading district of Moscow which used to occupy this site ('*za ryad'ami*', or 'behind the trading rows'), can also be interpreted as a pun on the Russian word for appliance charger (*zaryadka*).

'What is our main role?' asked Trehleb. 'We charge people with positive energy, emotions … which allow you to live, to be joyful'. And this act of charging also carries with it an explicitly social function, even a patriotic one. The 'positive energy' emanated by the park allows people to 'change their attitude towards the city and the country'; it impacts on 'people's emotional state, on their social adaptability. Even if you have financial problems at home, or family or other life problems, nevertheless you have [in the park] a source of energy, a place to charge yourself, you go there to suffuse yourself with useful energy'.

To cynically interpret these words, what Trehleb is trying to say is that if you – the inhabitant of Moscow – are feeling down, or if you are feeling poor, don't bother going out onto the streets to make a racket, don't take it out on the government or the municipality. Instead, why don't you just come and suffuse yourself with positive energy in your local public private Putinist paradise?

The social function of the social condenser, then, is interpreted here in precisely the opposite way to the sense in which the architects of the 1920s meant it. For Trehleb, the paradisiacal 'parkscape' becomes a transformer not for intensifying social energies, but for dulling or relaxing them. The social condenser becomes a social decondenser. The park is here conceived not as a political machine, but as an antipolitics machine.

Crucially, the social condensation of the High Line and of Zaryadye is an intensely theatrical experience; it is about showing off to your fellow paradise-dwellers and interacting with them on an aesthetic rather than a political level; and this type of theatrical sociality lends itself extremely well to various forms of technological mediation. Most prominently, via the medium of the selfie, social condensation can be broadcast to the whole world; and architecture becomes selfie-tecture (Figure 14.1 and 14.2).[6]

Arguably, the more social condensation becomes mediated through technology, the more it begins to herald the act of social distancing. We can see this, for example, in London's The Tide. Unlike the high lines of Paris and New York, which are actually built atop former, repurposed pieces of urban transport infrastructure, The Tide is a 1-kilometre chunk of fake high line, awkwardly composed into an enormous private housing development, adjacent to the former Millennium Dome in North Greenwich. The Tide's PR materials make a point of over-emphasising the possibility of sensuous, spontaneous social, ecological, paradisiacal, commercial, creative and artistic interaction that is possible atop and beneath the elevated parkway. Craft markets are held. Mediocre blue-chip public artworks – including offcuts by Damien Hirst, Antony Gormley and Richard Wilson – populate the peninsula. Users are encouraged to download and avail themselves of smartphone apps to

Figure 14.1 Selfies in Zaryadye, 2017.
© M. Murawski.

Figure 14.2   Selfies on Hudson Yards, 2019.
© M. Murawski.

aid them in every aspect of the 'peninsula experience' – even meditation. One app in particular was described as a 'portal that blends the power of meditation with the beauty of the world. Simply open the OPO app, be guided to an OPO portal near you, have a seat and immerse in the OPO soundscape. Relax and breathe in the view'.

I visited The Tide during its opening weekend in July 2019. A 'pop-up' music festival was taking place at the entrance to the elevated promenade. A short distance away, a young couple were seated on a bench with their eyes closed. They had their headphones in and were availing themselves of the OPO meditation experience. Another man was sitting on the opposite edge of the same bench at a safe social distance from the couple. He had arrived before them and was having a video call on his phone. The couple, distracted from their mindfulness experience, occasionally cast disapproving glances in his direction, before eventually asking him, quite rudely, to decrease the volume of his phone call. In the social decondenser, social meditation trumps social communication (Figure 14.3).

Social distancing

Consultancy firms, developers, ad agencies and municipalities frequently measure the success of an architectural or planning project by comparing the number of selfies and other photographs uploaded to Instagram at a given site before and after its completion. Given the fact that Zaryadye and the High Line were both closed during the first Covid-19 lockdowns in spring 2020, one might have expected the volume of selfies to grind to a halt. But city dwellers continued to post 'throwback' images from their

Figure 14.3   Asocial meditation on The Tide, 2019.
© M. Murawski.

archives, pining after pre-Covid social condensing. User Bvalchisen's photo from Zaryadye's 'Soaring Bridge' is accompanied by a long paean to unfulfilled ambitions: 'CORONAVIRUS. Oh, what plans we had for March, April and the whole summer.' @Natali_grakovich, posing in a series of locations around Zaryadye, writes: 'Sitting at home, I've been enveloped by nostalgia for walks around the city (*progulki*)', before going on to criticise – in a no-less nostalgic tone – the customer service in the park's (then-closed) media centre. At the High Line, meanwhile, @sarandezutter bemoans, 'I just wanna go back to when I wasn't over-analyzing every aspect about my life, when oh when will that happen'; while @amiraalkayyali comments, simply, 'missing this'.

What does this global outpouring of nostalgia for social condensation suggest? It seems to portend, on the surface at least, that people are aching to go back to normal, to a life of intense and sensuous, paradisiacal parkland interactions. As I have been trying to suggest, however, the type of social condensation cultivated and practised in the world's ppparadises over the past two decades is deprived of certain key ingredients. It adds up to a caricature of the socially-transformative, collectively-intense type of condensation propagated by Ginzburg and comrades in Moscow of the 1920s. It is proprietorial (as evidenced by Koolhaas's patent for his La Villette project), self-focused rather than substantively intersubjective, and in many ways, *anti*-social. It is built atop the remnants of the infrastructure of twentieth-century high modernity (or it pretends to be built atop an imitation of this kind of infrastructure), yet it effects a disavowal or negation of these infrastructures. It reduces social interaction to the superstructural or sensual, while apparently repressing the physical infrastructure as well as the political and economic conditions which allow for these projects to come into being. The High Line, of course, is a bullet of gentrification running through Manhattan, the direct effect of whose construction has been an exponential increase in land values in its immediate vicinity and the attendant process of class, race and social cleansing. The Tide is a desperately overwrought façade for a privately-built housing development, which creates low-quality, rabbit-warren dwellings for mortgage-bound, middle-income (predominantly White) house buyers at the lowest reaches of the 'property ladder'; while shunting the less-than-legally-required quantity of (predominantly non-White) social housing tenants into a badly-designed poor enclave several hundred metres removed from the riverfront (and the above-bemoaned pseudo high line which abuts it).[7] Each of these ppparadises, of course, was built by minimally-reimbursed migrant labourers, distinct from its users in class and race – most visibly so in the case of New York, where the greater share of the labour force were Hispanics from Central America; and in Moscow, whose construction workforce is mainly from the poor former Soviet republics of Central Asia, and who work in Russia under dreadful conditions and face constant racism.

Perhaps, acting out their stymied desire for human interaction following the eventual lifting of the long Covid lockdowns, people will take over the world's selfie-tectural post-parks to indulge in a more expansive, substantive, critical, generous type of public social condensation on the terrains of these sterile, highly-surveilled paradises. But I wouldn't bet on it. The three hundred muzak-blasting speakers constituting Zaryadye's public-address system (many of which also have surveillance cameras attached to them) will continue disciplining the movements of park visitors; while White middle-class couples will continue to blissfully and silently meditate amidst the generic shrubbery of the socially-cleansed Greenwich Peninsula, passively-aggressively shushing the conversations of people sitting in their vicinity. The infrastructure itself, the Marxian *basis*, 'the economic structure of society, the real foundation, on which arises the superstructure [*überbau*]' will remain hidden from view in these greenwashed ppparadises of somatic capitalism.[8]

Notes

1. Murawski, 'Falshfasad', 2022.
2. Murawski, 2020; for a comprehensive theorisation of new forms of enclosure and primitive accumulation, see Federici, 2018.
3. Mishkova and Daskalov, 2013.
4. For background on the origins and subsequent mutations of the social condenser, see the contributions to Murawski and Rendell, 2017.
5. Preciado, 2019. Of interest here is the fact that Preciado's volume appears as part of the 'Critical Life Studies' series.
6. Perhaps the most egregious and monstrous piece of selfie-tecture built hitherto, British designer Thomas Heatherwick's multistorey 'Oracle' – aka 'Shawarma' – in the Hudson Yards section of the High Line was indefinitely closed in February 2020 following a spate of suicides.
7. Wainwright, 2015.
8. This text was written before Russia's full-scale invasion of Ukraine and, like the remainder of the contributions to the Atlas, it has not been changed. It is essential, however, to note here the extent to which, following February 2022, the portents of war planted amidst the wild grasses of Zaryadye came into sharp relief. Grotesquely, the conduct of Russia's war and its self-declared conquest of temporarily-occupied Ukrainian territories has been reflected in the composition of the park's flora itself. Zaryadye has become the site for the condensation or crystallisation not of any kind of progressive sociality, but of the fascist, military public sociality of Russia in the time of 'culture Z'. See Murawski, 2022, 'From culture tree to culture Z'.

Bibliography

Federici, Silvia. *Re-enchanting the World: Feminism and the politics of the commons*. Oakland, CA: PM Press, 2018.

Mishkova, Diana and Roumen Daskalov. 'Forms without substance: debates on the transfer of Western knowledge to the Balkans'. In *Entangled Histories of the Balkans*, Volume 2: *Transfers of Political Ideologies and Institutions*, edited by Roumen Daskalov and Diana Mishkova. 1–97. Oxford: Brill, 2013.

Murawski, Michał. 'Wild capitalisms: The political ecology of the post-socialist city, from pyramid to PPParadise', PiraMMMida.life. 2020. Accessed 22 July 2024. https://www.pirammmida.life/michal-murawski.

Murawski, Michał. 'Falshfasad: Infrastructure, materialism and realism in wild capitalist Moscow', *American Ethnologist* 49(4) (2022): 461–77.

Murawski, Michał. 'From culture tree to culture Z: War, empire and Putin-era urbanism', *Soniakh Digest*, 22 October 2022. https://soniakh.com/index.php/2022/10/17/culture-tree-culture-z/.

Murawski, Michał and Jane Rendell. 'The social condenser: A century of revolution through architecture, 1917–2017', *The Journal of Architecture* 22(3) (2017): 369–71.

Preciado, Paul B. *Countersexual Manifesto*. New York: Columbia University Press, 2019.

Wainwright, Oliver. 'Revealed: How developers exploit flawed planning systems to minimise affordable housing', *The Guardian*, 25 June 2015. Accessed 22 July 2024. https://www.theguardian.com/cities/2015/jun/25/london-developers-viability-planning-affordable-social-housing-regeneration-oliver-wainwright.

15
Peripheristan
Francisco Martínez

In this entry, Francisco Martínez sketches the outlines of a transnational continent of the (semi-)fringes. Less Moscow or London, more Leicester, Tampere and Tallinn, as his own career evidences. The much-attested disadvantages of peripheral status, including the centres' refusal to see such locales on their own terms, are here compensated by the advantages (ambiguity and distance) of relative remoteness – though peripherality can be as much a political condition as a state of mind and a geography of displacement.

On Tuesday, 17th of January 2006, I entered Kazakhstan by train. Those who have travelled by train in Russia, the empire of peripheries, know what kind of suspension of knowledge the railroad experience entails there. Passengers become threshold people and a form of communitas arises.[1] Conversations with your neighbours in the wagon often emerge over a cup of tea. The film *Compartment Number 6* (2021) shows well the intricacies of this experience. (By the way, that film was made by a Finnish director, Estonian screenwriters and Russian actors.)

Back then I very much looked like a foreigner, so one of the fellows on the third-class *Platzkart* asked me about the purpose of my travel to a semi-remote country. Subsequently, they were very surprised at my reply. 'Tourism? I think you chose the wrong place for this. There is nothing to see here around', said a middle-aged woman who was visiting relatives in Aktau (a former Scythian settlement that has had four different names in the twentieth century).

When I arrived at Atyrau, the temperature was −45°C. I went out of the station but just for a few minutes; I soon gave up on the idea of visiting this (probably beautiful) town, previously famous for its fish cannery and nowadays known for being surrounded by oil refineries. Quickly, I came back to the station to buy a ticket for the next train, which happened to go to Alma-Ata.

In 2014, the (now resigned) President Nursultan Nazarbayev was in Atyrau when he proposed to attract more tourists by changing the name of the country to Kazakh Eli. In his view, Kazakhstan has as much tourist potential as Mongolia, but people do not come here because the name of the country ends with the suffix '-stan'. This change was not finally approved; alas, just a few days after Nazarbayev's resignation (after nearly three decades in power), the capital of the country, Astana, was renamed as Nur-Sultan. In September 2022, the new President Kassym-Jomart Tokayev reverted the change and the capital of Kazakhstan is called Astana again.[2] Also, he has announced a transition to a Latin-based Kazakh alphabet, instead of the Cyrillic one, a plan that includes efforts to promote the use of the Kazakh language over Russian in the local media. Neighbouring Kyrgyzstan is considering similar legislation.

There are seven countries in Central Asia with the suffix '-stan': Kazakhstan, Tajikistan, Uzbekistan, Kyrgyzstan, Turkmenistan, Afghanistan and Pakistan.[3] This suffix comes etymologically from Persian, and it means the 'place of'. The Latin 'stare' and the Sanskrit *sthā́na* come from the same root, meaning 'to stand'. It later evolved in English into 'state' and 'status' (a manner of standing).

The same year, when Nazarbayev announced his intention of erasing the '-stan' of his country, the ambassadors to the UK of Lithuania, Latvia and Estonia expressed anger about being included in *The Guardian*'s 'New East' network. The Lithuanian ambassador, Asta Skaisgirytė-Liauškienė, claimed that it is 'solely in factual terms we were a part of the Soviet Union'. In a similar vein, Latvian ambassador, Andris Teikmanis, called the 'post-Soviet world' category misleading and deluded, suggesting it was turning the clock back to the USSR.

In April 2019, the comedian Volodymyr Zelens'kyǐ (with no political experience) won the presidential elections of Ukraine with 73 per cent of the vote.[4] In his first speech, Zelens'kyǐ proclaimed: 'I am not yet officially the president, but as a citizen of Ukraine, I can say to all countries in the post-Soviet Union: look at us – anything is possible!'[5] But what kind of community is that, coined by Zelens'kyǐ – 'the post-Soviet Union'? Is it just another name with as much political weight as the Commonwealth of Independent States (assembled after the break-up of the USSR)?

Still, the imaginary geography of the 'post-Soviet Union' might not be limited to the boundaries of the former empire. That political kinship is instead mutable, multiple, and change-oriented; in some cases, it upgrades itself as semi-periphery, inhabited by liminal Europeans of all sorts. Further on, such a condition of relative remoteness can also travel – dependent on its connections to and separations from other places.[6] Both processes, mutating and displacing, are based on normative influences (coming from elsewhere) as well as on political aspiration.

In this piece, I propose the term 'Peripheristan' to conceptualise this kind of territory; a semi-remote location where Prada products still cannot be directly shipped and whereby funding, standards and legislation from the core arrive with difficulty, despite the local will to have them; and also, an area that can potentially be considered as its own 'sphere of influence' by aggressive powers at the core. Because Peripheristan is made up of border states, those standing in the middle of something, half existing in the eyes of big neighbours that relate to them through a sort of crypto-colonialism.[7]

In this speculative imaginary geography, we could argue that some countries could fit into the category of inner-periphery; other regions could rather be conceptualised as outer-centralia, as the very limen of the core;[8] some others, could be termed as para-peripheria – alongside, in front of and beside a given centre. And finally, there is also a place called 'Peripheristan of the core', which is the one made invisible or ignored despite being located in the centre. As an example, in my recent encounters with colleagues working in global capitals, I was surprised to hear about the difficult working conditions there, with a great number of people peripheralised in the centre of things.

Etymologically, the term periphery comes from the Greek *peripheres,* referring to a circumference and the act of revolving around. In medieval times, the term acquired the meaning of boundary, as the outside line of a surface. Nowadays, periphery still denotes an outer edge, but also a marginal or secondary position in relation to other subjects. Besides its geographical connotations, peripherality often refers to a condition of invisibility, presenting certain people as belonging to non-history, those who are not genuinely invited to the party.[9] According to this notion, the periphery might have multiple identities, but it is always defined in relation to a given core. This has been the traditional understanding of political science, presenting the periphery as a place that nobody is interested in and is nominally or practically dependent on some centre. For instance, in Immanuel Wallerstein's understanding, peripheries are areas that suffer from geographical isolation, with poor access, distant from core spheres of activity, and therefore precarious, unstable and dependent within the system of relationships.[10]

In anthropological studies, however, the focus on peripherality reveals complex dependencies that reach both ways – to and from centres and edges. Peripheries are thus more than a no-man's land, yet it remains unclear to what extent they offer themselves as a specific political or epistemic terrain.[11] Peripheries are often presented as being misinterpreted by a centre or hidden in the process through which things are made to seem clear, bounded and fixed.[12] They exist outside any focus, described as full of unrealised potential and as imbued with ambiguity. The gaze from there is more perspectival, resisting definitive categorisations, not fully adhering to any script. Peripheries present, therefore, a particular way of thinking about problems, as a zone where traditional methodological codes fail to guide our action.[13] We are talking of a view that allows us to observe what is not readily apparent when attested from the centre.

If reconsidering the autobiographical link between my fieldwork and the locations of my academic affiliations, I could present myself as an expert on peripheries, holding a Peripheristani passport and CV. That is, indeed, my anthropological nationality.[14]

The relationship between places and personalities affects knowledge, in the sense of influencing what can be known. One of the things I have learned is that the condition of peripherality depends on the question asked. For instance, when I moved to Leicester I heard a similar argument to one from a visit to Jyväskylä (Finland): 'this place is very central', 'you can go anywhere from here', and 'just look at the map!'. In the case of Leicester, we can observe that this town is right in the middle of the UK, appears at the top in terms of life quality, and is experienced as one of the most culturally diverse cities in this country despite the self-deprecation of some of its inhabitants.

Globalisation has turned peripherality and remoteness into a more complex, relative issue.[15] Helsinki and Tallinn are another example of this; these semi-peripheral cities are deemed as successful European capitals, yet their wealth partly comes from concentrating the resources coming from its surrounding areas and dubious foreign investments.[16]

Peripheral centres might ratify themselves both in opposition to the metropolis and by locating further peripheries – even weaker and more helpless, which still need some kind of centre to acquire a certain subject position.[17] The centre–periphery opposition can be also presented as a verticality that can have, as in the case of Russia, many levels. In that country, disputes are most often resolved through a vertical line, while the different peripheries of the assemblage have little direct contact between them.[18]

Today, we are seeing the destabilisation of core and periphery as historically constituted traditions and geographies. Terms such as aboriginal or Eastern Europe mark negatively how things were apprehended as instruments of modern (Western) epistemology.[19] By contrast, Peripheristan is here presented as an Other without borders, one which extends alterity almost to the infinite and might open up interesting lines of comparison. This is an ex-centric, transnational continent, not Moscow, not Mecca, not Berlin, not London,[20] a fertile third space, showing an ambiguous kinship, one radically contingent, in which things hardly last but experimentally endure, instead.

Notes

1. Turner, 1973.
2. The town holds the Guinness World Record for the capital city with the most name changes in modern times. In the last two hundred years, it has been called: Ақ мола, Akmolinsk, Tselinograd, Akmola, Astana, Nur-Sultan, and finally Astana (for now).
3. However, as Soviet republics, some of these countries were referred to with the Latinate suffix '-ia': Turkmenia, Kirghizia, and Uzbekia.
4. The name Ukraine (Україна) was first used in the twelfth century referring to the borderlands between the Polish and Kyivan Rus' territories. Etymologically, the name comes from the proto-Slavic *krajь*, which meant edge, fringe, or an area defined by certain boundaries.
5. See for instance: 'Posmotrite na nas, vse vozmozhno'.
6. Green, 2013.
7. Herzfeld, 2002.
8. For more on these terms, see Stromberg, 1999.
9. DiGiacomo, 1997.
10. Wallerstein, 1974.
11. Simone, 2019.
12. Green, 2005.
13. Martínez, Di Puppo and Frederiksen, 2021.
14. Martínez, 2019.
15. Martínez et al., 2021.
16. See for instance the Reuters coverage of money-laundering cases in the region. https://www.reuters.com/article/idUSKCN1QL11R/. Accessed 4 August 2024.
17. Iarskaia-Smirnova and Romanov, 2001.
18. Azrael and Payin, 1998.
19. Mignolo and Tlostanova, 2006.
20. Paraphrasing the artist group Slavs and Tatars.

Bibliography

Azrael, Jeremy R. and Emil A. Payin, eds. *Conflict and Consensus in Ethno-Political and Centre-Periphery Relations in Russia*. Santa Monica, CA: RAND, 1998.

DiGiacomo, Susan M. 'The new internal colonialism', *Critique of Anthropology* 17(1) (1997): 91–7.

Green, Sarah. *Notes from the Balkans: Locating marginality and ambiguity on the Greek–Albanian border*. Princeton, NJ: Princeton University Press, 2005.

Green, Sarah. 'Borders and the relocation of Europe', *Annual Review of Anthropology* 42 (2013): 345–61.

Herzfeld, Michael. 'The absent presence: Discourses of crypto-colonialism', *South Atlantic Quarterly* 101(4) (2002): 899–926.

Iarskaia-Smirnova, Elena and Pavel Romanov. 'At the margins of memory: Provincial identity and Soviet power in oral histories, 1940–1953'. In *Provincial Landscapes: Local dimensions of Soviet power 1917–1953,* edited by Donald J. Raleigh, 299–326. Pittsburgh, PA: University of Pittsburgh Press, 2001.

Martínez, Francisco. 'An expert in peripheries: Working at, with, and through the margins of European anthropology', *ANUAC* 8 (2019): 167–88.

Martínez, Francisco, Eeva Berglund, Rachel Harkness, David Jeevendrampillai and Marjorie Murray. 'Far away, so close: A collective ethnography around remoteness', *Entanglements* 4 (2021): 1–30.

Martínez, Francisco, Lili Di Puppo and Martin Demant Frederiksen, eds. *Peripheral Methodologies: Unlearning, not-knowing and ethnographic limits*. London: Routledge, 2021.

Mignolo, Walter and Madina Tlostanova. 'Theorizing from the borders: Shifting to geo- and body-politics of knowledge', *European Journal of Social Theory* 9 (2006): 205–21.

'"Posmotrite na nas, vse vozmozhno": Rech' Zelenskogo posle oglasheniia dannykh ekzit-polov' ['Look at us, everything is possible': Zelenskyï's speech after the announcement of exit poll data.], *tvrain.ru*, 21 April 2019. Accessed 4 August 2024. https://tvrain.ru/teleshow/vechernee_shou/rech_zelenskogo-484298/?fbclid=IwAR3C0N1IT3g_aUv3GYNQGf-5reQ2mPQcNyFQDqIEkk0pICMJ7RcIZZ_oQbY.

Simone, AbdouMaliq. *Improvised Lives: Rhythms of endurance in an urban South*. London: Polity, 2019.

Stromberg, Joseph. 'The Cold War', *Mises Daily Articles*, 1 June 1999. Accessed 4 August 2024. https://mises.org/library/cold-war.

Turner, Victor. 'The centre out there: Pilgrims' goal', *History of Religions* 12(3) (1973): 191–230.

Wallerstein, Immanuel. *The Modern World System*. New York: Academic Press, 1974.

16
The plus one dimension
Katalin Cseh-Varga

The artistic movements of the inter-war avant-garde were often interested in new ways of conceptualising space, exploring the potential of the artwork to capture a high-velocity, fragmented, post-Einsteinian world. Cseh-Varga presents one such movement, Sirató's Dimensionism, and its exploration of the borderless 'plus one'. She shows how, many decades later, Hungarian artists of the 1960s and 1970s rediscovered Dimensionism, finding in it a tool with which to dismantle the rigid borders of the Cold War.

A while after the passionate era of avant-garde thought, in Paris of the 1930s there remained a committed group of artists who had not given up on the symbiosis of life and art. Hungarian poet Károly Tamkó Sirató joined this circle and, based on his own artistic experiences and observations, in 1936 he authored the *Dimensionist Manifesto* (Figure 16.1a and b).

Inspired by the non-Euclidean law of physics, Tamkó Sirató drafted a law for the arts that no longer operated based on separate categories of space and time. Avant-garde art, the manifesto explained, transcends the borders of the known and the conventional. Leaving the geometry of two and three dimensions behind could lead to the 'vaporisation' of the artwork.[1] Some decades later when ideological contours started to determine everyday and cultural life alike, this avant-garde spatial fantasy gained a new significance in undermining the Cold War era of binary rigidity. Different avant-garde generations shared a creative interest in overcoming limitations for the sake of dynamic absolutism when circumstances in socialist states often dictated the opposite.

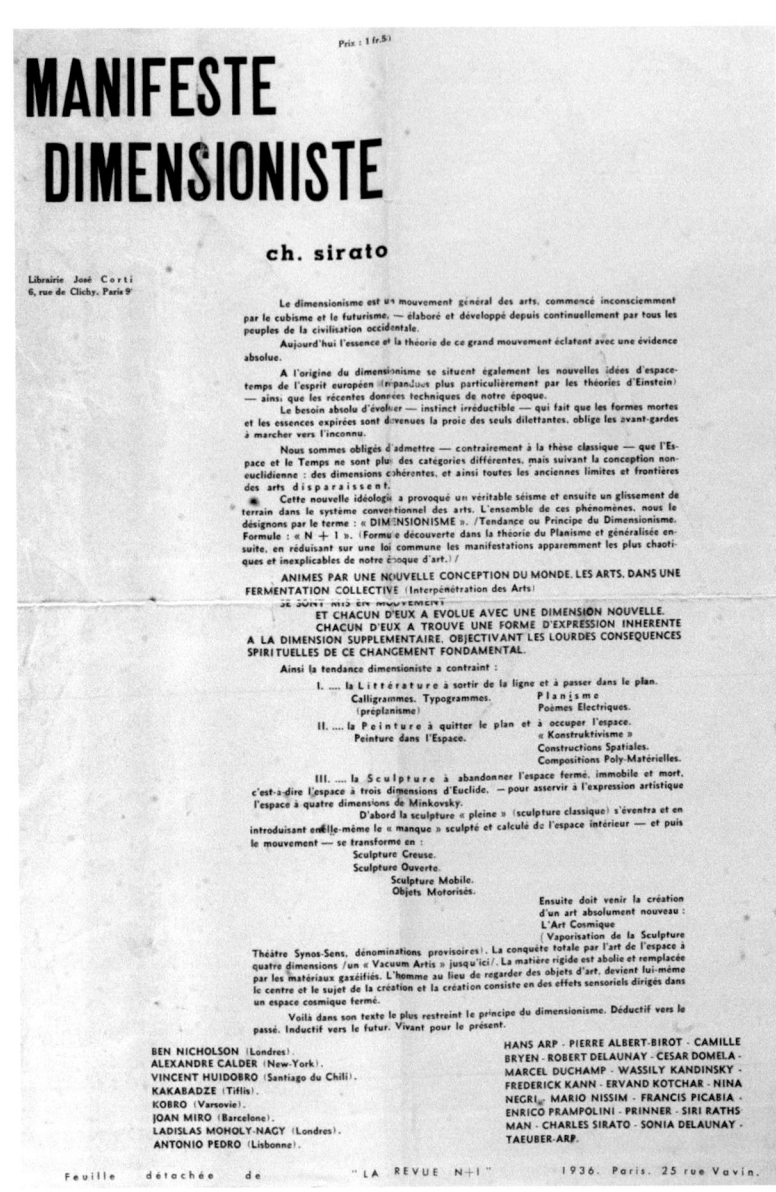

Figure 16.1a and b   The first edition of the *Dimensionist Manifesto*, 1936. Photo of the original document, dedicated by Károly Tamkó Sirató to Lázár Endre Bajomi.

Courtesy of Artpool Art Research Center, Budapest.[2]

Figure 16.1a and b (continued)

Tamkó Sirató, one pioneer of borderless thinking, felt that poetry in its linear, self-explanatory form was no longer satisfactory, so he added one more dimension to the line: that of height. In this way, he developed the poetry of plane geometry. The same happened with other artforms, too: the collage moved painting into the third dimension and kinetic sculptures conquered the fourth dimension. Tamkó Sirató borrowed the idea of the 'plus one dimension' from Einstein and the Minkowskian theory of spacetime.[3] This reflected scholarly debates of the beginning of the twentieth century that centred on bent space and hyperbolic and elliptic geometry. Albert Einstein introduced his special theory of relativity in 1905, which was geometrically applied two years later by Hermann Minkowski as a theory of four-dimensional spacetime. Minkowski argued that space and time in themselves are relative, but when united they become absolute.[4]

Dimensionism was a concept of thinking on the one hand, and a guidance for art production on the other. Tamkó Sirató (Figure 16.2) imagined dimensionism to be a slow process of realisation, in terms of becoming aware of how progression in science influenced progression in art. The dimensionist attitude and artwork were about extension and border-crossings.

The *Dimensionist Manifesto* might have been too enthusiastic and persistent about avant-gardist utopias. Its declaratory tone did not differ much from that of other art movements' manifestos. Some critics mentioned the phantasmagorical and transcendental voice of the text,[5] while others questioned the originality of Tamkó Sirató's proposed concept. Those latter critics suspected that the poet had simply recycled El Lissitzky's 'Proun' conception that set out a step-by-step transition from two-dimensional painting to three-dimensional installation and architecture.[6] Despite the mixed reception, the long list of important avant-gardists who signed the manifesto represented proof of its relevance.[7]

The list indicates something else, too: a global non-Euclideanism. Among the signatories there were, among others, British, Chilean, Hungarian and Polish artists. Tamkó Sirató imagined dimensionism as an international, borderless phenomenon of a shared interest among artists in expanding artwork into space and time simultaneously. In this interpretation, the dimensionist attitude existed beyond physical and temporal boundaries of any kind.

Because of the extensive nature of spacetime and a definition of art that neglected limitations, the re-evaluation of dimensionism in the Hungary of the 1960s and 1970s challenged the era of blocs

Figure 16.2 Károly Tamkó Sirató after his return to Budapest in 1936.
Courtesy of Artpool Art Research Center, Budapest.

and curtains. The arguments being made to turn attention back to dimensionism were grounded in its actuality and its compatibility with socialist progression.

Tamkó Sirató believed that the atomic and space age required an adequate art that did not correspond to the aesthetic norms which had been defined in the nineteenth century.[8] Because the Soviet Union and its satellites were playing a leading role in the Cold War race for technological advantage, he argued, they should not settle for aesthetic conservativism. In the 1962 draft foreword to the monograph entitled *Dimenzionizmus I. albuma* – first album of dimensionism – Tamkó Sirató argues that a realist, naturalist and impressionist style was not in line with contemporary technological progression. Instead, he saw the model of historical avant-garde as potentially suitable, mostly because it was contemporary, experimental and seeking the new, with the help of which it could be possible to reach the socialist commonwealth.[9] Despite these seemingly convincing arguments, the genealogy of the manifesto's emergence and Tamkó Sirató's explanatory remarks on the relevance of dimensionism in working towards the communist project did not matter to the Hungarian authorities. The *First Album* was not released until 2010.

In contrast, the *Dimensionist Manifesto* was first published in Hungarian translation by the Vojvodina-based magazine *Bridge* (*Híd*) in 1966. Looking around the art world, Tamkó Sirató experienced a feeling of self-affirmation. He, like the editors of *Bridge*, recognised that the law of the plus one dimension had become everyday practice in avant-garde circles; for instance, the art object turned ephemeral and the fleeting action occasionally replaced the static artwork. Border-crossings became manifest in the popular entanglement of diverse artistic genres and materials. The new generation of avant-gardists preferred dynamic art production with performative and intermedia-like tendencies.

Serbian-born Hungarian poet, art writer, artist and performer, Bálint Szombathy, belonged to the most important rediscoverers of dimensionism. He had a deep understanding of Tamkó Sirató's concept. In around 1971 and 1972 Szombathy became acquainted with Tamkó Sirató's two-dimensional grapho-visual works and republished some of them in *New Symposium* (*Új Symposion*), where he was a graphics editor (Figure 16.3).[10]

In an extensive 1977 paper entitled *Pathways of Concrete Poetry* (*A konkrét költészet útjai*) he summarised dimensionism's basic pillars for his generation through the looking glass of contemporary experimental poetry.

One of the main arguments Szombathy makes in the *Pathways of Concrete Poetry* is that writing against linearity and the explosion of the Gutenberg galaxy represents much more than just the reform of literature. Any activity connected with language is done through the avant-garde spirit of renewal and is affected by transformation.[11] Szombathy introduced a poem by Tamkó Sirató, from between 1963 and 1968, in which the 'dimensionist' draws a conclusion about dimensionism's relevance via a thirty-year perspective. In *Appeal to the Point-Man* (*Szózat a Pont-emberhez*), Tamkó Sirató describes the point, the line, the plane and the space alive and interconnected in four-dimensional spacetime. Spacetime is a continuity which defines the direction of progress in relation to the 'plus dimension'. Like many of his fellow poets, Tamkó Sirató began his career with the letter, before starting to arrange it in a non-linear form on paper. Later on, he added graphics to the written word and observed how his contemporaries applied similar techniques in their own art making. These observations, in combination with the achievements of modern geometry, physics and mathematics, allowed him to absolutise. With the help of abstraction, Tamkó Sirató designed a complex system for avant-garde art that obeyed one rule only: that of spacetime.

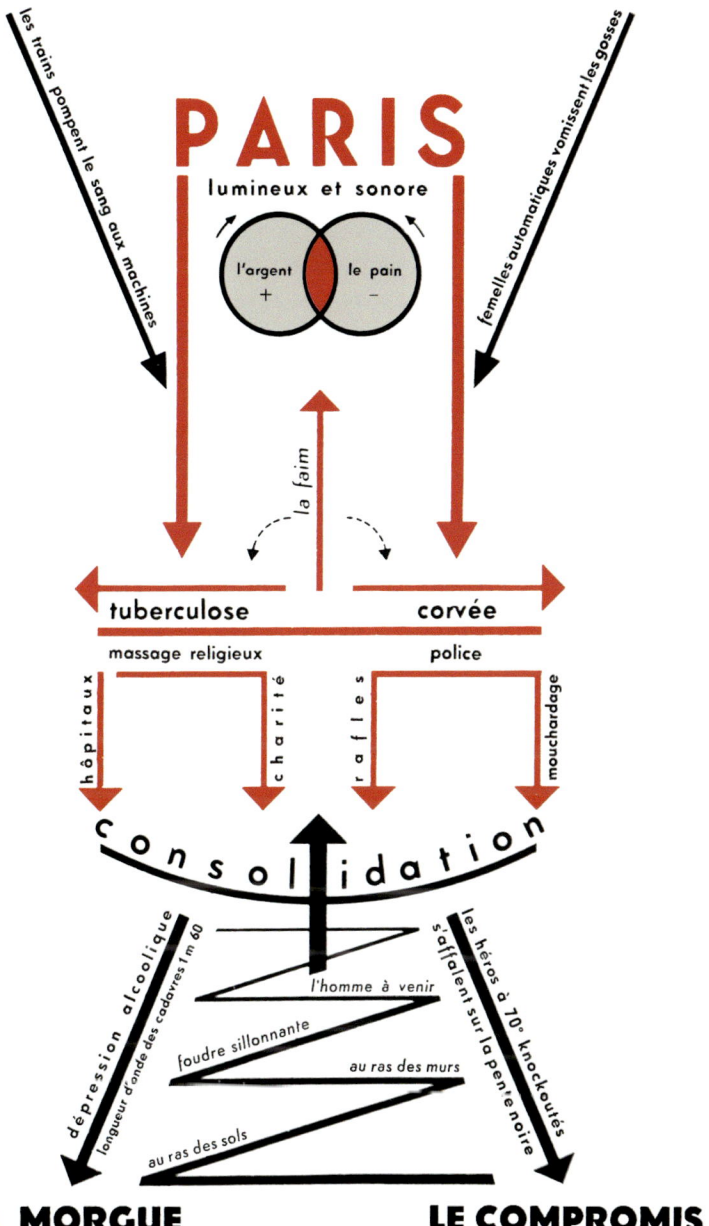

Figure 16.3 Károly Tamkó Sirató: *Paris*, 1936. Electric poem (Dim. I.).

Courtesy of Artpool Art Research Center, Budapest.

The temptation to revisit dimensionism in the 1960s and 1970s lay exactly in this. In the era of clearly defined frontiers, the perspective of spacetime opened up a completely different point of view. Shifting borders for this generation of avant-gardists not only came to the fore in event-based and intermedia art, but in the phenomena of travelling artists, artworks and ideas that undermined the rigidity of borders between the First, Second and Third Worlds. The list of examples is long, reaching from the extensive mail-art network during the Cold War, study and exhibition trips made by East-Central European artists to the United States or West Germany, to the reception of cybernetic theory in communist Romania.

If dimensionism, as Tamkó Sirató pictured it, was as absolute as the Minkowskian conception of spacetime, then it expanded from the artwork to the lives of artists and the territories in which they lived. Bálint Szombathy, one of the main supporters of dimensionism in the 1970s, was himself an author who has overwritten the contours of political and economic margins. He crossed the border between Hungary and Yugoslavia many times and was well connected beyond the Soviet zone of influence. Szombathy was engaged in experimental poetry, graphic design, art theory and conceptual and action art – a personification of the dimensionist attitude. In two, three or four dimensions, he developed a critical (indirect) position towards binary areas of East and West, socialist and capitalist.

Notes

1. Tamkó Sirató, 2018.
2. Based on the contract concluded between the Artpool Art Research Center and the legal successors of Charles Tamkó Sirató (dated 28 March 2010), Artpool holds all image rights for figures published in the *History of the Dimensionist Manifesto* book in the case of publications realised in cooperation with Artpool.
3. Tamkó Sirató, 2010, 58, 62, 65.
4. Gecső and Glaser, 2003, 139.
5. Lengyel, 2011.
6. Gecső and Glaser, 2003, 144.
7. The list of signees included: Hans Arp, Pierre Albert-Birot, Camille Bryen, Robert Delaunay, Cesar Domela, Marcel Duchamp, Wassily Kandinsky, Frederick Kann, Ervand Kotchar, Nina Negri, Mario Nissim, Francis Picabia, Enrico Prampolini, Anton Prinner, Siri Rathsman, Károly Tamkó Sirató, Sonia Delaunay, Sophie Tauber-Arp.
8. Hernádi, 1971, 116.
9. Tamkó Sirató, 1988, 4–5.
10. Szombathy, 2007.
11. Szombathy, 2018.

Bibliography

Gecső, Tamás and Judit Glaser. 'Egy fejezet a magyar avantgárd történetéből. Tamkó Sirató Károly: A dimenzionizmus I. albuma' [A chapter in the history of the Hungarian avant-garde. Károly Tamkó Sirató: Dimensionism's first album]. In *A nyelvleírás lehetőségei és határai: Segédkönyvek a nyelvészet tanulmányozásához XIX* [Possibilities and Limits of Language Description: Reference books for the study of linguistics XIX], edited by Tamás Gecső, 136–46. Budapest: Tinta Könykiadó, 2003.

Hernádi, Miklós. 'Tamkó Sirató Károly'. In *Látógatóban: Kortárs Magyar írók vallomásai* [Visiting: The confessions of contemporary Hungarian authors], 113–19. Budapest: Gondolat Kiadó, 1971.

Lengyel, Imre Zsolt. 'Prokrusztész vagy Prométheusz? Tamkó Sirató Károly: A Dimenzionista Manifesztum története, Petőcz András: Dimenzionista művészet' [Procrustes or Prometheus? Károly Tamkó Sirató: The story of the Dimensionist Manifesto, András Petőcz: Dimensionist art], *Jelenkor* (October 2011): 1099–103.

Tamkó Sirató, Károly. *A dimenzionizmus albuma*. Manuscript. Courtesy of Gyula Tóth, material sent to Magvető Kiadó, 1988.

Tamkó Sirató, Károly. *A Dimenzionista Manifesztum története: A dimenzionizmus (nemeuklidészi művészetek) I. albuma: Az avantgárd művészetek rendszerbe foglalása* [The History of the Dimensionist Manifesto: The first album of (the non-Euclidean art of) Dimensioninsm: Systematisation of the avant-garde arts]. Budapest: Artpool/Magyar Műhely Kiadó, 2010.

Tamkó Sirató, Károly. 'The Dimensionist Manifesto'. Translated by Oliver A. I. Botar. In *Dimensionism: Modern art in the age of Einstein*, edited by Vanja V. Malloy. Cambridge, MA: MIT Press, 2018.

Szombathy, Bálint. 'A konkrét költészet útjai' [The paths of concrete poetry]. 1977. Accessed 28 July 2018. https://www.artpool.hu/Poetry/konkret/bevezeto.html#0.

Szombathy, Bálint. Statement on how he got in touch with Tamkó Sirató. Email correspondence with Júlia Klaniczay, 2007. Source: Artpool Art Research Center.

17
The Red Adriatic: the Global East in Trieste
Chiara Bonfiglioli

Is Trieste – a quintessential frontier city – East, West, both or neither? In the nineteenth century this cosmopolitan port city was the point of connection between a vast imperial hinterland and the routes of global commerce; today it is, according to one famous travel writer, 'nowhere'. This account draws special attention to Trieste's Cold War entanglements, which made it simultaneously a beacon for the future of socialist internationalism and a bastion against 'barbarian slavo-communist hordes' – each version evoking a very different image of a Cold War Global East. Here Trieste embodies a micro-version of the Cold War, but with its own distinctive character. One place, but many different maps, each reflecting specific, not always congruent histories, dreams, projects and memories.

The twentieth-century experiment of a Global East, aimed at creating communism on a global scale,[1] was declined in very specific ways in the harbour city of Trieste during the Cold War. Due to its border status, Trieste has been the site of considerable nationalist investment from the Italian side, from its 'liberation' from the Austro-Hungarian Empire in 1918, to the 'Italianisation' of its Slavic minorities under fascism in the 1920s and 1930s, to the strenuous defence of Trieste as a bulwark of freedom and civilisation, from 1945 to 1954, when the city's contested status between Italy and Yugoslavia stirred nationalist sentiments. These nationalist sentiments are still very much present, alongside nostalgic attachments to the age of the Empire, when Trieste was a prosperous harbour under Austria-Hungary.

When looking below the surface, however, a less known and marginalised legacy emerges, namely the role played by Trieste in the utopian imaginary of international communism, an imaginary that was shared by communist activists of different nationalities in the period between 1945 and 1948. In these years, Trieste was at the centre of an unfulfilled geopolitical project linked to the newly established communist country in its vicinity. This project, in fact, involved the inclusion of the harbour city as the Seventh Republic (Settima Repubblica Federativa) of the Federal People's Republic of Yugoslavia. While short-lived and ultimately ended by the Soviet-Yugoslav split of 1948, this project had long-lasting consequences for the remapping of political and national identities in the Italo-Yugoslav border region.

As scholars have underlined, the Italo-Yugoslav border region became an early laboratory for 'borderland fascism' in the 1920s and 1930s, generating various forms of political and cultural repression against the Slovene minorities in Trieste and its hinterland, as well as against the local Italian working classes. During World War II, the area witnessed harsh confrontations between Axis forces and the local multiethnic antifascist movement, which strongly relied on the support of Yugoslav partisan formations. Both in the border region as well as in Istria and Dalmatia, assigned to Italy in 1919, fascist authorities legitimated their repressive politics through the idea that Slavic peoples were inferior races without history or culture. In the course of the war, the Italian nationalist imaginary strongly relied on sexualised racist imagery as a way to delegitimise 'slavo-communists', including female partisans.[2] Because of its Slovene hinterland and because of its strategic position on the Adriatic Sea, the city of Trieste assumed a mythical status for the Slovene liberation forces, and for Yugoslav forces more generally. The inclusion of Trieste within the Yugoslav federation was seen as a legitimate form of national liberation from the Italian Fascist oppressor and was welcomed by the majority of the local working-class Italian population, who looked forward to the idea of a socialist 'popular government' under Yugoslavia and, by extension, under the Soviet Union.[3]

Remapping attempts were frequent in the propaganda documents produced at the end of the war by communist organisations, striving to relocate the city within the geopolitical orbit of the new 'Global East'. During a meeting organised by the Italo-Slovene Women's Union in the nearby harbour city of Monfalcone in October 1945, the following description of a map of Europe was presented:

> Comrade Romea gives a political overview showing how Europe today is divided in two Democracies: 1) Popular Democracy, coming from the East, illuminating all the Balkans with a new light, with

peace and work and reconstruction, giving land to the peasants and raising the wages of the workers … 2) Imperialist Democracy coming from the West, which has a number of consequences in our Region, of which we can see some examples: strikes, lay-offs, higher prices, a life that is not very satisfactory for the popular masses.[4]

After the Yugoslav Partisans' triumphal entrance into Trieste on 1 May 1945 and 40 days administering the city, Tito's forces had to retreat when the Allied Military Government (AMG) took office. The Yugoslav Partisans' presence, together with a strengthening of left-wing associations and movements, led to a series of retaliations against fascist collaborators and alleged opponents.[5] The pro-Italian press in Trieste and Italy described the 40 days of Yugoslav administration as an invasion of the city by hordes of 'Orientals' and as a fate worse than German occupation, exploiting previous anti-Slavic and anti-communist feelings.[6] Triestine communist militants attached to the Yugoslav project, on the other hand, equated the Allied presence to 'colonialism' and 'imperialism', and were keen to have the 'popular powers' established by the partisans restored. Eventually, two occupation zones were established in July 1946: Zone A, which included Trieste, under the AMG, and Zone B, which included part of Istria and was assigned to the Yugoslav administration. These two zones were formalised with the peace treaty between Italy and Yugoslavia in February 1947.

The actual redefinition of national borders, alongside ideological and national divides, transformed the demographic configuration of the region. Most of the Italian-speaking inhabitants of Istria decided to leave their homes in what has become known as *esodo*, or exodus, in Italian historiography. Hundreds of thousands of citizens left, in what has been considered as a form of forced migration, if not of ethnic cleansing, spurred by Yugoslav authorities' repressive apparatus and by the phenomenon known as *foibe*, namely natural sinkholes which became a synonym for massacres and mass graves.[7] In the meantime, a smaller *controesodo* or counter-exodus took place in the opposite direction. Fascinated by the neighbouring socialist republic, a number of Italian workers and former partisans – particularly those living near Italy's Eastern border, in the region of Friuli – decided to move to Yugoslavia in the years 1946–7, in search of job opportunities and a better life. A particularly poignant case was the one of the 2000 shipyard workers from Monfalcone, who moved to the Rijeka and Pula shipyards.

The tentative remapping of Trieste as part of the socialist 'Global East' project continued throughout 1946 and 1947 with the onset of the

Cold War. The various multiethnic associations established in the city, such as the UAIS, the Italo-Slovene Antifascist Union, the already cited UDAIS, the Italo-Slovene Women's Union, or Sindacati Unici, the United Trade Unions, kept equating the Allied Military Government's presence to the instauration of a dangerous imperialist colony in the Adriatic. A brochure published in Italian for Women's Day in 1947 stated that the AMG 'treats our population in the same way that Anglo-American imperialism is accustomed to consider and treat the colonial population'. Instead, the establishment of Trieste as a Seventh Republic was presented as a way to establish true democracy, while redeeming Italian identity:

> With Trieste as Seventh Autonomous State, we'll adhere to Yugoslavia, not to become Slovenes, but to be truly Italian, finally free; and our victory will weaken the reactionary forces of the world, making it possible for the democratic forces, especially the Italian ones, to follow us on the road of justice and freedom.[8]

An underlying theme of left-wing propaganda was the idea that Italian antifascist forces should learn from the Yugoslav revolutionary experience. Accordingly, while Yugoslav national demands were portrayed as a legitimate compensation for their suffering under fascism, and were equated with the advancement of socialism, Italian national feelings were by definition reactionary. In another 1946 document from the local women's organisation, we read:

> [T]he national feeling expressed today by the Slavic peoples cannot be classified as a chauvinistic feeling. Rather, it expresses the attachment of those peoples to the fruits of their revolution, to the new world that has emerged from the sacrifices and the effort of millions of people. Conversely, the nationalism coming from the Italian side must be condemned. It is a damaging feeling, since it leads the people to defend a world that is long gone.[9]

The representation of Italian nationalism as necessarily reactionary, ultimately, did not sit well with Italian communist activists. A specific feature of the 'Red Adriatic' is the complex entanglement of national and ideological conflicts.[10] The Italian Communist Party strongly criticised the multiethnic Communist Party of the Julian Region (PCRG) for supporting the annexation of Trieste by Yugoslavia. While Yugoslav authorities were keen to enlarge their revolutionary struggle across the Balkans under Soviet patronage, and embraced a militant vision of communism, Italian communists, then part of the antifascist coalition government in a Western country, followed a more moderate course, which was also preferred by the Soviet Union and Stalin when it came to Western Europe. With time, many Italian activists in Trieste grew tired of Slovene and Yugoslav leaders' attempts to dictate the local agenda, and judged that the campaign for a Yugoslav Trieste alienated the sympathies of the Italian workers, while deepening the rift between 'Slavo-communism' and the anti-communism of the Italian middle classes. Also, the possibility of Trieste as a Seventh Republic seemed less and less plausible after the establishment of the Free Territory, which the Yugoslav authorities had endorsed.

Trieste's putative place in the socialist Global East was finally put to an end by the first major intra-communist divide, namely the Cominform Resolution of June 1948, which condemned Yugoslavia for 'nationalist deviation'. Supported by the Italian Communist Party, the resolution also seemed to reflect many Italian activists' everyday experience in Trieste. The resolution strengthened the power of communist leader Vittorio Vidali, a Moscow strongman who had been active in the Spanish Civil War, and who came back to Trieste in spring 1947. The local party committee split between a majority of followers of the Cominform Resolution (both Italian and Slovenes), led by Vittorio Vidali, and a minority of followers of the Yugoslav Communist Party (mainly Slovenes), led by Branko Babič.[11] After the Resolution, Triestine communists took up the task of defending pro-Soviet internationalism against 'Tito-fascism', as it was often called. On the other side of the border, Italian activists who had earlier migrated to Yugoslavia also tended to side with the Cominform. The majority of them managed to return to Italy, while others were put on trial, sentenced and suffered many years on the infamous prison island of Goli Otok and in other prisons.

Trieste was fully reintegrated within Italy in 1954. Ironically, even without becoming the Seventh Yugoslav Republic, the city continued to play a significant role in Yugoslav everyday lives and popular imaginaries. The experience of collective shopping in Trieste, from the 1960s onwards, became a rite of passage for ordinary Yugoslav citizens and is still fondly remembered across the post-Yugoslav region. The possibility to access an abundance of consumer products in Trieste illustrated the specificity of the Global Socialism project in its Yugoslav variant, while allowing Yugoslav citizens to experience the Global Capitalism just across the border.[12] With the fall of the Berlin Wall in 1989, and the start of the Yugoslav Wars in 1991, Trieste lost its place as a trading centre for Yugoslav citizens, as well as its close and yet contested entanglement with next-door communism.

The legacy of such entanglement periodically resurfaces as a controversy, notably during 1 May demonstrations, when exiles' associations protest at the waving of Yugoslav flags, or during the annual Italian Day of Remembrance for the victims of *foibe* and *esodo*, when state-sponsored condemnations of Yugoslav partisans' crimes and communist 'totalitarianism' are countered by denunciations of Italy's fascist crimes and appeals to antifascist and internationalist values, showing Trieste's lingering connections with the former Global East.

Notes

1 Müller, 2020.
2 Ballinger, 2003.
3 Sluga, 2001.
4 Comitato Centrale, UDAIS Monfalcone, 10.10.45, collection 1576, Glavni Odbor Slovansko-italijanske antifašistične ženske zveze. Box 1, folder iia., Slovenian State Archives (AS), Ljubljana, SI.
5 Ballinger, 2003.
6 Sluga, 2001.
7 Ballinger, 2003.
8 UAIS meeting, 5.11.45. collection 1576, Glavni Odbor Slovansko-italijanske antifašistične ženske zveze, box 1, folder IIA. Slovenian State Archives (AS), Ljubljana. SI.
9 'Programma che dovrà servire nelle riunioni per preparare le donne per il congresso regionale', undated, Trieste, box AFŽ – ZSZ – DAT, third folder, Slovenian National Library (NSK), Ljubljana, SI.
10 Terzuolo, 1985.
11 Terzuolo, 1985, 145.
12 Luthar, 2006.

Bibliography

Ballinger, Pamela. *History in Exile: Memory and identity at the borders of the Balkans*. Princeton, NJ: Princeton University Press, 2003.
Comitato Centrale, UDAIS Monfalcone, 10.10.45, collection 1576, Glavni Odbor Slovansko-italijanske antifašistične ženske zveze [Central committee of the Slavic-Italian anti-fascist women's union], box 1, folder IIa. Slovenian State Archives (AS), Ljubljana, SI.
Luthar, Breda. 'Remembering socialism: On desire, consumption and surveillance', *Journal of Consumer Culture* 6(2) (2006): 229–59.
Müller, Martin. 'In search of the Global East: Thinking between North and South', *Geopolitics* 25(3) (2020): 734–55.
'Programma che dovrà servire nelle riunioni per preparare le donne per il congresso regionale' [Programme to be used in meetings to prepare women for the regional congress], undated, Trieste, box AFŽ – ZSZ – DAT, third folder. Slovenian National Library (NSK), Ljubljana, SI.
Sluga, Glenda. *The Problem of Trieste and the Italo-Yugoslav Border: Difference, identity, and sovereignty in twentieth-century Europe*. Albany: State University of New York Press, 2001.
Terzuolo, Eric. *Red Adriatic: The Communist parties of Italy and Yugoslavia*. Boulder, CO: Westview Press, 1985.
UAIS meeting, 5.11.45. collection 1576, Glavni Odbor Slovansko-italijanske antifašistične ženske zveze [Central committee of the Slavic-Italian anti-fascist women's union], box 1, folder IIA. Slovenian State Archives (AS), Ljubljana. SI.

18
The Second World: building (for) emancipatory futures
Daria Bocharnikova

To move in a city and to engage with its buildings is to encounter different visions of the past and, Bocharnikova suggests, different visions of the future. Narrating her own movement in a now-unified Berlin on her way to the Haus der Statistik, an architectural relic of the DDR, Bocharnikova uncovers traces of the 'Second World' and its alternative and unfulfilled ambitions, ambitions that were in conflict with both Moscow-centred and Western-capitalist visions of modernity. For Bocharnikova, this perspective from the Second World can be a powerful methodological tool for scholars who want to work to build emancipatory futures.

Every morning for two weeks I take the same route. I get off an S-Bahn train on Alexanderplatz, today one of the most important transport hubs in Berlin, with more than 360,000 visitors per day. I walk through the square dominated by department stores and shopping malls that have popped up like mushrooms since the reunification of Germany in 1990. Then I head to the intersection of Otto-Braun-Strasse and Karl-Marx-Allee, commemorating the German Social Democracy of the interwar years and the German Democratic Republic that renamed the central street of its capital city first after Stalin and then after Karl Marx. These are streets at right angles that intersect only once in the urban canvas, denying the many entanglements and shared aspirations of Otto Braun and the founders of the GDR. The configuration insists that these two roads lead in different directions. One to Switzerland, into exile after the Nazis seized power in 1933. Another to Moscow, into the alliance with the Soviet Union that defeated fascism in 1945. Fascism is not named; it is in the air. I stop here. I wait for the green light, to traverse this intersection of non-aligned leftist projects, and their clashes with fascism.

I lift my eyes up and they encounter the monumental ruin of socialist modernism – the Haus der Statistik (House of Statistics, Figure 18.1). It looks back at me with its empty eyes of broken windows and screams: 'STOP WARS'.

I finally make it across and walk along the Western façade to the entrance of the Haus der Statistik, where the Making Futures School takes place. This year, on the occasion of the Bauhaus centenary, the school is set up to experiment with possible futures for architectural practice and education. Situated exactly at the crossroads of Otto Braun's reformism and Karl Marx's critique of capitalism, it attempts to work out scripts to revolutionise the everyday. For two weeks we build the school, work the garden, trap resources, study our collective metabolism, debate and cook, assemble and disassemble, launch silent conversations, exercise and dance, run a *späti* and a bar, open doors to welcome others, lock ourselves in and pour outside. We naively hope to hack the infrastructure of socialist modernity, to unfake the world and to stage possible futures. 'Fake it until you make it!', says the graffiti on the entrance to the building.

The Haus der Statistik was built only 50 years ago as one of several high-rises framing the Alexanderplatz, including the iconic Haus des Lehrers (House of Teachers). In 2008 the building was emptied and

Figure 18.1 Haus der Statistik, view from the Otto-Braun-Strasse and Karl-Marx-Allee intersection.

Photo: Gianfranco Albergo, Wikimedia Commons. https://commons.wikimedia.org/wiki/File:Stop_Wars_(210761511).jpeg.

progressively transformed into a ruin to be demolished and sold. In 2015 a group of artists and activists organised a fake opening of the Haus der Statistik as a new cultural and social institution. This initiative allowed the renegotiation of the status of the building not only as a valuable property in the context of a growing deficit in the Berlin real-estate market, but also as a precious resource for the collective production of alternative futures. Since 2019 the Koop5, uniting activists, the Mitte district authorities, the Berlin Senate and two state-owned housing companies, launched an experimental redevelopment project that will preserve the existing structure and enrich it with mixed uses. I wonder, are these new rituals of faking possible futures for buildings capable of bringing them back to life? What kind of life? How else can we activate these monuments of a bygone era without transforming them into zombie projects? Can this urban subaltern speak for itself? Or to put it differently, how can this unloved urban ruin participate in the transformation of the city? How can humans and nonhumans assemble futures?

At my first sight, Haus der Statistik is a splinter of the Second World, one of many material fragments sustaining and disturbing the everyday life of millions of people across the globe, from the Baltic Sea in the North to the Adriatic in the South, from Hanoi and Vladivostok in the East to Berlin and Havana in the West.[1] It is a remainder and a reminder of the world that is no more. It is also a partisan in an undeclared war on the hegemonic world order, beating it with its red wedge (Figure 18.2). But wait, why Second World? I encountered only the ruins of past leftist projects on my morning walk from Alexanderplatz S-Bahn station to the dreamworld of Making Futures enthusiasts. In seeing and recognising them as Second World, I smuggled an alternative, a different life into Berlin.[2] I brought it in my luggage of personal belongings and academic mental habits. I addressed this ruin as my peer in enacting emancipatory futures. Let me unpack this suitcase right here in the middle of the Alexanderplatz.

I came to the Making Futures School as a scholar of Second World urbanity interested in radical pedagogies. It is rare to be welcomed to an action-oriented research project as a historian of a region that fewer and fewer people in the world care about. The history of state socialism, as well as the larger field of Slavic, Eastern European and Eurasian Studies, has for several decades been the academic field of the few who choose not to forget, and who honour this history and territory, nurturing their sense of belonging. There are also a small number of international enthusiasts fascinated by its otherness.[3] I, like many of my colleagues,

Figure 18.2 'Beat the Whites with the Red Wedge' (Klinom krasnym beĭ belykh!), a 1919 lithographic Soviet propaganda poster by El Lissitzky.

El Lissitzky, Wikimedia Commons. https://commons.wikimedia.org/wiki/File:Klinom_Krasnym_Bej_Belych.JPG.

however, believe in the global relevance of knowledge produced by this field and seek to rescue it from the ghetto of conventional area studies. Conventional area studies, justly criticised for relying on imperial epistemology and ideological raison d'être, produce knowledge *about* the Other from a particular geographical region rather than *with* the Other. They often contribute to sealing off the object of study from the rest of the world, instead of exploring the entanglements that blur regional borders, and hence unavoidably undermine the legitimacy of area studies expertise. One trick, Viktor Shklovsky whispers, is to use alternative terms that allow the 'defamiliarisation' of the object of study, meaning upsetting automated perception and disturbing the set of certainties and knowledges inherited from the past.[4] That is why I call the world I find at the Haus der Statistik 'the Second World'.

The Second World is not a new term unburdened by historical connotations. It is a category inherited from Cold War vocabulary. Unlike the terms First and Third World, the notion of the Second World was relatively underused throughout the twentieth century. Together with my collaborator Steven Harris, I propose to hack this term and rework it into a novel category of scholarly inquiry.[5] Instead of replicating the model of three worlds racing to modernity at different speeds, we suggest re-crafting it to better grasp the specificity of socialist modernity on one hand, and to dissect the possibilities for emancipatory futures in our present on the other. The potential of this category to help make futures present comes from two intertwined methodological promises.

First, it permits us to overcome the political and methodological nationalisms that have shaped the field of Russian, Eastern European and Eurasian studies since 1989. The ideas and practices of socialist internationalism were an important backdrop for developments in such diverse places across the globe as Albania, Czechoslovakia, or Uzbekistan. These multiple exchanges and entanglements deserve not to be obliterated by the research focus on the political processes of building nation states on the ruins of an empire. Yet for us the performative task of the term Second World is not limited to rendering these interlinks visible.[6] It is a tool to think through a 'differentiated and divided, even if highly interconnected, world', and to imagine how nomads, goods and the energies of international solidarity and exchange become resources for building local communities.[7] There are certainly other internationalisms and models of translocal cooperation beyond the scope of Second World history, but we focus on this specific experience.

Second, it seeks to account for the complexity of hierarchies and superimpositions of competing visions that govern this diverse yet highly interconnected space. The Second World in our definition is not a monolithic political, military and economic bloc with its centre in Moscow. It is rather *a place of alterity* (aspiring to be a nation in a time of empires, building socialism as a challenge to the hegemony of capitalism, imagining alternatives to American, European, Soviet, or Russian models of development) and *a space in-between* (between capitalism and socialism, Western and vernacular modernities, colonial or imperial pasts and emancipatory futures). This interesting positionality of the Second World enables us to trace the antagonistic forces and visions, local, national and global, shaping concrete places. This helps us demonstrate the diversity of Second Worlds, often overlooked, and their multiple variations of global aspirations to social equality and modernisation. These variations in the pasts lived by the Second World (or rather by Second Worlds) open up space for future experimentation beyond the simplistic predicament of 'failed communism'.

Therefore, we propose to approach the Second World as neither a fixed spatial category designating everything east of the river Elbe, nor a limited time period (like 1945–91), albeit one intrinsically intertwined with the conditions of modernity.[8] For us it is a loose category that unites different places across the globe, that at different moments in their modern history found themselves at the intersection of competing universalisms (under the names of socialism, capitalism, or liberal democracy) and acted from the position of alterity. As a result, the focus of our research is often on local agency and the processes of forging urbanity that allow us to examine in detail the superpositions of competing visions and power dynamics.

This is what my Second World attempts to grasp and to help me think through. I came with this uncanny device in my pocket, to Otto-Braun-Strasse, 70–72, to the Haus der Statistik. How does it allow me to pin down the specificity of Haus der Statistik and its power in the context of imagining new life? Taken together, these two ruins to be resuscitated – the Haus Der Statistik and the Second World – produce a new encounter. I no longer see it only as a subversive remainder and reminder of the past. I rather think of Haus der Statistik as a global production site of emancipatory futures activated through the entanglement of local initiatives and international exchange. It is a social condenser, to use a Second World vocabulary, that intensifies the powers of locals and nomads through its infrastructures. It is a place of alterity and a space in-between that balances competing visions and produces the disruption of movement into the predictable future of global catastrophe and despair. It is an agitprop, a prop for agitating others, that opens up the space for experimentation with alternative futures. From a hushed urban subaltern decaying at the intersection of non-aligned leftist projects, the Haus der Statistik emerges now as a vociferous assemblage of humans, concrete, waste, dust, wires, aspirations, malfunctions, yeast, lichens and birds making alternative futures present. It reveals the power of humans and nonhumans to upset the order of things and to build emancipatory futures.

Notes

1. On the role of socialist infrastructure in the postsocialist cities, see Zarecor, 2018; Murawski, 2018.
2. Kulić, 2019.
3. The Association of Slavic, Eastern European and Eurasian Studies, ASEEES, one of the biggest scholarly societies in the field, counts 3300 members.
4. Shklovsky, 2016, 416.
5. See the introduction to the special issue, Bocharnikova and Harris, 2017.
6. Likewise, global historians argue against seeing global history as simply a history of networks and connections. For a synthesis of the debates on global history, see Conrad, 2017; Semyonov, 2017.

7   Bocharnikova and Harris, 2017, 5.
8   In that we follow the definition proposed by Gerasimov et al., 2011.

Bibliography

Bocharnikova, Daria and S. E. Harris. 'Second World urbanity: Infrastructures of Utopia and really existing socialism', *Journal of Urban History* 44(1) (2017): 3–8.

Conrad, Sebastian. *What is Global History?* Princeton, NJ: Princeton University Press, 2017.

Gerasimov, I., A. Glebov, M. Kaplunovski, M. Mogilner and A. Semyonov. 'On the Second World, for the last time', *Ab Imperio* 4 (2011): 10–14.

Kulić, Vladimir, ed. *Second World Postmodernisms: Architecture and society under late socialism*. London: Bloomsbury, 2019.

Murawski, Michał. 'Actually-existing success: Economics, aesthetics, and the specificity of (still-)socialist urbanism', *Comparative Studies in Society and History* 60(4) (2018): 907–37.

Semyonov, Alexander. '"Global history is more than the history of globalization": Interview with Sebastian Conrad', *Ab Imperio* 1 (2017): 23–43.

Shklovsky, Viktor. 'Art as device (1917/1919)'. In *Viktor Shklovsky: A reader*, edited and translated by Alexandra Berlina, 73–96. New York: Bloomsbury Academic, 2016.

Zarecor, Kimberly Elman. 'What was so socialist about the socialist city? Second World urbanity in Europe', *Journal of Urban History* 44(1) (2018): 95–117.

19
Sharovarshchyna: sonic contestations of Ukrainian wildness
Maria Sonevytsky

This piece introduces us to the Ukrainian phenomenon of sharovarshchyna *that has manifested itself recently in the mining of the wildness and sonic exoticism of traditional folk music to create something that sells on the international market – evidenced most notably in Ukrainian success at the Eurovision Song Contest. Arguing against the derogatory associations of the term and against the accusation that such music peddles a version of Ukrainian culture rooted in provincial liminality and kitsch, Sonevytsky suggests that drawing on* sharovarshchyna *might be a means of putting the margins at the centre of the global stage.*

Where is *Sharovarshchyna*? In Ukrainian, the suffix *-shchyna* (-щина) often denotes a place. It is perhaps most commonly used to describe regions: Lemkivshchyna, in the far west, spills over into Poland and Slovakia; Poltavschyna is the heartland, just east of Kyiv; Luhanshchyna lies in the fractured east, and so on. In this usage, the suffix demarcates a concrete territory. But it can also be used to delimit more conceptual terrain: *Panshchyna* referred to the feudal political-economic order by which serfs paid labour dues to their landlords. The term *Azarovshchyna* arose in the 1990s to describe a flagrant regime of corruption – specifically, the use of tax investigations to silence political enemies and curtail freedom of the press – that flourished during Mykola Azarov's tenure as head of the state tax administration. The suffix appears not only in Ukrainian but also in Russian and other East Slavic languages: *Zhdanovshchyna* was used to describe the postwar Soviet cultural policy introduced by Andrei Zhdanov, a member of the Politburo and Central Committee secretary, whose bifurcated view of the world pitted virtuous Soviet culture against the decadent bourgeois expressions of the non-communist world, adding a further chill to the onset of the Cold War. In contemporary Ukrainian usage, the suffix *-shchyna* is as likely to refer to zones of abstraction as it is to concretely territorialised places. We might locate *Sharovarshchyna*, then, as a hotly contested conceptual regime grounded in territorialised regional cultural symbols of affiliation and rurality.

Sharovarshchyna traffics in ideas of what I have previously termed 'Wildness' – that is, in discourses of the exoticised, rural, unknown or understudied sounds and expressive forms of Ukraine, a quintessential borderland country so often depicted as teetering on the threshold of East and West.[1] The dilemma of Ukraine's in-betweenness has defined its political culture for centuries, and especially since the fall of the USSR. Its ambiguous status vis-à-vis geopolitical centres and peripheries has been perhaps most vociferously argued by scholars who debate whether Ukraine is postcolonial or not, sometimes by projecting this question back into history, a thousand years or more.[2] Furthermore, as Alexei Yurchak has recently argued, the intellectual trend in critical area studies towards carving the world into a Global North and a Global South 'reproduce[s] multiple liberal distortions' that 'relegate the history of world socialism to an inconsequential aberration in the history of liberal capitalism'.[3] Yurchak points out that Russia 'does not fit into either the Global North or Global South; its past and present are rendered invisible by this terminology'.[4] Ukraine, then, is perhaps one step further displaced because it has been and continues today to be provincialised by Russia, while – like Russia – it also defies the binary parsing of the world into North or South, East or West. Yet it is the very fact of Ukraine's liminality – of its unsettled border status, of its historical narratives so overdetermined by outsiders, of its easy elision into Russia when politicians and pundits reduce the Soviet Union to Russia, of the fact that it was largely excluded from the knowledge-production paradigms of Cold War area studies – that allows Wildness as a representational resource in Ukrainian culture to flourish today.

If *sharovarshchyna* traffics in ideas of Wildness, however, it tires them out by rehashing the most worn-out tropes of territorialised identity. The term itself derives from *sharovary*, the billowy silken pants originally developed for ease in riding by Persian horsemen, which were, by the sixteenth century, integrated into the wardrobe of the Ukrainian Cossacks. Through Soviet cultural policy practices that standardised ethno-national costumes, these pants became emblematic of a kind of monolithic picturesque Ukrainian-ness, though evidence exists to suggest that the discourse of *sharovarshchyna* had already started to coalesce in the late nineteenth century.[5] No longer simply representing warriors of the premodern Ukrainian 'wild field', the glimmering crimson pants became symbolic of daredevil male dancing in state-sanctioned folk dance troupes. Today, many Ukrainians would agree, *sharovarshchyna* thrives in Soviet legacy institutions such as the Virsky Ukrainian National Folk Dance Ensemble, or the Veryovka Ukrainian Folk Choir, which present regional Ukrainian songs and dances in a seamless, highly professionalised medley. *Sharovarshchyna*, then, should be understood as a representational regime that domesticates heterogeneous and heterophonic gestures of Wildness by trapping them in the box of essentialised national culture.

In contemporary usage, *sharovarshchyna* is deployed to call out the banal and indiscriminate mixing of regional folkloric symbols (often the very same overused symbols codified in state-sanctioned cultural expressions of the Soviet era).[6] Vlad Trebunia, also known as the 'Hutsul-Punk' impresario Mokh, explained the term in the following way:

> The term *sharovarshchyna* has a negative meaning. That's the term we apply to culture of a low quality, which speculates on national motifs. It was especially active in developing and being cultivated by the government in the Soviet times. The motivations of the regime were understandable: on one hand, complete control over creativity, on the other – throw a bone to those who still want to hear, see and create his or her native art … Today's times are different. Ukraine is independent, there is no control over creativity. Nevertheless, *sharovarshchyna*, as the unprincipled Hutsuls sing, 'lives and flourishes' ('жиє й процвітає').[7]

Musical sounds have been especially fertile sites for such contestations over what is or isn't *sharovarshchyna*, especially when musicians successfully market their music for audiences outside of Ukraine. Vocal timbres, yawps and yelps that index the mythical 'village'; horns, hammered dulcimers or drums not found in a conventional orchestra or rock band; costumes that draw on and often exaggerate traditional garb – all may or may not enter the subjective, shifting, contentious zone of *sharovarshchyna*. Most Ukrainian musicians who draw on territorialised sonic tropes must navigate through the terrain of *sharovarshchyna*, fending off interpretations of their work as pseudo-patriotic 'fakelore'. So perhaps we can locate *sharovarshchyna* by the distance artists and critics mark between their aspirations for the representational force of their creative works, and this most damning allegation of inauthenticity.

Two of post-Soviet Ukraine's most visible musical exports in Western Europe – Ruslana, who won the Eurovision Song Contest in 2004 with a song called 'Wild Dances', and DakhaBrakha, the 'ethno-chaos' band who have become darlings of the lucrative world music markets in Western Europe and North America – have deflected accusations of *sharovarshchyna*. Ruslana's kitschy repacking of sonic gestures from Hutsulshchyna – the blurting *trembita* horns, hammered dulcimers and wooden flutes associated with the Carpathian mountaineers known as Hutsuls – married with the sounds of generic dance-pop, led her to triumph in the annual pageant of gussied-up geopolitics. DakhaBrakha emerged years later from the hip world of Kyivan experimental theatre and takes a somewhat more reserved – yet cartographically more expansive – approach to hybridising regional sounds. Anyone who has heard these two performers would likely agree that an aesthetic gulf separates them, yet neither can inoculate themselves from charges of *sharovarshchyna*, that their use of regional sounds is exploitative, superficial or haphazard.

Take, for example, the attack on Ruslana's 'Wild Dances' by Western Ukrainian intellectuals (convened by Trebunia) in the journal *Halyts'skyĭ Korespondent*. Here, the writer Yurko Izdryk identifies Ruslana as the current paragon of the lamentable continuation of *sharovarshchyna* from Soviet times:

> I don't know how it seems to the miner from Donetsk, but to me, for example, it is very hard to identify myself with the pederastic youth in raspberry-colored pants, with their sado-mazo bracelets, their *oseledets*' flapping in the wind, doing some cosmopolitan dance move in the background of the national deputy to Ukraine, the winner of some kind of Eurovision, Ruslana Lyzhychko.[8]

'Now then, here's the definition: "*Sharovarshchyna* – this is a kind of *lyzhychka*"'.[9] Izdryk shrewdly manipulates the pop star's rarely used last name – Lyzhychko – into a neologism that redefines *sharovarshchyna* for post-Soviet times. By equating the then-most prominent contemporary purveyor of Ukrainian ethno-national pop-rock with *sharovarshchyna*, Izdryk bitterly eulogised the state of expressive culture in Ukraine.[10]

Compare this to a 2019 interview with the members of DakhaBrakha, in which a journalist for the Ukrainian media organisation Hromadske TV asked them what differentiates their music from *sharovarshchyna*.[11] Marko Halanevych, one of the band members, responded confidently: 'DakhaBrakha begins where *Sharovarshchyna* ends'. The interviewer pushed him to clarify and Halanevych elaborated a bit, explaining that '*Sharovarshchyna* is not just a stylistic marker of something, but a worldview on that marker'. The other band members began to chime in to explain the perils of *sharovarshchyna*: the problem, they say, is when one believes that 'Ukrainians are the best, that our song is inimitable in the world', when there is a lack of moderation in using local sounds, or, in band member Nina Harenetska's words, when a performance feels 'the need to show everything at once ... as much as possible'. Halanevych goes on to explain that a particular kind of attunement to the world, a balanced approach to demonstrating the uniqueness of Ukrainian culture that is also in sync with the contemporary world, is what makes him confident that DakhaBrakha is not *sharovarshchyna*. They begin to joke that, given the oversized hats (*shapky*) that are part of their visual brand, perhaps they have introduced *Shapkivshchyna* to Ukraine. Or perhaps, another band member offers, what they offer is wholly uncharted territory, for which she proposes the term *DakhaBrakhivshchyna*.

Urban musicians who auto-exoticise through the incorporation of rural musical gestures that invoke the exotic lure of Wildness are especially susceptible to accusations that they widen the domain of *sharovarshchyna*. But Ukrainian musicians still persistently return to regional or local sound markers for inspiration. For those who seek to carve out a space in international music markets, marking their territory as unique and worthy is of paramount importance, and sonic gestures of Wildness offer one enticing path towards establishing this significance. Thus, by mining provincial sounds as source material, these musicians follow a paradoxical route towards deprovincialising Ukraine. Musical self-orientalisation (or, to play on Larry Wolff's formulation, 'self-demi-orientalisation')[12] becomes not a strategy of resistance so much as a technology of attachment. Amplifying sounds that evoke Ukrainian Wildness – and accepting the risk that they might be perceived as further expanding the reach of *sharovarshchyna* – is a musical method of centring Ukraine, of claiming that this liminal place occupies a legitimate place on the map.

Notes

1 Sonevytsky, 2019.
2 See, for example, Spivak et al., 2006; Snyder, 2015; Hrytsak, 2015. For a broader overview of how Eastern Europe was constructed as a space of 'demi-orientalism', see Wolff, 1994. Karnes, 2018, 75 extends Wolff's thesis into the realm of music and audition.
3 Yurchak, 2018.
4 Yurchak, 2018, 93.
5 Yermolaeva and Nikishenko, 2017.

6   For a comparison as to how 'positive Balkanism' has been incorporated into 'new political usages of discourses of regionalism' in postsocialist Balkan music, see Hofman, 2014.
7   Trebunia, 2010.
8   The *oseledets* (also called *chub* or *khokhol*) is the typical hairstyle associated with Ukrainian Cossacks, or Kozaky. It features a forelock at the front of the scalp, with the rest of the head shaved. In the context of a performance of 'Wild Dances' that Ruslana claims draws on Hutsul sources (from far Western Ukraine), the presence of Kozak imagery (associated with Central Ukraine) stands as an example of the mixing of regional symbols that many would call *sharovarshchyna*.
9   Trebunia, 2010.
10 Ruslana denied that her project succumbed to the banality of *sharovarshchynna*. She responded to critics by explaining: 'We turned to *ethnos*, not to *sharovarshchynna* … I am a contemporary singer with ethnic interests who has seen [ethnic material] through fresh eyes'. Quoted in Pavlyshyn, 2006, 480; As an alternative to *Sharovarshchyna*, *ethnos* deserves more explanation. For an overview of Soviet *ethnos* theory and its place in post-Soviet identity-making, see Bassin, 2016; Oushakine, 2009.
11 DakhaBrakha, 2019.
12 Wolff, 1994.

Bibliography

Bassin, Mark. *The Gumilev Mystique: Biopolitics, Eurasianism, and the construction of community in modern Russia*. Ithaca, NY: Cornell University Press, 2016.

DakhaBrakha. '"DakhaBrakha" pro sharovarshchyna, trampivsku Ameryku, Suprun ta vibory/Pochuiu kozhnoho' [DakhaBrakha on sharovarshchyna, Trump's America, Suprun and the elections/I will hear everyone]. Hromadske, 28 February 2019. Accessed 7 August 2024. https://www.youtube.com/watch?time_continue=1366&v=7tz-KIWuC84.

Hofman, Ana. 'Balkan Music Awards: Popular music industries in the Balkans between already-Europe and Europe-to-be'. In *Mirroring Europe: Ideas of Europe and Europeanization in Balkan societies*, edited by Tanja Petrović, 41–63. Boston, MA: Brill, 2014.

Hrytsak, Yaroslav. 'The postcolonial is not enough', *Slavic Review* 74(4) (2015): 732–7.

Karnes, Kevin C. 'Inventing Eastern Europe in the ear of the Enlightenment', *Journal of the American Musicological Society* 71(1) (2018): 75–108.

Oushakine, Serguei Alex. *The Patriotism of Despair: Nation, war, and loss in Russia*. Ithaca, NY: Cornell University Press, 2009.

Pavlyshyn, Marko. 'Envisioning Europe: Ruslana's rhetoric of identity', *Slavic and East European Journal* 50(3) (2006): 469–85.

Snyder, Timothy. 'Integration and disintegration: Europe, Ukraine, and the world', *Slavic Review* 74(4) (2015): 695–707.

Sonevytsky, Maria. *Wild Music: Sound and sovereignty in Ukraine*. Middletown, CT: Wesleyan University Press, 2019.

Spivak, Gayatri, Nancy Condee, Harsha Ram and Vitaly Chernetsky. 'Are we postcolonial? Post-Soviet space', *PMLA* 121(3) (2006): 828–36.

Trebunia, Vlad. 'Sharovarshchyna', interview with GK Press 2010. Translated by Maria Sonevytsky. Accessed 7 August 2024. https://gk-press.if.ua/x2166/.

Wolff, Larry. *Inventing Eastern Europe: The map of civilization on the mind of the Enlightenment*. Stanford, CA: Stanford University Press, 1994.

Yermolaeva, Viktoriya and Yuliya Nikishenko. 'Iavyshche "Sharovarshchyna": Poshuk definitsiï' [The phenomenon of 'Sharovarshchyna': In search of a definition], *eKMAIR* 68 (2017). Accessed 9 August 2024. https://ekmair.ukma.edu.ua/server/api/core/bitstreams/ec829c2e-2788-4ffb-8f98-1cc6b4c6b2a1/content.

Yurchak, Alexei. 'Fake, unreal, and absurd'. In *Fake: Anthropological keywords*, edited by Jacob Copeman and Giovanni da Col, 91–108. Chicago, IL: HAU Books, 2018.

20
Extracting the future: the socialist Anthropocene through artists' eyes
Maja Fowkes and Reuben Fowkes

What was the relationship between actually-existing socialism and nature? Did socialism 'destroy' nature? Did it seek maniacal 'mastery' over nature? Or was there in fact a lived, practised (and centrally planned) ecological, even proto-anthropocenic, sensibility to the socialist project, even in its most seemingly vicious Lysenkoite phases? This entry by Maja and Reuben Fowkes – gathering its 'data' from an analysis of socialist realist artworks – profiles the 'socialist Anthropocene' as a fluid but discrete spatial terrain; a continent on which the high modern project of conquering and accommodating nature ran a corollary but distinct course from that of the Western capitalist world.

The year 1948, recorded in the political history of Eastern Europe as a watershed in the consolidation of communist power, was equally momentous in the environmental history of the region when plans for a vast project of urban, industrial, infrastructural, agricultural and geoengineered transformation were launched. The Great Stalin Plan for the Transformation of Nature, which was unanimously adopted by the Communist Party that autumn, contained three key elements: the 'sculpting of rivers', including the Volga, Don and Dniepr, by building dams and turning them into a service for industry, agriculture and cities; the planting of large forest belts to protect farmlands from drought and hot dry winds; and the construction of an extensive network of roads and railways.[1] The setting in motion of geoengineering on a colossal scale revealed the abrasive merging of utopianism and pragmatism in Soviet attitudes and practices towards the natural environment. It also coincided with the high tide of socialist realism, when the official artistic doctrine spread beyond the borders of the Soviet Union to transform the artworlds of the Eastern bloc, with artists sent out into the field to collect visual evidence of the rapid transformation of rural and urban environments. Their celebration of the heroic achievements of the building of socialism also left an inadvertent record for posterity of the environmental impact of the socialist version of industrial modernity.

The notion of the Anthropocene, which was introduced into scientific circles more than half a century later to denote the scale and planetary implications of human interference in Earth systems, was significantly prefigured in the work of Vladimir Vernadsky in the 1940s. It was the magnitude of the destructive power unleashed by the Second World War that led the Russian-Ukrainian scientist to conclude that the extent of our interference in the biogeochemical manifestations of the planet had rendered humans not just a biological factor, but also 'a mighty and ever-growing geological force'.[2] In his prescient analysis, the biosphere, or life-supporting layer of the planet, was now subject to material changes, originating in the human mind, that accelerated with the technological developments of the twentieth century. He developed the term 'noösphere' for the biotic envelope of the Earth that has been transformed by the influence of human thought, holding out the promise of an 'immense future' in the 'geological history of the biosphere', as long as humankind does not use its power for 'self-destruction'.[3] The dose of sanguinity that emanates from the words of the Stalin Prize-winning scientist could be assigned to his genuine belief in technological progress, although there might also be an element of the proscriptive utopia of Soviet socialist realism encoded in his message.

The obligatory social and technological optimism of the official artistic style of the Stalinist era was abundantly evident in the large touring exhibition, *Szovjet festőművészet* (Soviet painting), that was dispatched with didactic intent to the countries of Eastern Europe in 1949. Reverberations of the extractivist ethos of the Great Stalin Plan for the Transformation of Nature can be detected in the catalogue introduction, which noted the 'closeness of the art of Soviet masters to the reality of their environment', visible in their portrayal of 'the new man and woman building communism, the glorious past of the Soviet peoples' and 'the unlimited transformations of the natural diversity of their native land'.[4] Many of the selected paintings also dramatically illustrated the dizzying scale of the Stalinist project to extend the reach of socialist modernisation to the far-flung corners of the largest country on the planet. Among the paintings on show was *The Conquerors of the Steppe* (1948) by Lutfulla Abdullaev, depicting four young Uzbeks, equipped with maps and scientific instruments, surveying their unspoiled country, while the heavy machinery, painted prominently in as much detail as the human figures, stands as a guarantor of their mission to turn ostensibly unused wilderness into productive arable land. As was often the case in socialist realism, a glaring discrepancy existed between the visualisation of the ideals of expeditious progress and the boundless plenitude of the natural world and what was actually taking place in the countryside. Environmental historians have pointed out that in their 'effort to bring the modern machinery of tractors, combines and harvesters, as well as fertilisers, to the countryside', Soviet agronomists and planners encouraged 'profligate use of land, accelerated erosion, and poisoned the soil', while hastening the decline of local cultures and communities.[5]

Similarly, Kondratiĭ Belov's landscape painting *Timber Rafting down the Irtysh* (1948) took as its overt subject the large-scale undertaking of tying logs together into rafts and sending them downstream for industrial use. The painting can however also be regarded as an unwitting document of the 'highly damaging practice of the spring timber float', since much of the wood sank during transport, to the river bottom, damaging riverbeds and banks, while as a result of the huge losses the process of deforestation was accelerated.[6] In the painting *Hunters* (1948), by Vasiliĭ Iakovlev, the frozen tundra is a mere backdrop for a group of warmly dressed hunters, with guns in their hands, returning from an implausibly successful kill, each with numerous plump birds, including wild geese, ducks and even a large swan hanging across their shoulders. While the hunting scene might have been intended to illustrate the promise of abundance of life under socialism, a potent message at a time of hunger and scarcity, it also corresponds with a particular moment in the environmental history of the largely indigenous Russian north, when 'Soviet colonisation meant increasing use of guns to hunt animals, leading to overhunting and some extinctions'.[7]

A key question raised, when considering the practices and attitudes to the natural world epitomised in socialist realist painting, is whether they should be taken as evidence of the exceptionalism of the socialist path to modernity. Environmental historians have singled out the Soviet approach to the natural world for its 'fetishistic embrace' of scientific planning as a means to reduce nature to a machinelike state of subjugation, bureaucratic preference for 'hero projects of Soviet power' that created vast technological infrastructures to service heavy industry, and 'constant struggle against enemies' that extended to a 'war against capricious nature itself'.[8] Revision of such stark views of Soviet environmental attitudes, that were formed under the sway of Cold War ideological polarities, has led to a more nuanced appreciation of the persistence, even at the height of Stalinism, of an 'independent, critical-minded, scientist-led movement for nature protection'.[9] Alongside the rise of policies to control, exploit and overpower nature, the Stalin era also saw the establishing of special protected territories, or *zapovedniki*, where pristine natural communities could flourish without human interference.[10] Although the Great Stalin Plan for the Transformation of Nature, as a whole, is generally regarded as a failure, the scheme to plant six million hectares of forest has also been characterised as 'the world's first state-directed effort to reverse human-induced climate change', in a study that made a provocative claim for a thriving Stalinist environmentalism.[11]

It is in light of the far-reaching challenges posed by the notion of the Anthropocene that the Stalinist, Soviet and 'actually existing' socialist approaches to nature can now be more decisively situated within the overarching logic of a global industrial society based on resource extraction and economic growth. The apparent similarities between the capitalist system's fixation on ever increasing production and profits and that of 'growth-oriented socialism, which closely resembles it', were observed decades earlier by Austrian theorist André Gorz, in his *Ecology as Politics*, which revealed the two rival economic and social orders of the Cold War era as equally enthralled to the unsustainable logic of technological progress.[12] However, this Cold War perspective accentuates the universalising discourse of the Anthropocene and could be seen as indicative of a levelling tendency with a blind spot for the specificities of the socialist model of development, not least its orientation towards collective goals rather than private profit. The economic programme of five-year plans could be taken as a starting point for charting the distinctive socialist path through the Great Acceleration, tracing social, political and environmental modalities in the unfolding of socialist modernity with its colonial undertones and eco-socialist potentialities.

The proposition of the socialist Anthropocene as a critical tool that intervenes, interacts with and transforms the existing debates around the Anthropocene, contributes to the dismantling of its West-centric narratives in dynamic relation with Black, Indigenous and decolonial critiques.[13] More specifically, through recuperating the distinctive environmental histories of the socialist system, reconstructing its eco-socialist epistemologies and reassessing the visual evidence engendered by its environmental art history, this emergent framework accommodates self-determining practices addressed to its conflicted pasts and possible ecological futures. The art practices of the socialist era, by disclosing the tension between progressive social programmes and centralising colonialist agendas, the divisiveness of environmental policy and the resourcification of nature, illuminate the entanglement of political temporalities and geological timescales in socialist modernity. The socialist Anthropocene, by insisting on a systemic rather than a geographical approach, could also serve as a template for how to think critically about area at a time of engulfing environmental crisis in which human and natural histories are revealed as inextricably linked.

Notes

1. Josephson et al., 2013, 119.
2. Vernadskǐ, 2014, 79.
3. Vernadskǐ, 1945, 8.
4. *Szovjet festőművészet*, 1949.
5. Josephson, 2013, 73.
6. Josephson, 2013, 169.
7. Josephson, 2013, 17.
8. Josephson et al., 2013, 22.
9. Weiner, 1999, 1.
10. Weiner, 1999.
11. For its conservation measures and legislative protection of forests from industrial exploitation, especially in the prewar period, see Brain, 2010.
12. Gorz, 1980, 11.
13. See the website of the Socialist Anthropocene in the Visual Arts (SAVA), a European Research Council/UK Research and Innovation (UKRI) supported research project (2022–7) led by Maja Fowkes, available at: www.sava.earth.

Bibliography

Brain, Stephen. 'The Great Stalin Plan for the transformation of nature', *Environmental History* 15 (2010): 670–700.

Gorz, André. *Ecology as Politics*. London: Pluto Press, 1980.

Josephson, Paul. 'War on nature as part of the Cold War: The strategic and ideological roots of environmental degradation in the Soviet Union'. In *Environmental Histories of the Cold War*, edited by J. R. McNeill and Corinna R. Unger, 21–50. Cambridge: Cambridge University Press, 2013.

Josephson, Paul, Nicolai Dronin, Ruben Mnatsakanian, Aleh Cherp, Dmitry Efremenko and Vladislav Larin. *An Environmental History of Russia.* Cambridge: Cambridge University Press, 2013.

Szovjet festőművészet [Soviet painting]. Budapest: Műcsarnok, 1949. Exhibition catalogue.

Vernadsky, Vladimir. 'The biosphere and the noösphere', *American Scientist* 33(1) (1945): 1–12.

Vernadsky, Vladimir. 'Some words about the noösphere'. In *150 years of Vernadsky*, Volume 2: *The Noösphere*, edited by Jason A. Ross, 79. Leesburg: 21 Century Science Associates, 2012.

Weiner, Douglas R. *A Little Corner of Freedom: Russian nature protection from Stalin to Gorbachëv.* Berkeley: University of California Press, 1999.

21
The stalked zone: late capitalist logics and state socialist models
Jonathan Bach

What is the relationship between the 'socialist city' and the Special Economic Zone? This text sketches the many levels of contrast and commensurability between these two seemingly diametrically opposed models of urban life, organisation, governance and imagination. In the 2020s, as Xi Jinping announces a reboot of China's old SEZ model by rebranding Shenzhen as a 'model demonstration area for socialism with Chinese characteristics', Bach's juxtapositions – which bring to consciousness the fact that SEZs have as much in common with Tarkovsky's zones of desolation and Soviet secret cities as they do with the free city or the porto franco – acquire an eerie prescience.

In Andrei Tarkovsky's famous film *Stalker*, the Zone is the only open space left capable of transformation and possibility, a dangerous place with an irresistible mythic room at its core that can fulfil dreams.[1] When the film came out in 1979, China was about to transform both socialist and capitalist development by readying its first Special Economic Zones (SEZs). As national spaces of exception, zones are like secret rooms that promise to fulfil the dreams of countries. As part of the geographic imagination of capital, they form a distributed continent separate from, but parasitic on, conventional geographies of sovereign states. Usually considered strictly capitalist formations, could they also be thought of as a type of hybrid socialist legacy, bridging late socialism and early twenty-first century global capitalism?

At first glance, the phenomenon of the special economic zone seems diametrically opposed to socialist planned urban spaces. After all, the modern special economic zone is a poster child for free markets and neoliberal dream space, luring foreign direct investment through low taxes, light regulation, easy repatriation of profits, low tariffs and reliable infrastructure. And yet, zones exhibit a similar logic to other state-led projects of experimentation, transformation and emulation, requiring complete legal and spatial control by the state over the territory. Above all, they are explicitly or implicitly tied to the transformation of society as a whole, whether through neoliberal or classic socialist invocations to fundamentally reshape and revolutionise.

Thus while from an economic point of view zones exist to export products, from a political point of view they exist to transform societies: zones are regularly invoked by governments and advocates to lead the country in the direction of future harmonious prosperity or, as the World Economic Processing Zones Association puts it: 'to lead both poor and rich countries to their wealthier destinies'.[2] As catalysts for the future, zones, like earlier model cities, appear as fresh starts for institutionalising new, universal subjectivities and rationalities, adapting the modernist impulse to embrace the future by starting from as close to a blank slate as possible. Intimately connected to historical aspirations of industrialisation, the zone is an experimental space in which new forms of production, living and working are enacted with the intention of turning the exception into the rule.

Seen thus, zones refract three basic dynamics familiar from the socialist model of urban planning. First and foremost, they share an ontological commitment to state-led development, a practice most often associated with socialist countries but also visible in postwar East Asia, in early export zones in South Korea and Taiwan and the developmental state more generally, and of course China's SEZs. Second is the concept of the test space, where a state-led project selects an existing village, city, commune or other space as an experimental site. In China, early experiments with market reforms often took place in rural settings (for example, Township and Village Enterprises), and the first special economic zones were placed not in existing economic centres such as Shanghai or Tianjin, but in areas such as Shenzhen, Xiamen and Hainan, where failure could be more easily contained, among other strategic reasons. Most importantly, these experimental spaces allowed for the testing of new policies and plans.

Third is what Kimberly Zarecor calls 'infrastructural thinking', in the service of 'total societal transformation'.[3] By connecting material production with social transformation, infrastructural thinking shows how state-chosen experimental spaces achieve their transformative goals through a combination of local impact, aesthetics and, crucially, emulation, which requires that test spaces be symbolically and materially portable if the experiment is to be emulated. Emulation can take the form of highly visible campaigns exhorting citizens to 'learn from X or Y', the promotion of new construction techniques or materials, establishing new policy guidelines or through technology transfer. While many model cities were made to be as visible as possible, the logic could also encompass less visible forms, such as Soviet 'secret' cities designed for weapons and other forms of industrial production. These secret cities both drew from, and in a sense perfected, the idea of the 'model' city.

The socialist model city and the neoliberal economic zone both embody national and global aspirations, and they converged in China's Shenzhen Special Economic Zone, established in 1980 as the cornerstone of a massive economic and social experiment to create a post-Mao society by developing 'material and spiritual civilisation'. For the former, exports and foreign direct investment were key, but for the latter, new subjectivities were needed. What came to be called 'Shenzhen spirit' became the method to create the new form of worker for the post-Mao era. As Eric Florence details, the government exhorted this new worker to simultaneously 'sacrifice themselves and their whole lives' to the nation, while following an official list of values from the city's communist party to build spiritual civilisation: 'deciding for oneself, strengthening oneself, autonomy, competition, taking risks and facing danger, equity, effectiveness and legality'.[4] Shenzhen spirit, in turn, should contribute to the 'four haves new person', who should have: 'ideals, culture, virtue, and discipline'. The zone model, with its new worker subjectivity and spirit, was meant to transform the entire country, and it did. In 1980 there were four new special economic zones in China. Today, nearly every city in China has a variation of a zone which exists to attract foreign investment and shape the modern citizen. Not every city can become Shenzhen (which went from a largely rural area to over 20 million people in one generation), but the imagination of Shenzhen came to serve as a national and global model, from India to Africa.[5]

China's special economic zones arose before the collapse of the Soviet Union, and zones later became prominent in postsocialist spaces, making the connection between socialist legacies and zonal practices less far-fetched than it might seem. Vietnam has been exploring SEZs since the early 1990s. Russia, in its post-Soviet incarnation, has embraced the idea, with 36 of its own special economic zones, and former Soviet Republics have also pursued them (with mixed results), while Poland, Hungary and the Czech Republic created their own zonal versions.[6] For all their free-market dreams, the legacy of socialist model making thus peers over the shoulders of these zones. For example, while the original Chinese special economic zones reflected lessons from the 1970s export model of the 'Four Tigers' (South Korea, Taiwan, Hong Kong and Singapore) the practices of planning the new zones drew on generations of planners, architects, policymakers and residents whose point of urban reference was Soviet-style planning. As Jacob Dreyer writes about Soviet influence in Chinese urban development: 'the Soviet model city could be realized on Chinese soil, when it could not be in Russia, because there were fewer impediments … Soviet architectural typologies and the models of Soviet urban planners constituted the first vision of cities ever glimpsed by Chinese peasants in a rapidly modernising society'.[7]

In a similar vein, Christina Schwenkel has written extensively on the analogous role played by the German Democratic Republic for Vietnam, and Łukasz Stanek has detailed how socialist countries shaped urban development across West Africa and the Middle East.[8] In Eli Rubin's description of the East Berlin district of Marzahn as an 'amnesiopolis' – a place with no past but only futures – we see another hallmark of the zones, where tabula rasa planning is meant to avoid the messiness of existing urban centres, allowing the state to proclaim new urban spaces as proverbial blank slates and elide their histories.[9] For example, China's Shenzhen sought to promote its new city narrative by physically and discursively erasing the traces of its many villages.[10] Thus the zone as a test space covers its experimental tracks by laying claim to its status as a teleological harbinger of a better time to come, whether East or West. As a consultant proudly pronounced to geographer Bridget Martin in the South Korean zone of New Songdo City: 'It's not an experiment, it's the future!'[11]

The zone thus appears as a kind of scaffolding in Zarecor's sense, 'a basic infrastructure for future growth onto which other systems – economic, social, political, environmental – can attach'.[12] Like the socialist urban planning Zarecor discusses, the zone can 'activate' discrete, state-controlled urbanised spaces through material production in the service of a teleological transformation. For true believers of neoliberal dogma, the zone accordingly serves as a catalyst for a harmonious future. Yet as with the lived reality under socialism, many zones are hollow promises, with unfinished infrastructure and 'ghost cities' of uninhabited high-rises serving as visual markers of corruption, vanity projects and plans gone astray. At the same time, zones have become a fundamental form of urban development, evolving from a kind of entrepôt into a global urban form(ula) with infrastructure at its core.[13]

If we learn to see the traces of socialist cities in the spread of economic zones worldwide, what might this mean for our understanding of both socialist planning, capitalist logics and the zone as a space? Perhaps across the spectral continent, stitched together by zones, we can discern both 'zombie socialism' – that convenient alloy of anti-communism and neoliberalism that Liviu Chelcea and Oana Druţă see as justifying present inequalities – *and* 'still-socialism', Michał Murawski's term for noncapitalist enclaves persisting in the heart of capitalism, reverberating with revolutionary pasts and untamed futures.[14] At the end of Tarkovsky's fable of modernity, no one dares to enter the mythic room that grants wishes at the centre of the Zone, despite having undertaken dangerous journeys to seek it out, preferring instead to live with its (safer) eternal potential. The world's many zones that make up a shifting continent of exceptional spaces are, perhaps, held together as much by the eternal potential of their dream-inducing power as by their networked global economic infrastructures.

Notes

1. An earlier version of this essay originally appeared in 'What kind of model? Thinking about the Special Economic Zone and the Socialist City', *Made in China Journal* 4(2) (2019): 72–8.
2. World Economic Zones Processing Association (WEZPA), n.d.
3. Zarecor, 2018.
4. Quotations in this paragraph cited in Florence, 2017.
5. See Singh, 2015; Bräutigam and Xiaoyang, 2011.
6. See Maslikhina, 2016.
7. Dreyer, 2014.
8. Schwenkel, 2014; Stanek, 2020.
9. Rubin, 2016.
10. Bach, 2017.
11. Martin, 2013.
12. Zarecor, 2018, 5.
13. See Easterling, 2014; Bach, 2011.
14. Chelcea and Druţă, 2016; Murawski, 2020; see Bach and Murwaski, 2020.

Bibliography

Bach, Jonathan. 'Modernity and the urban imagination in economic zones', *Theory, Culture and Society* 28(5) (2011): 98–122.

Bach, Jonathan. '"They come in peasants and leave citizens": Urban villages and the making of Shenzhen'. In *Learning from Shenzhen*, edited by Mary Ann O'Donnell, Winnie Wong and Jonathan Bach, 138–70. Chicago, IL: University of Chicago Press, 2017.

Bach, Jonathan and Michał Murwaski. 'Introduction: Notes towards a political morphology of undead urban forms'. In *Re-Centring the City: Global mutations of the socialist modernity*, edited by Jonathan Bach and Michał Murawski, 1–14. London: UCL Press, 2020.

Bräutigam, Deborah and Tang Xiaoyang. 'African Shenzhen: China's special economic zones in Africa', *Journal of Modern African Studies* 49(1) (2011): 27–54.

Chelcea, Liviu and Oana Druţă. 'Zombie socialism and the rise of neoliberalism in post-socialist Central and Eastern Europe', *Eurasian Geography and Economics* 57(4–5) (2016): 521–44.

Dreyer, Jacob. 'Maximum city: The vast urban planning projects of Soviet-era Russia are being reborn in modern China', *The Calvert Journal*, 26 June 2014. Accessed 9 August 2024. https://www.calvertjournal.com/articles/show/2760/soviet-era-urbanism-russia-reborn-in-modern-chinese-cities.

Easterling, Keller. *Extrastatecraft: The power of infrastructure space*. New York: Verso, 2014.

Florence, Eric. 'How to be a Shenzhener: Representations of migrant labor in Shenzhen's second decade'. In *Learning from Shenzhen: China's post-Mao experiment from special zone to model city*, edited by Mary Ann O'Donnell, Winnie Wong and Jonathan Bach, 87–105. Chicago, IL: University of Chicago Press, 2017.

Martin, Bridget. 'Welcome to the Zone: Place-making and place-breaking in New Songdo, South Korea'. Paper presented at the *Asian Cities: Colonial to Global* Conference, Leiden, Germany, 5 April 2013.

Maslikhina, Veronika. 'Special Economic Zones in Russia: Results evaluation and development prospects', *International Journal of Economics and Financial Issues* 6(1) (2016): 275–9.

Murawski, Michał. 'Palatial socialism, or (still-)socialist centrality in Warsaw'. In *Re-Centring the City: Global mutations of socialist modernity*, edited by Jonathan Bach and Michał Murawski, 104–14. London: UCL Press, 2020.

Rubin, Eli. *Amnesiopolis: Modernity, space, and memory in East Germany*. Oxford: Oxford University Press, 2016.

Schwenkel, Christina. 'Traveling architecture: East German urban designs in Vietnam', *International Journal for History, Culture and Modernity* 2(2) (2014): 155–74.

Singh, Priyanka. 'UP to be developed into China's Shenzhen Model', *Times of India*, 29 January 2015. Accessed 7 August 2024. https://timesofindia.indiatimes.com/india/UP-to-be-developed-into-Chinas-Shenzhen-model/articleshow/46058212.cms.

Stanek, Łukasz. *Architecture in Global Socialism*. Princeton, NJ: Princeton University Press, 2020.

World Economic Zones Processing Association (WEZPA). 'The WEZPA Family', n.d. Accessed 12 September 2018. http://www.wepza.org/history.

Zarecor, Kimberley Elman. 'What was so socialist about the socialist city? Second World urbanity in Europe', *Journal of Urban History* 44(1) (2018): 95–117.

22
Supercontinents and superdeep boreholes: area studies in three dimensions
Douglas Rogers

The inhabitants of the Global East have a common affinity, it is often claimed, for seeing the true reality of things beneath or behind the observable surface. The impulse to ask 'kto za etom stoit' (who is behind this) is often ridiculed as conspiratorial or paranoid by Western observers. There is also something peculiarly postsocialist about this geometry of knowledge, commensurable as it is to Marx's well-known duality of determining economic base or infrastructure and determined superstructure. But this geometry is particular not only to the socialist world, but to the epistemology of high modernity writ large. This impulse to dig for the truth and to dig for power, Rogers's entry insinuates, is necessarily tied to the development not only of high modern geology (and geo-prospecting) but also of high modern area studies. Critical area studies – whether it is high or low, modern, postmodern or metamodern – should take these connections seriously, and pursue its investigations in all available dimensions, burrowing deep into the many thousand shadowy boreholes constituting the deep conjunctures of our scholarship.

Area studies as it grew up in the twentieth-century West was, in retrospect, surprisingly one-dimensional – concerned with events, actors, knowledge and movements on and over the surface of the Earth. Topics and approaches have varied tremendously within this surface-level plane but rarely moved above it into the atmosphere or below it into the depths of the Earth, much less questioned its commonsense. This one-dimensionality can be glimpsed, for instance, in the massive social science output on nation-states and their borders in the 1980s and 1990s; more recent research on globalisation and transnationalism has troubled these lines on the map, but still sticks closely to ground-level movements.

Even when Cold War-era social science metaphors seemed to embrace the three-dimensional, in the international relations language of 'spheres of influence', those spheres usually turned out to be rather flat, reduced to (or just another way of talking about) one-dimensional geographical areas.

All of this remained the case even as other contemporaneous domains of knowledge were charting new worlds in and beyond the Earth's atmosphere, far below its seas and in the depths of its subsoil. The exploration of these spaces remained largely the province of the atmospheric and geological sciences, which rarely entered into the social science and humanities discussions that comprised area studies at the time. Returning to these fields with the benefit of more recent perspectives offered by the history of science affords some new ways to think about area studies in three dimensions, both as it developed in the Cold War era and as we contemplate its ongoing transformations.[1]

Consider, as one example, the trajectory of twentieth-century debates about the existence and movement of the ancient supercontinents. The proposition, that the arrangement of the earth's continents as we know them now is the outcome of millions of years of continental drift, dates to the early twentieth century. It is chiefly associated with the German geologist Alfred Wegener, who elaborated his ideas in a series of publications beginning in 1912 and ending with his death on an expedition to Greenland in 1930. It was Wegener who suggested that the single supercontinent from which our present-day continents drifted apart should be named Pangaea (see Figure 22.1). More recent research has charted the movements of even earlier supercontinents, such as Rodinia and Pannotia, and the post-Pangaea continents of Gondwana, Laurasia and others.

As Henry R. Frankel has recounted in his exhaustive *The Continental Drift Controversy*, Wegener's original ideas met with widespread criticism for many decades before they congealed into the modern geological consensus around plate tectonics.[2] But Wegener nevertheless set the terms of debate for global geology, well into the second half of the twentieth century. Alongside the growth of social science area studies, that is, geologists the world over were engaged in their own area studies debates, played out over longer timescales and focused on deeper strata of the Earth. Were similarities between widely dispersed geological, palaeontological or other phenomena evidence that parts of today's continents were once adjacent? Was the general principle of the geology of continents the older model of 'fixity' or Wegener's new 'mobilism'?

Figure 22.1 Palaeogeographic map of Earth ca. 260 million years ago, showing the supercontinent Pangaea during the Permian period of the Palaeozoic era.

Ron Blakey © 2016 Colorado Plateau Geosystems Inc.

The Bolshevik Revolution and, especially, the Cold War, played no small role in shaping these debates. After some initial interest in theories of continental drift, mainstream Soviet geology largely rejected Wegener's hypotheses. Most Soviet geologists, chief among them V. V. Beloussov, countered the theory of continental drift with theories emphasising vertical movement within the Earth's crust; horizontal movement was, in this view, at most a byproduct of vertical movement. The Soviet rejection of continental drift seems to have been, in part, related to the main evidence they were working with: the basic geology of the Soviet Union afforded fewer opportunities to glimpse continental movement 'in action' than other parts of the world. But Bolshevik ideology played a role as well, and early Soviet geologists who cited or agreed with Western scientists could quickly find themselves on the wrong side of state officials. Indeed, 1929 saw the Geological Commission Affair, in which dozens of geologists were accused of a variety of anti-Soviet activities – with fifteen of them found guilty.

One pivotal moment in these international debates came in 1957–8, proclaimed as the International Geophysical Year, which coincided with Khrushchev's de-Stalinisation and the thaw in the Cold War. A team of Soviet geologists travelled abroad extensively that year, bringing with them a gift for their fellow geologists – the most detailed tectonic map of the Soviet Union ever made. In eight massive handcrafted panels, the map was, among other things, a two-dimensional argument for Soviet geological theory at the time, especially Beloussov's insistence on continental fixity and vertical geological forces.[3] The delegations and exchanges of data in 1957–8 turned out to be an important opening for collaboration among Western and Soviet scientists on a number of fronts, most notably the exploration of Antarctica. It was one route by which plate tectonics entered the Soviet conversation with greater influence than in the past. Beloussov, however, remained unimpressed and unconvinced, and his overwhelming influence in Soviet geology delayed significant Soviet contributions to plate tectonics for decades.

A more headline-grabbing scientific accomplishment timed for the International Geophysical Year was the launch of *Sputnik* into low earth orbit in 1957. This evidence of Soviet leadership in space was a catalysing – and also three-dimensional! – event for area studies in the West, prompting the 1958 National Defense Education Act in the United States and, with it, the creation of region-focused, state-sponsored National Resource Centers at United States universities. The associated explosion of Cold War science funding breathed new life into stagnating debates about continental drift, eventually solidifying the science underlying plate tectonics.[4] Seismic instrumentation that enabled the United States Department of Defense to 'listen' for underground nuclear tests also provided data on earthquakes and other movements of the Earth's crust. The defence imperative of understanding magnetic fields for submarine navigation – and potential warfare – helped advance the new science of palaeomagnetism, the geological specialty that played perhaps the largest role in discerning the movements of ancient continents.

It was not, however, just state science funding or Cold War ideologies that connected the debates about these two varieties of area studies, one social scientific and decidedly ground-level, one scientific and trained on the Earth's crust. Indeed, a rapidly proliferating series of holes in the Earth connected these two planes of area studies in quite consequential ways. Turning their eyes in the opposite direction to that of the space race, for instance, geologists in the Soviet Union and the United States competed, beginning in the 1960s, to dig the deepest hole in the Earth's crust. The Kola Superdeep Borehole – begun in 1970 and capped only as funding dried up in 1994 – eventually reached over seven miles into the Earth's crust beneath the Murmansk region. The United States' counterpart, Project Mohole, off the coast of Mexico, began earlier, in 1960, but was also abandoned more quickly, in 1966; it nevertheless stands as an early experiment in the now-common practice of offshore deep-water oil drilling.

These are but two holes from tens of thousands that linked these two planes of area studies, for one of the things geologists came to understand was that most of the earth's hydrocarbon deposits were formed in the time of Pangaea, and especially during the breakup of the supercontinent around 175 million years ago. The twentieth century's ever-increasing, ever-deeper and ever-more-global oil and gas drilling operations connected the ancient supercontinent with the continents of the Cold War – and therefore all of the global and regional politics that swirled around oil, the twentieth century's most important commodity. Fascinating links between the geological science of continental drift and plate tectonics and the twentieth-century oil industry, are, in fact, legion on both sides of the Cold War. In the United States, it was not uncommon for the geologists closely involved in development of theories of continental drift and plate tectonics to have spent the summers of their early careers working for oil and gas companies.[5] In the Soviet Union, the chief proponent of mobilist theory, Alekseĭ Khramov, worked not at the Academy of Sciences (where geology research was still controlled by the dedicated fixist Beloussov), but at the All-Union Oil Research and

Geological Prospecting Institute at the Ministry of Geology, and it was on the basis of communication with the oil prospecting activities of his institute that his work developed.[6]

Examples of this sort could be multiplied, fleshed out and further analysed. For the moment, however, it is instructive to note that deep holes in the Earth continue to connect Pangaea to the political economy of world areas today. As the continental and offshore oil deposits that supplied so much of the world's energy in the twentieth century are depleted and abandoned, oil companies have increasingly looked to deep-water, even 'ultra-deep-water' projects. One of the key exploration strategies of this era is 'analogous exploration': if oil has been struck in deep-water off Morocco, it also makes sense to drill off the coast of Nova Scotia, for Halifax and Rabat were, in the time of Pangaea, a

Figure 22.2 *Pangaea Politica* by Massimo Pietrobon, 2012. An artist's arrangement of the countries of the twenty-first-century world into the approximate shape of the ancient supercontinent Pangaea.

Used by permission.

mere 300 miles distant from each other (see Figure 22.2).[7] The same logic applies for the coasts of Argentina and Namibia, Newfoundland and Ireland, and so on, up and down the Atlantic basin. The role of hydrocarbons in the making of today's world areas – whether that be African entanglements with international oil companies, the potential 'energy independence' of the North American continent, or other topics – proceeds in part through deeper and deeper holes drilled into an ancient supercontinent. We miss these important connections when we stick to the surfaces of area studies. If some of the most powerful and influential corporations on the planet are seeing the world in three dimensions, then so, too, must area studies.

Notes

1 See also Elden, 2013.
2 Frankel, 2012.
3 Paul, 2016.
4 Siever, 1997.
5 Siever, 1997, 149.
6 Frankel, 2012, Volume 2, 131.
7 Bryant et al., 2012.

Bibliography

Bryant, Ian, N. Herbst, Paul Dailly and John Dribus. 'Basin to basin: Plate tectonics in exploration', *Oilfield Review* 24 (2012): 38–57.
Elden, Stuart. 'Secure the volume: Vertical geopolitics and the depth of power', *Political Geography* 34 (2013): 35–51.
Frankel, Henry R. *The Continental Drift Controversy*, 4 Volumes. Cambridge: Cambridge University Press, 2012.
Paul. 'Door 18: The tectonics of the Cold War'. Geological Society of London blog, 18 December 2016. Accessed 8 August 2024. https://blog.geolsoc.org.uk/2016/12/18/door-18-the-tectonics-of-the-cold-war/.
Siever, Ray. 'Doing Earth Science research during the Cold War'. In *The Cold War and the University: Toward an intellectual history of the postwar years*, edited by Noam Chomsky, Laura Nader, Immanuel Wallerstein, Richard C. Lewontin and Richard Ohmann, 147–69. New York: The New Press, 1997.

23
When Yugoslavia was the Wild West
Natalie Koch

In the Atlas, the Wild West is placed firmly on the map (if mutably, in historical terms) on the forward edge of expansion across the North American continent, and its narratives of frontier conquest, individualism, resilience and violence form one of the defining myths of North American (particularly US) identity. The Anti-Atlas recognises that this mythic landscape belongs to many others, far removed from the US West, and has shaped their identities in equally powerful ways, whether for filmgoers across the socialist bloc, as discussed below, or children in Yugoslavia avidly consuming (Italian) comics about the Arizonan Texas Ranger, Tex Willer, or Czech 'trampers' playing at cowboys and Indians in the Brdy hills. Surprised by these unfamiliar 'Wests'? Good – that surprise is a means of reshuffling the divisions of the world and seeing beyond the taken for granted.

I'm doubtful that my mother was paying much attention to international affairs when she snapped this photo of me and my brother in 1989 (Figure 23.1). I certainly wasn't. Just three-and-a-half years old, this was my first rodeo. (Yes, really.) In Tucson, the annual February rodeo is quite an ordeal and I dutifully donned my cowgirl attire. All the rituals of the Wild West were ingrained in me from an early age, even if the formal rodeo attire was only for special occasions. Growing up in Arizona, life for me little resembled the Wild West, save the intermittent visits to Tombstone, Bisbee or their Hollywood knock-off at Old Tucson Studios, just outside town. Old Tucson and the surrounding desert has been used in hundreds of Hollywood westerns, including some of the genre's best known, like *Gunfight at the O.K. Corral* (1957), *Rio Bravo* (1959), *El Dorado* (1966), as well as famous western-themed television

Figure 23.1 The author, exercising her scepticism from an early age, and her brother in Tucson, Arizona (1989).

Photo from author's collection.

series like *Bonanza* and *Little House on the Prairie*. By 1989, the Sonoran Desert setting of my hometown had become the most iconic landscape representing the Wild West in English-language film and television.

But what my mother and I were not paying attention to in 1989 was the changing political order of Eastern Europe and, with it, the crumbling of another iconic Wild West – Yugoslavia. Before its eventual unravelling, parts of the country had become synonymous with the Wild West in German imaginations, East and West. *The Treasure of Silver Lake* (*Der Schatz im Silbersee*) (1962) marked the beginning of a long partnership between Jadran Studios in Croatia and the West German director Harald Reinl. The film was the first in a series depicting the stories of an Apache chief Winnetou (played by Pierre Brice) and his German comrade Old Shatterhand (played by Lex Barker), chronicled in the popular novels of Karl May (1842–1912). Based on numbers of books sold, May is said to be the most popular German author of all time. Reinl's films carried this popularity to a new generation, with new fictions, fantasies and fancies conjured for postwar entertainment appetites in the West. Yet like any appetite, there is a cost to feeding it. For the budding West German film industry, that was the cost of shooting in western-looking landscapes. Old Tucson Studios – or anywhere in the US South-west for that matter – was completely out of the question.

In Yugoslavia, however, the price was right: Croatia's Zrmanja Canyon would stand for the Apache ancestral lands in Arizona and New Mexico, teepees would be erected and Yugoslav extras would play the part of unspeaking but ubiquitous Native American residents, and an occasional fake cactus would be positioned just so (see Figures 23.2–5). It apparently made no difference that the karst canyons of Paklenica, the valleys of Grobnik, and the waterfalls of Krka would look completely wrong to anyone familiar with the American South-west – not just because of the unusual rock formations and the flora, but also largely because of the colour schemes. Most notably, the dramatic *white* rocks of Zrmanja,

Figure 23.2 Screenshot from *The Treasure of Silver Lake*.
© Rialto Film GmbH.

Figure 23.3 Screenshot from *The Treasure of Silver Lake*.
© Rialto Film GmbH.

Figure 23.4   Screenshot from *The Treasure of Silver Lake*.
© Rialto Film GmbH.

Figure 23.5   Screenshot from *The Treasure of Silver Lake*.
© Rialto Film GmbH.

which figure so centrally in Reinl's Winnetou films, have no counterpart in a region best known for its dramatic *red* rocks (see Figures 23.6–7). Of course, the original novels by Karl May had little to do with historical, cultural or geographical accuracy. It was well-known in Germany that he never visited the US West and he never exhibited a great interest in learning about its intricacies. German fans of the books and the movies are known to kindly correct the errors or joke about them, but few would ever consider them a fatal flaw.[1] The stories were fiction, and everyone knew it.

Of course, this also applies to the entire genre of westerns made in America. So while my home state of Arizona was the site for the 'real' drama of US territorial expansion and colonisation of Native lands, in all its violence and masculinist world-writing and world-erasing, this was carefully curated on screen for filmgoers.[2] Just as in the German westerns in Yugoslavia, the American westerns set in the Sonoran and Mojave deserts harness the rugged, untamed and foreign-looking landscape

Figure 23.6   Rocks in Paklenica, Croatia.

Filipa Beroš, Wikimedia Commons. https://commons.wikimedia.org/wiki/File:Paklenica_2017_(212250711).jpeg.

Figure 23.7   Rocks in Monument Valley, Arizona.

Jon Sullivan, Wikimedia Commons. https://en.m.wikivoyage.org/wiki/File:Monument_Valley.jpg.

as a backdrop to amplify the spectacle of brutal expansionism, frontier masculinity, and to ground specific moral geographies about resource extraction. Like the German westerns, the conflicts often revolve around who has rightful access to gold, silver or territory, and the landscape is consistently read through the lens of certain men's lustful fantasies – mostly of power and wealth, but also the occasional female seductress. These are familiar fantasies anywhere in the colonised world, but the audience's perception of rugged terrain as *foreign* breathes novelty into the pedestrian.

Filmed constructions of the Wild West in Yugoslavia and Arizona are thus bound by how they use the sheer scale of the landscape and curate its 'otherness' to make the familiar foreign. The idea of 'making the familiar foreign' is something of a mantra in academic anthropology, guiding scholars to develop the critical eye to pick apart the political and cultural layers to all that we take for granted. This is the ethos I have discussed in my framing of critical area studies as a way of *hearing beyond* – beyond traditional cognitive and interpretative frames, beyond commonplace metanarratives about certain parts of the world, beyond the trendy lines of inquiry of the day – and being open to surprise.[3] Escaping the strictures of conventional area studies assumptions and investments, glimpsed in this book 'through Eastern eyes', also demands scrutinising one's own assumptions and investments. Here, my surprise came from spending a great deal of time in Germany and discovering that 'their' Wild West was not 'my' Wild West.

Tracing the filmic construction of Yugoslavia as the Wild West has also forcefully dislodged any pretensions I may have had to *know* the Wild West. Despite my precocious scepticism apparently on display in Figure 23.1, the fact that I was shown at such an early age what it 'really' meant to grow up in Arizona, home of the 'real' westerns and the 'real' history fictionalised in countless tales about the US South-west, disposed me to perceive my own Wild West imaginaries as those that were more accurate. And here we return to the power of the landscape: the physical backdrop of westerns filmed in places like Arizona, New Mexico or Utah is not just about adding spectacle and drama. It is also about adding a veneer of truth to the nationalist storylines that these films advance. Whoever the bad guys are and whoever the good guys are, the South-west is the US South-west; this land is 'our' land; our *American* land. What makes the time when Yugoslavia was the Wild West so jarring for an American sensibility (or at least this American's sensibility) is that these nationalist storylines were not only distinct in the German portrayals, there were actually *two* German portrayals: West and East.

In the early years of divided Germany, the German Democratic Republic (GDR) stamped out most direct references to Karl May, who was popularly referred to as Adolf Hitler's 'cowboy mentor' because of the Nazi leader's fandom and apparent efforts to convince his generals to read May's books for battle insights. In the Soviet Union, meanwhile, access to American and West German westerns was restricted – despite (or perhaps because of) the roaring success of *The Magnificent Seven* (1960), which Nikita Khrushchev had permitted from 1962–4.[4] After growing complaints among Party officials, who saw the film as Western/imperialist propaganda, the film was removed from distribution. Yet Soviet leaders saw a chance to promote their own ideology through the film genre and began developing 'Red westerns' of their own and encouraging other Eastern bloc countries to do the same. Thus, in 1966, the GDR's state-owned film studio, DEFA (Deutsche Film-Aktiengesellschaft) released its first such film: *The Sons of Great Bear* (*Die Söhne der großen Bärin*).

The film was directed by the Czech filmmaker Josef Mach and launched the career of Gojko Mitić, who played the lead, Chief Tokei-ihto (Figure 23.8), and many other valiant Native chiefs in the *osterns* or *Indianerfilme* that followed. Mitić's immense popularity notwithstanding, the East German plots always placed Native Americans as the unequivocal heroes and the White settlers as villains. This was in stark contrast to the storylines of the West German Winnetou films, in

Figure 23.8 Gojko Mitić as Chief Tokei-ihto in *The Sons of Great Bear*.
© DEFA-Stiftung/Waltraut Pathenheimer.

which Winnetou was the 'blood brother' of Old Shatterhand (famously portrayed in *Winnetou – Part 1,* see Figure 23.9), and the two would join forces with the 'good' White people to fight the 'bad' White people. For the two strands of German westerns, the ideological narratives of the Cold War were played out in how American history was treated: either as an exemplar of selective, noble expansion and spreading the Enlightenment ideals of progress and civilisation (the West German western) or an exemplar of the violence and bloodshed resulting from the rapacious appetites of American imperialists in the lands of others (the East German *ostern*).[5] Both, of course, romanticise the figure of the Native American in a deeply troubling and colonial manner.

Yet like the landscape as backdrop, the historical plight of the Native American communities is fodder for the spectacle and the moral geographies written in and through these stories. As in so many narratives *about* Indigenous peoples, rather than *from* Indigenous peoples, Yugoslavia's Wild West was just as colonial as Old Tucson's. Ventriloquised or silenced, the genre preempts speech and reduces it to a theatre for someone else's political and ideological debates. And in some strange way, just as these debates were collapsing in Eastern Europe, this is precisely what was beginning for me as a small child dressing up for a rodeo in 1989. I was blissfully unaware of the Cold War moment I was born into, of the colonial origins of my home state of Arizona, and of the cultural meaning ascribed to my desert surroundings by East and West Germans, Yugoslavs, Soviets, Americans and of course, the Navajo, Hopi, Apache, Pima and Tohono O'odham, and countless others who knew it – through fact or fiction, mediated or unmediated – before me.

Figure 23.9 Winnetou and Old Shatterhand in *Winnetou – Part 1*.
© Rialto Film GmbH.

I dressed like a good cowgirl should and revelled in it. I learned US history through visiting places like Tombstone and Old Tucson Studios and revelled in it. I ran around the desert collecting cactus and plant specimens, feeling the texture of my native soil underfoot, and revelled in it too. I *knew* the South-west. Yet I was raised on myth: I was ultimately an actor in the theatre of someone else's political and ideological debates about whose 'native soil' this really was. Of course, I knew no other soil or other mountains or other flora. This was my home. Such experiences of home are always interwoven with myth and there is no one to blame for my happy childhood as a cowgirl. Myths are what give *place* meaning and their associations with landscape begin early. Whether this landscape has red or white rocks, cacti or none, Indigenous presences or erasures, the lessons I take from when Yugoslavia was the Wild West is that we, as critical area studies scholars, have more choices than being ventriloquised or silenced. We can unravel our own expectations and our own fantasies of good and evil and, just maybe, know the world differently.

Notes

1   Glachen, 2012.
2   See Slotkin, 1992.
3   Koch, 2016; 2020.
4   Lavrentiev, 2013.
5   Gemünden, 1998; Lavrentiev, 2013; Goral, 2014.

Bibliography

Gemünden, Gerd. 'Between Karl May and Karl Marx: The DEFA Indianerfilme (1965–1983)', *Film History* 10(3) (1998): 399–407.
Glachen, Rivka. 'Wild West Germany', *The New Yorker*, 2 April 2012. Accessed 8 August 2024. https://www.newyorker.com/magazine/2012/04/09/wild-west-germany.
Goral, Pawel. *Cold War Rivalry and the Perception of the American West*. London: Palgrave Macmillan, 2014.
Koch, Natalie. 'Is a "critical" area studies possible?', *Environment and Planning D: Society and Space* 34(5) (2016): 807–14.
Koch, Natalie. 'Deep listening: Practicing intellectual humility in geographic fieldwork', *The Geographical Review* 110 (2020): 52–64.
Lavrentiev, Sergey. 'The Balkan westerns of the sixties', *Frames Cinema Journal* 4 (2013). Accessed 8 August 2024. https://framescinemajournal.com/article/the-balkan-westerns-of-the-sixties/.
Slotkin, Richard. *Gunfighter Nation: The myth of the frontier in twentieth-century America*. New York: Maxwell Macmillan, 1992.

24
Zwischeneuropa: mapmaking as image-making

Katarzyna Murawska-Muthesius

Looking at the two maps displayed below, the area studies scholar might ask: how did the vast, apparently self-confident reaches of nineteenth-century Pan-Slavism's 'Slavic Europe' shrink to the twentieth-century interwar's unstable and tentative 'lands between'? But an equally fruitful question for critical area studies would be: what mechanisms activated these maps and the projects that produced them? Critical cartography and visual culture provide the tools – including shading, orientation, or genre – that allow us to read such maps not just as ideologues' plans or historians' records, but as images that follow (or transgress) their own conventions and convey their own information.

There is no point reaffirming yet again that maps are instruments of power and that space is not given but produced.[1] Those once groundbreaking claims of critical cartography have already become established truths. They today are both contested and supplemented by post-constructivist approaches, which redefine the map as process rather than product, contingent, corporeal and performative.[2] Theoretical cartographic discourse, however, has seldom focused on Europe's eastern peripheries, where the map, both as tool of power-knowledge and script of resistance, constitutes an intrinsic component of the region's identity. Not only does it precede the territory, but it is the area's 'ur-metaphor'. The post-World War I launch of the first 'cartographic mandate' of the region identified the area with the 'small states of Europe', drawn by 'the mapmakers of Versailles' on the bodies of the empires. The Yalta conference's subsequent arbitrary redrawing of Europe's map in 1945 conjured up both the territory behind the Iron Curtain and competing geographical metaphors, from the 'Communist Bloc' to 'kidnapped Europe'.

The 'fall of the wall', an instant metaphor in its own right, was followed by new maps redefining Europe's eastern periphery. The map is here to stay, and it is in need of critical interrogation. The intermediality of cartographic language, utilising both text and image, makes it particularly open to visual studies. If the map precedes the territory, is it the image that precedes the map?

Almost forty years ago, Brian Harley turned to the methods of art history to advance his critique of the map. His conceptualisation of the map as an image drew from visual culture, a new approach to studying images, which contested the positivist aims of art history. Developed in parallel to Harley's critical cartography, visual culture shared its social constructivist outlook, attention to exclusion and commitment to theory. Harley's interdisciplinary gesture, however, has hardly been followed. If the 'artness' of cartography has attracted cartographers, cultural geographers and artists, the 'artless' mechanisms of visuality as the modus operandi of any map have failed to ignite comparable debates.

This entry looks at maps of East Central Europe (or what the editors of this volume have asked me to call in the title, by way of reflection of the volume's spirit, *Zwischeneuropa*). It approaches maps of East Central Europe as images, focusing on a large map of Slavic Europe published by the Slavonic philologist Pawel Josef Šafářik in 1842 (Figure 24.1),[3] and a small thematic map from 1916, 'The New Europe on a Basis of Nationality' (Figure 24.2), from a book authored by another Slavist, the historian R. W. Seton-Watson, the founder of the School of Slavonic and Eastern European Studies, known as 'the maker of a New Europe'.[4] Can visual analysis uncover unwritten affiliations and aspirations, affections and aversions, activated by these maps? More broadly, can visual culture contribute to rethinking area studies?

Both maps advance arguments about the spatial dimension of East Central Europe, and both are propositional in nature. They aim to activate the territory and are driven by emancipatory aims. 'Slovanský zeměvid' is an unprecedented cartographic vision of Eastern Europe, which had never before been presented as a separate space worthy of its own map.[5] It reclaims the region occupied by the European empires as an imagined linguistic community of Slavs. 'The New Europe on a Basis of Nationality', published by Seton-Watson more than seventy years later, during World War I, is the next step of this pro-Slavic manifesto. It presents an idealist vision of post-World War I Europe, in which once enslaved nations of East Central Europe would be liberated and granted their own states, a vision soon to be realised at the Paris Peace Conference.

Figure 24.1 Pawel Josef Šafařík, 'Slovanský zeměvid', in *Slovanský Národopis* (Prague: Wydawatele, 1842), hand-coloured engraving, 53 × 63 cm.

Figure 24.2 R. W. Seton-Watson, 'The New Europe on a Basis of Nationality', in *German, Slav and Magyar: A study in the origins of the Great War* (London: Williams and Norgate, 1916), 146.

In spite of their similar agendas, the maps differ in almost every respect: the historical circumstances of their production, the area covered, medium, dimensions and format, targeted audiences and impact, as well as their kinship to a broad family of images. 'Slovanský zeměvid' belongs to the genre of ethnographic surveys, habitually included in nineteenth-century atlases. It is based on the exceptionally accurate topographical maps of Europe made for the Prussian army by the German cartographer Gottlob Daniel Reymann. All the place names are Slavonicised and spelled in Czech, including German sites. The name of the map is rendered in strikingly ornate lettering, evoking Slavic ornaments. Its elaborate legend lists all the ethnic groups, classified by their languages, and asserts Slav domination over the region. Published initially in 600 copies, the map was attached as a fold-out to Šafářik's *Slovanský národopis* (Slav ethnography), his survey of Slavic languages and folk songs.

By contrast, *The New Europe* is a small thematic map, made of lines and dots, no more than an illustration on a page of Seton-Watson's book, based on another ready-made map of Europe to which he added the proposed boundaries of the new states. *The New Europe* does not aspire to cartographic accuracy, but to rhetorical effect. Driven by an anti-German spirit, it was directed against the spectre of *Mitteleuropa*, revived by Friedrich Naumann in 1915. A small legend at the bottom, indicating 'existing' and 'new' frontiers, plus 'Free Ports', and especially its overblown title, form an important part of the image, a manifesto for a 'regenerated' Europe.

If Seton-Watson's map was buried in his book, to be seen by historians and perhaps by Versailles mapmakers, Šafářik's map attracted an incomparably wider audience. *Slovanský národopis* went through two editions in the first year, and was immediately translated into Polish and Russian, in the latter case including the map. The map literally activated an imagined community of Slavs, launching ethnic pilgrimages across Slavdom. Stanko Vraz, a leader of the Illyrian movement, recorded its impact: 'When I brought a copy of this map, the local patriots and even non-patriots almost tore it out of my hands. All of them cannot get over the fact that the Slav nation is spread so far. The map arouses more patriots here than a whole literature could do'. Superimposed on the cartographic matrix of *Mitteleuropa*, and vested in the Herderian glorification of language and folk culture, 'Slovanský zeměvid' was a conscious act of counter-mapping, a powerful script of cultural resistance, a rallying call for Pan-Slavism. It set the cartographic code for representing the region adopted in standard atlases and disseminated throughout the nineteenth century. The effectiveness of the map stemmed from its visual rhetoric, sanctioned by the authority of cartography. As testified by Vraz's enthusiasm, the map provided an image of an inhabitable Slavic collective identity, of the desirable Slavonic Self, but also a visible record of Slavic power. The act of unfolding the map was tantamount to the discovery of the legitimacy of Slavic Europe, spreading from Berlin to the Urals.

The physical features of the territory were largely de-emphasised, but much of the rhetorical power of the map came from its association with landscape, widespread, uniformly green, agrarian and welcoming. The Czech term *zeměvid*, which means 'map', combines *země* (land) and *vid* (aspect), thus connoting the act of viewing a land. The affinity between map and landscape is much discussed in cultural geography, and in visual culture, both pointing to the tension between the aesthetic values of landscape as an artistic genre and claims to ownership of the land it represents, whether on the part of landed gentry or communities defending their shared territory – their ethnocultural links to the soil. It is from this perspective that 'Slovanský zeměvid' reveals its double nature, emancipatory and discriminatory at the same time. The cartographic gaze, the mapmaker's commanding view from above, so clearly implied here, is an instance of the disembodied gaze, controlling access to knowledge and power. The vastness of the Slavic land is enhanced by the use of colour, the same shade of green standing for all Slavic people, without any divisions into northern, western or southern. While the linguistic boundaries between the Slavs are marked by dainty dotted lines, the thick state borders of the occupiers, highlighted in red, resemble scars on the Slavic body. The isolated areas inhabited by non-Slavs, such as Hungarians and Romanians, let alone Germans, are rendered in yellow, and in garish shades of pink, which clash and distort the sense of green serenity. The use of Slavic names restored and confirmed Slavic rights to the land in much the same way in which German names on the maps of *Mitteleuropa* gave authority to Teutonic expansion. Inclusion is always, and inevitably, related to exclusion. The counter-map turns into a map of domination.

Seton-Watson's map presents an entirely different image. In spite of its relative obscurity, it did contribute to the rise of a new cartographic regime, of representing East Central Europe in the totally changed political configurations of World War I. By then, Pan-Slavism had already been compromised as a tool of Russian expansionism. The *New Europe* had to exclude Russia, absorbing instead all the countries liberated from imperial subjugation, both Slavic and non-Slavic. A new cartographic code was needed, an image which would abandon the rhetoric of vastness and cultural affinity stemming from linguistic commonality, and generate a new common denominator for these diverse European states. In *The New Europe*, the horizontal landscape format, no longer suitable or tenable, was now replaced by the vertical portrait format. This had to incorporate a whole cluster of yet-to-be-established political bodies within the stretch of land separating Germany from Russia. Slavic vastness shrivelled to a narrow belt of *Zwischeneuropa*. From the critical cartography perspective, Seton-Watson's *New Europe* is a striking example of an arbitrary 'geo-body', Winichakul's term for the colonial cartographic invention of the still unmapped territory of nineteenth-century Siam, undermining the validity of local knowledges and generating its own historical narrative.

There is no doubt that Seton-Watson's *New Europe* was intended as emancipatory, restoring sovereignty to the oppressed nations, and its vertical format simply corresponded with their position on the map of Europe. However, as in Šafářik's map, it was the rhetorical power of the image itself which invested the map with additional layers of meaning and activated its socio-political status in the twentieth century. The genre of portrait, as much as landscape, makes extra-aesthetic claims pertaining to the social status and power of the sitter. Its subspecies, the group portrait, comments on the relationship between individuals, emphasising marks of shared identity, based on legal contract, blood ties or social affiliation. Most often it uses the horizontal format of a multi-figure composition and, like a single portrait, is essentially celebratory. The most evocative feature of Seton-Watson's *New Europe*, however, is the disparity between the conventions of a group portrait and a single portrait format. In contrast to its celebratory caption, it shows an anxiety-ridden image of a chaotic array of new states, small and insecure within their unfixed boundaries, and crowded uncomfortably, one on top of another. What they share, the image seems to say, is their 'newness', smallness, instability and propensity to discord. Another feature of *The New Europe* is the suggestion of separateness. The new states seem to occupy an isolated region which, in order to be represented, had to be excised from the map of the continent and framed as an independent territory, that of the 'New Europe', the 'shatter zones', the 'middle tier' or 'the belt of political change', positioned between Europe and Asia.

If 'Slovanský zeměvid' prompted the long-standing regime of representing Eastern Europe as bound to Russia, revived during the Cold War, Seton-Watson's map established another enduring cartographic trope, that naturalised understanding East Central Europe in terms of inherent political instability and fragmentation. Both were intended as maps of resistance, and both were liable to be read also as visual documents of domination and subjugation. It was their affinities to landscape and portrait that contributed to their opacity and ambiguity, generating oppositional readings.

Mapmaking and image-making are parallel processes, at the level of both production and consumption. Maps and images are in constant dialogue, borrow from each other, develop against each other, correct and supplement their visual accents, 'foci, zooms, their highlights, their blinkers and blindnesses'.[6] The image activates the map, and the map activates the image. The territory plays a secondary role. Likewise, cartography, critical art history and visual culture travel along parallel routes, raise similar doubts and benefit from glancing over each other's shoulders. East European area studies have an unexhausted potential to contribute.

Notes

1   Harley, 2001.
2   See Dodge, 2011.
3   Šafařík, 1842; on Šafařík, see Kirschbaum, 1961; Tibenský, 1975; Kovačka et al., 2004. Šafařík's name is spelled differently in Czech and Slovak. I am following the original transcription of his name, as on the title page of his book.
4   Seton-Watson, 1916, 146; on Seton-Watson, see Seton-Watson and Seton-Watson, 1981.
5   Hůrský, 1955.
6   Rose, 2003, 35.

Bibliography

Dodge, Martin, ed. *The Map Reader: Theories of mapping practice and cartographic representation.* London: Wiley, 2011.

Harley, John Brian. *The New Nature of Maps: Essays in the history of cartography,* edited by Paul Laxton. Baltimore, MD: Johns Hopkins University Press, 2001.

Hůrský, Josef. 'Vznik a Poslání Šafaříkova Slovanského Zeměvidu' [The origin and purpose of Šafárik's Slavic map]. In *Slovanský Národopis*, edited by Hana Hynková in cooperation with Josef Hůrský and Luboš Řeháček, 218–88. Prague: Československá akademie věd, 1955.

Kirschbaum, J. M. *Pavel Jozef Šafařík and His Contribution to Slavic Studies.* Cleveland, OH: The Slovak Institute, 1961.

Kovačka, Miloš, ed. *Personálna bibliografia Pavla Jozefa Šafárika* [Personal Bibliography of Pavel Jozef Šafárik]. Martin: Slovenská národná knižnica, 2004.

Rose, Gillian. 'On the need to ask how, exactly, is geography "visual"', *Antipode* 35 (2003): 35.

Šafařík, Pawel Josef. 'Slovanský zeměvid' [Slavic map]. In *Slovanský Národopis* [Slavic Ethnography]. Prague: Wydawatele, 1842.

Seton-Watson, Hugh and Christopher Seton-Watson. *The Making of a New Europe: R. W. Seton-Watson and the last years of Austria-Hungary.* London: Methuen, 1981.

Seton-Watson, Robert William. 'The New Europe on a Basis of Nationality'. Map in *German, Slav and Magyar: A study in the origins of the Great War.* London: Williams and Norgate, 1916.

Tibenský, Ján. *Pavol Jozef Šafárik: Život a dielo* [Pavol Jozef Šafárik: Life and work]. Bratislava: Osvetový ústav, 1975.

Part II
Wandering critics

This part foregrounds some figures who are emblematic of Eastern Europe (Ovid; komunistki; Natasha). Others, outspoken critics of essentialism, nonetheless trace conventional narratives by rejecting them (Gryczełowska; Chatterjee). Some of these lives highlight connections across conventional area borders and throw its blind spots and assumptions about global hierarchies into relief (Griffith and Butler; Polish architects; Sherlock Holmes); others focus on local knowledge and expertise and the ways these draw circles of belonging and exclusion (kraeved(ka); raja; Crni Srbi). We are, however, also interested in those who take advantage of spaces and frontiers in ways that we (or others) might consider opportunistic, reactionary or reprehensible (migration brokers; projectariat): critical area studies (CAS) is not solely concerned with heroes and victims.

In short, this Anti-Atlas is particularly concerned to highlight trajectories that area studies often fails to capture, and those lives that the conventional atlas doesn't always know what to do with – hence our interest in peripatetic scholars, people traffickers, transhumant shepherds, professional translators and practical polyglots, refugees, exiles, and the children of diaspora. We have concentrated here on people whose routes, divagations and dead ends throw into relief the very real constraints and boundaries that confront them (CAS is scarcely 'area studies without borders'), but we are also concerned to understand the individual motives, interests and desires that guide their endeavours. Because of these preoccupations, CAS is well suited to struggle fruitfully with the interrelations of context and actors, or structure and agency, without either launching into abstract theorising or taking refuge in an insistence on the particular and specific. But more than that, this then provides the means to consider commonalities and divergencies across societies and cultures in a comparative framework. This is one of the ways forward for a CAS with aspirations that are wider than the area covered in this volume.

25
The accidental transnationalist: an autobiographical manifesto
Choi Chatterjee

As scholars, we tend to leave ourselves – and the biographical and intercultural entwinings and enmeshments of which we are made – on the sidelines of our academic activity. Chatterjee's autobiographical reflections on a trajectory that takes her from Kolkata to Russian literature in California suggest that accidental and everyday transnationalism of this sort might be a route to a new form of collaborative and engaged scholarly and pedagogical practice. And they also indicate that we – the Anti-Atlas makers – do not stand on the sidelines of our project but may also feature in it as, albeit minor, characters.

As an Indian married to a Pakistani while teaching Russian history to a primarily Latino population in Los Angeles, the transnational part comes fairly easily to me; but on my bad days, I have trouble understanding what truly constitutes the national.[1] Growing up in an India that had recently won its independence from British rule, we had a complicated understanding of European and, by extension, of world history. We read Lenin and Sartre, E. P. Thompson and Alexander Solzhenitsyn, and Anna Akhmatova and Simone de Beauvoir, without fully understanding the intellectual fault lines that separated Eastern and Western Europe. We treated it rather uncritically as a common European intellectual heritage that, as former subjects of the British Empire, we could quite rightfully claim as 'ours'. I accepted confusion as my natural lot early in life, an emotional state that was easy to maintain in Kolkata, a multiethnic and multilingual city, where stolid British-colonial era buildings sheltered a rabidly Maoist-Leninist government from the 1960s to the recent past. A city so surreal, that it has compelled generations of respectable academics, Amitav Ghosh being only the latest representative, to take up fiction in order to understand the global crosscurrents that created the city in the twentieth century and then almost destroyed it in the decades following Indian independence in 1947.[2]

As a graduate student in the United States in the late 1980s, I learned about the many differences that apparently separated the East and the West, the First World from the Second. But when I went to the Soviet Union in 1991, as a member of the Third World I was less annoyed by the inconveniences of the late socialist system than some of my colleagues. I was used to unhygienic bathrooms, crumbling masonry and uncollected garbage disfiguring historic buildings and remarkable works of architecture and design. My Russian friends appreciated my premodern sensibilities as they opened their hearts and homes, while I saw echoes of my Indian past in the brilliant improvisations that constituted Soviet daily life. But by the late 1990s and early 2000s, when a second Gilded Age became a worldwide phenomenon, I saw that my friends who had made good in Los Angeles, Moscow, Karachi and Kolkata had all learned to fluently speak the language of neoliberalism. Their lives, regardless of the metropolitan city that they inhabited, were curiously similar. They were the double income couples, folks that we now call the one per cent, who sent their children to private schools, deeply distrusted the state and power of unions, and truly believed that their financial and career success was a product of their hard work and dedication.

During this period, I taught at California State University, Los Angeles. On this remarkable campus on the border of East Los Angeles, my students came from different parts of Mexico, Central and South America, Asia, Eastern Europe and even parts of the former Soviet Union. Some of them were undocumented immigrants, buffeted by the cruel winds of globalisation. Clear-eyed members of the working class, they read critical theory with interest and novel insight. They had experienced Foucault's biopolitics at the hands of border guards, prison officials and bureaucrats, and as such, they recognised the politics of postcolonial theory with uncanny prescience. They were in transit between empires and nations, rendered homeless by the political fictions of both colonial and postcolonial elites! While they dutifully repeated Dipesh Chakrabarty's dictum that we should provincialise Europe, in their hearts they knew that it was only a matter of time before a new world hierarchy was created, and new boundaries were drawn.[3] Rather than see the world set on an East–West axis, as Edward Said had claimed, they reinterpreted orientalism as the many ways that the powerful misrepresent the powerless. Having never belonged to a polity that actually represented them, my students intuitively recognised that nationalism was a constructed phenomenon, empires a constant historical reality, and knew to their bitter cost that class identities could be devastatingly flexible. Despite their realistic appraisal of their conditions, they also believed in the power of self-knowledge and that of resistance.

While deploying what we academics like to call strategies of survival, they also ascribed meaning to their everyday lives, to their actions and their life choices. Above all, my students hungrily coveted the power that authenticity, morality and integrity endowed. And like Svetlana Boym's subjects, they dreamed of 'another freedom'. These were subalterns who could actually speak, and they aspired to speak an authoritative language, one that the governing elites could understand.[4] They devoured selections from the Russian intellectual tradition, especially socialist-realist literature, revolutionary memoirs and prison-camp testimonials. Our discussions on *What Is to Be Done?* (Nikolai Chernyshevsky), *The Law of Love and the Law of Violence* (Leo Tolstoy), *Mother* (Maxim Gorky) and *Within the Whirlwind* (Evgeniia Ginzburg) were epic and interminable. I saw that my students drew two important meanings from these texts. First, that it was possible through the exercise of will and reason to refashion oneself, to overcome the harshest of circumstances, and rise above one's assigned station in life: the classic Nietzschean/American/Bolshevik story. Second, and more important, they deeply believed that individual success had to also encompass the needs of what Mark Steinberg has so eloquently deemed as 'moral communities', and what the Buddhists refer to as the sangha.[5] As we read the works of Emma Goldman, Leo Tolstoy, Peter Kropotkin and other Russian anarchists, my students found proof for their deeply held conviction that the individual has to be embedded in a larger ethical universe. And I understood more clearly why pre-Bolshevik socialist thought has survived the downfall of the Soviet Union and is now animating the global Left in the twenty-first century in unimaginable ways.

Since few of my students read Russian, I found it impossible to teach research courses in my area of specialisation. In desperation, I delved into the history of Russian–American relations. I found out that Americans since the middle of the nineteenth century have been fascinated with Russia and Russian culture. I fell in love with Turgenev again after reading Henry James's rapturous exegesis of his works. Ekaterina Breshko-Breshkovskaia exercised the same fascination on my students in the twenty-first century that she had on the journalist, George Kennan, in Siberian exile in the 1890s. In a research seminar on

Russian–American relations, my student Sergio Maldonado discovered to his intense excitement that Flores Magón, a preeminent intellectual of the early Chicano movement in Los Angeles, had not only read the works of Peter Kropotkin but had also been inspired by Emma Goldman's anarchist politics. A pedagogical exercise became an overwhelming passion and I became a closet Americanist, reading works of American history and literature at night while professing Russian history by day. But what had started as a secret intellectual detour soon led me to new professional communities, as I realised that many colleagues and talented scholars, including the editors of the Anti-Atlas, were also crossing frontiers in exciting ways.

I apologise for this long digression about my personal life and career, but in writing this essay I have realised that transnationalism is not merely a trendy intellectual category, a new spin on traditional area studies, or even a new way of doing comparative history. It is a way of seeing the world and considering one's position within the many coordinates of power that crisscross the globe. Throughout the ages, we have repeatedly borrowed from each other's canons, pilfered ideas and re-presented them as richer and more complicated versions. While the accelerating forces of modernity have rendered transparent our borrowings, plagiarisms, transpositions and transfigurations, in the long run, the global circulation of ideas always leads to the accretion of value. In the eighteenth century, while the Russians learned to speak French, British traders dubbed 'White Mughals' learned to live the lives of Muslim grandees in India.[6] In the nineteenth century, as Russians rediscovered the joys of the Russian language after defeating Napoleon's invading forces, sons of Indian Rajahs, forsaking Farsi, learned cricket and Englishness on the 'playing fields of Eton'. In both cases, the cross-fertilisation created profoundly hybrid cultures with intertwined root systems that have proven hard to disentangle. But transnationalism is not simply an updated form of cosmopolitanism that elites have enjoyed through recorded time. My students seek knowledge of a past that emphasises processes, structures, events, ideologies and personalities that transcend the history of a single civilisation, country, empire, nation state or area. Rather than focus on immutable civilisational or national differences, they are keen to analyse historical processes across physical, political and intellectual boundaries. Like them, I see the world's intellectual fund as a common heritage that people in different places and at different times have accessed to understand themselves, to replenish their souls and to create political movements. It can be seen as a giant mall, where ideas are displayed by national categories, but I prefer to think of ideas spinning endlessly in the seven crystal spheres awaiting discovery and rediscovery.

Transnational understanding of historical processes takes time, patience and reflection on one's personal experiences and their relationship to academic categories. It is a rocky and perilous road as often this scholarship is at odds with the way our field is structured. It rarely fits the mandates of granting agencies, and scholars have to struggle to unlearn their deep training in area studies that posit the uniqueness of cultures rather than their relational, mediated and interdependent histories. There are few jobs available in these historical fields that are yet to be defined, and courses in this area are yet to be designed. But transnational history has the potential to liberate us from the tyranny of our self-imposed expertise, and it helps us evaluate historical narratives with fresh eyes. When we utilise this approach, we can clearly see the harsh inequalities created by free markets worldwide, along with the abundance that free trade promised individual nations. The chimera of development reveals the staggering environmental toll that modern lifestyles have levied on a global scale. Rather than acclaim the nation-state as the desired end of history, we understand the many ways that governing bodies coordinate repressive mechanisms at borders to control the movements of populations fleeing war, poverty and natural disasters.

In short, transnational approaches allow us to combine our academic research with progressive politics, to connect our teaching with the needs of the populations that surround our campuses, and to rediscover the public uses of history. It teaches us to collaborate in new ways, to learn new languages, and to discover communities that are based on shared passions and interests. It allows us to be graduate students again, to plan improbably large and wildly impractical projects that may take many years to complete. Transnationalism invites us to abandon the model of the heroic and lonely intellectual and undertake what has been the norm in the sciences for a long time: large-scale collaborative projects that yield insight into the human condition.

Notes

1 A longer version of this essay was previously published as 'The accidental transnationalist: An autobiographical manifesto', *Ab Imperio* 4: 29–41 (2018).
2 Ghosh, 2008.
3 Chakrabarty, 2000.
4 Boym, 2010.
5 Steinberg, 1992.
6 Dalrymple, 2003.

Bibliography

Boym, Svetlana. *Another Freedom: The alternative history of an idea*. Chicago, IL: Chicago University Press, 2010.

Chakrabarty, Dipesh. *Provincializing Europe: Postcolonial thought and historical difference*. Princeton, NJ: Princeton University Press, 2000.

Dalrymple, William. *White Mughals: Love and betrayal in eighteenth-century India*. New York: Viking Press, 2003.

Ghosh, Amitav. *Sea of Poppies*. New York: Farrar, Strauss and Giroux, 2008.

Steinberg, Mark. *Moral Communities: The culture of class relations in the Russian printing industry, 1867–1907*. Berkeley: University of California Press, 1992.

26
Crni Srbi and Ron Holsey
Catherine Baker

In this essay, YouTube music videos operate as one of those grey areas between the closely policed borders of the Greater Europe described above: a space where Black and Serbian hip-hop artists collaborate in narratives that suggest a transnational and transracial workingman's solidarity, against contemporary Serbian assumptions of ethnic primacy and assertions of European 'whiteness'. For the past quarter century, Eastern Europe has been seen in terms of Edward Said's Orientalism, with its imaginative geography and nesting alteritisms; Baker invites us to look through the lens of Paul Gilroy's Black Atlantic and to see instead lived geopolitical experience and peripheral solidarities.

Introduced by sampled 'oriental' strings and hip-hop beats, a Black baker heaving dough inside a sweltering kitchen turns to the viewer and bemoans his downtrodden lot in song, using the language, verse-forms and characteristic ornamented vowels of the newly-composed folk music with which decades of singers from Serbia, Bosnia-Herzegovina, Montenegro and the Dalmatian hinterland have described the hardships of the labour migration that endemic unemployment at home has forced millions of their compatriots to undergo. His lament, that the only momentary pleasure in his life of labour is drinking rakija on a penniless Saturday night, is taken up at once by a slightly younger Black man, working as a painter, rapping to the camera in a few brief seconds of illicit leisure before his older White foreman comes back and argues about the third shift he is supposed to work that day. They, and the White labourer who breaks from hurling debris across the dusty yard outside to rap about working for ten and a half hours without a break for lunch, then (as he drops his heavy wooden plank) about inviting his friends to the kafana, are characters in the kind of social drama of exploitation and precarity which newly-composed folk music has long offered its listeners, and to which post-Yugoslav hip-hop since the mid-1990s has, at its most socially engaged best, added postsocialist political critique.

The snatched moments of release that Crni Srbi and Ron Holsey's video 'Rintam' ('I'm toiling away'), published on YouTube in 2016, offer the viewer, when they finally come together to toast in the yard and sing outdoors with their rakija bottles in the evening light, are the same affective spaces that popular music in Serbia and the rest of South-east Europe has long invited peripheralised workers, gastarbeiters and disenfranchised postsocialist citizens to look forward to and find solace in. The brotherhood between the three men, two African-Americans and one White Serb, embodies a translocal class-based solidarity marginalised within dominant ethnicised frames of identity. It even allows its viewer to project a critique of neoliberal capitalism that is not confined within the boundaries of 'postsocialist' Europe into the story which the conventions of music video invite them to tell about its scenes.

Both the duo of Crni Srbi (The Black Serbs), otherwise known as David Brkljač from Novi Sad and Jibri Bell ('Jovan Crnović') from South Dakota, and Ron Holsey, an African-American singer from California, who began posting YouTube videos of himself singing classic newly composed folk songs in 2015, have been able to reach audiences and make enough money to produce professionally-edited music videos, as a result of today's grassroots digital economy. Their communication does not depend on, though they are sometimes featured in, a mainstream media where the novelty of Bell and Holsey as Black Americans fluent in Serbian linguistic and cultural codes is still the primary lens through which they are presented to the wider Serbian public:[1] headlines like 'Here's what a guy from Los Angeles who sings folk songs [narodnjaci] has to say about Serbia!', from a *Blic* interview with Holsey published online on 16 December 2015, imply that the boundary between African-American identity and the identity of those with an innate affinity for narodnjaci (supposedly reserved for members of the 'narod' or ethnic nation) is a fixed border of racialised ethnicity that it is remarkable for someone to be able to cross. Instead, they address listeners primarily through digital spaces they curate, where two Black musicians' participation in Serbian linguistic and musical culture appears as everyday sociality rather than exotic sight.

The history of the friendship between Bell and Brkljač, which inspired them to start posting comedy videos online in 2013, itself emerged from the entanglement of Serbia's postsocialist and post-conflict situation with the racism and social inequalities of South Dakota, where Bell grew up and Brkljač ended up living, after his mother married a US Air Force mechanic she had met in Hungary, in 1999, while the family were temporary refugees, escaping the NATO air strikes over Novi Sad. They became friends as teenagers after Bell started dating Brkljač's sister Luna (having been to a party and heard her sing in Serbian, Bell told a Denver sports news site in 2018), although had first met when Brkljač kicked Bell during a fight between rival schools some years before; the comradeship they forged as fellow outsiders outlasted the breakup of Bell's relationship with Luna and first inspired them to make a series of comedy videos for YouTube, then to turn to collaborations with Black and Latino singers that expressed transnational friendships between the Balkans and racially marginalised diasporas in the USA.[2] Their *Serbia Coming to America* videos (2013–14) had Bell play a stereotypically ultra-patriotic and confrontational Serb, in šajkača and opanke, puzzling Americans by speaking Serbian and picking fights at burger bars, basketball courts and other typical spaces of intercultural encounter. 'Rintam' was their second musical collaboration of 2016: their first, 'Balkan Latino', was filmed in Chicago with Joshua Lazu and mixed lyrics in Serbian and Puerto Rican Spanish, rap, reggaeton rhythms, and trumpets which could equally accentuate a Serbian or Latin pop song to celebrate Latino and Balkan friendship – the same musical flexibility with which, in mainstream pop, the Serbian singer Saša Kovačević has recorded reggaeton-inspired summer hits like 'Temperatura' (with a video filmed in Havana, featuring a dreadlocked Black rapper unnamed in the credits) that fit effortlessly on to the region's radio stations alongside global Latino hits like 'Despacito', which 'Temperatura' and 'Balkan Latino' both anticipated by a year.[3]

The everyday experiences of transnational migration and interracial sociality that Brkljač, Bell and Holsey translate into the *mis en scène* of 'Rintam' not only evoke present-day labour politics of working-class masculine precarity, but seem to reinterpret and rework a phrase that remains commonplace in the former Serbo-Croatian languages: 'raditi kao crnac', 'to work like a Black'. Their caption underneath the 'Rintam' video reads 'Priča mog života!!! Radim kao crnac a mala mi je plata' (the story of my life!!! I work like a Black and my wages are low). During one of the *Serbia Coming to America* skits (when the duo run into a street film crew and start negotiating payments with a hapless researcher from MTV), Bell, in character, similarly remarks, 'Radim kao crnac a plaće me kao Srbina!' (I work like a Black and I get paid like a Serb!). The phrase has embedded the history of the Atlantic slave trade in many European languages,[4] and testifies to the fact that imaginations of 'race' in the region certainly date back much further than postsocialist identifications with the whiteness of a 'Europe' fortifying itself against the Global South.

The continued currency of 'raditi kao crnac' often surprises Anglophone learners whose public culture at home performs the fiction that we have moved on from racism, so that the language of overt racial stereotyping ought to have been left behind (in fact, as White Anglophones like myself should be especially aware while comparing formations of race between regions, the language may have been left behind but the structural racism remains). In an article on regional, ethnic and racial slurs in Croatian, the linguist Gordana Čupković argues that 'crnac', when alluding to hard physical work, should be taken as an expression of 'empathy for the oppressed and the exploited', indeed an identification with the oppression that enslaved Africans underwent at White overseers' hands, and not as a slur, in contrast to its implied opposite, 'raditi kao Cigan' ('to work like a Gypsy').[5] The simile cannot be distanced from racism like this when the hegemonic gazes of popular culture in the region still project colonial fantasies on to Black bodies. In Bell's use, however, the linkage of blackness, exploitation, tiring manual labour and low pay seems to hint at a horizontal solidarity between Blacks and Serbs that might be closer to socialist internationalism than to postsocialist aspirations for unconditional access to the symbolic whiteness of the centre of Europe (or indeed openly racist arguments that east European nations are part of that symbolic White core and ought to be preserved as such).

Crni Srbi's productions might, indeed, be comparable to how the Belgrade hip-hop collective Bombe Devedesetih (Bombs of the Nineties) have used their own online videos rather than mainstream media and recording-industry channels to construct a 'left populism' which distances itself both from the Serbian cultural elite and from the presupposition that the ethnic nation ought to be the first focus of solidarity: African footballers and Black Power activists are all among the 'heroes' and 'brothers' in their lyrics, and the rapper Mimi Mercedez named the last song on her 2015 mix-tape after the footballer Diafra Sakho, linking the 'global problem – the Balkans and West Africa' ('svetska problematika – Balkan i Zapadna Afrika').[6] Holsey, a musician who has gone on to make solo videos and perform with mainstream Serbian stars (including an intimate duet of 'Jovano, Jovanke' with the Belgrade-based Macedonian singer Tijana Dapčević), meanwhile hints at affinities between the blackness of the African diaspora and the localised blackness of Roma that have already been imagined from the Romani side when he appears on a US metro system in the last section of the video, wearing a tuxedo and playing an accordion, while a young White boy presses a banknote to Holsey's forehead as guests would to a Romani musician at a traditional Serbian wedding (and elsewhere in South-east Europe where it is customary to hire Romani wedding bands).

The routes through which a Serb from Novi Sad moves to South Dakota, a young Black man from Rapid City discovers Serbia, and another African-American from California becomes a digital celebrity by mastering the conventions of Serbian folk song – until the sound and style of hip-hop offer all three a medium for commenting on young working-class men's precarity – are part of a 'Black Atlantic'[7] created by the historical legacies of colonialism and enslavement, and by transnational networks of resistance, critique and creativity, which extends well beyond Europe's Atlantic rim into its interior, even though few sociologists of race until recently have traced it so far. The solidarities that Brkljač, Bell and Holsey personify in 'Rintam' are subaltern ones which neither the identity myths of Euro-Atlanticism, nor those of chauvinistic ethnocentrism, would accommodate, but which stem not just from imagined transnational identification but also embodied geopolitical experience.

Note

This text was prepared in December 2018. The Bibliography also contains works by Sunnie Rucker-Chang and Samantha Farmer published more recently that advance discussions of their topics beyond what I articulated in this text.

Appendix

At the time of writing, all the videos mentioned in this entry were available on YouTube, including:

'Rintam' https://www.youtube.com/watch?v=tUcBWqzwN1k.
'Serbia Coming to America' part 1 https://www.youtube.com/watch?v=PkvektlQo6A.
'Serbia Coming to America' part 2 https://www.youtube.com/watch?v=YA_Ivo1CKns. 'Balkan Latino' https://www.youtube.com/watch?v=pWEnRnPDIv0.

Notes

1. See Rucker-Chang, 2024.
2. Wild, 2018.
3. See Farmer, 2019.
4. Giovannetti, 2006, 5.
5. Čupković, 2015, 223–4.
6. Papović and Pejović, 2016, 118.
7. Gilroy, 1993.

Bibliography

Čupković, Gordana. 'Diachronic variations of slurs and levels of derogation: On some regional, ethnic, and racial slurs in Croatian', *Language Sciences* 52 (2015): 215–30.

Farmer, Samantha. 'Turbotón: Negotiating musical transnationalism and authenticity in turbofolk'. In *Old Beats, New Verses: 21 newly composed essays on turbofolk*, edited by Vladislav Beronja, Michelle Daniel and Ian Goodale. 2019. Accessed 15 April 2024. https://scalar.usc.edu/works/turbofolk/turbotn-negotiating-musical-transnationalism-and-authenticity-in-turbofolk.

Gilroy, Paul. *The Black Atlantic: Modernity and double consciousness*. London: Verso, 1993.

Giovannetti, Jorge L. 'Grounds of race: Slavery, racism and the plantation in the Caribbean', *Latin American and Caribbean Ethnic Studies* 1 (2006): 5–36.

Papović, Jovana and Astrea Pejović. 'The potential of popular culture for the creation of Left populism in Serbia: The case of the hip-hop collective "The Bombs of the Nineties"', *Contemporary Southeastern Europe* 3 (2016): 107–26.

Rucker-Chang, Sunnie. 'The "perpetual foreigner" in Serbia: On being marked and unmarked in a "raceless" state'. In *Off White: Central and Eastern Europe and the global history of race*, edited by Catherine Baker, Bogdan C. Iacob, Anikó Imre and James Mark, 293–310. Manchester: Manchester University Press, 2024.

Wind, Harrison. 'The incredible story of a Serbian refugee, a misplaced South Dakotan and a mission embodied by Nikola Jokic', *BSN Denver*, 29 May 2018. Accessed 13 August 2024. https://thednvr.com/the-incredible-story-of-a-serbian-refugee-a-misplaced-south-dakotan-and-a-mission-embodied-by-nikola-jokic/.

27
Arthur Griffith and Hubert Butler: the rhetoric and inspection of historical parallels between Ireland and Central Europe
Aidan O'Malley

Ireland in this Anti-Atlas stands as an example of a 'peripheral' nation that has both served as a model for Eastern Europe's small nations (see Archer, above), and has sought its own parallels there. Sinn Féin founder Arthur Griffith's use of Hungary as an inspiration for Irish politics has been read in a celebratory and anticolonial mode, despite the historical inaccuracies of his interpretation. However, a comparison with the views of another Irish critic of Hungary's own colonial relationships highlights the fact that emancipatory politics for some (Magyars in Hungary, Irish Republicans) are not necessarily emancipatory for all. More generally, periphery–periphery encounters do not necessarily work to challenge hierarchies and power relations: more depends on the ends than on the rhetorical means.

The late Pascale Casanova's *The World Republic of Letters* (1999) has provided one of the most detailed recent maps of world literary history. Taking its bearings from Paris, the study charted the different approaches individual writers and national literatures pursued in order to establish themselves in a politically-charged and unevenly-stratified world literary system. Focusing in particular on the relationships between peripheral cultures and metropolitan centres, Casanova turned to Ireland as a key test case of how an outlying culture negotiated this shifting, competitive, hierarchical space. The Irish Literary Revival of the late nineteenth and early twentieth centuries was, in this telling, a transnational cultural project that saw Irish writers forge channels of communication between Ireland and the metropoles of London and Paris. This dynamic contributed to the disruption and reframing of Ireland's colonial relationship with Britain, as did the manner in which Irish authors sought out examples that might be emulated from other peripheral regions of Europe.

One such writer was the journalist and political thinker, Arthur Griffith, whose *The Resurrection of Hungary: A parallel for Ireland* (1904) urged Irish politicians, in Casanova's terms, to follow 'the example of Hungarian deputies in boycotting the Austrian parliament, noting that efforts to revive the use of the Magyar tongue had led to an agreement with the Austrian monarchy on the language issue and a real measure of political autonomy for Hungary'.[1] In short, the manner in which Hungary forced Austria in 1867 to accept the legitimacy of Hungarian rights and so create the Dual Monarchy became the model for Sinn Féin, the party Griffith founded the year after the publication of the first edition of his tract. A third edition with a new preface was published in 1918, and in the United Kingdom elections of that year Sinn Féin swept the board in Ireland and put these tactics into practice, by not travelling to London and instead establishing an Irish parliament in Dublin in January 1919, thus precipitating the War of Independence. To this day, Sinn Féin deputies elected in Northern Ireland do not take their seats in Westminster.

These tactics were pursued in Hungary in order to pressurise Austria into re-establishing the country's constitution, which Vienna had suspended in the aftermath of the Lajos Kossuth-led rebellion of 1848. Policies crucial to Hungarian life, such as taxation, language and military affairs, must be debated and decided upon in Budapest, insisted Ferenc Deák, the demure leader of this nonviolent abstentionism. Deák is the hero of Griffith's treatise: he promoted a form of self-sufficient nationalism rooted in constitutional rights that Ireland should follow. In Griffith's analysis, Ireland had already gained constitutional sanction to have its own parliament, under the terms of the 1783 Renunciation Act. All it required now was a figure like Deák to reassert this right in a resolute fashion and encourage others to abandon the two main options, being pursued in 1904, to change Ireland's status: home rule, which Griffith saw as an insufficient compromise, and paramilitary activity. In Griffith's portrayal, Hungary flourished in the years after 1867 as a result of its policies of political, economic and cultural self-sufficiency. These did not denote disengagement from the world, but instead allowed international links to be established on the country's own terms. Notably, in terms of Casanova's argument, Griffith argued that Hungary disproved prognostications that extricating itself from the hegemonic grip of the German language and making Hungarian the state language would also leave it adrift from world culture, and he saw no reason why the use of Irish should cause the new Irish state to be cut off from international transactions.[2]

To this degree, *The Resurrection of Hungary* is a fine example of a trade in political and cultural ideas and strategies between peripheral European nations struggling to assert their rights in colonial frameworks. Having said that, this polemic's parallels between Hungary and Ireland are also deeply flawed on many different levels, as has been long noted by historians, in particular. For instance, Griffith outlines how the threat of Prussian expansionism played a major role in forcing Austria to accede to Hungary's demands.[3] His suggestion that Ireland held a comparable geopolitical importance in terms of the British Empire in the period of the American War of Independence is questionable, to say the least.[4] But, as Seamus Deane has neatly underlined, historical accuracy was never the force propelling this text: 'The pertinence or otherwise of the analogy does not matter in the least now and did not matter a great deal then. The comparison was a rhetorical device to stimulate the public into thinking of an alternative to Home Rule and to make economic sufficiency a priority of this new departure'.[5]

This 'rhetorical device' is steeped in a distinctively Victorian marinade, as Griffith recounts a heroic, poetic and masculine history – a story of great and weak men, with adjectives like 'virile' and 'manly' employed as terms of laudation. His ultimate objective is also remarkably conservative: the Anglo-Hibernian dual monarchy he advocates would be 'master of the world'.[6] This aspiration to participation in imperial power renders the uninterrogated invocation of this text problematic in *The World Republic of Letters*, informed as it is by postcolonial thinking and an attention to centre–periphery dynamics. Moreover, and crucially, Griffith's positive attitude to Hungarian colonial pretensions led him to overlook and denigrate the situations of the more precisely peripheral members of the Habsburg empire.

In the same moment as Griffith exposes the comparable racist stereotyping of the Hungarians and Irish by the Austrians and British, he offers a reading of Habsburg history that echoes Balkanist attitudes.[7] He describes, for instance, the Serbs and Croatians who worked for the Austrians to quell the 1848 rebellion in Budapest in these terms: 'Scarcely had the country [Hungary] started on its career of freedom when Wallach and Serb and Croatian swarmed over the borders, fed with stories of Hungarian designs to oppress and destroy them, and instigated to pillage and massacre'.[8] These 'marauders' are dismissed as gullible Austrian stooges, just as their post-1867 territorial and national claims are summarily shrugged off as nothing more than a strategy concocted in Vienna to disrupt Hungary's natural boundaries: they were simply 'the Slav hordes who had been taught by unscrupulous and cunning statesmen to regard Hungary as an enemy to them'.[9] Tellingly, this paragraph ends by drawing a comparison with Ireland that claims it could not be held to imperial ransom by border issues: 'The frontier of Ireland has been fixed by nature. Whatever Britain statesmen may do, they can never use the frontier question to raise up enemies for this country other than Great Britain itself'.[10] Originally written in 1904, these words are left unchanged in the 1918 edition of *The Resurrection of Hungary*, when the issue of Ulster Unionism played an urgent role in Irish political debates. In fact, the situations of Ulster Unionists and, in particular, those of Croatia could be said to have had points in common: both perceived themselves to be dependent on the imperial centre to stave off what they discerned as the aggressive intentions of the section of the empire that was moving towards independence. If Unionists ultimately never had to face direct hostility from the Free State/Republic of Ireland, Croatia was not so fortunate. As Rebecca West laconically recounts: 'the Croats had saved the Austrian Empire. They got exactly nothing for this service … When the Dual Monarchy was framed to placate Hungary, the Croats were handed over to the Hungarians as their chattels. I do not know of any nastier act than this in history' (pointing out in a footnote that 'It must be remembered that this journal was written in 1937').[11] West's opinions were by no means unique, as Hungary's rule over the Balkan regions it had been granted under the terms of the 1867 *Ausgleich* had garnered it considerable international notoriety in the years leading up to World War I, yet none of this was registered in *The Resurrection of Hungary*.

Griffith's attitudes, in fact, echo a tradition of metropolitan disdain towards Balkan claims to statehood; Karl Marx, for instance, similarly denounced the actions of these minor nations in 1848, imperiously dismissing them as 'dying nationalities'.[12] The Balkans, it might be said, seem to mark the limits of emancipatory discourses, as the Irish essayist Hubert Butler noted in his 1947 'Yugoslavia: The cultural background', which coldly dissects and historicises Griffith's stereotyping:

> Unfortunately there is no trade union of the oppressed. The brave little Hungary which inspired Sinn Féin by its nimble resistance to the Austrian oppressor used its new freedom to oppress the Croats even more than before … A genteel snobbism has often kept oppressed nations apart and attracted them to the oppressors

of others … The Irish have … always rated the Austrian above his uncouth Slavonic subjects and for centuries the Irish Wild Geese assisted the Habsburgs in oppressing them.[13]

While Griffith was a central figure in the founding of the new Irish state, Butler was a determinedly peripheral writer who published articles and essays in a series of newspapers and journals, many of which, such as *The Church of Ireland Gazette*, had limited readerships. But if Griffith's idealised, rhetorical, Hungary functions, in part, as a model of how Ireland might participate in a world-dominating empire, Butler lived in Yugoslavia, spoke its language, and wrote of it in a manner that let his Irish audiences reflect on how lives lived on the other side of Europe were not so very different: having been warped by colonisation, both locations subsequently underwent a repressive interweaving of religion and nationalist politics. Frequently working from localised instances – conversations while waiting for a tram in Zagreb, plaques on a Sarajevo bridge – Butler fashioned far-reaching ethical insights that extolled the neighbourhood, the provincial and the small nation as more fertile sites for a liberal, enabling, nationalism than might be found in larger political constructions.

However, despite his professed nationalism, his criticism of both empire and the postcolonial Irish state, and the manner in which he brought Irish experience into a meaningful dialogue with the successor states that emerged from the Habsburg and Ottoman empires after World War I, Butler has held a marginal position in Irish historical, political and cultural scholarship. In contrast, just as Hungary operated as a metaphor for Griffith, it might almost be said that *The Resurrection of Hungary* has assumed a commensurate – in other words, not fully examined – symbolic significance in cultural histories such as Casanova's, that seek to unearth transnational traffic between peripheral nations. But employing Griffith's tract in this shorthand fashion ultimately impedes the excavation and exploration of meaningful historical and cultural interactions between Ireland and other peripheral European nations. However, thinking of it together with Butler's diagnosis of its power biases, and in discussion with his more sober reflections on these two regions, produces complex readings of these exchanges that might also serve as a productively complicated model of peripheral encounters for a contemporary critical area studies.

Notes

1. Casanova, 2004, 250–1.
2. Casanova, 2004, 72–5.
3. Griffith, 1904, 36–7.
4. Griffith, 1904, 84.
5. Deane, 1989, 213.
6. Griffith, 1904, 103.
7. Griffith, 1904, 68–75.
8. Griffith, 1904, xxviii.
9. Griffith, 1904, xxviii and 70.
10. Griffith, 1904, 70.
11. West, 1994, 54.
12. Marx, 1907, 137.
13. Butler, 2016, 110.

Bibliography

Butler, Hubert. 'Yugoslavia: The cultural background'. In *Balkan Essays*, edited by Chris Agee and Jacob Agee, 109–25. Belfast: The Irish Pages Press, 2016.

Casanova, Pascale. *The World Republic of Letters*, translated by M. B. DeBevoise. Cambridge, MA: Harvard University Press, 2004.

Deane, Seamus. 'Political writings and speeches, 1850–1918'. In *The Field Day Anthology of Irish Writing*, Volume 2, edited by Seamus Deane, 209–14. Derry: Field Day Publications in association with W. W. Norton, 1989.

Griffith, Arthur. *The Resurrection of Hungary: A parallel for Ireland*. 3rd edition. Dublin: Whelan and Son, 1904.

Marx, Karl. *Revolution and Counter-Revolution: Or, Germany in 1848*, edited by Eleanor Marx Aveling. Chicago: C. H. Kerr, 1907.

West, Rebecca. *Black Lamb and Grey Falcon: A journey through Yugoslavia*. Harmondsworth: Penguin Books, 1994.

28
Krystyna Gryczełowska maps a moving Poland
Eliza Rose

How does an Anti-Atlas incorporate time in its presentation of space? Scholars of Eastern Europe have been used to conceiving of the opposition of rural and urban culture in their region in relatively fixed terms, one a space of the past and the other a space of the future. Rose's piece examines the Polish documentary maker, Krystyna Gryczełowska, whose pioneering practice maps not territory, but movement, and the way that, in the everyday trajectories of peasants, workers and administrators in 1960s and 1970s Poland, that relationship between the city and the countryside is constructed by conflicting and multidirectional narratives of modernisation, regression and flight.

Krystyna Gryczełowska spent her career producing social diagnostics in the documentary film form. Gryczełowska joined Warsaw's Documentary Studio after finishing her degree in 1955 at Moscow's All-Russian State University of Cinematography (VGIK). She belonged to a fleet of Moscow-trained filmmakers (such as Jerzy Hoffman and Edward Skórzewski) and a cadre of women (Danuta Halladin, Irena Kamieńska, Maria Kwiatkowska and editors Agnieszka Bojanowska, Lidia Zonn and Jadwiga Zajiček) shaping a new generation of Polish documentary. Several of them were Vilnius-born (Zajiček, Zonn, Gryczełowska herself) and rode the wave of Polish migration from eastern Kresy – a region whose multiethnic composition lessened after postwar territorial realignments.

Gryczełowska and her Moscow classmates imported into the Polish scene a commitment to the documentary form as sociological probe. Their arrival in Poland was timely. The National Film School, founded in Łódź in 1948, was turning out its first graduates, and Warsaw's

Documentary Studio (established that same year) offered infrastructure for early-career auteurs. In 1955, the Polish film industry splintered into five production units, opening a conducive landscape for regionally engaged film and a heterogeneous national cinema compared to the more consolidated Soviet model.[1]

October of the following year brought a paradigm shift in political and social life that recalibrated documentary film's task within socialism. First Secretary Władysław Gomułka's public pronouncement, that 'words had not found their reflection in actual reality', called into question the status of the documentary image. These words, part of the speech with which Gomułka inaugurated the Polish thaw, were an authoritative admission of a discrepancy between façade and fact, image and experience – a discrepancy that documentary newsreels, purporting to a privileged claim on truth, had obfuscated rather than exposed.

The Black Series (*Czarna seria*) movement, with which Gryczełowska was affiliated, coalesced in the wake of that October and interpreted Gomułka's performance as licence to relieve documentary film of its palliative duties to the state. Black Series filmmakers sourced aesthetic cues from Italian neorealism, British socially engaged documentary of the 1930s and the Soviet pedigree of their training. Documentary's new task was to compile evidence of the gap between reported success and the political system's actual ability to articulate and satisfy its constituents' needs. The voiceover of Włodzimierz Borowik's *Article Zero* (1956), a film calling for legislation to regulate prostitution, reports: 'We are collecting material for sociologists and lawyers'.

Gryczełowska's *Siedliszcze* (1960) self-reflexively confronts the exploitability of its medium. The film's first minutes show a 1954 Polish Film Chronicle newsreel celebrating the revitalisation of the eponymous village, now equipped with sidewalks, sports facilities and a hospital. The cited footage slides smoothly into Gryczełowska's intervention on the same (exerting opposite effects to collision montage). Six years later, Gryczełowska surveyed the same sites, employed an eerily similar voiceover and even emulated the newsreel's ratio of establishing shots to vignettes of local heroes. This time, however, the same formula uncovers an under-resourced, struggling town. Carrying over the newsreel's discursive style, Gryczełowska critiqued her genre's historical duplicity without parting from its syntax, thus modelling the course corrections her films demanded of the state. If she could massage documentary into an instrument of honest critique, couldn't the state bring the same acuity and humility to its reforms?

Favouring the surgical strike over sweeping condemnation, *Siedliszcze* and the films that follow are spot analyses of administrative shortcomings. Mikołaj Jazdon and others have argued that metonymic or *pars pro toto* critique was a camouflage strategy meant to placate censors by targeting critique to discrete institutions.[2] Yet we can also read this tactic as an earnest attempt to generate implementable suggestions for change. By acquiescing to the parameters of her industry, Gryczełowska retained the state as her (listening?) addressee. Her films show us what it looks like for critique to inch toward reform by identifying concrete problems and possible solutions. In this way, they supplemented the glitchy monitoring system of a Party administration slow to remediate its mistakes. In Gryczełowska's hands, documentary became a conduit for relaying grievances from below to above and from periphery to centre.

The film *…In February, 1971* (*…W Lutym, 1971*) continues this work by mapping negative power zones within the state's machinery of response. A group of deputies descends on a village outside Krakow bearing promises, projections and plans. The local population greets them with distrust. Gryczełowska considered titling the film *Five Weeks After December*, to make explicit its link to the December 1970 protests at the Gdańsk shipyards.[3] The film's objective, then, was to verify the Party's capacity to respond to crisis by feeding bottom-up critique into the decision chain. Legislative decisions can be fast, but their effects are felt over time. Gryczełowska's films are often anchored in one year but reference a previous one (*Siedliszcze*; *In February 1971*), plotting the two points necessary to measure rate of change. She was more interested in the months following unrest than cataclysmic oppositional events.

Gryczełowska's preference for temporal peripheries (aftermath over event) had a geographical analogue in her favouring of rural subjects. With her sharp eye for overlooked time periods and land tracts, she issued a career-long reminder that the centre is best monitored from its (bleeding) edge. Her films were in dialogue with the Russian Village Prose movement and 'Little Realism' (*mały realism*) in Poland. In the 1950s context, rural cinema countered the medium's obsession with urban hubs as the face of a reconstructed and rejuvenated postwar Poland. Today, the rural fixation persists in films by Anka and Wilhelm Sasnal (*Alexander*; *It Looks Pretty from a Distance*; *Swineherd*). The land serves this tradition as a migrating metaphor with uneven ideological uses. While work by her contemporaries (Włodzimierz Borowik's *Stony Earth*; Władysław Ślesicki's *Family of Man*) tends to accentuate ethereal pastures and the human face nobly ravaged by time, Gryczełowska favoured a straightforward talking-head format and often filmed her subjects at work. In her films, it is not the land that speaks but the people who cultivate it, subsist from it and feed it in turn. Rarely do her landscape shots wax poetic. Her idiom consists of soggy fields, skeletal trees, stone-choked soil and a muddy horizon bleeding into grey sky. This makes poor fodder for cults of blood and soil. These rural portraits cannot be leveraged to justify territorial claims on Poland as a rooted or ethnically discrete unit.

Gryczełowska's films dispel the illusive perception of the journey to the country as a regression in time. 'Backwards?', asks the narrator of *Krzeczowice: Fall* (1972). 'No, no, no. You can't call this backwards. These people have two, three hectares of land. Enough that tending it is hard work, but too little to modernise.' Following land reforms in 1944–8, the smallholder farmer became an increasingly unviable class category and gave way to a new class of *chłoporobotniks* – farmers forced to commute to jobs in industrial hubs. Gryczełowska's villages had not been left behind in time, nor had they dropped off the map. They were networked into the city grid, supplying it with workers. Their contribution of labour power yoked them to a system that inadequately attended to their needs.

For Gryczełowska, the farmer-worker's circumstances were man made, changing and changeable in turn. She reckoned with the farmer-worker's status as the proletariat's uneasy ally, revealing how the dialogue developing between managers and the managed in the industrial workplace left agricultural workers unspoken for. Gryczełowska filmed the journey from village to city but concentrated on the return home (never overdetermined as a return to origins): workers disembarking from the train after work, and sons and daughters renovating their parents' houses with income earned in the city.

Gryczełowska trained her camera on lines of flight, migration patterns and the traffic of those shuttling between village and city as work in both waxed and waned with harvest and production cycles. *His Name is Błażej Rejdak* (1968) follows a railroad signalman taking leave to farm his land. Błażej concludes his night shift with a shower at the station restroom, as if he must slough off one identity before transitioning to the next. 'Man divided', he muses, later, bent over his land, breaking up clods of hardened soil as winter thaws and growing season begins. The peasant-worker experience is somewhat specific to the Polish socialist context, where the collectivisation of agriculture never spread to the Soviet scale. To the extent that it did, Gryczełowska was there, watching: *Pegeerowcy* (*The PGR-ers*, 1970) documents work at the Łankiejmy state farm. Still, her sustained attention to small-scale landowners foregrounds the unevenness of social life that can trail behind economic changes.

'Backwards? No, no, no', we hear in *Krzeczowice*. Dissociating peasant experience from the future is a fallacy. John Berger has emphasised peasant farmers' continuous interface with the future: 'Everything they do is anticipatory – and therefore never finished'. In 'a sequence of repeated acts of survival', they maintain an open pact with a future whose conditions they continuously fulfil.[4] This pact binds them to a community-to-come populated by agents human (progeny) and nonhuman (crops, livestock, soil). The protagonist of *His Name is Błażej* bikes circles around his yard, his son perched behind him on the seat, their dog running alongside the wheel. The triumvirate's laps cut against the zig-zag routes of Błażej's railway shifts – visual figures of circular versus unilinear time.

If we extrapolate from Gryczełowska's surgical strikes to an indictment relevant today, it might be this: her films problematise the segmentation of Poland into zones more and less worthy of investment as parts of Poland's future. Such segmentation presumes society to be an organism whose parts hang together in equilibrium. Gryczełowska hovered over those parts that did not benefit from the growth of the whole. Socialism's promise included the equalisation of living standards across regions. Gryczełowska's films are nearly quantitative indices of the uneven availability of social services (housing, health services, sports clubs, swimming pools) in underserved regions. Any vision of Poland that allots its regions unequal stakes in the future implicitly imagines an immune system for the state within which resources naturally flow from parts that are healthy to those that are unwell. The countryside becomes the remainder of an equation that does not quite balance, serving the city as hygienic outlet and labour supply.

Gryczełowska's films resist this logic. Her meticulous storytelling, poised at fault lines between unsynchronised Polands, indicts how we segment space to construct narratives that serve us. One such narrative is the figure of progress as the journey from village to city. Gryczełowska's films instead visualise progress as a staggered series of lurches and lags. They remind us that for every train passenger who experiences the journey between cities as fluid flight, comfortably cushioned, bucolic fields blurry behind a pane of glass, there is a signalman like Błażej Rejdak experiencing this same passage as jolts felt in a body uninsulated from turbulence, jumping off and on a train in motion.

Notes

1 Sørenssen, 2012, 191.
2 Jazdon, 2014.
3 Kołodyński, 2009, 95.
4 Berger, 1992, xvii and xix.

Bibliography

Berger, John. *Pig Earth*. New York: Vintage International, 1992.

Jazdon, Mikołaj. 'Część zamiast całości, czyli sposób na cenzorów. *Szkoła podstawowa* Tomasza Zygadły – wzorcowy film kina "nowej zmiany"' [Part instead of the whole, or a way to cope with censors. Tomasz Zygadło's primary school – a model film of the 'new change' cinema], *Images: The International Journal of European Film, Performing Arts and Audiovisual Communication* 15 (2014): 281–6.

Kołodyński, Andrzej. 'Krystyna Gryczełowska: 1931–2009', *Kino* 43 (2009): 95.

Sørenssen, Bjøn. 'The Polish Black Series documentary and the British free cinema movement'. In *A Companion to Eastern European Cinemas*, edited by Anikó Imre, 183–200. Hoboken: Wiley-Blackwell, 2012.

29
The engineer as indispensable critic
Jelena Prokopljević

Across the many different times, spaces, phases and 'new natures' of the state socialist project, the figure of the engineer occupied a fraught, tense but central role: utterly critical to the construction of socialism as an indispensable agent of its infrastructural modernity, but also consistently critical of its mode of implementation, vulnerable to persecution but also voluble and impactful in consequence of her infrastructural indispensability.

The task of the engineer in socialist culture spanned various fields, from the control and exploitation of natural resources to all types of transportation, communication and construction. Their services were exported internationally and used to forge connections between nations within the socialist bloc and beyond. The works of hydraulic, aerodynamic, structural or mechanical engineers were critical to the implementation of the socialist project, while their precision and professionalism inspired both political discourse and artistic creation. However, in a number of cases, their very professionalism revealed the shortcomings of socialist planning, placing engineers in a contradictory relationship with the socialist system. Unintentionally or not, the work of engineers rendered a critique of the implementation of the socialist project, making them both critical *to* and critical *of* it.

For the realisation of the socialist project, technological progress was pivotal and the basis for the system's legitimacy, limiting its subversive potential, but at the same time scientific and technological development continually threatened the institutional framework within which technology operated. This duality grants technology a critical capacity that situates it in the realm of political ideology.[1] In the socialist bloc the indirect critique based on technical excellence – often beyond proper understanding by the powers that be – was rarely openly formulated, therefore almost never directly confronted. (This does not mean that some renowned engineers didn't experience purges and imprisonments, although they were mostly charged with strictly political crimes and not for their scientific or professional work.) Nevertheless, the perfect execution of a project can open a discussion – in line with Mannheim's paradox – that confronts the congruence of a political ideology with the dynamic reality it frames.[2]

For public opinion, engineers were the authentic builders of socialism: their structural improvements allowed for larger and taller constructions; research into the characteristics and production of materials made it possible to build more and faster; innovative interventions in the natural environment brought about more efficient exploitation of resources. The critical capacity of the engineer derived from the magnitude of their tasks in both the material and ideological sense; and it diminished as their projects were reduced in scale and importance. The meaning and the consequences of their actions varied depending on their moment in the history of socialism, while an appreciation of the critical content of those actions derives from a contextual reading of the plan and its realisation.

In the early post-revolutionary years, engineers and constructors inspired the proclamation of the death of 'art for art's sake' in favour of a new, technologically inspired art, critical of history, tradition and culture.[3] Structure and machine defined the beauty of the new epoch, exemplified by the first large-scale permanent structure in Moscow built during the civil war, the Shabolovka radio tower, a technologically innovative work by the structural engineer Vladimir Shukhov. The figure of the engineer was at the centre of the transformation of nature, through great hydraulic works, railway and highway network construction, and high-rise buildings that symbolised the progress of the socialist world. The poetic – utopian – potential of the engineer was used as a compliment and exhortation in Stalin's speech at the reunion of Soviet writers at Gorky's house in the fall of 1932: 'Man is reshaped by life itself, and those of you here must assist in reshaping his soul. That is what is important, the production of human souls. And that is why I raise my glass to you, writers, to the engineers of the soul!'[4]

The meeting at Gorky's house resulted in an unprecedented expedition of 120 Soviet writers to the construction works of the White Sea Canal and the subsequent elaboration of a 600-page collective book that blurred the individual style and authorship of its contributors in emulation of the engineering project it depicted. This document of the construction of a 200-kilometre-long navigable connection between Leningrad and the White Sea, built by convict labour, was the inaugural volume for a special genre of socialist realist 'hydraulic' literature praising the figure of engineer and constructor. However, the construction of navigable canals provoked varied adverse ecological consequences, among them the inversion of river flows and the extinction of local ecosystems, even the disappearance of the Aral Sea.[5] The perfect execution of these large-scale works proved problematic in the long run.

The Soviet hydraulic works inspired similar feats throughout the socialist world. The construction of the Three Gorges Dam on the Yangtze River, an enormous project that took over five decades to realise, led to the flooding of 1,300 archaeological sites, 13 cities and 140 towns, provoking the relocation of over a million inhabitants from the surrounding territories and substantially altering the natural environment. During the 1950s Hundred Flowers Campaign, in which Mao promoted the benefits of the dam, a hydraulic engineer named Huang Wanli openly questioned the project. He was then charged with belonging to a right-wing party, imprisoned, sent to a re-education labour camp and publicly humiliated. A similar, but smaller scale, project was the Yugoslav-Romanian Djerdap hydroelectric power station, built on the Danube's Iron Gate in the 1980s. The opening ceremony featured Tito and Ceaușescu greeting each other and crossing the dam together, overlooking the reservoir that flooded Lepenski Vir, the most important Mesolithic and Neolithic archaeological site in the central Balkans.

The early postwar architecture of many socialist countries was marked by socialist realism, incorporated into the triumphalist discourse of the victory of socialism over fascism and capitalism. However, as early as 1947, as Moscow's first monumental skyscrapers were opening, architect and engineer Vitaly Lagutenko was developing the first experimental system for prefabricated housing. Over the next decade it would evolve into the famous K7 system. The prefabricated construction questioned Stalinist monumental rhetoric, through its use of identikit industrialised concrete panels rather than richly decorated neoclassical façades, but was extensively applied after Khruschev proclaimed, in 1954, the urgent need for economically efficient housing construction. Lagutneko's prefabs, and the improved types that followed, became the model for residential neighbourhoods throughout the socialist bloc and were exported to Asian and African non-aligned nations. As the *Khruschevka* began to dominate the cityscape,[6] the engineer became the central figure in the creation of modular elements, structural solutions and new materials. Architecture and construction became the product of a collective effort that effectively critiqued individual authorship.

Prefabricated construction systems triggered the rapid development of the building materials industry, especially reinforced concrete components. These were dependent on heavy industry, the ideological base of the socialist economy. Countries faced varying degrees of difficulty in implementing the new system while satisfying the number of new housing units demanded by the five-year plans. During the 1950s, North Korea suffered from a huge housing shortage after the disastrous Korean War. Mandated by Kim Il Sung, who was forging his own political legitimacy through housing for the broad population, prefabricated construction was elevated to the national political agenda. The leader's personality cult grew as a function of industrial modernisation, new systems of construction and the new image of cities. The process went largely unquestioned, except by one voice: Kim Sung Hwa, a Tashkent-born and Moscow-trained structural engineer, who at the time was Minister of Construction of DPRK. He argued that the lack of relevant industries would result in poor quality new construction and that, at least for short-term planning, traditional methods would bring better results. This ended his career, and he was exiled to Moscow under accusations of instigating a pro-Soviet conspiracy. His successor, Choe Jae Ha, the first worker to ascend to a ministerial position, was responsible for implementing the Chollima movement – the North Korean version of the Great Leap Forward – based on industrialisation and prefabrication. The effects of accelerated building and production competition to surpass the established quantitative norms led to poor-quality structures that required improvements or reconstruction during the five-year plan.[7]

Concrete became the new nature of the socialist city. In Yugoslavia, starting in the 1950s, important advances were made in prestressed concrete structures, developed by the engineer Branko Žeželj and the Institute of Materials of Serbia. The prestressed prefabrication system, called IMS-Žeželj, was capable of covering large spans with thin and elegant concrete arches or beams. These were exported to various socialist and non-aligned countries.[8] Žeželj himself talked about the engineer as the tamer of this new 'natural' element.[9] Especially in the 1960s and 70s, when prestressed concrete structures became common in mass construction and new solutions overtook outdated building regulations, construction engineering articulated the need for a scientific renewal of production systems, more efficient communication and more freedom in decision-making. State bureaucracy and interventionism became the target of professional critiques, but they were rarely pronounced publicly. Instead, Žežel's collaborator Branislav Vojnović remembers the 'alternative diplomacy' that Žežel had to use in order to obtain permission for an innovative bridge foundation on the Danube in Novi Sad. He included experts linked to the administration in the design team and drew on his friendship with Tito, with whom he sometimes went hunting, to persuade politicians in the evaluation committee.[10] As Jovanović explains through the example of construction in New Belgrade, the quality of housing projects was undermined by spreading building commissions among multiple state building companies, regardless of the feasibility of their proposed solutions. When critique was solely private, and led only to compromise, quality suffered.

In the midst of the economic crises of the early 1980s, socialist Romania was building its new administrative headquarters, the huge People's House (now Palace of the Parliament), set at the end of the monumental Boulevard of the Victory of Socialism, in central Bucharest. Inspired by his trip to Pyongyang, Ceaușescu himself supervised the execution of the young architect Anca Petrescu's design and issued orders to facilitate the construction, including the demolition of existing urban quarters. The name of the engineer Eugeniu Iordăchescu – who invented a system for relocating buildings, among them important Orthodox churches and monasteries – became ingrained in the collective memory of the city. Iordăchescu's technological intervention in favour of historical and religious heritage represented a bold criticism of this monumental project, while allowing the construction of the monument to Ceaușescu's dictatorial regime to continue according to plan.

Engineering and construction were the main exports of some socialist countries to the non-aligned world. Energoprojekt and Union Inženjering, the largest Yugoslav construction enterprises, and the Polish Energoexport and Miastoprojekt, were involved in infrastructural, hydraulic and construction works throughout Africa, the Middle East and South America. A wide range of state-owned construction firms carried out similar projects: Bulgarian Technoexport or Bulgarprojekt, Hungarian Közti, Stroj Projekt and Armbeton from Czechoslovakia.[11] More liberal working conditions in the former colonial and capitalist states accentuated the need to revise domestic regulations in terms of patents, permits, taxes and control. Efficient and profit-oriented construction and reduction of state control were imported from construction sites in the non-aligned world and, especially in the case of Energoprojekt, contributed to the early transition towards capitalism in Yugoslavia.[12]

In the 1980s, the first laws permitting private entrepreneurship highlighted the rigid bureaucracy of the public and productive realm.

Perestroika and other anti-bureaucratic revolutions were, among other things, processes of repositioning the engineer and rescaling their role as social and political actors. The free market economy, privatisation and reduction of state companies diminished the figure of the structural, hydraulic or aeronautic engineer as condenser of the functional critique of state socialism.

Documenting the relations between important engineering projects and the political decisions behind them, as well as the consequences of the finished works, broadens the analysis of the implementation of socialism at its different stages. These cases highlight the double sense of being critical: both indispensable and judgemental or even condemnatory, although both meanings were not usually expressed simultaneously. They also reveal the complicated, even frustrated dialogue between the realms of politics and technology, despite their mutual dependency for legitimation and realisation. The position of engineers in socialism was unique: like a mirror, their work had the ability to reveal systemic shortcomings in scale, distribution, spatial and work organisation, multidisciplinary planning and social and ecological impact.

Notes

1. Habermas, 1970.
2. Breiner, 2013.
3. Gan, 2014; Chernikhov, 1990.
4. Westerman, 2005, 49.
5. Westerman, 2005; revisited by Fatland, 2019.
6. Hatherley, 2015.
7. Mateos Miret and Prokopljević, 2012.
8. Jovanović, 2017.
9. RTS-TVB, 1978.
10. Vojnović, 2015.
11. Stanek, 2020.
12. Sekulić, Krstić and Dolinka, 2013.

Bibliography

Breiner, Peter. 'Karl Mannheim and political ideology'. In *The Oxford Handbook of Political Ideologies*, edited by Michael Freeden and Marc Stears, 38–55. Oxford: Oxford University Press, 2013.

Chernikhov, Y. *The Construction of Architectural and Machine Forms*. Serbian edition [Konstrukcije arhitektonskih i mašinskih formi]. Belgrade: Gradjevinska knjiga, 1990.

Fatland, Erika. *Sovietistan: A journey through Turkmenistan, Kazakhstan, Tajikistan, Kyrgyzstan and Uzbekistan*. Spanish edition. Barcelona: Tusquets editors, 2019.

Gan, Aleksei. *Konstruktivizm*. Spanish edition. Barcelona: Tenov, 2014.

Habermas, Jurgen. 'Technology and science as ideology'. In *Toward a Rational Society*, translated by J. Shapiro, 81–122. Boston: Beacon Press, 1970.

Hatherley, Owen. *Landscapes of Communism*. London: Penguin Books, 2015.
Jovanović, Jelica. 'Mass heritage of New Belgrade: Housing laboratory and so much more', *Periodica Polytechnica Architecture* 48(2) (2017): 106–12.
Mateos Miret, Roger and Jelena Prokopljević. *Corea del Norte – Utopía de Hormigón: Arquitectura y urbanismo al servicio de una ideología* [North Korea – Concrete Utopia: Architecture and urbanism in the service of an ideology]. Brenes, Sevilla: Muñoz Moya Editores, 2012.
RTS-TVB. 'Čarobnjak prednapregnutog betona' [The wizard of prestressed concrete]. RTS-TVB, 1978. Accessed 12 August 2024. https://www.dailymotion.com/video/x3924r6.
Sekulić, Dubravka, Katarina Krstić and Andrej Dolinka, eds. *Three Points of Support: Zoran Bojović*. Belgrade: Museum of Contemporary Art, 2013.
Stanek, Łukasz. *Architecture in Global Socialism: Eastern Europe, West Africa, and the Middle East in the Cold War*. Princeton, NJ: Princeton University Press, 2020.
Vojnović, Branko. 'My encounters with Branko Žeželj'. Republic of Serbia Intellectual Property Office (2015). Accessed 2 April 2021. https://www.zis.gov.rs/intellectual-property-rights/patents/famous-serbian-inventors.1099.html.
Westerman, Frank. *Engineers of the Soul: The grandiose propaganda of Stalin's Russia*. Spanish edition. Madrid: Siruela, 2005.

30
Il'f and Petrov
Lisa A. Kirschenbaum

In analysing the American experiences of two Soviet satirists, Il'f and Petrov, Kirschenbaum here advocates for a critical area studies that looks beyond bounded geographical regions and instead maps individual lives, zones of contact, cultural exchanges and hybrid identities. Following this guidance upends not only the canonical division between the socialist and capitalist worlds, but also the rigid, enemy-obsessed binaries of Western Cold War area studies: to quote the often-censored American cartoonist, Walt Kelly: 'We have met the enemy, and he is us'.

> Where does the Russian lady live? The village of Rio Chiquito, New Mexico, United States.
>
> Il'ia Il'f, letter to his wife, Mariia Nikolavena Il'f, 26 November 1935

In 1935, in the midst of the Great Depression, the Soviet satirists Il'ia Il'f and Evgenii Petrov, already famous for their novel *The Twelve Chairs*, set off on a ten-week, ten-thousand-mile road trip across the United States. They documented their search for the 'real America', beyond the skyscrapers of New York, in a series of photo essays in the popular magazine *Ogonëk* and in the book *Odnoetazhnaia Amerika* (Single-storey America), published in 1937 in both the Soviet Union and the US, where it appeared under the title *Little Golden America*.[1]

Finding America proved challenging in part because, as the letter quoted in the epigraph suggests, the writers met Russians in places like New Mexico, that they imagined as a world away from Russia. Sometimes these meetings were unplanned, as in the case of their chance encounter with the 'Russian lady' Alexandra Fechina (the former wife of the Russian émigré painter Nicolai Fechin) in Taos.[2] Additionally, to an extent unacknowledged in their published texts, Il'f and Petrov relied on Russian Americans – and Americans who had spent time in Soviet Russia – as hosts, translators and guides. Although Il'f and Petrov's published work concluded with a canonical emphasis on the 'distance' that separated 'the capitalist world' from 'the world of socialism', their letters home, Il'f's diary and significant sections of *Odnoetazhnaia Amerika* itself offer a model of critical area studies. Their search for 'real America' took them though an archipelago of immigrant, exile and fellow traveller communities that stretched from Hartford, Connecticut to Los Angeles, California. In these communities, among people who identified as both Russian and American, who sympathised with the Soviet Union even as they sometimes made prosperous lives in the US, Il'f and Petrov tracked the transnational trajectories of people and ideas that traditional area studies can obscure.

Il'f and Petrov travelled as reporters for *Pravda*, and their travelogue had to clear the Soviet censors, but their account was not straightforward anticapitalist propaganda. The America they described was at once the spiritually impoverished antithesis of the socialist utopia under construction in the USSR and, even during the Depression, a 'phenomenally rich' model of efficiency and modernity. As many analyses of *Odnoetazhnaia Amerika* note, the authors, drawing on a long-standing Russian and Soviet appreciation of *Amerikanizm*, found much to admire in American technology and in the no-nonsense American attitude that allowed Henry Ford's employees to greet him by his first name.[3] Certainly the book provides plenty of sweeping, even condescending, generalisations about Americans: they are loud and always laughing; they have a strange affinity for drinking orange juice; they prefer trashy movies to good books. Il'f and Petrov's American translator highlighted the contrasts they noted between the Soviet Union and the US, titling the book's penultimate chapter 'They and We'. But Il'f and Petrov also found plenty of 'Americans' who did not fit the stereotypes. Their own more ambiguous title for their valedictory chapter is 'Bespokoĭnaia zhizn' – unsettled life.

Engaging with instability, the inadequacy of canonical categories, and the illusion of fixed boundaries, Il'f and Petrov demonstrate how to move beyond a 'know your enemy' framing of area studies that, while politically useful, slights historical complexities.[4] The most important and central 'complex hybrid' in their story is Mr. Adams, their 'guide-chauffeur-interpreter-altruist'. As the literary scholar Milla Fedorova notes, Mr. Adams and his wife blur the boundary between *svoi* (one's own) and *chuzhoe* (the Other): They are Other because they are Americans; at the same time, they are 'ours', not 'ethnically', but because they 'share socialist ideals'. Il'f and Petrov introduce Mr. Adams as an American engineer who worked for General Electric in the Soviet Union; like Mrs. Adams, who actually did the driving, he spoke excellent Russian. What they neglect to mention is that Mr. Adams's real-life counterpart, Solomon A. Trone, was born in 1872 in the Russian Empire (Mitau, now Jelgava, Latvia), and in 1916 emigrated to the US. After Il'f and Petrov returned to Moscow, Trone wrote to them that he and his American wife Florence 'would very much like to settle in the Union and work there'. By turning Trone into the American Mr. Adams, Il'f and Petrov evaded uncomfortable questions about why a Russian engineer, whose expertise was needed in the Soviet Union, chose to remain in the United States. Yet even as an American, he troubles the divide between 'ours' and 'Other', as do other American acquaintances. The muckraking journalist Lincoln Steffens, who in 1919 famously wrote of Soviet Russia, 'I have seen the future, and it works', tells Il'f and Petrov that his last wish is to die in the Soviet Union. When revealed as a Russian American, the 'hybrid' Mr. Adams becomes even more 'complex', and the line between capitalist and socialist 'areas' becomes increasingly fuzzy.

Often interacting with people who lived 'at the blurry juncture of two worlds', Il'f and Petrov suggest a means of reconceptualising area studies as a study of the relationships between globalisation, regional particularities and individual lives – what I have elsewhere called 'area studies without borders'. This approach allows us to rethink what constitutes the 'area' – or how we 'map difference'.[5] Rather than delineating geographically bounded 'regions', critical area studies maps the personal and institutional networks that constitute transnational 'regions' or zones of contact, highlighting cultural exchanges and hybrid identities.

In Il'f and Petrov, this critical approach to area studies is in tension with the canonical emphasis on 'us' and 'them'. The tension is clearly visible in the Hollywood episode of their journey, only part of which they narrated in their published work. In both *Odnoetazhnaia Amerika* and their letters home, Il'f and Petrov disparage the American film industry, dismissing the bulk of its products as vulgar, violent and formulaic 'trash' (*drian'*). However, this judgement did not prevent them from seeing as many movies as possible. They tell readers that they went to the cinema almost every night in New York City and every night on the road, viewing by their own estimate more than a hundred feature films and at least as many newsreels, shorts and animated cartoons over a span of four months. It seems they retained to the end a 'vestige of hope', as they wrote in *Odnoetazhnaia Amerika*, that the films they saw in the US would match the quality of the films of Hollywood's 'best' directors – Lewis Milestone, King Vidor, John Ford and Rouben Mamoulian – that they had seen in Moscow. Indeed, these same directors privately screened 'the best' films for Il'f and Petrov, movies that compared favourably to (and were to some extent models for) the best Soviet films.

What Il'f and Petrov left out of *Odnoetazhnaia Amerika* was the story of how they themselves became small players in the American movie industry. Indeed, their story suggests that the Hollywood movie industry was not narrowly 'American' at all. As they documented in their letters home, they worked frantically over five days at the end of December 1935 to produce a twenty-two-page treatment of their novel *The Twelve Chairs*. They worked at the invitation of Lewis Milestone, who Petrov characterised as 'very Soviet-minded'. The transaction was likely facilitated and perhaps in part motivated by the fact that Milestone was a Russian American immigrant (born Leib Milstein in 1895 in Bessarabia). Il'f and Petrov received an advance of about 600 dollars and were promised a minimum of 3,000 dollars if Milestone succeeded in selling a screenplay based on their treatment.

Like many of the Russian Americans they met in Hollywood, Il'f and Petrov appear to have had both commercial and artistic ambitions. Both wrote ecstatically to their wives that the sale would make it possible to take 'our trusty Ford' to Moscow. Petrov looked forward to buying a second Ford with the proceeds from the screenplay. But their motivations, like those of their Hollywood peers, were not entirely mercenary. Both were pleased with their work and seemed to think that in the right hands the scenario might turn out to be one of the (alas, few) good Hollywood pictures. From directors and actors they admired, Il'f and Petrov learned that the problem was, as Petrov reported without apparent irony, the 'brutal censorship (church and political)' and the studio bosses, who prevented artists from 'breathing freely'. Although Il'f and Petrov distanced themselves from the complaints of the 'Hollywood serfs', they had similar experiences with the Soviet film industry. Before leaving for the US, they had demanded their scriptwriting credit be removed from Grigorii Aleksandrov's American-themed movie musical, *Circus*, because they objected to the director's decision to turn what he characterised as a 'light-hearted eccentric comedy' into a 'melodrama' better suited to the propaganda needs of the moment. What Il'f and Petrov did not know (or did not report) was that their Hollywood sojourn coincided with the directors' growing resolve to stand up to the studios. On 23 December 1935, thirteen directors met, according to the *New York Times*, 'in great secrecy' at King Vidor's house to lay the groundwork for the Screen Directors Guild, which, like the pioneering Screen Actors and Writers Guilds (and unlike the Union of Soviet Writers) worked to protect creative workers' financial and artistic interests. Vidor became the Guild's president and the 'very Soviet-minded' Milestone its first vice president.

In Il'f and Petrov's encounter with the movie business in Hollywood – and indeed with the United States in general – neither the players, the productions nor the problems were entirely Other. At the end of their road trip, they affirmed that 'throughout the entire journey we never once stopped thinking of the Soviet Union'. But the constant presence of an imagined Soviet Union did not dictate a strictly canonical story of the fundamental distinctiveness and superiority of the Soviet 'socialist arrangement of our life'. Even in New York City, the capital of capitalist hell, where they expected Mephistopheles to spring out of one of the steam vents, they found people like Trone, who shared their sensibilities and dreams. Thus, within the canonical text they provided a counter-canonical story of personal, ideological, artistic and commercial intersections and exchanges. Looking for 'real' America, they found (and relied on) a far-flung community of Russian Americans, who blurred the boundaries between 'us' and 'them'. Il'f and Petrov's Soviet American road trip points the way to a globalised area studies that focuses on transnational connections and the permeability of the lines between worlds, even the possibility of the Other being very much like us.

Notes

1. Il'f and Petrov, 1937; All quotations are from the English translation. Their photo essays have been translated as Il'f and Petrov, 2007.
2. All letters cited are from Il'f, 2003.
3. Fedorova, 2006, 73–92.
4. Engerman, 2009.
5. Greenstein, 2014, 263; Kirschenbaum, 2018; Morris-Suzuki, 2000, 20.

Bibliography

Engerman, David. *Know Your Enemy: The rise and fall of America's Soviet experts.* New York: Oxford University Press, 2009.

Fedorova, Milla. *Yankees in Petrograd, Bolsheviks in New York: America and Americans in Russian literary perception.* DeKalb: Northern Illinois University Press, 2006.

Greenstein, David E. 'Assembling Fordizm: The production of automobiles, Americans, and Bolsheviks in Detroit and early Soviet Russia', *Comparative Studies in Society and History* 56(2) (2014): 259–89.

Il'f, Il'ia and Evgeniĭ Petrov. *Odnoetazhnaia Amerika* [Single-storey America]. Moscow: Khudozhestvennaia literatura, 1937.

Ilf, Ilya and Eugene Petrov. *Little Golden America: Two famous Soviet humorists survey the United States*, translated by Charles Malamuth. New York: Farrar and Rinehart, 1937.

Il'f, Il'ia and Evgeniĭ Petrov. *Odnoetazhnaia Amerika: Pis'ma iz Ameriku* [Single-storey America: Letters from America], edited by A. I. Il'f. Moscow: Tekst, 2003.

Ilf, Ilya and Eugene Petrov. *Ilf and Petrov's American Road Trip: The 1935 Travelogue of Two Soviet Writers Ilya Ilf and Evgeny Petrov*, edited by Erika Wolf, translated by Anne O. Fischer. New York: Cabinet Books, 2007.

Kirschenbaum, Lisa. 'Reframing Slavic studies and the global impacts of 1917'. In *Russia's Great War and Revolution: The wider arc of revolution*, edited by Choi Chatterjee, Steven Marks, Steve Sabol and Mary Neuberger, 345–58. Bloomington, IN: Slavica, 2018.

Morris-Suzuki, Tessa. 'Anti-area studies', *Communal/Plural* 8(1) (2000): 9–23.

31
Komunistki: Polish communist women
Agnieszka Mrozik

In late capitalist (or wild capitalist) Poland, several categories of people are aggressively excluded from the official register of full-fledged humanity, whether present-day or historical, as promoted by the current regime: migrants, Muslims, foreigners, Jews, non-heterosexual people, women and people of left-wing persuasion (in particular, communists from the period of the Polish People's Republic). Communist women, then, are not well-positioned for a place in the national pantheon. Many communist women were also of Jewish heritage (but almost all are imagined by the official discourse to have been Jewish), some were foreign and some were gay. In this text, Mrozik explains the particularly vicious demonisation attached in the Polish language to the epithet komunistka; and tells short stories about the real lives of several komunistki – Róża Luksemburg (Rosa Luxemburg), Wanda Wasilewska and Zofia Dembińska – as embodiments, both in their own time and today, of the figure of the boundary-crossing but barricade-building activist-critic, each of whom played a central, positive role in the formation of the modern world.

At the 2017 Budapest conference *Ruptures, Empires and Revolutions*, the name of Polish Marxist Rosa Luxemburg (1871–1919) arose in connection with the 1968 student rebellion in Japan: 'Red Rosa' was an icon of radicalised Japanese youth. The German researcher moderating the discussion admitted that she had forgotten Luxemburg's Polish roots. She remembered her involvement in the German communist movement, and so as anchored in German political memory and present, one of 'their own'. A few months later, following legislation meant to decommunise Poland, the Polish Right took it upon itself to rid Polish history and memory of Rosa Luxemburg, by removing a commemorative plaque from the house in Zamość, in south-eastern Poland, where 'Red Rosa' was born.

Another example: Wanda Wasilewska (1905–1964), a communist writer and politician, to this day remains one of the best-recognised Polish women in Ukraine. Unsurprisingly, as she lived in Kyiv after World War II, her grave is there, and Ukrainian anthologies of twentieth-century literature still contain her texts. Even though Wasilewska wrote in Polish her entire life, it would be pointless to search for her works in Polish libraries and curricula: they have been removed. After 1989, Wasilewska's name became, in Polish public discourse, a symbol of 'national treason'. She had been Chair of the Union of Polish Patriots, established in the USSR during World War II, a deputy to the Supreme Soviet of the USSR, and a postwar peace activist. Today, gossipmongers publish exposés of her alleged affairs with postwar political figures, including Stalin, interested only in whether she was 'submissive' or 'dominant'.[1]

A third example: Zofia Dembińska (1905–1989), a teacher before the war and then cofounder of the publishing house Czytelnik (The Reader) (1944–51), Deputy Minister of Education (1951–60) and member of the United Nations Commission on the Status of Women (1951, 1954–68), has today been 'discovered' by Western researchers as an important figure in the women's international movement, remembered as one of the main initiators and authors of the Declaration on the Elimination of Discrimination against Women (DEDAW) adopted by the United Nations (UN) in 1967.[2] In Poland, she has been all but forgotten, except for her connections with men important for Polish culture: Henryk Dembiński (1908–1941), a prewar Marxist publicist and her husband, and Jerzy Borejsza (1905–1952), father of the postwar publishing empire and Dembińska's boss at Czytelnik.

Who were these women whom Poland has taken such great pains to erase from its history and memory, except as 'dark characters' or 'prodigal daughters'?

A handful of facts: Wasilewska and Dembińska were a generation away from Luxemburg, but they had much in common. They all came from fairly well-off families. Luxemburg was from a Polish-Jewish bourgeois family; Wasilewska and Dembińska from patriotic Polish intelligentsia families. They considered religious dogmas and institutions to be a source of enslavement, especially of women. Only Dembińska had been active in Catholic youth organisations before becoming a Marxist. They were all well-educated. Luxemburg studied philosophy, economics and law in Zürich; she defended a PhD thesis. Wasilewska completed a doctorate in Polish Studies in Krakow. Dembińska took Polish Studies in Vilnius. They combined teaching, writing and political activities. Wasilewska and Dembińska taught in schools; Luxemburg published *The Accumulation of Capital*, a seminal work of Marxism; Wasilewska debuted in 1934 with a critically acclaimed novel, *Oblicze dnia* (*The Face of Day*). Luxemburg was cofounder of Social Democracy of the Kingdom of Poland and Lithuania, the Communist Party of Germany, and headed the antiwar Spartacus League. Wasilewska was a member of the Polish Socialist Party, on its National Council in 1934–7; she argued for *rapprochement* with the communists in the People's Front; in 1940, she became a deputy to the Supreme Soviet of the USSR and joined the All-Union Communist Party (Bolsheviks) a year later; in 1943, she headed the Union of Polish Patriots, established in agreement with Stalin. Dembińska, in the 1930s associated with leftist Vilnius youth, after the war joined the Polish Workers' Party, and represented the Polish United Workers' Party at the UN Commission on the Status of Women.

The facts are significant not only because they anchor their biographies in time and place, but also because they act as scaffolding for their views and decisions, both political and private. Luxemburg, Wasilewska and Dembińska were all harshly critical of the nation state as supporting big capital, and thus a matrix for exploitation, class, ethnic and gender injustice. This criticism of nationalism, to be remedied by proletarian internationalism, was expressed in terms specific to Poland. Luxemburg argued with Polish socialists about the hierarchy of 'things to take care of': independence for Poland could wait, the priority was class struggle. She also criticised Lenin's doctrine of 'self-determination of nations'. In 1918, she was convinced that the Polish Left should fight to expand the Russian Revolution to Germany, instead of focusing on Polish independence.

Wasilewska, Dembińska and communist women of their generation chastised the interwar Polish nation-state for poverty, exploitation, social disparities, and in the 1930s, for 'fascist methods of action'. Wasilewska was disappointed that Poland, reborn after 123 years of enslavement, was 'a mother to factory and land owners, but a stepmother to peasants and workers'. She saw the Catholic clergy 'running rampant', and stigmatised Polish antisemitism. Before World War II began, she believed that progressive humanity must unite against fascism under the USSR's command. She continued to believe in the USSR during the war, as the only force capable of liberating Poland from Hitler's occupation and of building a new, egalitarian order, and afterwards, she represented the USSR in the international peace movement.[3]

While Poland was yearning for independence, and even afterwards, criticising the nation-state was the gravest sin a Pole could commit. Those who voiced such opinions were ostracised and accused of treason, all the more so if they acted on their opinions. Luxemburg, who risked prison for her socialism in Russian-annexed Poland, spent most of her politically mature life in Germany, becoming part of the international Left. Wasilewska did not return to Poland after World War II, staying in Kyiv. Her contemporaries could not forgive her for negotiating with Stalin to move the Polish border West, relinquishing the Eastern territories – including the formerly Polish cities of Vilnius and Lviv.[4] Dembińska stayed in Poland, but much of her political involvement as a UN activist for women's rights focused on the international arena.

To the women portrayed in this text, communism was not only a radical criticism of social inequalities and exploitation, but also a lifestyle. Trespassing boundaries was an inherent part of this; national boundaries, boundaries of Polishness, of the messianic ethos that had shaped generations of Poles in the nineteenth and twentieth centuries. Wasilewska mentioned that her positive attitude toward the USSR led to conflict with her father, Leon Wasilewski (1870–1936), the Minister of Foreign Affairs in the first Polish government after regaining independence, who negotiated the Polish–Soviet border in 1921. Class boundaries were also to be trespassed (suffice it to mention the minister's daughter Wasilewska's relationship with a bricklayer, Marian Bogatko (1906–1940)). Religious ones too: for Dembińska, who came from an avidly Catholic family, joining the Marxists must have been a shock. And finally, the traditionally female roles of wife and mother, in the romantic costume of Mother Poland. Importantly, these women, so active in men's worlds, did not turn a blind eye to the problem of gender inequality: they saw women's emancipation as an obvious element of the leftist agenda. They firmly believed that this would only be possible in conditions of true social and economic equality, where the church and the nation-state would have no say in the definition of the family and of the roles men and women should play in the public and private spheres. They not only preached, but also practised: they rejected the patriarchal family and bourgeois marriage as institutions that fossilised the enslavement of women; they chose relationships built on partnership with men, believing in the idea of a 'family of choice', not necessarily based on 'ties of blood'.

All of this is important, because it allows us to reconstruct a certain political environment, and especially the women from this environment, who took up the fight for a new world order in the late nineteenth and early twentieth centuries. It is also important because it allows us – at least partially – to understand the anger or even hatred felt by those who saw communist men and women as the main enemies of the 'natural' order. As shown by Klaus Theweleit in his seminal work *Male Fantasies*, twentieth-century anti-communism not only had strong antisemitic foundations, but also antifeminist ones.[5] A communist woman – the famous 'butch with a machine gun' – was the main object of hatred of the male proto-Nazis from the Freikorps, and Rosa Luxemburg's death at their hands was seen as punishment for both her private transgression and her political attack on the 'world as we know it'. Interpretations of Wasilewska's postwar fate have always been, and still are, sexist: her decision to stay in Ukraine described as motivated by the loss of Stalin's backing, and her withdrawal from active politics by marriage problems.[6] Loneliness, sickness, premature death – this is what awaits women who disrespect tradition, hierarchy, the natural order of things.

The communist women's project represents a political critique of a worldview segregated by sharp boundaries between genders, social classes and nations. As such – now disowned or forgotten – it may be considered a version of a critical area studies perspective. Interestingly, their enemies' anti-communism, antifeminism and antisemitism also hints at patterns that, for all their focus on the 'natural' boundaries of nation, patriarchy and religion, circulated in shared transnational loops that transcended such borders; this is still the case today, with the Far Right's global rise. It should not be forgotten, however, that while crossing boundaries, communist women also participated in delineating them, especially after World War II when the Left gained power in some regions of the world. Wasilewska co-created a new world order in its geographical (constructing a new map of Central and Eastern Europe) and ideological (acting for peace) dimensions, and Dembińska as a UN official worked to put an end to discrimination against women. The possibilities they had and the power at their disposal differed from what Luxemburg could afford. While she was thinking about boundaries in terms of barriers that could stop the march of the Left towards victory and as such needed to be overcome, Wasilewska and Dembińska transformed the concept of boundaries, making it part of a positive programme of socialism, perceived as the only possible end of inequality, injustice and exploitation.

Notes

1 Mrozik, 2017a.
2 De Haan, 2018.
3 Mrozik, 2017b.
4 Mrozik, 2013.
5 Theweleit, 1987.
6 Mrozik, 2013, 528–54.

Bibliography

De Haan, Francisca. 'The global left-feminist 1960s: From Copenhagen to Moscow and New York'. In *Routledge Handbook of the Global Sixties: Between protest and nation-building*, edited by Chen Jian, Martin Klimke, Masha Kirasirova, Mary Nolan, Marilyn Young and Joanna Waley-Cohen, 230–42. Abingdon: Routledge, 2018.

Mrozik, Agnieszka. '"Komuniści (nie) mają ojczyzny …" Wanda Wasilewska jako polska (anty)bohaterka narodowa' ['Communists (don't) have a homeland …' Wanda Wasilewska as a Polish national (anti)heroine], *Studia Litteraria et Historica* 2 (2013): 528–54.

Mrozik, Agnieszka. 'Beasts, demons, and cold bitches: Memories of communist women in contemporary Poland', *Baltic Worlds* 4 (2017a): 54–7.

Mrozik, Agnieszka. 'Crossing boundaries: The case of Wanda Wasilewska and Polish communism', *Aspasia: The international yearbook of Central, Eastern, and Southeastern European women's and gender history* 11 (2017b): 19–53.

Theweleit, Klaus. *Male Fantasies*, Volume 1: *Women, Floods, Bodies, History*. Translated by Stephen Conway, Erica Carte and Chris Turner. Minneapolis: University of Minnesota Press, 1987.

32
Kosmopolitka: an orphaned subject between home and abroad
Karolina Follis

In this text, Karolina Follis provides a deeply reflexive, firmly-grounded examination of the figure of the East European female kosmopolitka *– a woman whose globalist aspirations it is all too easy for the now-post-cosmopolitan Euro-American intellectual to dismiss as paradoxically parochial. Critical area studies, Follis's intervention reminds us, is not about denying other people's visions of borderlessness, but about attempting a substantive self-critique of our own visions.*

Critical area studies (CAS) pursues locatable subjects, mobile or emplaced, but always spatially and temporally situated. It is therefore expected that CAS would be sceptical of universalist philosophies and metropolitan perspectives. Cosmopolitanism is one such philosophy and perspective, and hence, it would appear, not of interest to CAS. And yet here I join those anthropologists and postcolonial scholars who argue that cosmopolitanism can be fruitfully studied as an embodied practice of specific subjects.[1] I propose that contemporary Eastern Europe is the home of one such cosmopolitan subject, whom I call *kosmopolitka*. I sketch her hypothetical profile and set it in a historical and geopolitical context, recognising the ambiguity of both the temporal and geographical boundaries of the space she inhabits. My claims about *kosmopolitka* are speculative, derived from anecdotal evidence and ambient knowledge gleaned from two decades of personal and professional encounters with women who have lived in 'the region' and abroad, and who share similar demographic character-istics. I explore patterns and intuitions rather than data, which remain to be gathered. My aim is to alert practitioners of CAS to the socio-cultural contributions of women who may fit the profile of *kosmopolitka*, and to argue in favour of systematic research into their experiences.

Recently, those experiences have included a sense of dislocation and disillusion. In the second decade of the twenty-first century, after twenty or so years of post-Cold War respite, cosmopolitanism, or 'citizenship of the world' once again is getting a terrible press. Almost anywhere they are, cosmopolites, whether they embrace the label or not, find themselves on the defensive, unfavourably compared to 'patriots', those ostensible paragons of virtuous citizenship. The backlash was crystallised in the words of the former British Prime Minister, Theresa May: 'If you believe you're a citizen of the world, you're a citizen of nowhere. You don't understand what the very word "citizenship" means.' These words came as part of the former PM's keynote speech articulating her vision of post-Brexit Britain at the conference of the Conservative Party, in October 2016. Yet they captured a sentiment which in recent years has fed renewed nationalism in the East and West of Europe, North America, parts of Asia and beyond. Cosmopolites are suspect. Mobile, affirmatively worldly individuals are portrayed as rootless, detached and possibly disloyal to where they come from, and/or to where they happen to live. This discourse is not very discriminating. It stigmatises the ill-defined 'global elite', which may encompass upper-class business and finance leaders and the 'faceless bureaucrats' of international institutions, but also academics, students and any member of the professional classes who takes advantage of the opportunities created by European integration and globalisation. My protagonist, *kosmopolitka*, is among those swept up by the anti-cosmopolitan backlash in the global North.

And yet, far from the caricature of the rootless 'citizens of nowhere', *kosmopolitka* has a distinctive genealogy and intellectual kinship network. She is a woman born between the late 1960s and the mid-1980s, somewhere roughly south of the Baltic, east of the Adriatic and north of the Mediterranean. (*Kosmopolita*, a man, is another story, as I explain below.) *Kosmopolitka* is endowed with considerable cultural capital. She came of age influenced by the secular, non-nationalist, in large measure Jewish East European intelligentsia. Her intellectual mentors were writers and political activists, some of them émigrés, people who inspired and drove liberal reforms in the region after 1989, who fostered an ethos of local social and political engagement combined with a keen interest in the wider world. In her formative years, *kosmopolitka* experienced the excitement of the Cold War's ending and the world 'opening up'. She took advantage of opportunities that became accessible to her as part of the political transformation. She embraced travel, education, love and employment across borders. Born and raised in a region where states routinely immobilised citizens within strict border regimes, she seized and was seized by the rhetoric of open borders, and perhaps by the thrill of personal liberation that she experienced as she left behind the roles and paths prescribed for her at home. Encouragement for *kosmopolitka*'s world-embracing choices came from sources that seemed trustworthy at the time. 'Travel, learn languages, study abroad, conquer the world', said authority figures who had spent their own lives resenting the closures imposed by communism, and who were now celebrating the freedoms accorded to the younger generation. 'You are a European now', was the diffuse message that *kosmopolitka* soaked up as she charted her path in the 1990s and 2000s, through universities, student exchanges, stints in London, Berlin or New York.

It is possible that to the extent that she did feel stigmatised as an Eastern European on her sojourns, this seemed temporary, a difference that could be overcome with a polishing of the accent and a fluency in the habits and mores of Western urban professionals. Eventually *kosmopolitka* would blend in among other cosmopolites, her origins reduced to a feature of her worldly self, not a determining characteristic. She would not let herself be embarrassed by where she came from, but she did not believe that her nationality defined her. She moved, after all, in inclusive transnational circles where everyone was from some place, yet they all shared the same joys and woes of life in late capitalism: diverse communities, exciting nightlife, but also high rents and scarce access to meaningful jobs. Whether in the EU or beyond, she negotiated this reality without thinking of herself as a 'migrant'. It jarred to hear of the Eastern Europeans who 'flooded' Europe, taking jobs and exploiting benefits. Surely those who complained about the Poles or Romanians in the UK or France meant other people, not her. She figured she was protected, by her education, cultural capital, salary and perhaps legal status. And yet as the anti-immigrant clamour intensified, the question 'where are you from?' became awkward. How to answer without giving the interlocutor the power to decide who she was and whether she belonged? This unease was the harbinger of doom. Soon, 'where are you from?' came to sound like an accusation, a demand to go back where she came from.

In the mid-2010s a series of political events in Europe and North America (Brexit, the so-called 'migrant crisis', the election of the 45th president of the United States) amounted to a revocation of the 1990s promise of open borders. The post-Cold War era ended to open up a new vista on uncertain times: the post-post-Cold War? Looking back at her experiences, *kosmopolitka* had to wonder if the hospitable cosmopolitan world that she had thought she inhabited was going through a temporary spasm, or was it on course to being destroyed? Did this world actually ever exist or was it a neoliberal sham, as many on the Left increasingly insisted? Was she a victim of deception or her own imagination? In the meantime, everything got complicated, above all the question of home and belonging.

If asked, *kosmopolitka* would share this story, offering CAS scholars insights into the contemporary configurations of East European diasporas, their intellectual and gendered history, notions of 'home' and 'abroad', and their political ambivalence. But where are CAS scholars to find her? Although technically a migrant or, within the EU, a free mover, *kosmopolitka* is not easily captured by statistics, nor is she well reflected in qualitative research. Sociologists of migration in the European Union have attempted a portrayal of EU mobile citizens, that is, those who take advantage of what is officially called 'intra-EU labour mobility'. However, in much of the research in this field, Eastern Europeans equal low-skilled workers and, in the case of women, they are associated mostly with care and sex work. More recent, area-focused research asks about the relationship between migration and cosmopolitan attitudes, cautiously indicating a positive correlation.[2] But where Favell, in the 2000s, gathered rich ethnographic data on the lives of Belgian, French and other West European middle-class 'free movers' in Amsterdam and London, no comparable study exists that would capture the experiences, epiphanies and identity dilemmas of Eastern Europeans from the middle class/intelligentsia.[3] Meanwhile, ethnography could yield rich insights into whether *kosmopolitka*, like her Western peers, escaped to the global city for '*refuge*: from the provinces, from the intolerant, the xenophobic, the small-minded'.[4] If so, what is at stake and what is different? To what extent does she feel that escape is possible at all, when countries of origin and countries of destination alike are in the process of disowning 'citizens of nowhere'?

Perhaps history is a better guide than sociology to *kosmopolitka*'s whereabouts. Denying cosmopolitans belonging in the national community is an old trope, particularly in Eastern Europe. In the eighteenth-century contest of ideas between Immanuel Kant and Johann Gottfried von Herder, the latter advanced his conception of nationhood in opposition to the Enlightenment's cosmopolitan rationalism. Beyond Germany, Herder's ideas of the *Volk* as the embodiment of the 'national spirit' were particularly influential east of his homeland, where they appealed to peoples whose identity was constantly threatened by foreign domination. The Polish, Czech, Lithuanian and other national movements drew on Herder's ideas, embracing national languages and regarding the nation as the primary cultural community. By the 1880s, the Herderian conception of the nation as a natural social unit had become so entrenched as to go almost unquestioned. In the twentieth century, as nationalism turned virulent and forgot Herder's principle of respect for cultural difference, cosmopolitans were portrayed as devoid of spirit and moral compass, beholden to foreign ideology, thinking of their homeland 'as a birthplace, nothing more'.[5] Later, in Soviet Russia, 'rootless cosmopolitans' – *bezrodnyi kosmopolity* – became the epithet of choice for people who were targets of Stalinist anti-bourgeois and antisemitic purges. In the twentieth century, disdain for 'citizens of the world', or rather, the practice of applying this label to political enemies, marked the overlapping fields between communists and the nationalist Right.

The cultural and intellectual traditions that informed *kosmopolitka*'s upbringing were Kantian rather than Herderian. They were positivistic rather than romantic and liberal rather than nationalist, though not in any way ideologically rigid. But she is also a woman, and cosmopolitanism is gender neutral only in abstract theory.[6] Ideas like open borders, meritocracy and post-national citizenship apply differently to men and women. *Kosmopolitka*, unlike *kosmopolita*, her male counterpart, instantly understood that in addition to ethnic prejudice and her own national/regional baggage, she also had to negotiate patriarchy in its distinctive home and abroad manifestations. At home, the resurgent patriots revived paradigms where women's bodies, sexuality and life choices were to be subjugated to the cause of preserving the nation. Abroad, #MeToo disabused *kosmopolitka* of her relatively optimistic assessment of Western gender equality and its possibilities. Ultimately, scarred by the anti-immigrant and anti-women upheavals of recent years, *kosmopolitka* found herself drained by the dead-end opposition between modernity and traditionalism, between the liberal cosmopolitan and the illiberal local. She wants to move on and address problems more pressing than whether 'citizens of the world' are really 'citizens of nowhere'. Orphaned by the liberal cosmopolitan framework that shaped her, *kosmopolitka* is a character of deep ambivalence and if she actually identifies as such, she does so only with bitter irony. When she returns 'home', she looks at the stone-cold faces of the patriots and mourns the world which never was, but which at least could be thought of as hospitable. In her estrangement from home and abroad, she is among the most reliable guides to the area known as Eastern Europe, and to its relations with the wider world.

Notes

1. Werbner, 2006.
2. White et al., 2018.
3. Favell, 2008.
4. Favell, 2008, 5.
5. Porter, 2000, 195.
6. Vieten, 2012.

Bibliography

Favell, Adrian. *Eurostars and Eurocities: Free movement and mobility in an integrating Europe.* Malden: Blackwell, 2008.

Porter, Brian. *When Nationalism Began to Hate: Imagining modern politics in nineteenth century Poland.* New York: Oxford University Press, 2000.

Vieten, Ursula. *Gender and Cosmopolitanism in Europe.* Farnham: Ashgate, 2012.

Werbner, Pnina. 'Understanding vernacular cosmopolitanism', *Anthropology News* 47(5) (2006): 7–11.

White, Anne, Izabela Grabowska, Paweł Kaczmarczyk and Krystyna Slany. *The Impact of Migration on Poland: EU mobility and social change.* London: UCL Press, 2018.

33
The *Kraeved(ka)*: a portrait of the Soviet citizen scientist
Sofia Gavrilova

Kraevedenie is yet another, context-specific project of area studies, with its agents ranging from the political exile of Tsarist times, through the centrally-directed Soviet-era citizen-researcher, to the contemporary independent enthusiast for all kinds of local knowledge. Gavrilova's study of these vernacular area-studies experts demonstrates just how multifarious the project of producing area knowledge can be, not just in its agents, but its purposes, methods, concepts of professionalism, and rewards. Today's kraevedka may not necessarily be a model for a critical area studies practitioner, but she shows us that there is not only one conceivable way of knowing the world.

'Ask him, he is a *kraeved*' – this is the answer one can expect to hear when seeking site-specific local knowledge across the post-Soviet countries. Every *krai*, every single half-abandoned settlement in the middle of Siberia or Central Asia, has a person referred to as a *kraeved* – who quite often runs a local museum and possesses specialised local knowledge about a place with which he identifies himself. The word *kraeved* in Russian refers to both men and women involved in the curation of local knowledge, though the Soviet authorities would never specifically have called the latter *kraevedka* (feminine), so that the historical contribution of the women *kraevedy* was dissolved. A *kraeved*, like *tovarisch* and *Stakhanovets*, doesn't have a gender, only a social role imposed by government.

Krayeved(ki) and the museums they run (there are still more than eight hundred across the former Soviet Union) are what have remained from the former socialist knowledge production system – *kraevedenie* – which emerged from unsupervised research activities in nineteenth-century Siberia and was turned into a large state-sponsored project of accumulating regional data for the needs of the socialist planned economy. *Kraevedenie* might be translated literally as 'the study of local lore' and has no direct analogy in Western academia or, more broadly, in Western society. The existing academic translations of *kraevedenie* into English, either 'local studies' or 'local histories', are both insufficient, as Soviet *kraevedenie* was a mixture of Soviet ideas about geography, ethnography and history.¹ These translations limit *kraevedenie* by attempting to fit it into Western-centred academia. 'Local histories' leaves out the geographical and ethnographic aspects of *kraevedenie*, while 'local studies' ignores the changing spatial dimension of *kraevedenie* as well as the intimate connotation of the word '*kraĭ*' (region or area) for the Russian-speaking public, widely used by the Soviet authorities to promote the connection between a *kraeved(ka)* and his/her 'little motherland'.

Kraevedenie has undeservedly received little attention in Western intellectual history. As a modernist state project of data production it has not yet been properly incorporated into area studies, nor has the changing role of the *kraevedka* as a vernacular, *narodnyĭ* (popular), scientist been critically discussed. However, both in-depth studies of *kraevedenie* and the role of the *kraevedka* could potentially widen our understanding of non-Western modes of knowledge production and the framework of citizen science, and contribute to debates on the position of a researcher with regard to the object and indigenisation of research.

So who is she, this *kraevedka*?

'A doctor, a merchant, a priest, a Russian, a Yakut, bishop Meletiĭ, a political exile, all these were among the first *kraeveds* in Yakutia.'² The type of person who would only come to be called a *kraeved* several decades later started to emerge as a male provincial intellectual activist exiled to Siberia in the late nineteenth century and was seen by the locals as an outsider who was researching his place of exile. The conventional Soviet history of *kraevedenie* tells us that these marginalised intellectual communities across Siberia triggered the establishment and development of intellectual life in these regions, as there was no cultural or intellectual life before that, apart from the 'primitive' knowledge of the indigenous population. That places the first *kraevedy* in quite an extraordinary position, one which merges the social roles of a marginalised political criminal, and an intelligent White man from Central Russia researching the territory of 'the Others'. The first pre-Soviet *kraevedy* are not anonymous: in the Soviet history of *kraevedenie* they are seen as the active forces of emerging scientific practice and their names are preserved in the intellectual history of *kraevedenie* (for example, the *kraevedcheskiĭ* museum in Yakutsk is still named after E. M. Iaroslavskiĭ, the political exile who started both the museum's collection and *kraevedenie* in Yakutsk in the nineteenth century).

The word *kraevedenie* itself first appeared in the Russian language only in the early twentieth century, at the First All-Russian Conference of Scientific Societies for Studying Local Regions (*Krai*), held in 1921.[3] That was the starting point for the centralisation of the administration of *kraevedenie*. Towards the 1930s it shifted from the Academy to *Narkompros* (the People's Commissariat for Education), with its tasks and agenda aligned to the government's needs and the planned economy. *Kraevedenie* began to be managed by guidelines for the whole circle of data production – from instructions on collecting various types of data to recommendations for the *kraeved(ka)*'s outfit. The *kraevedka* in this period remained the key person in the process of data collection for *kraevedenie*, but now she was no longer an exile, marginalised and illegal, but was instead officially acknowledged and recognised, becoming a valuable member of the scientific community. Therefore, the *kraevedka* of the first decades of the Soviet *kraevedenie* can be seen as a traditional colonial scientist, researching a place of the Others. However, the difference from the colonial members of the eighteenth- and nineteenth-century expeditions is that a *kraevedka*, once arrived, started to live on site and within the community. She was doing research, narrowing down her 'critical distance' from the subject and *becoming* local. The texts of the late-nineteenth- and early-twentieth-century *kraevedy*, however, have very little auto-ethnography and a critical attitude towards their own figures in local cultural and intellectual life. They are classical colonial texts of a researcher of the Empire's periphery.

So who were they, the Soviet regional activists, the pre-web modernist 'citizen scientists' who were gathering data for the majority of the state's projects from 1930 onward? The Soviet narrative of *kraevedenie* explains clearly the difference between the 'old bourgeois' proto-*kraeved* (who was a representative of the central Russian exiled intelligentsia) and the 'new Soviet' *kraevedka* (now a Soviet citizen). Against the backdrop of the early stages of the development of a new institutional system for *kraevedenie*, the formerly cohesive portrait of a *kraeved(ka)* split into two different social roles. The first is the 'new Soviet' *kraevedka*, who was seen as the successor to the prerevolutionary *kraeved*, and the second one was the emerging leader of *kraevedenie*. A *kraevedka* is no longer an outsider, but quite the contrary, a regional and local activist; the (male) leaders of *kraevedenie* are intellectuals, affiliated with Soviet academia, who debate the theory, methods and core of *kraevedenie* and issue guidelines for the work of local activists. The gap between 'vernacular scientists' and 'central professionals' grew rapidly through the 1930s and reached its peak in the early 1950s. The conventional Soviet history of *kraevedenie* is based on the theoreticians of *kraevedenie* and the Soviet authorities who wrote articles and issued guidelines. We know their names – they include Ivan Krezhin, Mikhail Levin, Sigizmund Shmidt, Vladimir Karpich and many others. But the vast majority of the other Soviet *kraevedki* – the regional activists – remain generalised, very often anonymous, and neglected by official history. If you search for 'famous *kraevedy*' you will either find prerevolutionary figures or the Moscow-based Soviet representatives of the institutions of *kraevedenie*. The personal input of regional activists, their practices and methods, as well as their role in the community have been, as yet, poorly studied.

The engagement of amateurs or nonprofessional scientists allows us to approach the *kraevedka* as a citizen scientist. Citizen science (or community science, crowd science, crowdsourced science, civic science) has recently become a very popular concept and is defined in various ways. The term first appeared in the work of US researcher Rick Bonney and the work of UK researcher Alan Irwin and has since become widespread.[4] According to the *Oxford English Dictionary*, 'citizen science' is: 'scientific work undertaken by members of the general public, often in collaboration with or under the direction of professional scientists and scientific institutions'.[5] *Kraevedenie* fits perfectly into these frames, alongside voluntary scientific associations in Tsarist Russia and other scientific practices of different periods.[6] It is important to note that despite popular attitudes to citizen science as bottom-up and 'democratic', *kraevedenie* was a very strict governmental modernist project, functioning according to stringent Soviet guidelines.

In 1932, 'a mass all-USSR geo-hike for studying the natural resources of the USSR' was organised by the central committee for *kraevedenie* to 'fill in the blank spots on geological maps'.[7] This triggered a wave of publications such as 'Organisation and practice of geological survey work for kraevedy' or 'Geohike' for minerals.[8] Later expeditions include the Geopokhod in 1936 organised by the Western Siberian Bureau, which resulted in the exploration of 150 new mineral deposits, including gold, iron and coal. The Phyto-expedition of 1935–6 resulted in finding massive resources of fibrous plants.[9] These are just some of the examples of the input of regional activists into state projects and plans.

The Soviet *kraevedenie* project was created in the first place to replace the nineteenth-century model of accumulating data based on expensive, longstanding and highly risky scientific expeditions. To make *kraevedenie* work, the Soviet authorities created an institutional infrastructure of *kraevedcheskiĭ* museums (regional research centres), which spread all over the former Soviet Union. Furthermore, the Soviet authorities developed a narrative linking *kraevedenie*, love towards the 'little motherland' and patriotic feelings toward the homeland, both to promote the importance of *kraevedenie* and to recruit people to this project.

During the most severe years of Soviet centralisation, the *kraevedenie* authorities used this narrative to accuse people, who hesitated to become *kraevedy*, of a lack of patriotism – something that could lead to punishment. The need for data, particularly concerning the five-year plans, shaped both the methodology of Soviet *kraevedenie* and the sort of people involved. The basic thesis, reflected in the guidelines for *kraevedenie*, was that the tasks of *kraevedenie* should be formulated so 'anyone can understand them and conduct Soviet *kraevedenie*' and the predominant critique was that they should not be too 'scientific'. All this shaped the Soviet 'civil scientists', who 'voluntarily' accumulated data according to governmental plans and needs, which were in turn strictly aligned with the five-year plans. The data collected by a *kraevedka* would be unique and hardly verifiable. That also creates a gap with the citizen scientists of the late-twentieth and twenty-first centuries, whose input would normally have been verified and be less specific. The *kraevedka* normally went on a field trip or expedition to inaccessible places and sent the findings back to the central governmental institutions. There were no resources, in time or money, to double-check this data. The guidelines, implemented from above, were vague and mostly referred to the practice's ideological core and purposes, rather than research techniques or methods of data collection. As a result, these methods, the instruments or the research techniques of the *kraevedy* remain unclear.

That gap between the central professionals of *kraevedenie* and the regional civil scientists, as well as the numerical imbalance between the former and the latter, leads us to the question: who was really shaping and defining *kraevedenie*? A dozen Soviet academicians in Moscow, or thousands of regional activists, doing *kraevedenie* on a daily basis? Western intellectual history is quite often written as the history of individuals – experts, professionals, men – and institutions, both of which are shaped by knowledge-production systems broadly understood, as well as by academic disciplines. This history however does not fit all forms of knowledge production; it excludes and simplifies other non-Western traditions, where the relationships between the process of knowledge production, actors and practices, or notions of professionalism might be different. And that is precisely the case with the split roles of Soviet *kraevedenie* (and of the *kraeved/kraevedka*). Through this optic, the professionals are the Soviet authorities and theoreticians of *kraevedenie*, and the contribution of the amateurs and nonprofessionals, the women and those outside the academies of Moscow and Leningrad, has never officially been acknowledged, nor approached from a critical perspective as citizen science.

So a Soviet *kraeved* was far more a coauthor in a research project than a volunteer in a project drawing on civilian input. But all the approaches to these key actors in data production for *kraevedenie* remain depersonalised and generalised within (post-)Soviet discourse. The vernacular knowledge of locals has become the most important content of *kraevedenie*, but the names of the people who gathered the data can scarcely be found in the archives, nor can their day-to-day research practices and methods. Moreover, as well as being forgotten by the conventional Soviet history of *kraevedenie*, the *kraevedka* is also absent from the Western intellectual history, which simplifies *kraevedenie* and therefore forgets its key contributors. The practices, expeditions, places and Soviet *kraevedki* themselves remain unnamed not only in the archives (as being unimportant) but in public memory (as being too common to remember), and their role in knowledge production and state planning is not acknowledged. Therefore, the history of *kraevedenie* that we know is the history written by the Soviet centre, which leaves aside personal contributions, the regional aspects of *kraevedenie* research practices, and the data itself.

The social and economic fluctuations of the twentieth century influenced *kraevedenie*, its role in socialist society, level of independence from the central authorities, research agenda and the people who were involved in it. The sort of person who was a *kraeved* in the late-nineteenth century would never be a Soviet *kraevedka* in the mid-1950s, and certainly not a *kraevedka* of the twenty-first century. Today, in one village, the *kraevedka* might be a (wo)man in their late 60s, marginalised by the local community and usually perceived as a 'holy fool', who runs a local museum out of their house. But equally, she might be the centre of the cultural and intellectual life of a small village and be treated with special respect. In a bigger city, the *kraevedka* might work at a '*kraevedcheskii*' job in a government-supported museum, doing research or curating the local exhibitions. Today the definition and meaning of the word *kraevedka* is vague and the definition of a '*kraevedcheskii*' position is also quite obscure.

Kraevedenie, as a project of Soviet knowledge-production, fell apart after Stalin's death, and the social role of the *kraevedka* and regional museums dissolved as well. Though the word '*kraevedenie*' still exists and is widely used in post-Soviet countries, the Soviet institutional framework has been almost completely demolished, leaving an unsupervised network of regional and local museums throughout the country. The State *kraevedenie* plan has come to its end, and there are no more governmental institutes of *kraevedenie*, or educational programmes. However, a bottom-up 'new kraevedenie' initiative is starting to emerge in various regions, led by new generations of *kraevedki*, who not only reshape local knowledge, but also propose a rethinking of the whole project. So despite the changes of gender, social role and knowledge produced, the *kraevedka* represents an important collective image of a Russian vernacular scientist, one who could be seen as potentially reviving local indigenous knowledge and, probably, civic area studies.

Notes

1 See Eytuhov, 2012; Johnson, 2006; Smith-Peter, 2004.
2 Shishigin, 1978.
3 Johnson, 2006, 4.
4 Bonney et al., 2009; Irwin, 1995.
5 *Oxford English Dictionary*, 2014.
6 Bradley, 2009; Könneker and Lugger, 2013.
7 Iakovlev, 1936.
8 Korobkov, 1933; Iakovlev, 1936, 2.
9 Krezhin, 1945.

Bibliography

Bonney, Rick, Caren B. Cooper, Janis Dickinson, Steve Kelling, Tina Phillips, Kenneth V. Rosenberg and Jennifer Shirk. 'Citizen science: A developing tool for expanding science knowledge and scientific literacy', *BioScience* 59(11) (2009): 977–84.
Bradley, Joseph. *Voluntary Associations in Tsarist Russia: Science, patriotism, and civil society*. Cambridge, MA: Harvard University Press, 2009.
Eytuhov, Catherine. 'Voices from the region: *Kraevedenie* meets grand narrative', *Kritika: Explorations in Russian and Eurasian History* 13(4) (2012): 877–87.
Iakovlev, A. A. 'Soderzhanie kraevednoĭ raboty' [The substance of local history work]. 1936. Russian Sate Archive, 10010, file number 4, p. 196.
Irwin, Alan. *Citizen Science: A study of people, expertise and sustainable development*. Abingdon: Routledge, 1995.

Johnson, Emily. *How St. Petersburg Learned to Study Itself: The Russian idea of Kraevedenie*. University Park: Pennsylvania State University Press, 2006.

Könneker, Carsten and Beatrice Lugger. 'Public science 2.0: Back to the future', *Science* 342(6154) (2013): 49–50.

Korobkov, N. 'Drevnie i starinnye rudnye razrabotki RSFSR' [Ancient and old ore mines of the RSFSR], *Sovetskoe kraevedenie* 10 (1933): 38–41.

Krezhin, I. P. *Puti i stadii razvitia sovetskogo kraevedenie (1917–1941)* [Paths and Stages in the Development of Soviet Kraevedenie]. Moscow: Mysl, 1945.

Oxford English Dictionary. 2nd Edition. Oxford: Oxford University Press, 2014. Continually updated at https://oed.com/.

Shishigin, E. S. 'Em. Iaroslavskiĭ i Iakutskiĭ kraevedcheskiĭ muzeĭ' [Emelian Iaroslavskii and the Yakutsk local history museum], *Polarnaia zvezda* 3 (1978): 112–15.

Smith-Peter, Susan. 'How to write a region: Local and regional historiography', *Kritika: Explorations in Russian and Eurasian History*, New Series 5(3) (2004): 527–42.

34
The 'last heroes' of perestroika (and their legacy in metamodernist Russia)
Maria Engström

The notion of 'metamodernity' is a curious example of a wandering concept. Initially popularised by an Iranian-American critical theorist (Mas'ud Zavarzadeh) and a Nigerian-American art historian (Moyo Okediji) it was appropriated and viralised by two Dutch cultural theorists in the 2010s as an alternative to the notion of 'post-postmodernism'. It prospers as an extremely widespread and popular term among scholars of culture and aesthetics in the postsocialist (and especially the ex-Soviet) world. Engström here proffers two figures – deceased rock icon Viktor Tsoĭ and fashion designer Gosha Rubchinskiĭ – as paradigmatic embodiments of a metamodern political-aesthetic continuum temporally stretching from perestroika to the present-day; and spatially demarcating the ex-Soviet space (centred on an increasingly assertive, aggressive, insular but also exportable vision of Russia) as the terrain across which these metamodern 'last heroes' strut. These protagonists delineate a new space that is modernisation without Westernisation. Engström's portrayal of this necromantic metamodernity and its icons acquires a disturbing timbre in the post-2022 world. Surviving members of Tsoĭ's band Kino are sent to the front in Ukraine to play for Russia's invading army, appearing on stage with a deepfaked hologramic avatar of Tsoĭ himself; while Rubchinskiĭ publicly consorts with prowar figures in Russia, among them fascist philosopher Aleksandr Dugin.

The era of post-Crimean polarisation – defined by the ideological and military standoff between Russia and the West – has created an atmosphere that was already very present within Russia's counterculture during the late 1980s and the first half of the 1990s.[1] Back then, in Russia's countercultural circles, the late-Soviet ideal of Russia as a future part of an imaginary West began to collapse, while the image of

Russia as part of an imaginary Anti-West took root: Aleksandr Dugin's neo-Eurasianism, Timur Novikov's New Academy and Eduard Limonov's National Bolshevik Party emerged on the fringe at this time.

The style and energy of perestroika-era Soviet counterculture fashion and music were largely determined by the protest aesthetics of the Leningrad underground movement – primarily the music of the band Kino and the image of its leader Viktor Tsoĭ (1962–1990), presented in Sergeĭ Solov'ev's movie *Assa* (1988). An equally strong political symbol of disappointment with the 1990s market reforms and the return to patriotism in the 2000s was the work of Yegor Letov and his band *Grazhdanskaia Oborona*, Vyacheslav Butusov and *Nautilus Pompilius*. Sergeĭ Bodrov Jr. (1971–2002), who created the image of a romantic Russian killer in Alexei Balabanov's movies *Brat* (*Brother*) (1997) and *Brat 2* (*Brother 2*) (2000), became the hero of the post-Soviet transition generation. Today, a utopian vision of an ideological and aesthetic Russian alternative to a Western 'first world' is leading to an accelerated, retrospective canonisation of a wide variety of countercultural icons and their anti-establishment pathos from the late perestroika years and the early 1990s.

In this contribution, I look at the contemporary fashion and music industries, which give clear indications of evolving ideological reinterpretations of late-Soviet and early-post-Soviet counterculture and demonstrate how the aesthetics of the Russian musical and artistic underground are being adopted by various ideological players – from Donbas separatists and ideologists of the 'Russian World' to Moscow hipsters and Parisian couture houses. The first part of this chapter is dedicated to Victor Tsoĭ and the second to fashion designer Gosha Rubchinskiĭ and the metamodernist aesthetics of alternative globalisation.

Viktor Tsoĭ: resurrection of 'the last hero'

The nationwide reverence for the leader of the band Kino began right after his death in 1990, when walls all over Russia were covered with graffiti reading 'Tsoĭ Lives'. The reverence remained steady throughout the 1990s and 2000s, and yet in recent years we have seen a new round of canonisation and appropriation of his symbolic capital (epitomised by both his music and visual images) by various political forces, ideological groups and communities. I would now like to look at two main types of reinterpretation of Victor Tsoĭ's legacy in contemporary Russian culture: the populist (or national-patriotic) and the elitist (or liberal).

Tsoï as a hero of the Russian world

During the perestroika years, Viktor Tsoï represented the myth of the 'last hero' – an individual set against the collective Soviet myth, and he became a symbol of resistance and freedom from surrounding oppression. Today the songs of Kino are becoming an important part of another ideological context: a patriotic narrative of Russia's resistance to 'the forces of evil' (meaning the West), while Tsoï himself morphs into a *skrepa* (spiritual bond) and a hero of 'the Russian world'. Two particular songs are of importance here: 'Gruppa Krovi' (Blood Group) and 'Kukushka' (Cuckoo).

Tsoï's song entitled 'Gruppa Krovi' (Blood Group), from 1987, is today frequently used as a war song by pro-Russian forces in Donbas. On YouTube we can find a number of video clips where images of Victor Tsoï performing this song are combined with documentary clips from the war in Eastern Ukraine. The extensive use of Tsoï's aesthetics of resistance by Donbas separatists was one of the reasons why the head of the Ukrainian Institute of National Remembrance, Volodymyr Viatrovych, made an appeal to ban Tsoï in Ukraine. He called Tsoï an 'exquisite tentacle of the Russian world', used by the Kremlin to preserve its imperial cultural hegemony.

Even more popular in the national-patriotic context is one of Tsoï's last songs – 'Kukushka' (Cuckoo), from 1990. In 2015 a 'Kukushka' cover, produced by Konstantin Meladze and performed by Polina Gagarina, was included in the soundtrack of the movie *Battle for Sevastopol* (2015), which tells the story of a Soviet maiden who turns out to be a natural-born sniper.[2] After the *Battle for Sevastopol*, Tsoï's song was reinvented as 'a song about the war', thus becoming a patriotic anthem of post-Crimean Russia, collecting over 185 million views on YouTube.

One of the latest covers of Kukushka is performed by 12-year-old Dasha Volosevich (2015).[3] The special twist of Dasha Volosevich's performance in this video, which has been viewed on YouTube more than 13 million times, is the fusion of childish innocence, aggressive militarisation, and a willingness/readiness for future sacrifice; while seven-year-old Iaroslava Degtarieva's 2016 cover was viewed more than 16 million times on YouTube.[4] The press release of the song tells us that the girl chose the song herself after viewing the film *The Battle for Sevastopol*.

Tsoï as a metamodernist hero

The patriotic reinterpretation of Tsoï's legacy is dominant, but it is not the only one. The liberal establishment resists the appropriation of Tsoĭ and Kino by national-conservative forces. For this segment of Russian society Tsoĭ and the late-Soviet underground is interesting as an example of artistic nonpolitical resistance during the period of late-Soviet 'stagnation'.[5]

In June 2017, to celebrate Tsoĭ's 55th birthday, the liberal news website Meduza and Russian-American journalist Michael Idov's label Kometa Music presented a tribute *My vyshli iz Kino* with twenty-five covers of Kino songs made by a new generation of musicians (Anton Sevidov from Tesla Boy, Antoha MC, Noize MC and others). Most of the covers emphasise the philosophical dimension of Tsoĭ's poetry or adjust his songs to contemporary metamodern youth culture and visuality (the so-called 'New East Aesthetics' or 'Eastern Bloc Aesthetics').[6] Metamodernism is the new cultural code that comes after postmodern antithetical critique and captures the new sensibility that emphasises a kind of integrated pluralism. It attempts to bridge the different sides of the culture wars, for example, between traditionalists and progressives, and synthesise perspectives of the Left and Right.

In sharp contrast to the militarised and heroic Tsoĭ in the populist discourse, Tsoĭ in the metamodern discourse is apolitical and lame. The best example of this reinterpretation of Tsoĭ's legacy is Kirill Serebrennikov's film *Leto* (*Summer*), which tells the story of the summer of 1982 and the love triangle involving Viktor Tsoĭ, Mike Naumenko (frontman of Leningrad underground rock band Zoopark) and Mike's wife Natalya. Serebrennikov tries to reconstruct the reckless atmosphere of the late stagnation years as an era of blessed timelessness, a time of hope and love.

Leto became a disappointment for those who hoped that Serebrennikov's new film would be about making political protest art under a strict and controlling regime. The movie does not present the heroism of the perestroika years or the revolutionary stance of Kino (something that was in demand among the liberal camp during the anti-Putin protests of 2011–12). Instead, *Leto* is about withdrawal into internal exile, proving that freedom is possible under any political regime.[7]

Gosha Rubchinskiĭ and the aesthetics of alternative globalisation

In recent years, we can see how the symbolic capital of the perestroika era and the youth culture of the 1990s is being revived by the fashion industry and included in the development of a new Russian style. The main agents of the new aesthetics, which have already been announced in the global fashion industry, are designers Gosha Rubchinskiĭ (b.1984), Demna Gvasalia (b.1981), the creative director of the House of Balenciaga and the co-creator of the Vetements brand, as well as Lotta Volkova (b.1984), the leading stylist of Vetements, Gosha Rubchinskiĭ and Balenciaga.

This post-Soviet trinity, who spent their childhood in the perestroika times in the USSR (Moscow, Sukhumi and Vladivostok, respectively), became leaders of a new round of avant-garde antifashion for the global generation of post-Millennials. They returned to the long-forgotten poor and squalid clothes of the post-Soviet street bazaars of the 1990s and created a new global style. The designers of the new Russian wave contrasted the old Russian style, with its Moscow beauties, the Romanovs, vodka, caviar and bears, with the cultural codes of the Eastern bloc from the period of disintegration, the style of perestroika and the post-perestroika decade, combining the energy of transition with the melancholy of unfulfilled expectations.

As part of the same phenomenon, we should mention Avdotya Alexandrova (b.1990), a movie director and owner of the agency of non-standard Russian models, Lumpen. Alexandrova searches around the world for young Russian men and women who have a counter-model appearance, creating a visual library of the global 'Russian world'. Those unconventional types attract the attention of leading fashion houses because they demonstrate a different beauty canon and individuality, and represent a challenge to the glossy standards of the First World. As Alexandrova herself says, in an interview given to the Dozhd TV channel, she is a Russian patriot and wants to present 'the Russian alternative' to the whole world and, unlike the official 'Russian World' project, she has been successful so far. The rough types from Lumpen's catalogue have a kind of ominous yet elegant subjectivity.

The first show of the 2008 Gosha Rubchinskiĭ men's collection, called *The Evil Empire*, defined the ideological profile of new Russian fashion: the reconstruction and remake of the transition era (1980s and 1990s), the role of 'the enemy of the free world' and 'the global hoodlum', and the creation of a radical aesthetic alternative. When building his own fashion narrative (which includes not only clothes but also exhibitions, photo albums, movies, soundtracks and show venues, models' personal stories, collaboration projects, and so on), Rubchinskiĭ appropriates and capitalises on all the clichés and stereotypes of the Cold War that became relevant again after 2014.

Very young models with the appearance of seductive criminals present ambivalent queer images of the standard bearers of the 'evil empire', a 'poor but sexy' subject of the Second World and alternative globalisation.[8] The signature characteristics of this style are phrases in the Cyrillic alphabet and references to the Soviet canon of military and sports style (inscriptions such as 'Russia', 'Enemy', 'Football', 'Ready to work and defend'), quotes from artists and musicians of the unofficial culture of the late-Soviet era (a collection with works by Timur Novikov and Erik Bulatov, inscriptions 'ASSA' or 'Russian Renaissance') or references to the Russian avant-garde (Malevich), homages to the rave club culture of the 1990s (Vostochnyĭ Udar – Eastern Impact). The shows are organised in public places that are associated with the disciplinary practices of Russia and the USSR (churches, stadiums, cultural centres), or with the main spaces of the 1990s youth counterculture (rave squats and dilapidated houses in cities).

Rubchinskiĭ's last three collections were shown in Russia (Kaliningrad, Saint Petersburg and Yekaterinburg), which is mould-breaking for the fashion industry that stays in Paris, Milan, New York and London. The choice of Kaliningrad, which is a militarised zone and the home base of the Baltic Marine Fleet, as the venue for the 2017 autumn-winter collection should be viewed not only as a marketing message, but also as an ideological gesture. The collection was created in collaboration with Adidas Football and contains aesthetic references to Soviet–German ties, to military dandyism, and the subculture of football fans with their aggressive nationalist rhetoric. Having initiated the decentralisation of fashion shows, Rubchinskiĭ began the subversive destruction of the symbolic domination of the West in the production of visual/ideological images: 'I chose Kaliningrad as a tribute to Adidas. In Russia and the USSR, sports teams always wore that brand. I want to prove that global ideas can be presented also in small Russian towns. I want to demonstrate the end of globalization.'[9]

Rubchinskiĭ's most recent collection (autumn-winter 2018) was presented in January 2018 in Yekaterinburg, which was one of the main centres of the alternative culture of the 1980s and 1990s. The Yeltsin Centre hosted the catwalk featuring Russian boys wearing Doc Martens boots, Levi's jeans, Burberry trench coats, Adidas sports suits bearing the inscription 'Россия' (Russia), military shirts and black sweaters reading 'Враг' (Enemy), which contained references to the 1990s Limonovtsy aesthetics (black shirts, red and white armbands on sleeves).[10] At the end of the show, the choir of models sang the song 'Goodbye, America' by Vyacheslav Butusov, a reference to the cult *Brother 2* movie: this song was used in the scene when the protagonist Danila Bagrov was flying home from America.

Conclusion

This 2018 collection by Rubchinskiĭ, which happened to be his last one as a solo designer, is interesting because it cites the cultural codes of the 1990s and reconstructs the context of the first disappointment after a close encounter with the West. The transnational Russian fashion avant-garde by Rubchinskiĭ and Gvasalia as well as the patriotic reinterpretations of Tsoĭ's legacy coincide with current Russian political overtones, which can be described as 'modernisation without Westernisation' – in other words, Russia's participation in the transnational market and post-industrial economy, accompanied with simultaneous isolation and 'enemy' status. This new image of a 'poor but sexy', 'new east' and even 'anti-West' Russia, as a zone free from conventions and restrictions of 'the civilised world', combines the idea of decolonisation with the affirmation of current Russian social and political order.

In the material discussed above (the appropriation of underground figures such as Viktor Tsoĭ in Russian nationalist narratives, the distinctive aesthetic and marketing practices of Rubchinskiĭ et al.) there is an attempt to re-anchor what was previously seen to be drifting off to become part of a liberal, global realm, into a reconfigured, bounded and distinctively Russian space of capitalist modernity. This contribution, then, and its protagonists, delineate this new space that is constituted by a critical attitude (anti-Western, anti-status quo), political ambivalence (both reactionary and progressive, or neither) and a geopolitical agnosticism (a commitment to modernisation without Westernisation).

Notes

1. This chapter is part of the research project 'No(w)stalgia of Modernity: Neo-Soviet Myth in Contemporary Russian Culture', Swedish Research Council, no. 2020-02479.
2. Gagarina, 2015.
3. Volosevich, 2015.
4. Yarolsava Degtyareva. https://www.youtube.com/@yaroslavadegtyareva.
5. The term was coined by Mikhail Gorbachev to describe the period between the Thaw (mid-1950s to the mid-1960s) and perestroika (1985–91).
6. The term is used in numerous publications about the fashion style of Generation Z, see more below.
7. The terms 'internal exile' or 'internal emigration' are broadly used in the Soviet and Russian context and describe distancing from the mainstream ideology and a method of resistance to the state of things.

8   See Pyzik, 2014.
9   *Elle* (Russian edition), 2017.
10 The term 'limonovtsy' refers to the members of the National Bolshevik Party (NBP, 1993–2007), founded by Russian writer and political activist Eduard Limonov (1943–2020). The NBP was popular during the 1990s; it was banned in 2007 as an extremist organisation.

Bibliography

Elle (Russian edition). 'Chto nuzhno znat' o pokaze Goshi Rubchinskogo v Kaliningrade' [What you need to know about Gosha Rubchinskii's show in Kaliningrad]. January 2017.

Gagarina, Polina. 'The Cuckoo (OST Battle for Sevastopol)'. StarPro, 31 March 2015. Accessed 14 August 2024. https://www.youtube.com/watch?v=fuPX8mjeb-E.

Pyzik, Agata. *Poor but Sexy: Culture clashes in Europe East and West*. Alresford: Zero Books, 2014.

Volosevich, Dasha. 'Dar'ya (Dasha Volosevich) – 12 let – Kaver V.Tsoy "Kukushka"' [Daria (Dasha Volosevich) – 12 years old – cover by V. Tsoï 'Cuckoo']. Posted 8 October 2015. Accessed 15 August 2024. https://www.youtube.com/watch?v=8bHloO3e32w.

35
Mediator sanitar
Charlotte Kühlbrandt and Mihai Surdu

Our Anti-Atlas is predicated on the idea that spaces are not simply out there in the world, waiting to be mapped, but that they are constructed by human actors and their social practices. Kühlbrandt and Surdu's piece focuses on one such figure, the Roma health mediator, and looks at the way that these workers – whose role is to provide a bridge between national health systems and the Romani communities in Central and East European states – delineate the space of the Romani world, in relation to the 'White' world that surrounds it, as one of unassimilable, cultural otherness, and as a problem that needs to be solved.

Who are 'the Roma'? Where do they come from? How many are there? We prefer to hold back from standard opening declarations about the Roma (or *țigani*, according to some). We want to resist geographies of groupness that conventionally make a link between the Roma and Eastern Europe. We lean towards this anti-encyclopedic stance because – as so many before us have shown – the quest for authoritative definitions of ethnicity can have dangerous consequences. Instead of trying to answer these opening questions, we follow the figure of the Roma health mediator (*mediator sanitar*) in Romania, to interrogate the political effects of persistent enquiries about the nature, origin and number of the Roma. We are not asking who the Roma are, but how and why the Roma are imagined as they are by public health discourses, and what these imaginations both reveal about the political economy of health systems, and conceal about the structural inequalities and the wider economic systems in which these are embedded.

Whether deliberately or inadvertently, two sensationalist metanarratives have formed, which present the Roma as an a priori category:

either as a public health threat (*pericol public*) or as victims of racist health systems. Different actors, such as the press, non-governmental organisations (NGOs), academics and international organisations, see the Roma as a troublesome group. The local and popular press paint an image of the Roma as a dirty, diseased and dangerously fertile population group. NGO reports stress how Roma patients are discriminated against by health professionals and the health system more widely, pointing to ethnically segregated maternity wards, refusals of treatment and systemic inequalities in insurance coverage. The academic literature on Roma health substantiates claims with epidemiological survey data, regression analyses and standard deviations, but the questions that are asked of this data often mirror the same kind of assumptions held by the popular press or the writers of NGO reports. Even though scholars admit that the Roma are a highly heterogeneous group who do not share language, religion, social status or cultural allegiances, the Roma continue to be reduced to a statistical average and considered as one people. Drawing as they both do on this understanding, popular and academic discourses on Roma health are preoccupied with the influence of Roma culture on health, in particular with regards to vaccination and reproductive health. Simultaneously, attention has also been focused on systemic barriers to accessing health care, including the lack of health insurance and discrimination by health care staff. Taken together, these themes consolidate a picture of Roma as a public health category of concern.

Roma health mediation

Roma patients seeking adequate treatment in times of medical need have instead long been met with a concerned gaze and analytic intention that has reduced them to the status of a problematic public health category. The 1990s saw the introduction of Roma health mediators across Eastern European countries, a targeted intervention that trains and employs women 'from Roma communities' to act as bridges between Roma and the health system. Some might assert that such targeted interventions are, at least in principle, 'well-intentioned', striving for genuine Roma–non-Roma integration. However, many Roma integration interventions led by European funding may in fact also be coupled with political agendas that cannot be said to be straightforwardly altruistic. We are thinking, for example, of the prevention of westward migration. Integration programmes have thereby prompted reiterations of those standard and delimiting questions: who are 'the Roma', where do they come from, how many are there – but also, where might they be going?

Mediators were introduced to mitigate the exclusionary effects of racist and/or victimising discourse about the Roma. But in the training manuals and handbooks produced for Roma health mediators, once again the Roma appear both as a public health threat and as victims of discrimination.[1] The *Health Mediator's Manual* refers to mediators as coming 'from the community', as figures who should 'build trust between two different worlds, i.e. the Roma community and the medical staff'. Mediators are expected to 'mediate the relationship between the Roma community and the local health authorities', helping the 'doctor understand the basic elements of Roma culture and traditions'. The manual asserts that Roma 'culture especially favours cleanliness' or that 'when people are forced to move from the traditional community, to live on the periphery of cities, in time they forget what they have learnt from their elderly'. The manual cautions that mediators should be aware that reproductive health is a 'quite delicate matter with Roma communities'. And perhaps most tellingly, mediators are expected to 'prevent unpleasant situations that may arise between the doctor and her Roma patients'.

What image of the Roma does this tool for Roma inclusion portray? The Roma *Health Mediator's Manual* fixes images of Roma as a distinct, homogenous and bounded ethnic group who dwell in 'Roma communities', who adhere to a specific, traditional 'Roma culture', who have specific traditional attitudes towards health, all of which results in different health needs from the general population. The Roma, in other words, are Other. It is the mediators' job to bridge the gap between this world of Otherness and the normative world of the health system. This, it is imagined, will result in Roma inclusion, and fewer 'unpleasant situations' arising in interactions between Roma and medical staff.

Roma health mediation in the Global East

Health mediation as a practice does not only exist in the context of Romania. Health systems in many other countries in eastern and in Western Europe employ mediators to work between health professionals and patients. In Western Europe, mediators tend to work with migrant populations to bridge language barriers. In eastern Europe, mediation almost exclusively targets the Roma in an attempt to bridge 'cultural barriers'. Setting up this binary between Roma and non-Roma health needs only further consolidates a construction of the Roma within the Global East as an unassimilated, culturally different Other. This kind of targeting insistently brings its practitioners back to those opening questions: who are 'the Roma', where do they come from, how many are there?

Roma health mediators are a cornerstone of the Roma inclusion agenda and the development industry that has formed around it in which global, European and regional organisations position Eastern Europe as an atavistic region in need of development. Since the end of communism, a whole economic sector, a network of governmental, intergovernmental and non-governmental organisations has sprung up to address the disadvantages that the Roma face, not only in health, but also in education, employment and housing. This development sector, fuelled by European and American funds, has provided new job opportunities for 'Roma experts', many of whom do not identify as Roma, who organise and attend workshops, training, conferences and who conduct research and write reports.[2]

One of the consequences of this enterprise has been the ceaseless counting and delineating of Roma as a population group in eastern Europe, a group that has to be constantly shown to be Other in order to justify targeted intervention.[3] This new 'inclusion industry' reinforces the position of Roma-as-Other that has been in place for centuries. In doing so, it returns again to those familiar questions: who are 'the Roma', where do they come from, how many are there?

Part of what makes Roma inclusion an economically productive field is the fact that these questions are in principle unanswerable. The European agenda for inclusion has for three decades generated endless strategies, innumerable expert meetings and many targeted programmes, of which Roma health mediation is only one example. Because nobody can say precisely who the Roma are, or how many there are, it is difficult for the success of Roma inclusion to be measured. Despite the uncertainty over the nature and number of the Roma, the inclusion industry calls for ever more Roma-targeting interventions.

Mediation in practice

In their day-to-day work, mediators observe how absence of health insurance impedes access to healthcare. They witness how lack of health insurance ties in with a wider lack of documents, itself related to a complex history of landlessness and being forced into illegal settlements.

Mediators see low-quality health care, especially in poor rural areas. They see people being offered different treatments or attention by medical personnel because they look poor or because they look Roma. They observe how health professionals lump these categories together. Mediators witness racial segregation in maternal wards and poor treatment by emergency services. They hear about cases in which ambulances refuse to come at all, where no-shows are justified by inaccessibility along crumbling roads. They see how medical services blame inattention on the very infrastructure that marks the structural inequalities that lead to poor health and medical emergencies. In other words, mediators encounter all those causes of health inequalities that appear to be invisible to those who insist on framing the situation in terms of the a priori category of 'Roma-as-problem'.

In all this, mediators are caught by their own insular working practices. Mediators work at the whim of mayors who can hire and fire them at will. They suffer from their marginal status in the health system, occupying a place where they are often tasked with activities that bear no direct relation to health at all. Even though the programme provides employment for a few hundred women, who very likely would otherwise be unemployed, the salaries for health mediators are small and their prospects for career development are uncertain. Without professional networks that have representation and influence, mediators can rarely act on what they see. They are obstructed by the very same institutions that employ them to address discrimination and health inequalities.

Mediators as agentic critics

The very existence of Roma health mediators consolidates 'Roma' as a public health category, both conceptually and in practice. The experiences of mediators at the margins of the Romanian health system are themselves characterised by deep structural contradictions and racisms. Mediators may not always see themselves as critics, but their work calls attention to critical flaws within the political economy and political culture of the health system and the broader economies within which this system is embedded. Despite targeted interventions, poor health outcomes in Roma communities persist. Instead of taking a broad societal approach, targeted policies are brought into existence to bridge gaps between two allegedly distinct and easily identifiable groups. This masks how unemployment, poverty, lack of educational opportunities, precarious housing and health problems affect not only those who identify or are identified as Roma, but people with a broad range of cultural identities. Attaching ethnic labels to problems which have structural roots and devising targeted policies is divisive and prevents solidarity among those affected. Drastic reductions in public spending have substituted more universal approaches and prioritised low-cost programmes, such as those focusing on Roma cultural identity as a cause of inequality. This reallocation of funds and attention interlocks with the growth of nationalism that seeks scapegoats in minorities and finds solutions by forcing *them* to change, often by means of symbolic and sometimes physical violence. The way in which Roma as a cultural group have been constructed as a problem barely veils racialised approaches to Roma inclusion. These approaches further marginalise and at the same time fail to attend to institutional forms of discrimination that are at the root of racialisation and marginality in the first place.[4]

Breaking with a priori categories

Health mediation builds on these assumptions, in that it frames Roma inclusion at a safe distance from systemic critique, where it tries to address health outcomes resulting from cultural clashes. Can we break away from these a priori categories? Instead of assuming 'Roma-as-problem', we might instead account for the ways in which people themselves frame what gets between them and a healthy life. This would involve paying greater attention to the political economy of health systems in their historical and regional context, rather than merely focusing on the cultural practices of certain minority groups. Attending to discourse, power and positionality, it is possible to see not only how mediation is built on a particular construction of 'the Roma' and the ways in which this justifies the cutting of public spending and provisions for poorer parts of the population. It is also possible to see how the Othering of Roma serves to attribute a developmental inferiority to the Global East more broadly. Mediators may observe and document the structural nature of inequalities (including the absence of health insurance, institutional racism, and so on), but their insular working practices and lack of institutional support mean that they are ill-equipped to act upon them. In their current formation, mediators are condemned to the role of agentic critic, rather than becoming agents of political change.

Notes

1 Nanu et al., 2008.
2 Trehan and Kóczé, 2009.
3 Surdu, 2016.
4 Kóczé and Popa, 2009.

Bibliography

Kóczé, Angéla and Raluca Maria Popa. 'Missing intersectionality: Race/ethnicity, gender and class in current research and policies on Romani women in Europe'. Budapest: Center for Policy Studies, Central European University, 2009.

Nanu, Lavinia, Daniel Rădulescu, Hanna Dobronăuțeanu, Cristina Jitariu and Corina Raicu. *Health Mediator's Manual.* National Agency for Roma. Bucharest: Human Dynamics Co, 2008.

Surdu, Mihai. *Those Who Count: Expert practices of Roma classification.* Budapest: Central European University Press, 2016.

Trehan, Nidhi and Angéla Kóczé. 'Racism, (neo)-colonialism and social justice: The struggle for the soul of the Romani movement in post-socialist Europe'. In *Racism Postcolonialism Europe*, edited by Graham Huggan and Ian Law, 50–73. Liverpool: Liverpool University Press, 2009.

36
The migration broker
Philippa Hetherington

Mobility alone does not make a 'wandering critic'. Even more than the migrants they served (or seduced), the migration brokers introduced below needed to understand the cosmopolitan economies of brothels, plantations or factories abroad, as well as the routes that would reach them most efficiently, but also the regulations that constrained movement across imperial frontiers (and how to evade them), as well as the motivations and resources of the would-be migrants. These people-movers reveal the interlocking (il)logic of state frontiers, a globalising economy, and the needs and desires that put people on the move, out of the tsarist empire into the world.

For women and men in Russia's western reaches in the late nineteenth century, the world often appeared to be getting smaller. Just as it did for many millions of subaltern peoples across the globe, the arrival of industrial travel and communications altered the perception of 'spacetime' experienced by peasants, *shtetl* Jews, small town merchants and itinerant labourers. Even for those who were resolutely immobile, modernity – with its proliferating penny press, intrusive train lines and pornographic picture postcards – compressed the time it seemed to take to move away, and thus the space you traversed to get there. Historians have argued that, as much as any concrete human movement, this new notion of spacetime typified the *fin-de-siècle* age of globalisation.[1]

If spacetime shifted, it did not, however, do so in uniform ways, and the vertiginous effects of compression often obscured the rootedness with which Eastern Europeans still lived their lives in 1900. In particular, for the many hundreds of thousands (or millions) of Russian subjects who wished to travel abroad for work or emigrate, in the late tsarist period, the network of laws, regulations and border controls prohibiting departure made the cross-border flows promised by globalisation impossible. Emigration was illegal from the Russian Empire. Going to work abroad temporarily was possible, and indeed the agricultural economy of Russia's neighbour Germany relied on cheap itinerant labour from the East. But even this was hedged by strict rules and encased in an array of paperwork that was difficult and complicated to obtain. Those who wanted to go further than Silesia, or who wished to leave behind the *shtetlakh* or the *sela* forever, often had to seek out clandestine ways to depart.

In this context, migrants often turned to third parties to mediate their experience of the border, to transform them from rooted objects to mobile subjects, and to connect their lives in Eastern Europe to the metropolises of Buenos Aires, Montevideo or Cape Town. These migration brokers – known as 'emigration agents' or 'traffickers', and coming closest to 'people smugglers' in today's derogatory parlance – became essential participants in the process of migration engaged in by millions in this time period. They were ubiquitous in settlements across the part of the empire now covered by Belarus, Ukraine, Poland and the Baltics. Migrant letters, memoirs and police investigations reveal that the vast scale of *fin-de-siècle* migration would have been impossible without them.

And yet they remain shadowy figures for the historian. As Adam McKeown has explained in relation to Pacific world migration management, the nineteenth century saw the figure of the broker placed in a 'black box' of deliberate ignorance. After Atlantic slavery was abolished in the first half of the century, government officials, journalists and commentators in the Americas increasingly relied on a strict dichotomy of free and forced migration, in which the only valid migrant was the one who moved without brokerage.[2] Of course, the spider's web of migration regulation necessitated by the very concept of the 'free migrant' in fact facilitated the continuation of brokerage: only now it was to take place underground. This situation continues to the present day, when, as contemporary migration scholars argue, researchers and officials' understandings of migration facilitation and smuggling suffer from the 'double disadvantage' of conceptual fuzziness and (often deliberate) empirical silences.[3]

Sifting through the archival record of the late tsarist world, we find, however, that migration brokers and third parties were ubiquitous features of the Eastern European landscape. While conceptual fuzziness was a feature of late-nineteenth- as much as twenty-first-century attitudes to brokerage, we can nonetheless begin to extract the migration broker from the black box. When we do so, we start to see a figure who existed (and exists) because of the dialectical interplay between the local and the global; between the need for deep knowledge of regional conditions and connectedness to global flows of capital, people and labour. In the taxonomy of *fin-de-siècle* observers, migration brokers fit into a fluid triad: emigration 'agents', shipping emissaries and traffickers in sex. Often rhetorically separated, in practice their roles overlapped. This entanglement of the roles of agent, trafficker and businessman points to the vast plane of migration assistance that was often benign, could also be malignant, and was frequently an uncomfortable combination of both.

The paradigmatic 'emigration agents' – a term used for those who undertook similar practices to the similarly demonised 'people smugglers' of today – were frontier locals who knew how to get across the borders frequently and had the local border guard in their pockets. Often, they were groups of Jewish or Polish men who worked to facilitate the mass departure of their coreligionists or co-nationals to a better life outside the Pale of Settlement or Congress Kingdom. Even in the tsarist police records there often seems to be little difference between these gangs of smugglers and a local emigrant mutual-aid society. They relied on the aid of friendly (and avaricious) border guards who took money to look the other way when suspect papers were presented or extra people hidden in luggage. In 1899, in Kretinga, an imperial customs point on the border of Germany and what is now Lithuania, one 'border guard Petrov' was arrested for aiding and abetting a group of five men who were regularly taking would-be emigrants abroad on false passports, for which Petrov received up to 60 Rubles at a time. Also helping them was a local woman, Girsha Neimana, who was caught attempting to cross the border with a passport under the surname 'Lipman' and was found to have three more false passports secreted away in her pockets.[4] As investigations such as these demonstrate, fundamental to the work of the broker was local knowledge, the ability to pass as a benign traveller (what could be more benign than a woman?). Just as important were informal contacts with representatives of the state whose palms were most eager to be greased.

At first sight, the shipping company emissary, sent into darkest Russia to sell tickets for the Hamburg or Dutch-American Lines, was a very different beast from the locally-rooted emigration agent. In contrast to the latter's local aura, he represented the dangers of foreigners and the marketplace. Tsarist officials complained to local diplomatic representatives that 'shipping delegations' from Germany, Belgium or Britain were just covers to entice would-be departees into emigration abroad.

In 1890, the chief of the local Odesa police met with the Dutch consul to complain that his compatriot, one Dominik Kemper, was travelling through rural areas outside the port and selling locals cheap tickets to America. He had even placed a notice in the local newspaper advertising the wealth to be found abroad. The Dutch consul protested Kemper's right to conduct legitimate business, noting as an aside that he would be happy to pay a 'fee' of up to 15,000 Rubles to continue it. The police chief was unmoved, insisting that such shipping agents seduced Russian subjects to break the law and must be expelled from the city.[5] It was not only those without Russian subjecthood who could be expelled for conducting the 'legitimate business' of the shipping companies, however. That same year, the railway police in Verzhbolovo, a border control point between Russia and Prussia, expelled over twenty 'Jewish agents' accused of working for a German government-run travel agency selling tickets for the German shipping lines just over the border. Again, protests that they were engaging in business, and not criminal, activities were dismissed. All but four of those expelled were Russian subjects, suggesting that embeddedness in the local communities of the frontier regions was equally central to the business side of migrant mobility.[6]

While brokerage was cast as criminal in both of the above cases, there was one category of intermediary for whom the most hatred was reserved: the border-hopping pimp, or trafficker in women. The late nineteenth century was the first flourishing of a global panic about sex trafficking that has been recapitulated many times since. In Russia, the virgin youth of the western borderlands was perceived as most vulnerable to this crime, a tacit acknowledgement of the mania for mobility raging within that space. And it was the men most familiar with that youth – their neighbours, fellow travellers and friends – who were seen as most suspicious. Trafficking was migration brokerage with the aggravating factor of additional pimping. Emigration agents who smuggled labour migrants abroad promised them work in factories or on plantations; prostitution was not, however, recognised as work and thus the trafficker smuggled a woman abroad to abandon her in slavery. If the 'third party' was abandoned to the proverbial black box when the dichotomy between 'free' and 'forced' migrant ossified, the status of a migratory prostitute's 'freedom' was even more under dispute. When police investigated trafficking cases in the western borderlands they found, however, that their suspects looked a lot like the emigration agents they were familiar with. If anything, knowledge of local conditions and circumstances appeared even more vital in cases of trafficking, as the third party needed to know the local brothel economy as well as the best paths out, in order to find victims (highlighting the extent to which most women trafficked abroad were already involved in the sex industry at home). In a 1908 case pursued by Russian consular officials in Istanbul, a man from Zhitomir, who had brought women to brothels in Port Said and Ceylon, was found to have plied his trade with the aid of deep knowledge of both the rural backwaters of north-western Ukraine and the sex industry of tropical Colombo.[7] The trafficker needed to navigate deeply regional and expansively global conditions as much as the emigration agent or the shipping emissary.

Perhaps even more than the migrants whose mobility they brokered, the emigration agents, shipping emissaries and even traffickers, constituted paradigmatic 'wandering critics' of area in late tsarist Eastern Europe. It was not merely their mobility that garnered them this status; their very coming-into-being depended on the knitting together of embedded localism and ambulant globalism. The exigencies of Eastern Europe, or Kovno province, or Kirbatai town, or the Verzhbolovo customs point where the train passed from Russia to Prussia, were definitionally central to the agent or trafficker. At the same time, he (or more rarely she) relied on cosmopolitan contacts with transatlantic shipping cartels, red-light districts in dazzling port cities and the ability to cross borders and pass as someone who belonged, in London, New York or Istanbul. It was the encounter between the local and global that produced the broker as a category, even as international legal regimes were increasingly attempting to make her or him invisible.

Notes

1 Koselleck, 2004.
2 McKeown, 2012.
3 Baird and van Liempt, 2016.
4 Politicheskii Otdel, 1899–1901.
5 State Archive of the Russian Federation, ll. 3–4.
6 State Archive of the Russian Federation, ll. 1–2.
7 AVPRI files. Foreign Policy Archive of Imperial Russia, Moscow.

Bibliography

AVPRI files. Foreign Policy Archive of Imperial Russia, Moscow.
Baird, Theodore and Ilse van Liempt. 'Scrutinising the double disadvantage: Knowledge production in the messy field of migrant smuggling', *Journal of Ethnic and Migration Studies* 42(3) (2016): 400–17.
Koselleck, Reinhart. *Futures Past: On the semantics of historical time*. New York: Columbia University Press, 2004.

McKeown, Adam. 'How the box became black: Brokers and the creation of the free migrant', *Pacific Affairs* 85(1) (2012): 21–45.

Politicheskii Otdel, 1899–1901. Lithuanian State Historical Archives. 'O chinovnik Petrov i drugikh dolzhnostnykj litsakh Kovenskoĭ gubernii, obviniaemykh v zlopotrebleniiakh po sluzhbe' [About the official Petrov and other officials of the Kovno province accused of abuse of office], Fond 378, Delo 27, ll. 68–9(ob), Vilnius.

State Archive of the Russian Federation. 'O kontorakh i parakhodnykh obshchestvakh, sposobstvuiushchikh k pereseleniiu raznykh lits v Ameriku' [On offices and shipping societies that facilitate the resettlement of various persons to America]. Fond 102, Deloproiz 2, Opis' 1890, Delo 104ch. 4, ll. 1–2, Moscow.

State Archive of the Russian Federation. 'O kontorakh i parakhodnykh obshchestvakh, sposobstvuiushchikh k pereseleniiu raznykh lits v Ameriku' [On offices and shipping societies that facilitate the resettlement of various persons to America]. Fond 102, Deloproiz 2, Opis' 1890, Delo 104ch. 4, ll. 3–4, Moscow.

37
Olga Brookman's everyday eyes: the Russian mail-order bride as ethnographer
Emily Curtin

The Soviet tradition of America-critique is better established than the Soviet discipline of American studies (Amerikanistika), and the critical Americalogues of Maksim Gorky ('City of the Yellow Devil') and the humourists Il'f and Petrov reached (and still reach) many millions of readers in the (former) Soviet space. California-residing Yekaterinburg born Olga Brookman – a so-called 'mail-order bride' and full-time YouTube vlogger – is in many senses their contemporary equivalent. Her videos, which attract an audience of tens of thousands, offer sardonic critiques of the everyday imponderabilia of American life. In this text, anthropologist Emily Curtin – a New York-residing anthropologist of Russia and Belarus – reflects on the distinctions and continuities between the labours of critique performed by the professional ethnographer and the professional YouTuber.

Yekaterinburg native and YouTube vlogger Olga Brookman is giving her audience a tour of the men's underwear section of a mid-range Californian department store when she is interrupted by her off-screen American husband. Switching from Russian to English, she explains haltingly, 'I make movie for … YouTube'. He mocks her pronunciation – which sounds more like 'ooo-tube' – and asks her loudly and slowly if she would like to buy anything for herself in the women's department. 'I don't know?' she says, before returning to the serious business of informing her Russian fan base what kind of shorts American men wear to golf and how they position their legs when they sit on the beach.[1]

    I stumbled onto Olga Brookman's YouTube channel a few years ago while living in Minsk and doing some preliminary ethnographic fieldwork for my doctoral dissertation. Charmed by the frank and artless way she documented her life in the US, I learned that Brookman had recently emigrated after meeting her husband through an internet matchmaking agency. Though older than the typical mail-order bride, at 44, in other ways Brookman conformed to the stereotype: beautiful, financially dependent and speaking virtually no English on arrival. Her channel, which has since grown to over 75,000 subscribers, presents a mix of personal narrative, observations about US culture and advice for other Russian women considering a similar migration strategy. As an American watching her videos from Belarus, that summer, I felt an affinity with her, as a fellow outlier struggling to make sense of my surroundings. Despite the not insignificant differences in our circumstances, we had both fashioned ourselves as cultural interpreters for faraway audiences. As I watched more of her vlogs, I came to appreciate Brookman, with her emic approach and heightened sensitivity for cultural minutiae, as a sort of 'outsider ethnographer'. With this framework in mind, I turn to some highlights from her ever-expanding body of observations.

Americans know little about Russia

Brookman is surprised to find out that although Russians consume American movies, music and television shows, this cultural exchange is not mutual. She describes the shock she felt learning that Americans were unaware of even the biggest Russian stars, like Alla Pugacheva and Nikita Mikhalkov. 'They have their own world, their own idols, their own athletes', she somewhat sadly informs her viewers.[2] She also admits that having assumed Russian food was universally considered the tastiest and Russian women the most beautiful, she was disappointed to find that neither seemed to register in the canon of local tastes.[3] The first time she went to church in the US, she says, people were surprised to learn her nationality, because to them the image of a Russian woman was not – as it is for her – one of glamour, but rather of a babushka wearing a headscarf and carrying a log.[4]

The American 'plastic' smile

Perhaps because her English is not very good, Brookman is particularly attuned to American gestures, appearances and body language. In one early video, Brookman defends the 'American smile' (plastic smile, or *plastmassovaia ulybka*), which in the Russian-speaking world is shorthand for everything that is perceived to be shallow and insincere about Americans. In her rather Durkheimian interpretation, the smile's primary function is to preserve harmony between the individual and society. When someone bumps into you or annoys you, a 'sorry' and a smile serves to dissolve the tension of the moment. 'Everyone has their own problems', Brookman says, 'but here you don't have the right to show that you're in a bad mood or that you don't like someone'. While acknowledging that it's difficult for Russians to smile at strangers, Brookman insists that this behaviour can be learned.[5] In later videos, we see Brookman embodying her new friendly persona as she films her daily walks, enthusiastically greeting people she passes along the way.

Socialising at home with Americans

While Brookman is happy to go native in some ways, she is critical of other local cultural practices, including American hospitality. In one video, Brookman describes an evening when she was sitting and chatting with some Russian girlfriends in her kitchen, only to have her American husband walk in and start tidying up, completely ruining the mood of the party. In Russia, Brookman says, people linger at the table for ages with company, talking, drinking endless cups of tea and perhaps continuing to snack on the remains of the meal or dessert. In the US, on the other hand, she finds that the hosts rise to clear the table as soon as people finish eating. This video ends on an uncharacteristically abrupt note, with Brookman imploring (unfortunately, preaching to the choir): 'So clean up *after* the guests leave!'[6]

Personal space

In an early video about American men and their preferences, Brookman talks about their need for personal space. When her husband comes home from work in the evenings, he likes to sit at the computer for an hour or two writing emails, and she knows not to bother him. She goes on to list other American habits: people change their clothes every day and brush their teeth every time they leave the house, even if they leave and come back five times in a day. Few American men, she adds (perhaps not entirely accurately), smoke or drink alcohol. Finally, she mentions that in the US, people don't thrust their opinions on you the way they do in

Russia – instead people are expected to make their own decisions about how to live their lives.⁷ While apparently free associating, Brookman in fact invites us to see how all these behaviours could be organised under the rubric of personal space, which implies not only physical distance from others, but freedom from the overflow of their bodily odours and unwanted advice. This video is characteristic of Brookman's output in that it plots intersections of cultural expectations that move from 'East' to 'West' and back again to her Russian audience, socialising its members in the US behavioural norms her American subjects themselves take for granted.

American mysteries

Sometimes Brookman does not explain so much as she poses interesting questions, which often say as much about Russia and post-Cold War geopolitics as they do about the US. In one video entitled 'I can't understand: Questions without answers', she asks: Why, when people eat so much unhealthy food, do Americans live such long lives? Why, when dental care is so expensive, do you never see anyone here without teeth? Given how little time American schoolchildren spend studying, how is it that the US has such prestigious universities? And finally, if Americans are so dimwitted, how is the US 'ahead of the rest of the planet'? 'If you have answers to any of these questions', she says earnestly, 'please let me know'.⁸

What do we do with Olga Brookman?

Although she exists quite outside of academia, Brookman's videos contain flashes of what we might recognise as an ethnographic sensibility in the Anglo-American tradition. Interestingly, it is precisely her 'outsider' status that allows her to, as she puts it, 'see things through regular, everyday (*bytovye*) eyes'.⁹ Had she been trained as a social scientist in the Soviet Union, it is unlikely that she would turn her gaze towards such seemingly trivial cultural phenomena as facial expressions and personal hygiene. Invested as anthropologists are with the conceit of outsider acuity, we crave foreign observations and analyses of American society. And yet – Brookman's lack of academic credentials, a consistent methodology, peer accountability and institutional networks mean that she is *too much* of an outsider to engage with academics or policy makers as a peer. This points to a larger problem with the wandering critic: however much we need the perspective and originality of the marginalised voice, we rarely hear it when it does not come on our terms.

If Brookman's output is confusing, her subject position also defies categorisation. As a so-called 'mail-order bride', it is tempting to see her as a victim of an exploitative capitalist system. Yet Brookman is more cheerful opportunist than sad captive, living a life which, by all appearances, is the picture of comfort and freedom. She does not work outside of the house, nor, by her own admission, does she cook or do any housework. She claims to be happy with her husband and fills her time with shopping, dining out and trips abroad. And of course, Brookman is far from voiceless, having a platform to express her thoughts to an audience considerably larger than those engaged by most 'real' anthropologists.

That said, Brookman's observations and reflections on American culture are unlikely to reach an Anglophone audience, which in multiple respects does not speak her language. Her lack of fluency in English limits her assimilation and autonomy from her husband and her status as a mail-order bride carries considerable social stigma in mainstream American society. We might locate Brookman at an intersection of privilege and marginalisation created by overlapping global and local inequalities: on the one hand, uneven development between Russia and the US; and on the other, gender inequalities which create a market for mail-order brides in the first place.

Conclusion: framing vlogs as ethnography

The popularity of Brookman and other Russian immigrants' vlogs, some of which have been viewed hundreds of thousands of times, have tapped into a demand on the part of Russian speakers for more authentic representations of the US than those circulating in the media or in American pop culture. Through the medium of personal narrative, these vloggers produce ethnographic knowledge which introduces many Russian speakers to the US cultural environment and influences their migration decisions. As with traditional Euro-American anthropology and area studies, economic and geopolitical factors shape these practices of gathering and disseminating data about the 'other'. While many Western researchers have undertaken fieldwork in the postsocialist world, it is still rare to find Eurasian scholars doing social scientific research in the US and Western Europe. Although Russian immigrants' vlogs do not satisfactorily bridge this gap, they are nonetheless rich with interpretative possibility. By framing Brookman as an 'outsider ethnographer', I have tried to draw attention to an emerging genre which has the potential to hold up a mirror to North American society, reveal the norms and categories of value held by its producers, and unsettle received wisdom about what counts as ethnography.

Notes

1 Brookman, 2013a.
2 Brookman, 2013c.
3 Brookman, 2017c.
4 Brookman, 2013c.
5 Brookman, 2013d.
6 Brookman, 2017b.
7 Brookman, 2013b.
8 Brookman, 2017a.
9 Brookman, 2014.

Bibliography

Brookman, Olga. 'SSHA. Pochemu muzhiki smeiotsia nad shotami moego muzha-Amerikantsa. Zamuzh za inostrantsa' [USA. Why do people laugh at my American husband's shorts? Married to a foreigner]. Brukman zhena Amerikantsa [Brookman, wife of an American]. Posted 2 July 2013a. Accessed 15 August 2024. https://www.youtube.com/watch?v=MxN OKfIxc58&t=13s.

Brookman, Olga. 'SSHA. Amerikanskiye muzhchiny. Kakiye oni? Revy-korovy. postoyanno v dushe moyutsya' [USA. American men: what are they like? Roaring cows. Always taking a shower]. Brukman zhena Amerikantsa [Brookman, wife of an American]. Posted 27 July 2013b. Accessed 15 August 2024. https://www.youtube.com/watch?v=e9E-fnJZObk.

Brookman, Olga. 'SSHA. Chto znaiut obychnye amerikantsi o Rossii?' [USA. What do ordinary Americans know about Russia?]. Brukman zhena Amerikantsa [Brookman, wife of an American]. Posted 10 August 2013c. Accessed 15 August 2024. https://www.youtube.com/watch?v=DM4Tem3WGfs.

Brookman, Olga. 'Amerika. O znamenitoĭ 'plastmassovoĭ ulybke' amerikantsev' [America. On the famous American 'plastic smile']. Brukman zhena Amerikantsa [Brookman, wife of an American]. Posted 14 August 2013d. Accessed 15 August 2024. https://www.youtube.com/watch?v=V9DznL_7Edw.

Brookman, Olga. 'SSHA. Pochemu u Amerikantsev krasivye, zdorovye, belye zuby? Zakazat' poloski ssylki pod video' [USA. Why do Americans have beautiful healthy white teeth? Links to order strips below]. Brukman zhena Amerikantsa [Brookman, wife of an American]. Posted 18 March 2014. Accessed 15 August 2024. https://www.youtube.com/watch?v=L8DbvEtJ2S8&t=238s.

Brookman, Olga. 'SSHA. Ne mogu poniat' voprosy bez otvetov pochemu tak to?' [USA. I can't understand questions without answers; why are things this way?]. Brukman zhena Amerikantsa [Brookman, wife of an American]. Posted 9 January 2017a. Video marked private. https://www.youtube.com/watch?v=CIB2_BZUprc.

Brookman, Olga. 'SSHA. Durnoi ton muzha ili ėto mentalitet? Razognal moĭ devichnik' [USA. Bad form on the part of my husband or just a cultural difference? He broke up my girls' night]. Brukman zhena Amerikantsa [Brookman, wife of an American]. Posted 11 February 2017b. Accessed 15 August 2024. https://www.youtube.com/watch?v=eILQeKJMqjo.

Brookman, Olga. 'SSHA. Proshchanie illiuziiami. Moia zhizn' pod kolpakom' [USA farewell to my illusions, My life under scrutiny]. Brukman zhena Amerikantsa [Brookman, wife of an American]. Posted 4 November 2017c. Video marked private. https://www.youtube.com/watch?v=4V_fZSUYDeY&t=16s.

38
Ovid in Tomis and the unreal space of literature
Tim Beasley-Murray

Beasley-Murray here uses Ovid to show that his place of banishment in Tomis (contemporary Romania's Constanța) – as well as the rest of the world – can only be apprehended through language, in this case, the genre of exilic poetry in particular. Ovid thus inhabits spaces which, though they may also be real, are 'inescapably imaginary'. At the same time, though, the example of Ovid demonstrates the tangible effects of these imaginary spaces in the real world, in the bronze statue that embodies nineteenth-century Romanian claims to a Latin heritage. The real and the imagined are not opposites, but twins: to accept this is to better understand the worlds we inhabit.

Ovid at the Romanian seaside

In the centre of the Romanian city of Constanța, set back a little from the Black Sea waters of the ancient port, in front of the National Archaeological Museum, on the square that bears his name, stands a statue of the Roman poet, Publius Ovidius Naso. Ovid, in darkened bronze, broods in pensive, perhaps melancholy fashion, his eyes most likely cast down too far to be able to see the sea. On the pedestal is inscribed the bittersweet and ironic epitaph that Ovid had penned for himself:

> Hic ego qui iaceo tenerorum lusor amorum
> Ingenio perii Naso poeta meo
> At tibi qui transis ne sit grave quisquis amasti
> Dicere Nasonis molliter ossa cubent

> I, who lie here, with tender loves once played,
> Naso, the bard, whose life his wit betrayed.
> Grudge not, O lover, as thou passest by,
> A prayer: 'Soft may the bones of Naso lie!'[1]

This statue, by the Italian sculptor Ettore Ferrari, was unveiled with much fanfare in 1887, the tumultuous year in which Romania won its independence from the Ottoman Empire. The Romanian notables of the city, who sponsored the statue, in celebrating Ovid as their city's most illustrious one-time resident, sought to lay claim to national distinctiveness and European filiation by reference to Ovid and, with him, a notion of Romanian Latin heritage. As witness to, and guarantor of, this heritage, Ovid – along with his statue – has acquired a symbolic function in Constanța (and in Romanian national and cultural discourse more generally) where he has, inter alia, lent his name to the city's university and has become something of a symbol of the city as a whole.[2]

There is, of course, a deep irony to this Constanțian and Romanian celebration of Ovid. Ovid was no willing visitor, and, by his account, he detested the place. In the year 8 CE, at the age of 50, Ovid was exiled from Rome, by fiat of the Emperor Augustus, to Tomis, as it was then called, a city that lay at the far-flung and war-torn edges of the Roman Empire, where he would die in 17 or 18 CE. The works that Ovid produced in his Tomisian exile, above all, the *Tristia* and the *Epistulae ex Ponto*, are letters, to friends and allies in Rome, that bitterly lament his conditions of exile and desperately seek a means of return.[3] Exiled in a wilderness where, according to his account, no-one has a real command of Greek, let alone Latin, Ovid's writings speak of an extreme cultural isolation where – in one of his most striking similes – to write poetry that no one will hear is like dancing in the dark.[4] He describes it in the following terms:

> I busy my mind with studies beguiling my grief, trying to cheat my cares. What else am I to do, all alone on this forsaken shore, what other resources for my sorrows should I try to seek? If I look upon the country, 'tis devoid of charm, nothing in the whole world can be more cheerless; if I look upon the men, they are scarce men worthy the name; they have more cruel savagery than wolves. They fear not laws; right gives way to force, and justice lies conquered beneath the aggressive sword. With skins and loose breeches they keep off the evils of the cold; their shaggy faces are protected with long locks. A few retain traces of the Greek tongue, but even

this is rendered barbarous by a Getic twang. There is not a single man among these people who perchance might express in Latin any common words whatsoever. I, the Roman bard – pardon, ye Muses! – am forced to utter most things in Sarmatian fashion.[5]

In contrast to longed-for Rome and the nourishing warmth of its civilisation, Ovid uses relentless hyperbole to portray Tomis, its environment and inhabitants, as a freezing cultural and climatic wasteland:

> Yet while the warm breezes blow we are defended by the interposing Hister [the Danube]; with the flood of his waters he repels wars. But when grim winter has thrust forth his squalid face, and the earth is marble-white with frost, and Boreas and the snow prohibit dwelling beneath the Bear, then 'tis clear that these tribes are hard pressed by the shivering pole. The snow lies continuously, and once fallen, neither sun nor rains may melt it, for Boreas hardens and renders it eternal … With skins and stitched breeches they keep out the evils of the cold; of the whole body only the face is exposed. Often their hair tinkles with hanging ice and their beards glisten white with the mantle of frost.[6]

In his exile writings, then, Ovid provides us (particularly those of us who work on the region of Eastern Europe) with a vivid image of his Northern, Eastern exile among the wild Sarmatians and Gets, an image whose coordinates of metropolitan civilisation and peripheral barbarism have continued to shape discourse about the region and are familiar to us today. This is a discourse in which later Romanian discourse about Ovid and the supposed Latin heritage of Romania takes part, albeit as a dissenting rejoinder. Taking the two phenomena together – Ovid's writing in exile and the nineteenth-century statue that commemorates that exile – we can see that Ovid in Tomis is invested with the role of sign or border-post in two similar but importantly variant projections of space that come to stand in ironic disjuncture: on the one hand, Ovid's writings map out the terrain of today's Romania as barbaric borderlands, literally at the edge of the world, all the better to exclude it from the sphere of civilisation; and, on the other hand, the Romanian statue of Ovid functions as a flag, planted in the ground, that claims that same territory as an integral, albeit peripheral part of the civilised centre, and that suggests that barbary begins yet further away, beyond Romanian national and cultural borders.

Ovid's 'unreal' spaces

It is a commonplace, one that we have learned from Derrida and from the new historicism that drew inspiration from him, to say that 'il n'y a pas de hors-texte'; that everything that we know about the world is given to us in language and is mediated discursively, and that that mediation in discourse involves narrative structures, rhetorical devices, literary tropes, and so on. This insight tells us there is no strictly policeable boundary between the literary and the non-literary and that everything that we know about the so-called real is always bathed in a suspicion of the fictional and unreal. All this is most definitely not to say that there really *is* nothing but text and that there is no such thing as a referential world. It does say, however, that – while this referential world exists, somewhere in the shadows – we are only able to know it as it presents and represents itself to us in the light of language.

These insights are more than pertinent when looking at Ovid and his exile, the factual and historical basis of which remains hazy, shrouded in the fog that rises from the Black Sea. For centuries, scholars have debated the exact nature of the reason for the poet's exile. Ovid himself speaks enigmatically of 'carmen et error', where the carmen (song) most likely refers to his *Ars amatoria*, a poem that is thought to have offended Augustus since it did not sit well with his programme for moral restoration.[7] Intriguingly, moreover, so little is known about the circumstances of Ovid's exile that scholars, at different periods, have even gone so far as to cast doubt on the historicity of Ovid's exile itself, as much as to say, that all that we know of Ovid in Tomis is mere fabrication and fiction.[8] Many of these arguments for Ovid's exile as auto-mythology are made on the basis of the striking incompatibility of what we know must have been the objective features of Tomis at the time (its climate and so on) and their hyperbolic depiction in Ovid's verse. As Jan Morris bluntly puts it in a 2005 review of a new translation of the *Tristia*:

> As many a Black Sea tourist knows, nowadays the climate of Constanța is pleasant (average annual temperature 54F), but in Ovid's descriptions it was a perpetual wintry nightmare of cold, fog, bitter winds, wine frozen into bottle-shapes and snow allegedly lying all the year round (at the same latitude as Florence!).[9]

By way of riposte to such arguments, scholars like Claassen have sought to underline the pathetic aspect of Ovid's verse-making, countering that the admittedly wild discrepancies between any verifiable truth and

Ovid's poetry can be attributed to the way that the poet 'realistically externalises inner suffering in concrete, physical terms'.[10]

Nonetheless, the faint possibility that Ovid's reader is the victim of what would be one of the greatest literary hoaxes of all time is alluring. An extreme response to what Williams terms the 'unreality' of Ovid's Tomis, this possibility corresponds to the sense of the reader that Ovid's exile is not so much about movement in 'real' space as about a journey in literature. 'Exile' facilitates a movement, less from Rome to Tomis, than away from his previous works: a movement to inhabit a different form of literary genre (the genre of exilic poetry) and a different form of (exilic) subjectivity. Whatever the case, 'exile' enables Ovid to explore – as much as, if not more than any genuine Sarmatian wastes – a landscape of topoi and form that are, in large part, already pre-given to him in the Ancient literary tradition: the Callimachean genre of invective, the topos of the frozen, barbarian North that finds its roots in Herodotos and Strabo, the genre of lament of exile, well established in both Greek and Latin poetry, and so on.[11] Thus, by way of a particular example: Ovid's description of his thundery arrival in Tomis, tossed by waves and winds, echoes, is mediated and, indeed, made possible by the analogous arrivals on rocky shores of the literary heroes Aeneas and Odysseus, in Virgil and in Homer, respectively. As much as to say: whether or not Ovid ever actually reaches Tomis, the Tomis that he encounters is never entirely or solely real: any real journey he makes is always inseparable from, and unimaginable without, a voyage through and to spaces that, as much as they may be real, are also inescapably imaginary.

It might be possible to imagine – behind the veil of genre and its conventions, subject positions and expectations – an apparently real Ovid in Tomis. This Ovid consorts happily with his new-found friends among the 'trousered throng of Getae', composes witty drinking songs in their language in the local taverns, finds warmth in his goat-skin cloak, and appreciates the cool mist that rises from the Black Sea.[12] This Ovid, whose image is visible only in the light of speculation, inhabits an unmediated space that exists in a totally different dimension from the one that is defined by the opposition of the icy wastes of barbarism and the warmth of civilisation. But this real space can only ever be the product of imagination and fantasy. For the Ovid that we do know can only ever be the Ovid who returns to his rooms at the end of the evening and gloomily inserts himself into a lyrical subject position and a set of spatial coordinates that are not those of any real geography, but rather those of the literary imagination. What is instructive about Ovid in Tomis for a critical area studies – and what makes him a good standard bearer for it – is the fact that his work sets into motion a shadowy interplay of real and unreal spaces and places, an interplay that cannot be ignored. This foggy interplay and this mist-bound terrain are phenomena that traditional area studies often wishes to do away with. Critical area studies recognises, celebrates, and finds its exilic home in them.

Notes

1. Ovid, *Tristia*, III, 3, 73–6.
2. For more on the role that Ovid has come to play in Romanian national and literary discourse, including the claim that Ovid was the first 'Romanian' poet (based on a tendentious suggestion that the poet wrote a threnody in memory of Augustus in Getic, one of the local languages), see Ziolkowski, 2005, 112–24.
3. Strictly speaking, Ovid was not exiled, but rather subject to banishment (*relegatio*), meaning that he was allowed to keep his property in Rome, to correspond freely with his wife and friends, and could legitimately nurture hopes of pardon and homecoming.
4. 'Sive quod in tenebris numerosos ponere gestus, quodque legas nulli scribere carmen, idem est' – Because to dance in the dark and to write a poem that you may read to no one is the same thing. *Epistulae ex Ponto*, IV, 2, 33–4. My translation here departs from Wheeler's 'making rhythmic gestures'.
5. Ovid, *Tristia*, V, 7, 64.
6. Ovid, *Tristia*, III, 3, 24.
7. There is a voluminous scholarly literature on this subject. The classic study of the enigma remains Thibault, 1964. For a more recent assessment of trends in this scholarship, see Williams, 2002.
8. This thesis was first advanced by J. J. Hartman in 1915 and has been re-proposed by scholars periodically. See Van der Welden, 2019.
9. Morris, 2005.
10. Claassen, 2008, 6.
11. For more of Ovid's treatment of Tomis and its inhabitants and his use of Ancient literary models and tropes in his exile poetry, contributing to what Williams terms the 'unreality' of Ovid's Tomis, see Williams, 1994, 3–49. Something of an outlier in the scholarship, Batty argues for a much more realistic and geographically and ethnographically accurate dimension to Ovid's depiction of Tomis and its environment in Batty, 1994.
12. 'bracataque turba Getae', Ovid, *Tristia*, IV, 6, 47.

Bibliography

Batty, R. M. 'On Getic and Sarmatian shores: Ovid's account of the Danube lands', *Historia: Zeitschrift für Alte Geschichte* 43(1) (1994): 88–111.
Claassen, Jo-Marie. *Ovid Revisited: The poet in exile*. London: Bloomsbury, 2008.
Morris, Jan. 'Far away and long ago…', *The Guardian*, 18 June 2005. Accessed 24 July 2024. https://www.theguardian.com/books/2005/jun/18/featuresreviews.guardianreview11.
Ovid. *Tristia. Ex Ponto*, translated by A. L. Wheeler, revised by G. P. Goold. Loeb Classical Library 151. Cambridge, MA: Harvard University Press, 1924.
Thibault, John C. *The Mystery of Ovid's Exile*. Cambridge: Cambridge University Press, 1964.
Van der Welden, Bram. 'J. J. Hartman on Ovid's (non-)exile', *Mnemnosyne* 73(2) (2019): 336–42.
Williams, Gareth D. *Banished Voices: Readings in Ovid's exile poetry*. Cambridge: Cambridge University Press, 1994.
Williams, Gareth D. 'Ovid's exile poetry'. In *The Cambridge Companion to Ovid*, edited by P. Hardie, 336–42. Cambridge: Cambridge University Press, 2002.
Ziolkowski, Theodore. *Ovid and the Moderns*. Ithaca, NY: Cornell University Press, 2005.

39
Polish architects in the world socialist system
Łukasz Stanek

Architects from the People's Republic of Poland (and others from the Second World) working in the Global South during the Cold War, occupied a 'world system' – this entry shows – whose own centre–periphery dynamics were relatively autonomous and not reducible to those of Wallerstein's capitalist sphere of hegemony and dependency. This Socialist World System (SWS), Stanek's entry insinuates, did not die in 1989–91. Polish (and other) architects learned hybrid skills in the course of their functioning within it, which they then turned to their advantage while navigating the waters of the country's nascent postsocialist realities. The SWS's material legacies – and institutional path-dependencies – like those of the Second World, are still with us today.

'West Africa was as far to the West as we could get' – this is how Polish architect Grażyna Jonkajtys-Luba recalled her work in Ghana under its first independent leader, Kwame Nkrumah (1957–66).[1] Luba and other Polish and Eastern European architects and planners travelled to West Africa in the wake of Khrushchev's opening towards the newly independent countries, which included the world-wide promotion of the socialist path of development. In the service of state design institutions and contractors in Ghana, they contributed to the development of the country, including the construction of housing and social facilities, as well as the modernisation of industry and agriculture according to the Soviet model.

Yet Luba's motivation, and those of her Polish, Bulgarian, Hungarian and Yugoslav colleagues, to go to Ghana were rarely political. These architects were attracted by the opportunities of international travel and were eager to leave behind the austerity of post-Stalinist Eastern Europe.

If the former British colony appeared, on Luba's mental map, to be closer to Western Europe than Poland, it was because Ghana's cosmopolitan environment allowed for easier exchanges across Cold War divides. Such exchanges, including architectural ones, were important for her and her colleagues, who often accepted foreign contracts motivated by professional ambition. In particular, travels to Ghana offered them opportunities to work on prestigious projects in Accra, the country's capital, such as the State House Complex (1965) and the International Trade Fair (1967).[2]

Professional ambition comes to the fore in the personal dossier that Grażyna Jonkajtys-Luba submitted to the Association of Polish Architects in Warsaw (SARP). Her submission was part of the application for the status of 'architect-creator' that came with specific benefits in socialist Poland, including access to scarce commodities and working spaces. The application consisted of a professional curriculum vitae listing education, employment, awards, as well as a self-assessment of her 'main creative achievements', supported by a portfolio, in which Luba included her work in Ghana and her later designs for Nigeria. In compiling the dossier, she engaged in a delicate balance between the need to demonstrate her individual creativity and also to comply with the rules of professional collegiality: while highlighting her personal contribution to each design, she needed not to omit the contributions of others. They included her husband, architect Jerzy Luba, with whom she collaborated in Ghana and Nigeria, and who also submitted a dossier to SARP.

During the socialist period, hundreds of architects filed similar applications, and Luba's is one of 417 dossiers which include references to work abroad. They add up to a unique archive: self-curated, since it was compiled by its protagonists who chose the content of their files; and performative, since the role of each dossier was to demonstrate the creative labour of the applicant. As an archive of Polish architectural exports it is in no way complete, since the dossier submitted to SARP only included work up to the moment of the application (1984 in Luba's case). Furthermore, many architects who went abroad did not submit a dossier at all, and one of the reasons might have been the hiatus between the expectation of an individual architectural oeuvre in the application process and the reality of collective work in state-socialist design institutes.

However incomplete, when taken together, these dossiers can be used to map a preliminary geography of architectural collaboration between socialist Poland and the Global South. I mapped it by digitising the data from the SARP archive and feeding it to Gephi, a networks analysis software. Gephi produces force-directed graphs which consist of nodes connected by edges. The graphs show forces between any two nodes: each node exerts a repulsive force on all other nodes, while two nodes connected by an edge attract.

When using Gephi, I interpreted as nodes each of the 417 architects whose dossiers include at least one reference to designs abroad. In turn, I defined edges as countries where these designs were located. Accordingly, two nodes representing two architects are connected by an edge representing a particular country, if each of them worked on at least one design destined for that country. The architect in question could have worked on these designs either in their destination countries or in Poland at any time between the 1950s and the 1980s. By connecting architects through the territories in or for which they worked, the resulting graph begins to map the mobility of Polish architects within state-socialist networks during the Cold War (see Figure 39.1).

At the centre of this map are the countries receiving the greatest number of architectural designs from socialist Poland: Iraq, Libya and Algeria, followed by Syria, while countries visited by fewer architects are located on the fringes. (The map is limited to the twelve most actively involved destination countries.) The map is not time-sensitive, and it covers the whole period of Polish architectural engagements during the Cold War. Yet the centrality or peripherality of a particular country in the map often approximates the length of these engagements, which accumulated throughout the years. For instance, Ghana was a destination for Polish architects for not much longer than a decade (during and shortly after Nkrumah's tenure), while the UAE became a destination only in the 1980s. By contrast, Iraq, Libya, Algeria and Syria received them during longer periods and, for instance, Iraq was open to the socialist bloc between the coup of Qasim in 1958 and the first Gulf war in 1990.

In the wake of the 1973 oil embargo, Libya and Iraq became the main destination of Polish architects. This embargo was a game changer in socialist foreign trade, as some of the profits of Arab governments deposited in Western financial institutions were lent to socialist countries intent upon modernising their economies. Yet they did not achieve the envisaged industrial leap and, in order to finance their debt, Poland and several other Eastern European countries boosted their exports, including those of design and construction services. Put under pressure from state and party leadership, architects, planners and managers of construction companies actively sought commissions in booming oil

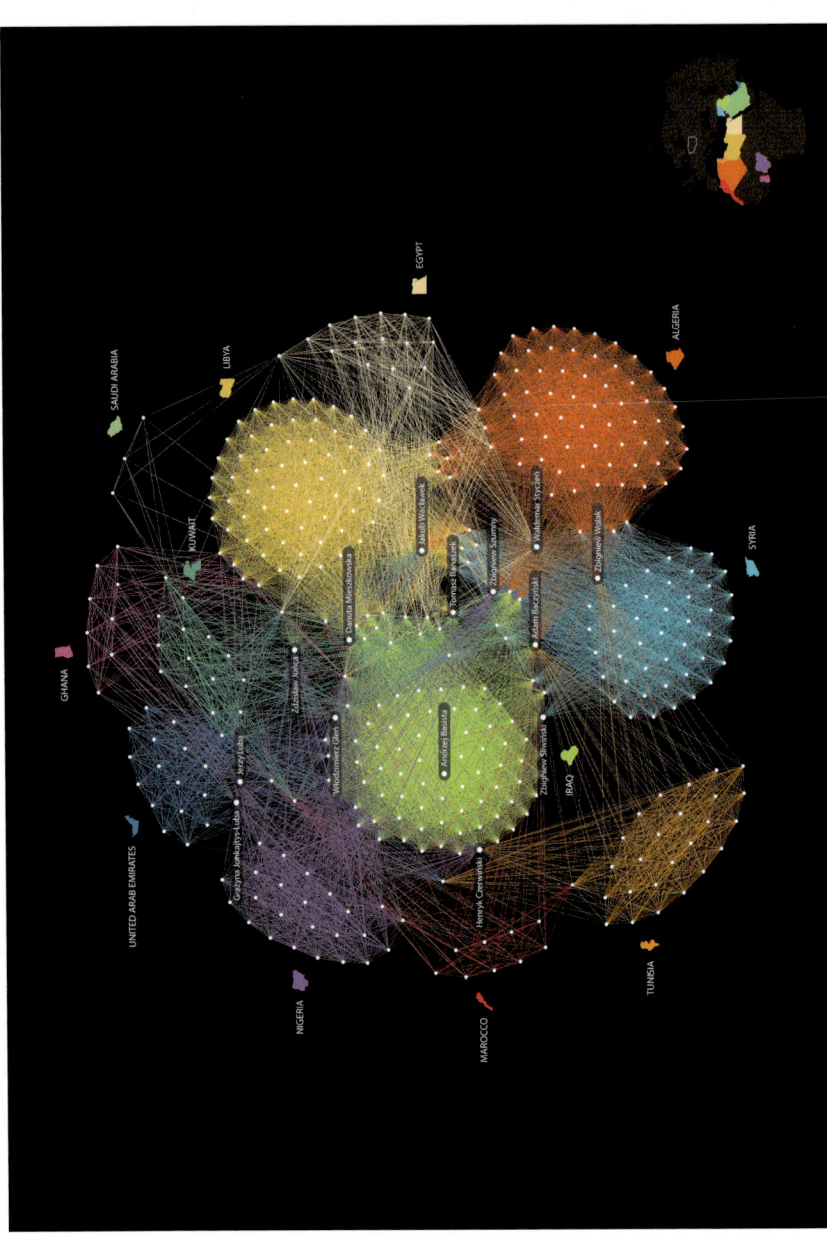

Figure 39.1 Patterns of geographic deployment of members of the Association of Polish Architects during the Cold War. The architects whose names are highlighted in the graph are discussed in the text.

Drawing © Lukasz Stanek; postproduction: Kacper Kępiński; data source: SARP Archive (Warsaw); software: Gephi.

producing countries in the Middle East and North Africa. The favourite principle of these exchanges was barter, or the exchange of goods and services without the mediation of money, and in particular the exchange of Eastern European goods and services for crude oil (petrobarter) from Iraq, Libya and elsewhere.

The geography of these exchanges is captured by the map, and it is at odds with the Cold War discourse about a world divided into two camps dominated by two 'superpowers'. Rather, at the map's centre are countries which were neither following the Soviet path of development, nor Soviet-supported Marxist-Leninist regimes. While often nominally socialist, Iraq, Libya, Algeria and Syria guarded their sovereignty against the Soviet Union and exploited East–West rivalries to advance their strategic priorities in security, state building and industrial development (and sometimes prosecuted their local communist parties). In this sense, the map shows what Soviet economists called the World Socialist System, or a community of countries trading with the socialist bloc on preferential terms. While the core of the system was the Council for Mutual Economic Assistance (Comecon), the system was not limited to the Soviet allies, and its theorists argued that it was open to all countries, irrespective of their economic and social orientation.[3]

Besides mapping the centres and peripheries of the World Socialist System as they were traversed by Polish architects, this map also tracks their trajectories. They reflect the organisation of the export of architectural labour from socialist Poland and its legal frameworks. In general, Polish architects and planners were mobilised by two types of contracts.[4] The first concerned specific design commissions which straddled all scales, from a regional plan to architectural blueprints, and they were sometimes packaged with the commission to construct the buildings designed. Polish design institutes such as Miastoprojekt Kraków established field offices to work on larger planning commissions, such as the master plans of Baghdad (1967 and 1973) and Iraq's General Housing Programme (1976–80). Many architects who are shown in the map as having worked in Iraq were based in Miastoprojekt's field office in Baghdad, headed in the late 1970s by Danuta Mieszkowska.[5]

The second type of contract was an employment contract signed between individual professionals and an institution abroad, including a planning institute, a university, a local or national authority and sometimes a private architectural office. Such a contract was signed by Andrzej Basista who first travelled to Baghdad for the master plan commission, and then stayed in Iraq to teach at the School of Architecture, Baghdad University. Mieszkowska, Basista and other members of the

Miastoprojekt team in Baghdad typically stayed for several years in Iraq. After the ending of their original commissions, some among them became employed in other countries in the region, as several nodes in the centre of the map show. One of them represents the trajectory of Włodzimierz Gleń, who relocated from Iraq to Kuwait.

By contrast, nodes in the map which are connected to multiple countries – and float between them – often represent experts who worked as consultants with various governments on behalf of international organisations, such as the United Nations. A case in point is Zbigniew Wolak, who worked for the municipal and planning departments in Syria, Tunisia and Algeria, but also in countries not shown on the map, such as Indonesia, Guinea, Qatar and Western Samoa. Others, like Zdzisław Jońca, were members of expert bodies in Poland, where they advised on tender submissions. Most frequently, however, people represented by floating nodes were designers in charge of international tenders within specialised design institutes, including BISTYP, or the Institute for Research and Type Projects in Industrial Architecture (Zbigniew Śliwiński), as well as chemical industry (Waldemar Styczeń, Zbigniew Szumny), health care (Tomasz Banaszek) and wood-processing industry (Henryk Czerwiński). Other such nodes represent architects who submitted designs to international design competitions (Adam Baczyński, Jakub Wacławek).

The map of the trajectories of Polish architecture in the Cold War challenges capitalist triumphalism that, after the end of socialism, reduced architecture's globalisation to Westernisation or Americanisation, and retroactively extended these narratives into a teleological development path of architecture after the Second World War. Against the Cold War propaganda and its afterlives, this map shows that global urbanisation and its architecture resulted from complex and uneven negotiations in which geopolitical aims, state-building objectives and national economic plans were combined with personal ambitions and desires. By the 1990s, much of this geography of architectural mobilities fell apart in the wake of the wars in Iraq, then Libya and Syria and the collapse of state-socialist institutions in charge of Polish construction export. In postsocialist Poland, few architects advertised their foreign engagements within state socialist networks, and in this sense, when looked at today, this map approximates a repressed memory of a profession that eagerly embraced the turn towards market economy. This memory sometimes haunts the architectures designed and built after the end of socialism in Poland. While embracing the postmodern idiom that was meant to herald Poland's 'return' to Europe, these buildings may also afford a more private reading: complex geometries that might have been drawn by a hand trained in arabesques; pastel panels that resemble those weathered under a desert sun; and references to 'traditional European urbanism' that had been carefully studied in the many 'little Parises' of the Maghreb and the Levant.

Notes

1   Jonkajtys-Luba, 2011; see also Stanek, 2020.
2   Stanek, 2015.
3   Zevin, 1976, 26.
4   Grzywnowicz and Kiedrzyński, 1972.
5   Stanek, 2012.

Bibliography

Grzywnowicz, Stanisław and Jerzy Kiedrzyński. *Prawa i obowiązki specjalisty* [Rights and Obligations of a Specialist]. Warsaw: Wydawnictwa UW, 1972.

Jonkajtys-Luba, Grazyna. Personal communication. June 2011.

Stanek, Łukasz. 'Miastoprojekt goes abroad: Transfer of architectural labor from socialist Poland to Iraq (1958–1989)', *The Journal of Architecture* 17(3) (2012): 361–86.

Stanek, Łukasz. 'Architects from socialist countries in Ghana (1957–1967): Modern architecture and Mondialisation', *JSAH* 74(4) (2015): 416–42.

Stanek, Łukasz. *Architecture in Global Socialism: Eastern Europe, West Africa, and the Middle East in the Cold War.* Princeton, NJ: Princeton University Press, 2020.

Zevin, Leon Z. *Economic Cooperation of Socialist and Developing Countries: New trends.* Moscow: Nauka, 1976.

40
Projectarians
Kuba Szreder

Projectarians of the world, unite! All that is solid melts into flows! It is not the nourishment of projectarians that determines their fleeting opportunities, but it is their (hypocritical?) climate-bashing frequent-budget-flying that determines their nourishment. Does it make sense to adapt the classical terminology of nineteenth-century Marxism in order to explain the lumpen faux-bourgeois realities of the non-fungible-token-chasing, non-invited but self-inviting, frequently but not necessarily always independently wealthy class of twentieth-century art projectarians? Fusing the classical Marxist concept with Boltanski and Chiapello's notion of the project, Kuba Szreder lends sharp definition to this emergent twentieth-century class-esque network, which is 'semi-connected, hovering at the borderlines', and whose existence jars with the still-dominant ideology of an 'open access and flat world'.

Eastern European clusters of the global networks of contemporary art are populated by throngs of freelance artists, curators, art critics and academics. The natives of this seemingly borderless circulation like to fashion themselves as if they were citizens of nowhere, joy riders of the flat world, as Pascal Gielen derides them.[1] The Eastern Europeans follow the flow, just as their Western European, American, Asian or African counterparts do. Or at least they try to, as much as they can afford it, but more about that later. The constellation of flows that they inhabit cherishes the illusion of boundless opportunities, essential for its own expansion and the maintenance of old and creation of new connections. This is a late, already slightly tarnished, stage of the brave new spirit of capitalism, which was analysed in its heyday by Luc Boltanski and Eve Chiapello.[2] Even now, the continual expansion of networks, where all that is solid melts into flows, capitalises on humans, infrastructures and cultural idioms, despite the failed promises of globalisation. Obviously, the prominence of international networks and promises of a frictionless world make one wonder about the relevance of terms like 'area' or 'region'. Taking the promises of globalisation at face value would risk unreflective repetition of the false ideology justifying the continuous expansion of the global circulation of capital (both economic and symbolic), which pretends to be the only remedy for the ills caused by its very expansion. This world is neither frictionless, nor is it horizontally organised. Neither the means nor fruits of circulation are distributed equally. Cultural producers operate in new cartographies of privilege, reproducing old and creating new boundaries and hierarchies. These developments do not render area studies obsolete. On the contrary, this situation requires a thorough, materialist critique of the political economy underpinning the metropolitan corridors that artists traverse and areas that they originate in and pass through. Such is the intended contribution of this short entry to the development of critical area studies.

Making a foray into the critique of the political economy of artistic circulation, one can risk a hypothesis that the natives of this circulation fall prey to a double bind. They are torn between the promise of unbounded freedom which the network offers, and the material reality of precarious life. Many find their imagination, aspiration and creativity utilised as a disposable resource for the sake of networked expansion and exploited for the individual pursuits of those who dominate hierarchies of this only superficially flat world. Quite a few of the aspiring joy riders are unlucky enough to be dependent on fleeting opportunities, the flow of which they need to monitor and chase, always on the lookout, swerving from one application, project, job to another, the only shared characteristic of which is their temporary nature. They become opportunists, in a sense dictated by Paolo Virno's materialistic, sober and non-moralistic definition of the term, denoting the flexible working conditions of post-Fordism.[3]

The inherent instability of this existence explains the growing indignation among cultural producers, who often denounce the precarity, injustice and exploitation inherent in the sector, reproduced mainly by the free labour of those who populate it. Artists exhibit without payment, curators organise their projects without even a glimpse of money, writers give their texts for free. They work only for the promise of future stability bound by the cruel laws of the artistic and academic universe. They circulate at any cost, just to keep afloat. In the circulation underpinned by the threat of forced exclusion one needs to carefully maintain one's own visibility, as only those who circulate can secure access to future opportunities. Those less successful in the art of navigating the flow of opportunities swell the ranks of artistic dark matter, a social mass of unrecognised human labour, which – as Gregory Sholette argues – underpins the gravity of the artistic universe, and at the same time is socially necessary for its reproduction and denied its rightful place in the distribution of resources, reputations and opportunities.[4] In this sense, artistic freelancers share the conditions inherent to the situation of the precariat, the new social class of temping workers, whose condition is analysed at length by sociologists, such as Guy Standing and Andrew Ross.[5] However, the situation of artists and other cultural freelancers is particular in the respect that their precarity is – at least seemingly – a result of their own decisions to pursue the promises of unbridled creativity and freedom which the networks offer. For this reason, theoreticians like Isabell Lorey prefer to talk about self-precarisation, while sociologists, among them Angela McRobbie, analyse the mindsets and risks intrinsic to the brave new world of artistic precarity.[6] It would be a mistake to think that the strategies entailing self-precarisation are doomed to fail, as many manage to realise their creative dreams, as long as they last. Guy Standing distinguishes precarity, an unwanted dependence on employers, from the freedom offered by flexible working arrangements to those who cherish privileged positions in the division of labour.[7] Those with better social backgrounds, education, capitals and contacts benefit from the same arrangements which are so detrimental to the ones less privileged. The artistic precariat seems – yet again – to be cast in between choice and circumstance.

Considering this ambivalence, I have proposed elsewhere to discuss the working conditions of artistic freelancers as 'projectarians'.[8] The projectariat is a theoretical detournement of the classic Marxist term, referenced not only in discussions about the perils of artistic circulation but also in critical management studies and analyses of international non-governmental organisations (NGOs), wherever people work on a project to-project basis.[9] Despite its somewhat ironic resonance, the term informs a materialist, critical and dialectical effort at understanding the labour conditions of the highly mobile artistic workforce. The baseline of this critique would be that projectarians are people who, in order to survive, have no choice but to make and implement projects, as many of them do not own much beyond their own capacity to circulate. In this situation, they are both similar and distinct from proletarians, who are defined by their lack of property. Similar to proletarians, who need to sell their labour in order to survive, projectarians are forced to chase temporary possibilities of employment, provided by projects or jobs structured as if they were projects (that is, temporary and task-oriented assignments). On the other hand, projectarians resemble micro-entrepreneurs (or to use Foucault's term, entrepreneurs of themselves), because projects enable them to capitalise their innate capacities, social connections and experiences – as if they were forms of capital – in exchange for monetary or reputational gains. In this sense, they are owners of their own means of production, even if they can capitalise only on themselves.

Such capitalisations are made possible by *projects*. According to Luc Boltanski and Eve Chiapello, the project is:

> ... a mass of active connections apt to create forms – that is to say, bring objects and subjects into existence – by stabilizing certain connections and making them irreversible. It is thus a temporary *pocket of accumulation* which, creating value, provides a base for the requirement of extending the network by furthering connections.[10] (italics original).

Projects are temporary assemblies of agents, things and relations that are oriented to realising a defined goal, after which they dissolve and dissipate in the network. Project-related modes of production are characteristic of post-Fordism, in which the dominant role is played by flexible labour arrangements, accelerated mobility and temporariness of relations. As projects are everywhere – festivals, exhibitions, biennials, but also temporary jobs in academia, media or in the NGO sector – the ranks of the projectariat expand.

Projects – these temporary pockets of accumulation – are excellent for expanding networks by forming new and mobilising old connections. The general flexibility of this system creates an illusion, already mentioned above, of the flat and glossy world of borderless intercultural exchange. But the costs and risks innate to the expansion and maintenance of cultural networks are not distributed equally. The meritocracy of this system is a convenient myth, or even a false ideology of merit-based access. The idea is that even if networks are competitive, eventually the wise and talented prevail. But, as already suggested, the difference between freedom and precarity derives from access to various forms of capital, as in order to circulate one needs to rely on privileged access to resources, funds and infrastructures. Family inheritance proves to be tremendously helpful for surviving long periods of unpaid or underpaid labour in culture and academia. It is essential to be able to source systems of public support, foundations or state institutions, to support one's own exploits. Not to mention fluency in English (as Mladen Stilinović, a Zagreb-based conceptual artist quipped in his work from 1992: 'an artist who cannot speak English is no artist') and an excellent understanding of artistic idioms, which derives from exceptional education. Affiliation with elite institutions is invaluable when it comes to making and presenting research, essential for keeping afloat in academic networks. Eventually, access in the flat world is determined by the good old hierarchies of class, nationality, race and gender.

Possibly the projectarians native to the eastern fringes of the European Union are more attuned to the paradoxes of this system. They are connected and privileged enough to revel in the sweet promise of circulation, enjoying the bliss of visa-free travel and unlimited access to the capitalist centres, but still not privileged enough to be sheltered from the risks inherent to circulation, in thrall to precarious labour markets, unfinished infrastructures and relatively weak welfare systems. It is a shared condition of global semi-peripheries, located somewhere on a transverse line between North and South, definitely not West, but also not far East. This paradoxical situation, despite its shortcomings, creates an opportunity for establishing trans-border solidarity networks. Being semi-connected, hovering at the borderlines, in flight from one temporary project to another, makes one question the ideology of open access and a level field. It is a matter of politics to change this sentiment into action towards the constitution of an actually-existing and not merely an illusionary borderless world.

Notes

1. Gielen, 2009; 2013.
2. Boltanski and Chiapello, 2005.
3. Virno, 2004.
4. Sholette, 2011.
5. Standing, 2014; Ross, 2009.
6. Lorey, 2006; 2011; McRobbie, 2015.
7. Standing, 2014.
8. Szreder, 2016.
9. Jałocha, 2016; Greer, Samaluk and Umney, 2019; Baker, 2014.
10. Boltanski and Chiapello, 2005, 105.

Bibliography

Baker, Catherine. 'The local workforce of international intervention in the Yugoslav successor states: "Precariat" or "projectariat"? Towards an agenda for future research', *International Peacekeeping* 21(1) (2014): 91–106.

Boltanski, Luc and Eve Chiapello. *The New Spirit of Capitalism*. London: Verso, 2005.

Gielen, Pascal. *The Murmuring of the Artistic Multitude: Global art, memory and post-Fordism*. Amsterdam: Valiz, 2009.

Gielen, Pascal. *Creativity and Other Fundamentalisms*. Heyningen: JAP SAM Books, 2013.

Greer, Ian, Barbara Samaluk and Charles Umney. 'Toward a precarious projectariat? Project dynamics in Slovenian and French social services', *Organization Studies* 40(12) (2019): 1873–95.

Jałocha, Beata. 'Projectocracy or projectariat?: How project work shapes working conditions in public, non-governmental and business sectors'. In *9th Annual Conference of the EuroMed Academy of Business: Innovation, entrepreneurship and digital ecosystems*, edited by Demetris Vrontis, Yaakov Weber and Evangelos Tsoukatos, 2022–5. Warsaw: EuroMed Press, 2016.

Lorey, Isabell. 'Governmentality and self-precarization', *Transversal* (2006), translated by Lisa Rosenblatt and Dagmar Fink. Accessed 16 August 2024. https://transversal.at/transversal/1106/lorey/en.

Lorey, Isabell. 'Virtuosis of freedom: On the implosion of political virtuosity and productive labor'. In *Critique of Creativity: Precarity, subjectivity and resistance in the 'creative industries'*, edited by Ulf Wuggenig, Gerald Raunig and Gene Ray, 79–91. London: MayFly Books, 2011.

McRobbie, Angela. *Be Creative: Making a living in the new culture industries*. Cambridge: Polity Press, 2015.

Ross, Andrew. *Nice Work If You Can Get It: Life and labor in precarious times*. New York: New York University Press, 2009.

Sholette, Gregory. *Dark Matter: Art and politics in the age of enterprise culture*. London: Pluto Press, 2011.

Standing, Guy. *The Precariat: The new dangerous class*. London: Bloomsbury, 2014.

Szreder, Kuba. *ABC Projektariatu: O nędzy projektowego życia* [The ABC of the Projectariat: About the misery of project life]. Warsaw: Bęc Zmiana, 2016.

Virno, Paolo. *A Grammar of the Multitude*. Los Angeles: Semiotext(e), 2004.

41
Raja: the not-quite critical subject of Sarajevo irony
Stef Jansen and Nebojša Šavija-Valha

Raja (Bosnian-Croatian-Serbian, through Ottoman Turkish from Arabic, 'cattle, flock, subject population'): historically, in Ottoman usage, a member of the Christian and Jewish tax-paying class, both safeguarded by Ottoman law (the Sultan's 'well-protected flock') and 'shorn' (taxed) to support the state. Hence, in Bosnian contemporary colloquial usage, either ordinary people, mob, rabble; or conversely, ironically, an in-group or a member of such a group. The discussion below dissects an 'anti-geography' that critiques any stable form of differentiation, but also hints that the display of area knowledge can itself be a means of inclusion or exclusion.

In Bosnia and Herzegovina, and particularly in its capital, Sarajevo, 'raja' denotes what is perceived as a kernel of truth about 'us'. Everyone knows what it is. Perhaps not quite. But they do know how it works, at least while it works in a here and now. Our entry draws on such presumably self-evident knowledge, interspersing it with quotations from interviews.

When pushed, interviewees defined 'raja' in various ways, as both subject and object of a social game, thus making it hard to pin down in any general terms. Raja was said to be 'a milieu', 'a *sui generis* form of society', 'a mentality', 'a code', 'a codex'. As a principle of practice unwritten in its own vernacular, in Sarajevo today, raja refers all at once to an incorporated individual who follows the principle of raja; to a community of such individuals; and to a milieu, a scene in which a drama of raja has unfolded.[1]

This contemporary usage of the term is both faithful and unfaithful to its etymology. As in the Turkish word of Arabic origin *râiya*, raja is indeed a flock (or a 'herd', as some interviewees said). As during

Ottoman rule, it denotes the common people in opposition to the ruling elite. However, as we shall see, the (self)naming of raja today includes a deconstruction of these (op)positions to produce an antielite elite which ultimately negates any social space beyond its 'herd'. All inhabitants of Sarajevo are (forcibly) invited to partake in a drama of reciprocal exchange, and it is precisely this potentially infinite reach that renders raja possible.

Alongside such antihistorical displacements of the term, we find, as befits an Anti-Atlas, frenzied anti-geography. At least from a Eurocentric perspective, due to relentless de- and re-territorialisation of the great powers of any given period, Bosnia and Herzegovina has been mythologised, dismissed, celebrated and lamented as the paradigmatic border zone: neither-nor/either-or West/East/South/North. This pertains to whatever bipolarity these cardinal directions might signify: civility/savagery, Islam/Christianity, socialism/capitalism, outside/inside, and so on. The one thing that holds stable is the notion of Bosnia and Herzegovina as border zone. In the process, contradictions are maintained.

For 'border zone' is a contradictory notion. Like a territory, a zone is two-dimensional, self-contained, centred and exclusive; a border is one-dimensional, shared, ex-centred and inclusive. A zone gravitates towards singularity of signification, a border towards its multiplicity. Imagine Bosnia and Herzegovina as a plane surrounded by various power-infused energy fields. Then, imagine a line that floats over the plane, advancing and retreating like – or actually being – a frontline that confronts armies affiliated with external powers. As it floats, the plane becomes saturated with leftovers, boundary stones of former conquests, now becoming cultural markers. Their abundance renders it impossible to differentiate between the zone and the border, as traces are not abandoned but put on standby. The borderline production machine is waiting to be activated.

From this perspective, Bosnia and Herzegovina is inhabited by survivors: those able to navigate such rough, uneven terrain, intersected by so many boundaries. 'Bosnians, particularly Sarajevans, I think it is a set of, not positive, but crazy and negative characteristics of our conquerors from times immemorial until today … We learned nothing positive from them.'[2] Survivors developed unbreakable affiliations with their conquerors, becoming guardians of their symbolic order. Yet, perhaps typically for such border zones, they also cultivated the ability to transgress this loyalty, those boundaries, and to affiliate with compatriots who acculturated with a competing conquering order. Incommensurable at first glance, the two affiliations are, nonetheless, complementary.

Both are kept at one's disposal for 'proper' use, for precise interpellation in a specific here and now.

Today, a resulting game of 'balancing' is identified as the core productive act of raja, extending its principles far beyond the imperial ethno-religious heterogeneity in which it originated. 'The mentality of people living here is such that there must be a balance, a balance within raja. Whoever goes down or up, he stands out … Everybody should be at the same plane.' Stereotypical? Essentialising? Sarajevo-centric? Mythologising? Sure. In fact, self-reflexive, ironic performances of all of these are key to the practice of raja. And raja is the champion of the balancing game, the elite player who lifts the game up to a next level. Balancing and the plane mutually reproduce each other as conditions and practices. And raja appears as their immanent result.

At the heart of such drama lies humour that spares no-one, especially not oneself. Irony is crucial:

> no matter how much people are ironic towards others … there is a tradition in Sarajevo to be self-ironic. Even appreciation and admiration are shown in a 'mild' ironic manner. Like those raja sitting in a café when Ivo Andrić passed by. And they called out: 'Hello, bridge over the Drina, is anything being written!?' [Halo, na Drini ćuprija, napiše li se štagod!?]. This is not to demonstrate their own primitivism – well, that's evident, har-har – but they also show that they recognised the great novelist, read his books, somehow respect him, and that they were interested in what he was doing, while teasing him.

What happens in this anecdote? Bosnian Nobel laureate Ivo Andrić's high status and the planetary recognition of his novel *The Bridge on the Drina* render him different from others and place him in different orders of power. This is recognised as a threat to the shaky balance, the glue of everyday life. Therefore, such differences must be displaced as an excess of signification. They are displaced to the sphere of privacy, where identities, accomplishments, stratified positions are acknowledged as relevant and, through their relation to the order of power, divisive. In contrast, the sphere of raja is constructed as 'a plane of consistency', in which no particularity – 'below' or 'above' – is permitted.[3] With successful displacement, the individual is relieved of the burden of various orders and s/he becomes one of us, simply raja. Potential divisions are disabled and sociality can operate: raja practices are a 'cohesive force – for good or for bad'. By adding markers of irony – quotation marks, facial expressions, nicknames, particular phrases – The Writer becomes 'the writer', deprived of excesses of signification.[4] So the Subject of raja is possible only as a *'S'ubject*, with Subjectivity suspended by irony.

And what does this ironic subject do? It socialises. Socialising (*druženje*) is raja's unique entry point. It is both its scene and its activity, configured around reciprocal exchange. A potlatch of wit and jests makes every order of power crumble, there and then, producing an outburst of pleasure.[5] Everybody must socialise. Yet the actual activity in which one socialises (hiking, playing ball, singing) is to be treated as secondary, even accidental: the real investment is in the socialising it allows. This is learned at an early age and articulated as it expands through neighbourhoods, schools, workplaces and leisure sites. All these settings serve as hubs which gather one's different rajas, each with specific traits: raja from one's street, raja from school, bicycling raja. Ultimately these can be imagined to cross-fertilise until this encompasses – colonises – the whole city. There is no social space beyond raja. And there is no place to hide: raja is a fully transparent, omnipresent, totalitarian community in which every person is exposed to everybody else, for good and for bad.

Refusal to de-subjectify oneself is swiftly punished by expulsion. 'The most terrible thing you can face is to be expelled from raja.' Now outside raja, that person comes to be labelled a *papak* (pl. *papci*). Literally this means 'cloven hoof': desocialisation here entails dehumanisation, expulsion into animality. A *papak* shows off and may even seek to impose his or her attitudes, identity, ideology, accomplishments, status and so on. Unforgivably, a *papak* takes himself or herself seriously. This is a pathology that raja does not tolerate. As an antielite strategy raja compulsively displaces any excellence into the realm of irony, or, failing that, literally beyond the city limits. In this very act raja constitutes itself as a paradoxical antielite elite which grounds its own excellence in the displacement of any other excellence.

However, there is no permanent distinction between raja and *papci*. Due to its immanence, the story of raja is always a story of a particular practice. In the endless reproduction of irony, only the here and now in which raja affirms its existence counts. Potentially anyone can be a *papak* and anyone can be raja. In that sense, raja is an ad hoc community of those who socialise here and now, deploying irony to temporarily displace any dangerous excesses of differential signification. Through this totalitarian ad hoc inclusion, enabling all kinds of *papci* to infiltrate it, different rajas competitively enrich the register of irony. This fires great productivity, particularly in popular culture. Yet no matter how vanguard, such production always remains rearguard, never leaving the embrace of its own circle of irony and celebrating nothing but itself.

As the antielite elite player of the balancing game, raja masterfully irons out the contradictions of the border zone and consequently any other divisions, demonstrating sustained pleasure in ironic unity. This severely limits its critical capacity: raja reiterates a society in which, if we are allowed to paraphrase and play with Marcuse: '[a] comfortable, smooth, reasonable [!?], democratic [!?] [*and above all humorous un-*] freedom prevails …'.[6] For all its subversive charm, raja is politically toothless. Any resistant power it could possibly wield is ironised, displaced into the private sphere, and all (identitarian, class or other) 'politics' are considered to be motivated by private interests.

Ultimately, within raja we may discern the very possibility of both East and West. In their urge to demarcate those two with cadastral precision, conquering powers always provoke raja's counterstrike. As an 'anti-geographer' extraordinaire, raja wittily denounces the ultimate futility of such 'geographical' efforts. Comfortably reclining in the armchair of its border zone, armed with relentless sedentary irony, raja displaces any defining and dividing property of the borderline to where it belongs – to the centre of power that is drawing it. It excels as a critic of the possibility of any articulation of both great and petty geopolitics. It ridicules them even when they are deadly serious here and now, expecting them to get lost in the abundance of ironic significations they suddenly encounter. However, taking nothing seriously, raja's expectation is futile too, so the game continues without changes – for better or worse.

Barth has taught us to focus on boundary drawing rather than on the stuff of identities.[7] No West without East, then. From the perspective of raja, however, they are both *papci*.

Notes

1 Šavija-Valha, 2017.
2 Unattributed statements in this part derive from private conversations with the author.
3 Deleuze and Guattari, 2004.
4 Hutcheon, 2005, 34.
5 Mauss, 1966.
6 Adapted from Marcuse, 2007, 3.
7 Barth, 1969.

Bibliography

Barth, F. *Ethnic Groups and Boundaries: The social organization of culture difference*. Oslo: Universitetsforlaget, 1969.

Deleuze, Gilles and Félix Guattari. *A Thousand Plateaus: Capitalism and schizophrenia*. London: Continuum, 2004.

Hutcheon, Linda. *Irony's Edge: The theory and politics of irony*. London: Routledge, 2005.

Marcuse, Herbert. *One-Dimensional Man*. London: Routledge, 2007.

Mauss, Marcel. *The Gift*. London: Cohen and West, 1966.

Šavija-Valha, Nebojša. 'Raja: The ironic subject of everyday life in Sarajevo'. In *Negotiating Social Relations in Bosnia and Herzegovina: Semiperipheral entanglements*, edited by Stef Jansen, Čarna Brković and Vanja Čelebičić, 163–78. London: Routledge, 2017.

42
Sherlock Holmes and his doppelganger: for an anti-atlas of world literature
Antonija Primorac

Doppelganger demonstrates vividly why even studies of the presumed 'core' areas of world literature demand a detailed contextual knowledge of territories, histories and relationships well beyond Paris and London. Without such knowledge, an absence of evidence (particularly in English-language sources) easily becomes evidence of absence, while assumptions about direct core–periphery relations of power and influence obscure more intricately plotted routes of transmission, let alone creative adaptations where the point of origin is less important than the new context. Any aspiration to grasp and analyse global patterns, including but not limited to world literature, needs to take local cultures and spheres of influence seriously, or risk the sort of partial and distorted conclusions that Sherlock Holmes warned against.

Hidden inside plain cardboard boxes in the Croatian National Library in Zagreb lie scores of yellowed, well-thumbed, early twentieth-century penny dreadfuls belonging to the series *Detektiv Sherlock Holmes i njegovi znameniti doživljaji* (Detective Sherlock Holmes and his famous adventures). Published between 1907 and 1908 under Arthur Conan Doyle's name, the series included translations of his Sherlock Holmes stories, alongside what prove to be pastiches churned out by anonymous writers hired by the Berlin-based publishing house, Verlagshaus für Volksliteratur und Kunst. The first eleven issues of these German pastiches were published as *Detektiv Sherlock Holmes und seine weltberühmten Abenteuer* (Detective Sherlock Holmes and his world-famous adventures) with the publisher soon selling the translation copyright across the globe. A lawsuit filed by Conan Doyle's German publisher in Stuttgart resulted in the series title being changed, to *Aus dem*

Geheimakten des Welt-Detektivs (From the secret files of the world detective), from the twelfth issue onwards.[1]

Outside Germany, these translations of Sherlock Holmes's sensational, action-packed adventures were published in locations where news of these court proceedings had not penetrated, often in the same format and series as translations of Conan Doyle's actual works, as is evident from the surviving Croatian titles.[2] This probably helped obscure the stories' provenance and delayed the discovery of fraud, helping disseminate the adventures of Sherlock Holmes's doppelganger as Conan Doyle's work, as far as Argentina.[3]

The story of *Detektiv Sherlock Holmes und seine weltberühmten Abenteuer* is more than just a story about unscrupulous publishers meeting demand for the globally popular Sherlock Holmes stories. This peculiarly successful pastiche also offers itself as an ideal case study of transnational literary dissemination through translation. If we trace the many different translations of the series (Danish, Swedish, Norwegian, Polish, Croatian, Slovenian, Serbian, Portuguese, French and Spanish Argentinian editions have been located thus far) we are faced with a map of the very broad sphere of influence that this German publisher of popular literature – and, by extension, German editors – had in the early twentieth century.[4] Moreover, the sheer scale of the translations' geographical spread in a relatively short period (there were Croatian, Serbian, Slovenian, Portuguese and Argentinian editions published between 1907–11, almost immediately after the German ones) confirms the proposition, put forward by Louise Nilsson, David Damrosch and Theo D'haen in the introduction to their edited collection, *Crime Fiction as World Literature*, that crime fiction is a world literature genre *par excellence* because of its global outreach via translation and because it 'fully illustrates what Marx and Engels enticingly describe as world literature's "intercourse in every direction"'.[5] This particular German doppelganger of Sherlock Holmes will be used to test some recent theories of world literature and the related method of distant reading, investigating received assumptions about literary dynamics east and south-east of the presumed literary centres in Western Europe. Conan Doyle's Holmes will be engaged on his doppelganger's case, his methods and proclamations providing the critical guidelines.

'It is a capital mistake to theorise before one has data' (*A Scandal in Bohemia*, 1891)

In his *Atlas of the European Novel 1800–1900* (1999), Franco Moretti posited London and Paris as the key European centres for the creation and dispersion of the novel and its subgenres across the European 'narrative markets' by analysing maps created with the help of available catalogues and bibliographies.[6] Moretti suggested that the translation routes on the maps revealed that 'at one extreme, a small group of countries ... exported furiously in every direction; at the other extreme, a very large group that imported a lot, and exported almost nothing'.[7] This led to his conclusion about 'two, three Europes. With France and Britain *always at its core*, most other countries always in the periphery; and in between a variable group that changes from case to case'.[8]

In subsequent work that championed the application of quantitative literary analysis, Moretti suggested that comparative literature had failed its early promises of studying world literature and proposed instead a formalist approach united with Wallerstein's world-systems theory, where literature substituted capitalism.[9] The stress was to be on the examination of unequal relationships in the literary world-systems, where the cultural and linguistic power of the 'core' dictated trends in the 'peripheries'. Moretti also provocatively proposed the method of 'distant reading', a quantitative analysis of large amounts of digitised literary works that included the forgotten and now unread contemporaries of works that would come to constitute the canon. Here distance becomes 'a condition of knowledge: it allows you to focus on units that are much smaller or much larger than the text: devices, themes, tropes – or genres and systems'.[10] Such an approach to the study of literature became possible due to advances in technology and improved computational methods, but was quickly misunderstood as an attempt to supplant close reading and other traditional critical approaches.[11] Yet the real problem of distant reading lies not in technological optimism or, as Ted Underwood astutely puts it, the conflation of 'new interpretive methods with new technologies', but in the limitations of the digital archives available for analysis.[12]

In the first of Arthur Conan Doyle's short stories featuring the famously rational detective, Sherlock Holmes pronounces: 'It is a capital mistake to theorise before one has data. Insensibly one begins to twist facts to suit theories, instead of theories to suit facts'.[13] Large-scale digitised literary data is still relatively scarce in South-East and East Europe, primarily due to different but persistent funding issues related to digitisation projects and digital humanities in general;[14] it is therefore no surprise it was also scarce in Moretti's maps tracing translations of English and French novels in nineteenth-century Europe. In his *Atlas* Moretti used only data from Hungary and Romania for the whole region south-east of German-speaking Europe, alongside a handful of other countries with 'reasonably good bibliographies': Denmark, Poland, France, Italy, the Netherlands, Great Britain and Spain.[15] However, even the data on Romania was incomplete, thanks to the fact that the available national bibliography stopped at 'R'. Moreover, the fact that Romania has considerably more translations from French than from English is interpreted merely as a problem deriving from the small size of its market; there is no attempt to consider historical, cultural or linguistic ties that might have affected this choice.[16]

What registers as an absence in the maps merely reflects a lack of data on the literatures and languages in question. Still, because the dearth of data ends up interpreted *as data*, the resulting maps of European narrative markets end up reinforcing, rather than challenging, assumptions about the literary history of the region, the development and/or diffusion of literary genres. This can be read as emblematic of the Anglosphere's blindness to literary or cultural trends outside its direct sphere of interest, which often goes hand in hand with a disconcerting disregard for the pivotal role played by translation in the processes of cross-cultural exchange even when, as is the case with Moretti's *Atlas*, translations are discussed. However, Moretti bases his analyses on the assumption that translations only ever travel one way – and directly – from the source text to the target language. But the translation process is not always so straightforward, especially in the nineteenth and early twentieth centuries.

'When you have eliminated the impossible, whatever remains, however improbable, must be the truth' (*The Sign of the Four*, 1890)

Perhaps unexpectedly, translations are not always based on the original, in the source language. The boundaries that a translation crosses, and the languages it travels through, all reflect complex power dynamics among different languages and cultures. Sherlock Holmes of *Detektiv Sherlock Holmes und seine weltberühmten Abenteuer* enters the literary scene as the always already translated doppelganger of Conan Doyle's Holmes – a translation, moreover, without an English original. Thanks to more or less convincing paratexts (bylines with supposed US copyright, for example), every subsequent translation poses as a translation from a spectral English original, yet each is more or less obviously translated from German; the final title in the Portuguese series, for example, does not even attempt to correct the German spelling of 'Scherlock'.

Translation-studies scholars often bemoan the paradoxical lack of attention to translation in Anglophone comparative literature studies, where translations are widely used but are rarely discussed as translations, created in particular times and social and cultural contexts, and for particular audiences. As Lawrence Venuti shows in his examination of the Anglophone bias in the study of comparative and world literature in the US, attitudes to translation can vary, from reductive commentary on translation processes defined by the rhetoric of loss, to studies of transnational literature that demonstrate 'the aggressive monolingualism of the US academy [that] entirely excludes foreign languages and literatures'.[17]

The speed with which the German Holmes appeared across and outside of Europe, together with the fact that it took some time for the pastiche to be exposed, reflects the powerful role played by the German language (and German publishers) as a cultural hub and purveyor of trends. Just as Shakespeare first appeared in Croatia through translation from German in the early nineteenth century, the first translations of Sherlock Holmes in Russian also came through German.[18] But while the texts featuring Sherlock Holmes's German doppelganger pose as translations from English, they also end up disseminating a wholly *new* Holmes – physically robust, adventurous and without Doctor Watson. Moreover, this new, always already translated, Holmes is not only relatively independent of the Anglophone Sherlock's 'core' norms: he also enters into direct competition with it in the 'periphery's' narrative markets.

The case of Sherlock Holmes's doppelganger thus points to this blind spot in the study of world literature, highlighted by Venuti: the role played by translation. To truly understand the history and development of world literature as an interconnected yet profoundly differentiated system, one must chart the complex journeys that translations make across borders and through languages and cultures. For this to happen, however, there needs to be a stronger engagement not only with translation studies but also with critical area studies, especially its insights on the spheres of cultural influence. The resulting anti-atlas would map translation routes, literary influence and reception trends that would contribute to a better understanding of transnational relationships between literatures and cultures, showing that assumptions about the presumed centrality of London and Paris at the end of the nineteenth and the beginning of the twentieth century ignore some rather interesting goings-on outside Western Europe and the Anglosphere.

Notes

1. Ritzheimer, 2016, 36.
2. More on this topic, including access to the digitised copies of the Croatian translations of the series in question, will be available through a virtual exhibition *Sherlock's Doppelgangers/ Sherlockovi dvojnici*, at the website of the Croatian National and University Library in Zagreb, planned for 2025. The exhibition is one of the outcomes of my research project entitled: 'What We Read When We Read Sherlock Holmes in Translation: On the theory and practice of translating popular literature' (*Što čitamo kad čitamo Sherlocka Holmesa u prijevodu: O teoriji i praksi prevođenja popularne književnosti*) funded by the University of Rijeka and produced in collaboration with the Croatian National and University Library (project details available at https://portal.uniri.hr/Projekti/Details/01099. Accessed 17 August 2024). I would especially like to thank Sofija Klarin Zadravec for her invaluable help with the digitisation and the setting up of the exhibition.
3. A hardbound Spanish translation of three stories from this series, published in Buenos Aires in 1911 as *Casos Secretos de Sherlock Holmes*, is held in Portsmouth City Library's Arthur Conan Doyle Collection, Richard Lancelyn Green Bequest. Special thanks to Michael Gunton, Senior Archivist at the Portsmouth City Library, for his assistance navigating the Arthur Conan Doyle Collection, and to Rachel Smillie who created the initial survey of the collection's holdings and thus made tracking down the French, Portuguese and Spanish editions possible.
4. Some were even republished until very recently: the French translations were reprinted as late as 1993 in Lausanne, Switzerland, and Croatian translations in 2007 and 2008 in Zagreb.
5. Nilsson, Damrosch and D'haen, 2017.
6. Moretti, 1999, 37.
7. Moretti, 1999, 173.
8. Moretti, 1999, 173–4 (emphasis added).
9. Moretti, 2013, 46.
10. Moretti, 2013, 48–9.
11. Underwood, 2019, 145.
12. Underwood, 2019, 156.
13. Conan Doyle, 1904.
14. A European Commission-funded COST Action entitled Distant Reading for European Literary History (2017–21) is currently trying to address some of these issues by creating a pan-European, multilingual, open access corpus of the nineteenth-century novel – the European Literary Text Collection (ELTeC). More on the project at: https://distant-reading.net. Accessed 17 August 2024.
15. Moretti, 1999, 176.
16. Moretti, 1999, 177.
17. Venuti, 2016, 183.
18. Lupić, 2010, 147; Piliev, 2019.

Bibliography

Conan Doyle, Arthur. 'A scandal in Bohemia'. In *The Complete Sherlock Holmes*, 119–35. London: George Newnes, 1904.

Lupić, Ivan. *Shakespeare između izvedbe i knjige* [Shakespeare Between Performance and the Book]. Zagreb: Globus, 2010.

Moretti, Franco. *Atlas of the European Novel, 1800–1900*. London: Verso, 1999.

Moretti, Franco. *Distant Reading*. London: Verso, 2013.
Nilsson, Louise, David Damrosch and Theo D'haen. 'Introduction: Crime fiction as world literature'. In *Crime Fiction as World Literature*, edited by Louise Nilsson, David Damrosch and Theo D'haen, 1–8. New York: Bloomsbury, 2017.
Piliev, George. 'A study in Russian'. Introduction. Accessed 30 July 2019. http://www.acdoyle.ru/about/study%20in%20russian.html.
Ritzheimer, Kara L. *'Trash', Censorship, and National Identity in Early Twentieth-Century Germany*. Cambridge: Cambridge University Press, 2016.
Underwood, Ted. *Distant Horizons: Digital evidence and literary change*. Chicago, IL: University of Chicago Press, 2019.
Venuti, Lawrence. 'Hijacking translation: How comp lit continues to suppress translated texts', *boundary 2* 43(2) (2016): 179–204.

43
Cartographies of Soviet childhood
Nataliya Tchermalykh

Atlases suggest that time as well as space can be frozen on a page. These frozen images then come to represent reality in the minds of readers – all the more so when they are part of childhood memories. Here the author conveys her own disorienting experience of seeing taken-for-granted maps reorganised by geopolitics so as to be unrecognisable and simultaneously analyses an artist's use of Soviet children's maps as political interventions: ones that recognise the long-lasting influence of familiar cartographies and deconstruct their implications and their emotional power. Not all mental maps conform to the geographies of power: artists' treatments (and individuals' reactions) show how critical and creative approaches can also give access to more personal, less officially sanctioned visions of the world.

In 2014 it seemed as though every season brought new political currents to Ukraine: the revolutionary winter followed by a Crimean spring, when everybody talked about 'referendum' and 'annexation'; then came the Donbas summer, when the word 'war' was for the first time on everyone's lips. At the same time, the contours of Ukraine were changing on the global map: first, the Crimean peninsula became shaded with a particular dense red-lined hachure, standing for 'disputed territories', then the Eastern regions of Ukraine were transformed into amorphous grey zones, flecked with broken lines, marking the areas controlled by the insurgent armies of the so-called People's Republics of Donetsk and Luhansk (DNR and LNR), the regular Ukrainian army, and the pro-Ukrainian paramilitary groups.

During those times, I was surely not the only one to be affected with a feeling of perplexity, one that sprang from the realisation that the maps registered in our minds from schooldays – and perhaps still stored in the same boring classrooms – are not accurate anymore (see Figure 43.1). This strange feeling of bewilderment was amplified even more by an incapacity to recognise the piece of reduced territory with partly stumped borders, referred to in the media as 'Ukraine', as a familiar country, or as one's home. How has this disruptive experience of territorial reconfiguration – an experience that is both cognitive and visual – been reworked and reimagined by local artists?

In this entry, I examine one case of artistic reworking of Soviet child-oriented cartography observed during my fieldwork conducted in 2014–15 in Ukraine and Russia.[1] My main objective was to document and analyse artistic and intellectual responses, produced within the artistic communities, to the ongoing political hostilities opposing the two countries. In such a controversial, rapidly changing context, the area of 'politically motivated art' becomes a locus of critical experimentation around such disputed concepts as the State, the Empire, the borders, the war – critical opinions and debates that are pushed to the margins of public awareness in a range of post-Soviet societies. I argue that, in the context of a rigidifying hegemony of attitudes, these artistic manifestations may epitomise and symbolically stand for voices, concepts and spheres of knowledge that are restrained from the socially accepted representations of political realities. These forms of artistic production are significant symptoms of a relentless, yet often unnoticed reflection and contestation unfolding in the margins of the states. Such creative responses and cultural redefinitions of political processes should fall under scrutiny of critical area studies, as they make sense of the ever-evolving contours of the Global East, that 'enormous, inchoate territory, encompassing myriad distinct political and economic systems, as well as cultural and aesthetic proclivities'.[2]

In 1999, Fernando Coronil had already asked similar questions, drawing from Borges, Chomsky and Said: 'And if we managed to freeze history and replicate geography in a map, wouldn't this representation be ephemeral? Since space too is located in time and is changing constantly, how could a map represent geography without apprehending its movement?' – a question which he answers a few lines later: 'Perhaps, this shows that maps do not mirror reality, but depict it from partial perspectives, figuring it in accidence with particular standpoints and specific aims'.[3] His text, and more specifically its subtitle – *Toward nonimperial geohistorical categories* – came to mind when I accidentally saw a Russian female demonstrator holding a banner that quite incredibly seemed to come straight from my childhood (Figure 43.2).

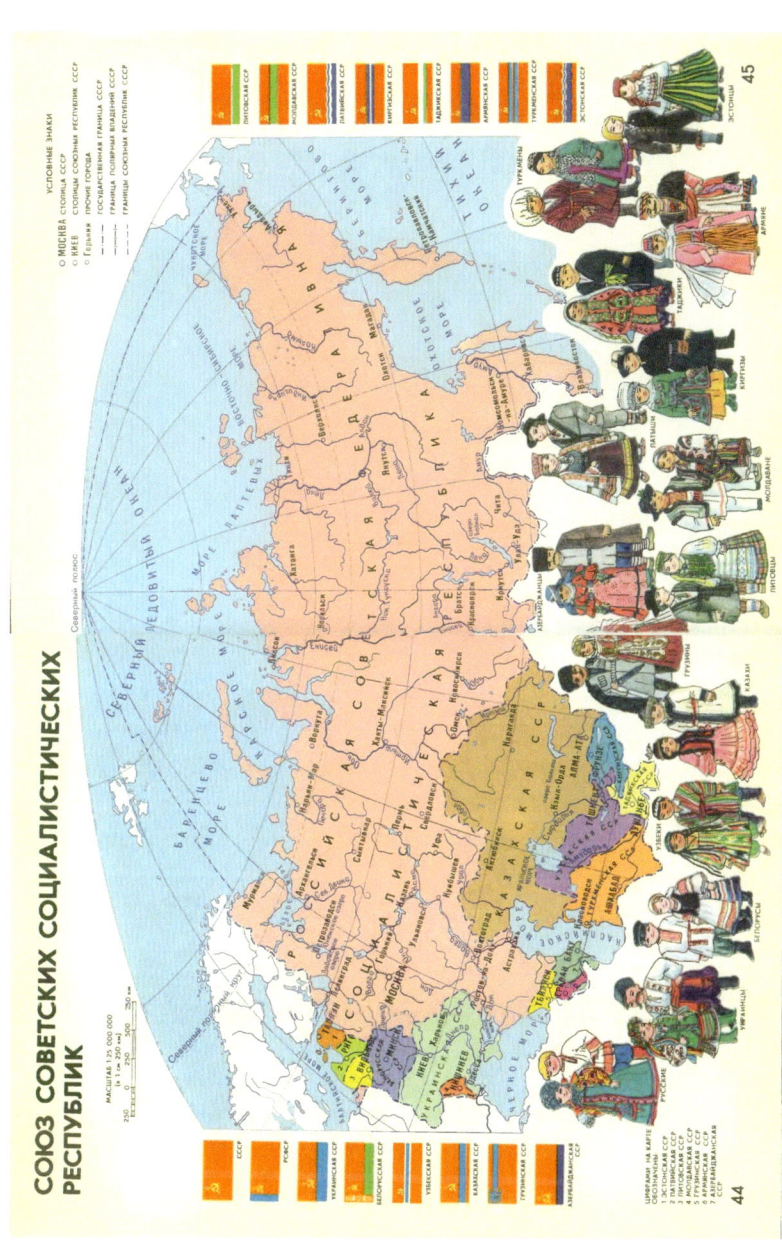

Figure 43.1 Political map of the USSR with national costumes and flags of Soviet republics. From geographic atlas *Mir i chelovek* [World and humanity], 44–5.

Inna Zhdanova and Tat'jana Aleksandrovich, 1988.

Figure 43.2 Viktoria Lomasko with banner: 'Imperial education leads to war', at a demonstration against the war between Russia and Ukraine, Moscow, 21 September 2014.

Photo: E. Yakhina, courtesy of Viktoria Lomasko.

Imperial education leads to war

The banner was carried by Viktoria (Vika) Lomasko (born in 1974), one of the important figures of both the artistic and the feminist scenes in contemporary Russia. She was one of those who gathered in Moscow on the 21st of September 2014 for the 'March for Peace', to protest Russian military intervention in Ukraine. These demonstrations, initiated by the extra-parliamentary liberal opposition in several cities across Russia, combined antimilitarist, pro-Ukrainian and anti-Putinist rhetoric, and brought together many protesters, variously estimated from 5,000 to 50,000.

Lomasko's favourite artistic genre is rapid graphic documentation, which she defines as 'social reportage'. It combines sketches and fragments of speech and is realised immediately in the thick of action. Using this semi-ethnographic strategy, she documented all the major anti-Putin demonstrations of the 2000s, the biggest trials of artists and activists, including those of Pussy Riot.[4] She has also completed several projects of high social value on undocumented migrants in Russia, victims of unlawful detention and slavery, the inmates of the penal colonies, as well as sex workers.[5]

The banner in the photograph that Viktoria was holding over her head presented a drawing and a slogan: 'Imperial education leads to war' (Figure 43.3). When I first saw it, it was only a matter of seconds for me to figure out why the images she used looked so familiar. They came from a book, or more precisely, a geographical atlas, entitled *Mir i Chelovek* (Human and World), designed for young readers and published in the USSR in 1987. I once owned it myself and cherished it particularly for its glazed paper, big format and colourful pages: even back then you could tell there was something not-so-Soviet about its form.

The atlas included a large double-folded page, representing the political map of the USSR and its 15 republics, their flags, and beneath them, the 15 'state nationalities', each represented by couples, man and woman, dressed in grotesque caricatures of national costumes. This map – a pure and somehow exaggerated illustration of what Gregory has defined as 'a landscape where historical ambiguity [is] reconciled through spatial order' – constituted an important element of the political imagination of Soviet children from the first post-Soviet generation.[6] This visual representation clearly 'colonised' the imagination of Lomasko as well. A flag, a colour, a costume, a couple, holding hands – far from being 'the Evil Empire', on the pages of child-oriented geographic maps, the Soviet Union looked like a cheerful Noah's Ark, floating in the middle of nowhere.

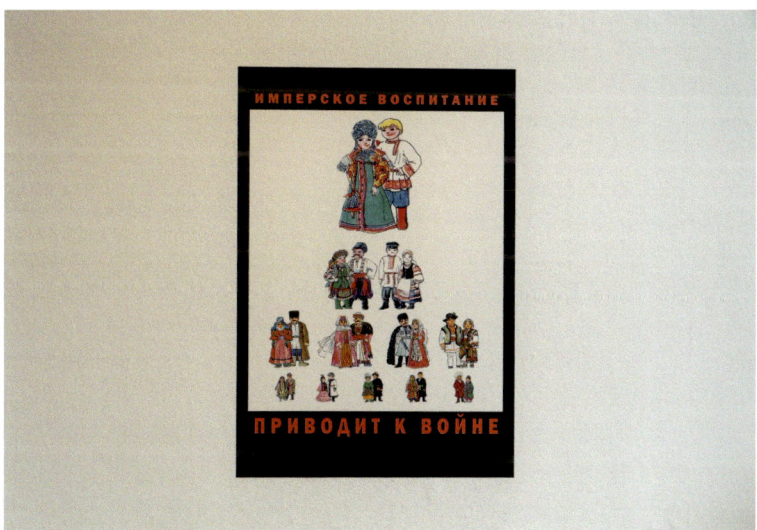

Figure 43.3   'Imperial education leads to war', banner by Viktoria Lomasko.
Courtesy of Viktoria Lomasko.

In September 2014, with the helping hand of an artist, those little characters reappeared at the demonstration against the armed conflict between Ukraine and Russia. Here, Lomasko used the Debordian principle of *detournement*, which consisted of rearranging recognisable images in order to convey a new political meaning, undermining the idyllic representation of the Soviet 'institutionalised multinationality'. As opposed to the horizontal egalitarianism claimed by the Soviet atlas, the artist proposes a pyramidal reconfiguration of nations: a geometric form that reflected more accurately the hierarchies she was observing around her. In Lomasko's drawing, the Russians occupy the top of the pyramid, then come the Ukrainians and the Belarusians (White Slavic peoples), then the peoples of the Christian Caucasus (Armenians and Georgians) and finally the republics of the Muslim Caucasus and Central Asia (these populations are racialised as 'Black, poor and Muslim'). Other ethnic groups and minorities (Tatars, indigenous peoples from the North and the Caucasus) are absent from her representation, as they were from the atlas. This pyramid, which Lomasko conceptualises as a simplified scheme of 'Imperial education', could be interpreted as an artistic representation of the essentialising habitus rooted in the Soviet cultural imaginary.

In fact, this seemingly naive banner calls for a much more complex hypothesis that traces the sources of the contemporary Russian neo-imperialist project back to the ethnocentrism and the declarative egalitarianism of Soviet 'multinationalism' (a similar argument can be found in socio-anthropological scholarship, starting from Verdery) – and demystifies both, by placing them in the context of the imaginary, associated with childhood.[7]

By asking why the 'Druzhby narodov nadezhnyĭ oplot' (Bulwark of peoples in brotherhood strong – a line from the Soviet national anthem) is by a single twist of the artist's hand so easily transformable into a hierarchy – or, in Coronil's words, why the Soviet geohistorical categories intended to be anti-imperial may so easily become imperial again, Lomasko pushes Soviet universalistic utopianism to its limits. By doing so, she highlights one of the key aspects of post-Soviet coloniality, that is the traceable genealogical relationship between the essentialising classificatory paradigm of the socialist past and the neo-imperial project of the present.

By means of this ambivalent visual statement, Lomasko hypothesised about the causes of the war. She thus addressed a question to her generation: 'You should probably remember how we thought it was? … Here where we are now – and the only thing we can do with it is to protest'.

Our Post-Soviet Land

Four years later, in 2018, Viktoria Lomasko's large-scale wall drawing *Our Post-Soviet Land* was exhibited in Oldenburg, Germany as part of the exhibition *Die Neunte Kunst: Unwanted Stories*, reflecting on novel reworkings of the graphic novel by contemporary artists.[8] *Our Post-Soviet Land* documents and represents in a symbolic form impressions from what Lomasko refers to as her 'investigative journeys' through former Soviet republics (Figure 43.4).

In the centre of the mural composition, one can recognise a statue of Vladimir Lenin, repainted in the colours of the Ukrainian flag (this practice of ideological reappropriation was widespread during the Maidan Revolution in 2014). Beneath the statue one can see three veiled faces, two of which belong to Muslim women, and one to a paramilitary soldier, wearing a black balaclava and holding a gun. The left side of the drawing shows a group of Russian religious nationalists, marching under the Kremlin walls towards the statue of Prince Vladimir, the baptiser of Kyivan Rus', recently added to the Kremlin architectural landscape. The right side of the artwork shows a range of Soviet buildings, a mosque,

Figure 43.4 *Our Post-Soviet Land*, wall drawing by Viktoria Lomasko, in the exhibition *Die Neunte Kunst: Unwanted Stories*. Edith-Russ-Haus for Media Art in Oldenburg, Germany, February–April 2018.

Courtesy of Viktoria Lomasko.

and a mural in Bishkek – which is itself a reworking of a famous Soviet painting *Daughter of Soviet Kyrgyzia*.⁹

An attentive eye would notice that Lomasko integrated two self-portraits into the composition: one can see her making sketches while sitting on a traditional Uzbek carpet and as part of a parenthetic image in the upper right corner, where she sits by the window in an aeroplane. This image is symmetrical, and very similar to the one located in the opposite corner, in which a young boy is also looking at the landscape through the window of an aeroplane. The presence of the child might seem insignificant for the viewer, but it is of great importance for Lomasko. The symmetry of her portrait and the portrait of the child suggests the almost imperceptible ties that connect Lomasko to her first aesthetic impressions, which were formative for her artistic gaze and method, and more generally to the Soviet past and its cultural codes.

In her artist's statement, she writes: 'When I was growing up, children's books … about the "friendship of the nations" among the fifteen Soviet republics made a big impression on me. I especially remember an issue of the cult magazine *Veselye Kartinki*,¹⁰ published for the 60th anniversary of the creation of the Soviet Union'.¹¹ This issue, published in December 1982, featured a short story, 'Strana, gde my zhivëm' (The country where we live), written by Sergeĭ Baruzdin.¹² Its protagonist, a five-year-old boy named Dimka, is invited by the author – a middle-aged man with a thick moustache and a tie – to fly over the whole Soviet territory in one day, travelling from one republic to another. As a child, Viktoria was fascinated by this magic journey and Dimka's encounters with children from other Soviet republics: 'an Armenian boy met him with songs about the mountains and grapes, a little Turkmen boy in a robe and *tiubeteĭka* sang about a canal in the middle of the desert …'.¹³ This fantasy of a one-day flight over the territory of the largest state in the world, from its centre to the periphery and back, chimes interestingly with the ideas of James Scott, who theorised the role of aerial photography in the consolidation of modern states and the ordering of their territories.¹⁴

In her wall composition, Lomasko resuscitates her first proto-political affects, stimulated by Dimka's breathtaking voyage, in order to resignify them in feminist and decolonial terms. She utilises Valentin Rozantsev's illustration to Dimka's story as an opening to her own graphic travelogue, one that is driven by a research question that may sound more ethnographic than artistic: 'What kind of political and social processes are taking place in these territories today?' – asks Lomasko and replies with her mural composition: 'it is not impossible that Dimka's friends from Moscow became radical nationalists, and his Turkmen and Kyrgyz fellows – undocumented migrants'.[15]

As an adult, Lomasko could dissociate the aesthetics of the ethnicised representations in children's press from the culturalistic hierarchies that they were vehiculating: she describes them as 'beautiful but brimming with orientalism'.[16] As she realises today, this trip could only be made by a generic Dimka – a privileged and apparently well-connected Muscovite boy, wearing a t-shirt and sneakers. 'One could never imagine such a trip "the other way around" – when a Tajik girl would travel to meet Dimka and admire his national Russian costume.'[17] Perhaps this was the reason why I was not particularly impressed by this issue of *Veselye Kartinki*: as a Ukrainian girl from Kyiv, I simply could not project myself into such a fantasy.

On the last page of this celebratory issue of *Veselye Kartinki*, the readers see Dimka and his guide landing at an airport in Moscow. The story ends with a dialogue in which the adult asks the five-year-old: 'What have you learnt about our country?', and immediately concludes everything on a strident ideological note: 'You are right, Dimka! It is big, rich, strong, friendly, kind, and will become even more so, because Soviet people under the guidance of the party of communists work hard to build a new, happy life. This new, happy life is called – communism!'[18] This ideological apotheosis is an almost line-to-line illustration from *The Table Book of the Primary School Teacher*, published in 1950, which clearly codifies the children's patriotic ideal of late Stalinism:

> Gradually, children create a concrete idea about our socialist homeland. They will find out that: our homeland is the Union of Soviet Socialist Republics; our country is the largest country in the world; there are no capitalists or landlords in the USSR; all people work for each other, for the common benefit; the USSR is a brotherly union of nations; there is no such friendship of nations in any country as in the Soviet Union. *The great Russian people have a leading role in the commonwealth of the USSR*.[19] (italics in the original)

What is worth our attention here, however, is that what the artist recalls is neither that the 'happy life is called communism', nor her revulsion towards dogmatic ideologemes, but the multiplicity and richness of graphic elements and the striking beauty of the images in *Veselye Kartinki*. Her narrative suggests that the iconic Soviet periodicals were much more complex semiotic objects than simple mediators of state-driven propaganda. *Veselye Kartinki*, despite devoting a significant amount of its space to exercises in child-oriented ideology, was exempt from censorship by Glavlit.[20] Every issue was produced by multiple voices and hands, some of which belonged to nonconformist artists such as Ilya Kabakov, Eduard Gorokhovskiĭ or Viktor Pivovarov, later associated with 'Moscow conceptualism'.[21] From this polyphony of artistic and poetic representations, distorting by its very multiplicity the ideological unity of Soviet high modernism, the child was able to pick the meaning she preferred.

It is also possible that what triggered a form of fascination in Lomasko was her first encounter with a map – a powerful cognitive tool and simultaneously an artistic and scientific object – a map in the very unusual form of a magazine, one keeping traces of the aerial journey of a child. While turning the pages of this issue of *Veselye Kartinki*, one can

Figure 43.5 Viktoria Lomasko in front of her wall drawing *Our Post-Soviet Land*, in the exhibition *Die Neunte Kunst: Unwanted Stories*. Edith-Russ-Haus for Media Art in Oldenburg, Germany, 30 January 2018.

Courtesy of Viktoria Lomasko.

find a set of separate maps of socialist republics, as imagined by Iurii Molokanov. They are very different from those of the atlas *Mir i chelovek*. For example, the map of the Ukrainian Socialist Republic features, alongside the inevitable couple in ethnic costumes in the centre, a range of grey Soviet bloc buildings, a statue of Bohdan Khmelnytsky, some traditional Ukrainian *haty* (houses), thatched with straw and surrounded by cows and sunflowers. The industrialised Donbas is represented by slag heaps, hydroelectric dams and the smoke of factory chimneys, while in the South one can see the sandy beaches of Crimea (in its borders of 1954–2014), surrounded by the sea, with a dolphin, a military flotilla and a seagull.

This artistic 'messiness' of natural and architectural objects, humans and animals, presenting a somewhat ironic entanglement of tradition and modernity and holding no intrinsic claim to scientific accuracy is situated much more closely to cartography-as-art than to cartography-as-science – these maps seem to be in an even closer relationship to Lomasko's art (Figure 43.5).

Notes

1. Tchermalykh, 2015.
2. Murawski, Mileeva and Maksimov, 2020.
3. Coronil, 1996.
4. Lomasko, Nikolaev and Frimmel 2013; Lomasko et al., 2014.
5. Lomasko, 2018a.
6. Gregory, 1994.
7. Verdery, 1993a; 1993b.
8. The exhibition took place in Edith-Russ-Haus for Media Art, 1 February–2 April 2018, featuring works by Victoria Lomasko, Wojciech Bąkowski, Ganzeer, David O'Reilly and Amir Yatziv.
9. Lomasko, 2018b.
10. *Veselye Kartinki* (Merry Pictures) was a monthly children's cartoon magazine launched by the Komsomol in 1956 and dedicated to children age 4–8. In the 1980s it was considered the most widely circulated Soviet children's magazine, reaching a circulation of 9.5 million copies. Gölz, 2019, 138.
11. Lomasko, 2018b.
12. Baruzdin, 1982.
13. Lomasko, 2018b.
14. Scott, 2008.
15. Lomasko, personal interview, 2 April 2020.
16. Lomasko, 2018b.
17. Lomasko, personal interview, 2 April 2020.
18. Baruzdin, 1982.
19. *Nachal'naia shkola: Nastol'naia kniga uchitelia* 1950, cited in Kelly, 2003.
20. General Directorate for the Protection of State Secrets in the Press under the Council of Ministers of the USSR was the official censorship agency established in 1922.
21. Hellman, 2013.

Bibliography

Baruzdin, Sergeĭ. 'Strana, gde my zhivëm' [The country where we live], *Veselye Kartinki*, 1982. Accessed 6 April 2020. http://www.barius.ru/biblioteka/book/4991.

Coronil, Fernando. 'Beyond Occidentalism: Toward nonimperial geohistorical categories', *Cultural Anthropology* 11(1) (1996): 51–87.

Gölz, Christine. 'Merry pictures of the little folk: The cartoon magazine *Veselye Kartinki*, or what's left of the Socialist "Children's World"', *Filoteknos* 9: 138–55 (2019).

Gregory, Derek. *Geographical Imaginations*. Cambridge, MA: Blackwell, 1994.

Hellman, Ben. 'Thaw in the World of Children (1954–1968)'. In *Fairy Tales and True Stories: The History of Russian literature for children and young people (1574–2010)*, 472–533. Leiden: Brill, 2013.

Kelly, Katriona. 'Malen'kie grazhdane bol'shoĭ strany: Internacionalizm, deti i sovetskaia propaganda' [Little citizens of a great country: Internationalism, children, and Soviet propaganda]. Translated by Y. Tokareva. *Novoe literaturnoe obozrenie* 2 (2003). Accessed 6 April 2020. https://magazines.gorky.media/nlo/2003/2/malenkie-grazhdane-bolshoj-strany-1-internaczionalizm-deti-i-sovetskaya-propaganda-2.html.

Lomasko, Viktoria. *D'autres Russies: Un reportage graphique de Victoria Lomasko* [Other Russias: A graphic report by Victoria Lomasko]. Poitiers: The Hoochie Coochie, 2018a.

Lomasko, Viktoria. 'Our post-Soviet land. Artist's statement for *Die Neunte Kunst*: Unwanted stories'. Viktoria Lomasko's personal archive, 2018b.

Lomasko, Viktoria. Interview by Nataliya Tchermalykh (online via Zoom, Moscow–Geneva) 2 April 2020.

Lomasko, Viktoria, Anton Nikolaev and Sandra Frimmel. *Verbotene Kunst: Eine Moskauer Austellung* [Forbidden Art: A Moscow exhibition]. Berlin: Mathhes and Seitz, 2013.

Lomasko, Viktoria, Anna Zaytseva and Gérald Auclin. *L'art interdit: Art, blasphème et justice dans la Russie de Poutine* [Forbidden Art: Art, blasphemy and justice in Putin's Russia]. Poitiers: The Hoochie Coochie, 2014.

Murawski, Michał, Maria Mileeva and Denis Maksimov. 'Perverting the power vertical: Politics and aesthetics in the Global East', (2020). Accessed 15 April 2020. https://www.ppv.life.

Scott, James C. *Seeing Like a State: How certain schemes to improve the human condition have failed*. New Haven, CT: Yale University Press, 2008.

Tchermalykh, Nataliya. *Paysages Instables: Des artistes ukrainiens entre révolution et guerre* [Unstable Landscapes: Ukrainian artists between revolution and war]. Kyiv: Rodovid, Galerie Pangée, 2015.

Verdery, Katherine. 'Whither "nation" and "nationalism"?', *Daedalus* 122(3) (1993a): 37–46.

Verdery, Katherine. 'Nationalism and national sentiment in post-socialist Romania', *Slavic Review* 52(2) (1993b): 179–203.

Zhdanova, Inna and Tat'jana Aleksandrovich. *Mir i chelovek: Geograficheskiĭ atlas* [World and Humanity: Geographical atlas]. Moscow: Glavnoe upravlenie geodezii i kartografii pri Sovete Ministrov SSSR, 1998. Accessed 6 April 2020. https://www.litmir.me/bd/?b=252084.

44
TINA and Natasha: mapping exploitation after history's end
Jennifer Suchland

This piece juxtaposes TINA – the slogan of capitalism's inevitability post-1989, 'There is no alternative' – with Natasha, the East European sex worker, stripper, and/or victim of human trafficking, who made her appearance in the cities of the West, likewise following the fall of Communism. Suchland's suggestion is that this pair must be seen as twins, as two sides of the same coin: where TINA declared the end of history and an end to the unfreedom of state socialism, Natasha told us the other side of the story and was testament to the emergence of new forms of patriarchal and racialised exploitation.

With the demise of the Cold War, two femmes emerged onto the global scene: TINA and Natasha. Who are they and why did they appear at roughly the same time? The rejection and collapse of state socialism in Central-Eastern Europe and Eurasia amplified an important deceit of capitalism – that economic violence is an aberration in the system. With the absence of a global alternative to capitalism, in the early 1990s political and economic elites declared 'There Is No Alternative' and thus TINA came to life. Of course, the idea behind TINA was not new, but her image grew in prominence, asserting that one world of capitalism had arrived. At the same time, another female name gained global attention – Natasha. From the streets of Ankara, Turkey to the newsprint of the *Washington Post*, Natasha – the sex worker, the stripper, the victim of trafficking – came to represent, not the failure of neoliberal states or the exploitation of markets and the need for alternatives, but the myth that capitalism's violence is an aberration rather than constitutive of it. Natasha, the pan-Slavic name which problematically represented the ethnic and nationally diverse Central-Eastern Europe and Eurasia, came to life at the same time as TINA. And, yet, Natasha's presence never challenged the belief in or dominance of TINA. Despite the prominence of both TINA and Natasha, these female names demonstrate the endurance of heteropatriarchy as it functions across different racialised and cultural contexts.

The emergence of these notorious femmes begins with the 'end of history', as Francis Fukuyama proclaimed at the end of the Cold War.[1] Previously, the world was starkly divided between the duelling modernities of state socialism versus capitalism, wherein exploitation was projected as an evil endemic to the other system. Capitalism was presented as the system of 'free markets', while state socialism was presented as the system of nonexploitative labour. While the tension and conflict between socialism and capitalism has a long history and varied locations, the metanarrative of socialism versus capitalism produced a map of the world that used the East–West or socialism–capitalism dyads to draw the lines of where exploitation resided. State forms of violence, such as settler colonialism, racial slavery and imperialism, were shrouded within the progress narratives of modernity purported by either side of the conflict. You could stand in Charleston, North Carolina in the United States, or in Tashkent, Uzbekistan in the USSR, and either way colonialism and racial capitalism were not the culprits of exploitation.[2] At the same time, the presence of state violence in other locations was either made ancillary to or ignored by the primary points of the East–West compass. Rather than the end of exploitation itself, the 'end of history' marks the closing of a grand narrative about how and where violence was made visible during the Cold War. The map of exploitation that was created by that grand narrative took the land and people for granted – the 'finding', taking and gathering of lands and the forced removal of peoples did not register as violence in the Cold War mapping of exploitation.

TINA is driving her car down the highway of neoliberal capitalism and it is now possible to see in the rearview mirror that the East–West dichotomy was primarily an antagonism within Eurocentrism. The Cold War was less world historical and more world catastrophic: capitalism and state socialism fought within the same racial and economic matrix produced by the 'modern world system', even if their differences appeared to be categorically unique. Looking at the end of the Cold War through TINA's rearview mirror, it appears that the 'end of history' was an end to the state sanctioned argument against capitalism. The end of history is really just the death of European Marxism.[3] As TINA is speeding along at greater velocity and accumulating human, nonhuman and environmental disasters, she laughs while rolling over discarded 'most wanted' posters, looking for 'TINA: posterchild of heteropatriarchal racial capitalism'. TINA is no fool; she understands that new maps of exploitation will be made and that she will need to navigate them. What will be the post-Cold War maps of exploitation? In the one world of capitalism there is no other system to blame, so exploitation is represented as an individualised problem that requires criminal laws, border patrols, detention centres, prisons and, most of all, market solutions. That map of exploitation, therefore, is not of geographic locations but consists of data points of risk factors that give evidence to the resilience and expansion of inequity, even if it never adds up to an argument against capitalism. Risk captures both the market's logic and the potential for exploitation. Everyone has to take risks; everyone is at risk.

And that is what Natasha did – she took a risk, devised a plan to make capitalism work. Natasha enters this story when capitalist transition puts the former Second World into the plotline of human trafficking.[4] The fact that women work in sexual and informal economies, and that this work can be forced or done without consent, became a new global fixation in the 1990s. While neoliberal development strategies and military bases had fuelled sexual commerce for decades, the entrance of the post-Soviet (seemingly) 'White' woman into those economies registered an alarm that would eventually be cast as the problem of 'modern day slavery'. The informal economies of hustling in contexts of state socialist scarcity proved to be beneficial strategies for survival, for mobility, for becoming capitalist. As women set out to make or find capitalist lives in the scattered monetary epicentres of the world (Dubai, New York City, Berlin or Ankara, for example) some of those experiences of force, fraud and violence brought attention to this (new) alleged aberration of the free market – human trafficking.

The map of exploitation, of modern-day slavery, is produced by national and global carceral regimes that first hunt criminality to find potential victims. Whether it relates to sexual or nonsexual labour, victims are essentially recategorised criminals. The expansion of the anti-trafficking apparatus in the name of human rights has extended and expanded the carceral reach of the state and its entities. Thus, this figurative map I am describing displays not only the numbers of people harmed by extreme exploitation, but the carceral logics of human rights that mobilise policing and state surveillance to draw the line between the deserving and undeserving. Within the old logics of the Cold War, Natasha was either the femme fatale of espionage or an image of the communist dispossessed. Her name now symbolises the worthy yet unlucky victim of human trafficking.

The data collected in annual reports from the US Trafficking in Persons Report to the International Labour Organization, reaffirm the carceral logic of mapping exploitation after the Cold War. The magnitude of trafficking increases concern and resources directed to trafficking, which then feeds a system that inevitably finds more victims. It is this feedback loop within the carceral logics that perpetuate the problem and the solution. At the same time, the political economy of borders, visa regimes, undocumented travel, repression and suppression of labour organising, criminalisation of migrants and migration, divestment from state support and survival strategies in formal and informal economies, are not viewed as the sources for this cartography; the market simply produces unlucky people and bad choices. The twinned appearance of TINA and Natasha brought about a supposedly 'post-racial' and hyper-individualised cartography of exploitation. This new map once again shrouds racial capitalism, as Natasha the 'White negro' deracialised unfree labour.[5] Her secondary whiteness simultaneously summoned the moral gravitas of 'old slavery' while detaching modern-day slavery from the historical and ongoing racial and colonial systems that constitute capitalism. Natasha could do this because the violence she experienced was in TINA's world – where violence is data, and where there is no alternative to capitalism.

Notes

1. Fukuyama, 1992.
2. The location of Charleston, North Carolina, is an example of a site created by settler colonialism and slavery. Similarly, Tashkent, Uzbekistan is a site of Soviet colonialism and imperialism. See Dunbar-Ortiz, 2014; Tlostanova, 2012.
3. Derrida, 1994.
4. Suchland, 2015.
5. In the nineteenth century, Russian thinker Alexander Herzen argued that Russian serfs were 'white negroes' and analogous to the Black negroes of concern in the debates about the trans-Atlantic slave trade.

Bibliography

Derrida, Jacques. *Spectres of Marx: The state of the debt, the work of mourning and the new international*, translated by Peggy Kamuf. New York: Routledge, 1994.
Dunbar-Ortiz, Roxanne. *An Indigenous Peoples' History of the United States.* Boston: Beacon Press, 2014.
Fukuyama, Francis. *The End of History and the Last Man*. New York: Free Press, 1992.
Suchland, Jennifer. *Economies of Violence: Transnational feminism, postsocialism and the politics of sex trafficking.* Durham, NC: Duke University Press, 2015.
Tlostanova, Madina. 'Postsocialist ≠ postcolonial? On post-Soviet imaginary and global coloniality', *Journal of Postcolonial Writing* 48(2) (2012): 130–42.

45
Yardsticks and shillelaghs: Croatian migrants to Ireland
Rory Archer

Accelerating and intensifying migration processes, here within the European Union, are often seen as erasing national borders and cultural difference, rendering area studies irrelevant. But Croatian migrants to Ireland reveal the potency of a popular, common-sense area knowledge, grounded in experience and in pre-existing tropes of cultural similarity and difference between peripheral areas, particularly in articulating social, economic and political criticism.

Since joining the European Union (EU) in 2013, Croatia has rapidly become one of the largest sources of immigrants to Ireland, relative to its population, with tens of thousands having moved to the republic by 2019. Such figures are still dwarfed by the many more Croatian citizens – perhaps up to 200,000 – who left for the traditional destination of Germany. Yet, the novelty of migration to Ireland has captured the imagination of many journalists and Croatian citizens and prompted news reports and flurries of social media activity (including instructional guides about moving to Ireland and a proliferation of Facebook groups facilitating migration). Ireland is routinely invoked both as a symbol of contemporary outward migration and as evidence of the failure of the Croatian state to facilitate a 'normal life' for many of its young people since EU accession.

Croatian migration to Ireland is characterised by hypermobility, individualism, personal choice, free access to the labour market and a fast-paced, flexible labour market – characteristics noted by studies of other migratory flows to the republic. Scholarship stresses that distinctions between economic migration and other forms of mobility, like tourism, commuting and student migration, have been breaking down.

Migrants are no longer bound by a residence or work permit restricting the employee to a particular employer or sector – as EU citizens, Croatian migrants can change jobs and domicile within Ireland rapidly. But this does not mean that concepts of distinct areas within the EU are vanishing, or that culture and politics float free of place. On the contrary – despite mobile, multidirectional flows, the purported levelling effects of globalisation do not render place and nation irrelevant.

This contribution conceives of recent Croatian migrants to the Republic of Ireland as late capitalist 'wandering critics', for whom a repertoire of narratives about one (still nationally framed) location informs understandings of the other. Ideas about two distinct areas are interlocking for the protagonists involved. While the centre–periphery division is clear on an economic level, the idea of Ireland as a periphery (or at least semi-periphery) helps explain the potency of Ireland as an empty signifier in recent Croatian discourses. The experience of labour migration to Ireland prompts discussions about work, deservingness, opportunity and attachments to the nation (despite alienation from an immoral state apparatus). For countries on the European peripheries, like Croatia, Ireland can serve as a shining example of a belatedly developed nation-state with a respectable international standing, punching above its weight culturally and economically on the global stage in recent decades, despite being a perennial European periphery itself. Indeed because of its (semi-)peripheral status Ireland forms a pertinent point of comparison for a (semi-)periphery like Croatia.

Positive accounts of working and living in Ireland are routinely contrasted to unfair and corrupt practices experienced in Croatian workplaces, often caustically. Boris V., a recent migrant to Ireland, wrote an extended Facebook comment in 2017 that subsequently went viral in Croatian digital media:

> If you are not a sponger [*uhljeb*], daddy's spoilt brat [*guzonjin sin*] or a political parasite of one of the leading parties, you can bet that you, just like me, have asked yourself how is it that here [in Croatia, *kod nas*] that people who are total idiots, rude [*nekulturni*], arrogant and uneducated have so much money, they are successful, famous and avoid the law and rules without any consequences […]
>
> Then, I had a completely EXTRAORDINARY experience in Ireland where to my astonishment my employer really appreciates my work, effort, engagement, honesty, fairness, responsibility towards the work and the client. F*ck, you cannot believe it […]

> In the guise of nationalism, [political elites] stole and sold our homeland. I am proud to be a Croat and will always love my homeland but the Croatian state. Yuck.[1]

For Boris V. and other wandering critics, a sense of fair play, meritocracy and advantages of a flexible labour market in Ireland is contrasted with corruption, deception and incompetence in Croatian workplaces and in public life generally.

How might a critical area studies approach the claims drawn from the migration experiences of critics like Boris V.? The discussions about Ireland taking place in Croatia serve as a reminder that 'common sense' popular knowledge about areas circulates widely, beyond the academy, and becomes interlaced with personal experience. Place and nation are of great salience in such discussions. The resulting critiques are deeply rooted in the ambivalent position of Ireland as both a perennial periphery and a globalised force to be reckoned with. Terry Eagleton writes that Ireland simultaneously signifies roots, belonging, as well as exile, diffusion, globality and diaspora. Although touted as a recent globalised success story, Honor Fagan reminds us that Ireland 'was always part of broader flows of people and ideas; it was always globalized, and it was always a floating signifier'.[2] Thus Ireland can be considered to have numerous often mutually contradictory characteristics – tradition, poverty, wealth, innovation, Catholicism, secularisation, (post)modernity, advancement. 'Irishness' in its many guises is 'a commodity available for trade on the open market', and this is true in Croatia as much as elsewhere.[3] While Ireland has the worrying potential to become 'Croatia's most populated island', due to migration, it also represents an aspirational model of neoliberal economic development, routinely cited in Croatia. For example, following a meeting in Dublin with Irish premier Enda Kenny in April 2017, President Kolinda Grabar-Kitarović declared that she would like Croatia to replicate the Irish model of investment in education and the IT sector, along with the implementation of tax reforms aiming to attract multinational corporations.

If Germany symbolises the perennial pull of an economically powerful centre in which migration was undertaken in the conditions of both Yugoslav socialism and postwar German social democracy, Ireland is emblematic of a liberal EU migratory experience. As a successful European (semi) periphery, it offers a more pertinent and powerful point of comparison to Croatia for the wandering critics and their attentive audience at home. That contemporary Croatian migration to Ireland differs from *gastarbeiter* migration is stressed in a 2015 report on Croatian state television, which claims it to be strikingly different from the migration of the 1960s. Involving well-educated young people in their prime, they reportedly are seeking not to build a house or obtain consumer durables but instead strive to participate in a fairer form of sociability underscored by meritocracy. Croatian public discourses do still frame migration in terms of economic rationale (many articles use the phrase *trbuhom za kruhom*, 'going with one's stomach after bread/wages', and compare income and unemployment rates between the two states). Nevertheless, hypermobility and circular forms of migration are stressed. As a consequence, 'toing and froing' between the two states tends to foreground comparisons with home, with mobility facilitating more constant dialogue between different forms of work, sociability and everyday life.

Initial reports on the experiences of migrants in Ireland tended to be very positive. The migrants quoted usually praised the rapid way one could find a job, the quality of life in Ireland, decent pay and sociability. A 2016 article in the Croatian daily *Slobodna Dalmacija*, about migrant life in Cork, Ireland, gave glowing reports of working conditions in Ireland. Croatian migrants in conversation with the journalist declared: 'You know what the situation is like at home [in Croatia], there are no jobs or prospects'. In contrast, the narrator found a job within three days of arriving in Cork and after a week's trial received a contract. The respondents emphasise a sense of fair play or meritocracy in the Irish labour market and stress the possibility of receiving a pay rise or promotion commensurate with effort made: 'In Ireland you do not need connections to find a job, you don't have to call a politician to start working. For the Irish, diplomas are important, but most important is practical knowledge. Effort and commitment will not go unnoticed by the employer. Raises follow'. A sense of sociability when living and working in Ireland is also emphasised. Recent migrants report Irish people as fun and gregarious: 'The Irish like fun, they are not at all anxious [*nervozni*], they are very approachable and at the weekends in particular they like to kick back [*otkače se*]'.[4] Such comparisons contain implicit criticisms that echo those of Boris V. – Croatia is an unfair society which makes its citizens anxious.

Predictably, not all Croatian print, digital and social media reports offer unqualified praise about living and working in Ireland. As a response to the unbridled enthusiasm about migration to Ireland, individual migrants began offering counter-narratives that highlighted not only economic problems, but also cultural clashes, distinctions and hierarchies between Irish and migrant workers. For example, also in 2016, a Zadar resident spoke to *Slobodna Dalmacija* about his disappointment with migrant life in Dublin and his speedy return to Croatia. He pointed out the difficulties in finding accommodation (in Dublin rents had risen to record levels). The narrator described 'army like' bunk beds in rooms with multiple occupants from Eastern Europe, being rented for 500 EUR per bed. He also claimed that working conditions for migrants from newer EU member states were notably worse than for Irish workers: 'We from the "Eastern Bloc" are paid less than Irish [workers]. They don't work for less than 25 EUR per hour but we work for minimal wage of 9.15 to 15 EUR per hour, except in the IT sector and in medicine'.[5] Criticising zero-hour contracts, the narrator claimed many Croatian acquaintances were being sent home unpaid when no work was available while Irish colleagues were not. 'They are better paid than us. We are better paid there than here [in Croatia] but accommodation and living costs are much higher. They take advantage of our situation in some way. The Irish make money out of us but not us from them.'

Such Croatian migrants resemble wandering critics between two European peripheries. Unemployment, corruption and a deficient sense of sociability in the workplace has induced Croatian citizens not only to migrate to Ireland, but to invoke the migratory experience to disparage public life and the labour market in Croatia. Imagined tropes as well as lived experience in two defined areas coalesce. In Croatia, discussions of migration to Ireland provide an example of the overlapping and simultaneity of Hirschman's categories of exit, voice and loyalty in migration studies.[6] Parallel to sustained outward migration (exit), the slogan 'I don't want to go to Ireland' is raised on banners by protesting shipyard workers in Croatia (voice), while national loyalty is not disputed but rather affirmed. Far from being a diffuse transnational affair, critique of life in Croatia is *inter*-national in nature. Nation and place matter, even within a theoretically undifferentiated EU and its single labour market. It hinges on Ireland and Croatia being sufficiently distinct places so as to stress difference, while relying on commonalities in terms of (semi) peripherality to make comparisons hit home. The experience of living and working in both Ireland and Croatia, in their varying conditions of late capitalism, serves as a yardstick to measure (and sometimes batter!) the other.

Notes

1 Jutarnji.hr, 2018.
2 Fagan, 2002, 141.
3 Mays, 2005, 9.
4 Primorac, 2016.

5 Kalajžić, 2016.
6 Hoffmann, 2010, 59–60.

Bibliography

Fagan, Honor. 'Globalization and culture: Placing Ireland', *Annals of the American Academy of Political and Social Science* 581 (2002): 133–43.

Hoffmann, Bert. 'Bringing Hirschman back in: "Exit", "voice", and "loyalty" in the politics of transnational migration', *Latin Americanist* 54(2) (2010): 57–73.

Jutarnji.hr. 'Mladić koji je pobjegao u Irsku opisao svoje neobično iskustvo "Uvijek sam se pitao jesam li zaostao, nesposoban, totalni idiot!?"' [A young man who escaped to Ireland described his unusual experience 'I always wondered if I was retarded, incompetent, a total idiot!?']. 2018. Accessed 31 July 2018. https://www.jutarnji.hr/naslovnica/mladic-koji-je-pobjegao-u-irsku-opisao-svoje-neobicno-iskustvo-uvijek-sam-se-pitao-jesam-li-zaostao-nesposoban-totalni-idiot-5646575.

Kalajžić, M. 'Dublin (ni)je grad iz snova: Donosimo priču Zadranina koji je uteka doma nakon deset dana' [Dublin is (not) the city of dreams: We bring you the story of a man from Zadar who ran home after ten days], *Slobodna Dalmacija*, 10 July 2016. Accessed 18 August 2024. https://www.slobodnadalmacija.hr/novosti/hrvatska/clanak/id/319201/dublin-nije-grad-iz-snova-donosimo-pricu-zadranina-koji-je-uteka-natrag-doma-za-deset-dana.

Mays, Michael. 'Irish identity in an age of globalisation', *Irish Studies Review* 13(1) (2005): 3–12.

Primorac, Mate. 'Planirate bolji život u Irskoj? Ponesite barem 2000 eura, trebat će vam' [Planning a better life in Ireland? Bring at least 2000 euros, you will need it], *Slobodna Dalmacija*, 12 November 2016. Accessed 18 August 2024. http://www.slobodnadalmacija.hr/novosti/svijet/clanak/id/449874/planirate-bolji-zivot-u-irskoj-ponesite-barem-2000-eura-trebat-ce-vam.

Index

Albert, Yuri 107
Amerikanistika (American studies) 210, 239–43, 287–92
Anthropocene, socialist 167–71
architects 121–4
    Polish 301–7
area studies
    in the Balkans, 8, 30–1
    critical area studies (CAS), 7–17, 20–2, 205–6, 25
    decolonial turn in, 16–17
    East European Studies/Russian, Eastern European and Eurasian Studies, 17–18, 20, 56, 155, 157
    future of, 2
    geology as, 179–85
    and power, violence, 1–3
    as three dimensional, 179–85
    traditional 1–2, 34, 76, 156, 179, 182, 210, 240, 300
    trans-area studies, 76
    vernacular, 68–9, 95–101, 239–43, 257–63, 287–92
areas, academic production of 30
    debates over area labels 8, 12
    political uses of 29–34
Artek 42–3
artists, 103–10
    circulation of 309–13
    countercultural 95–101
    Hungarian 137–44
    interwar avant-garde 137–44
Association of Slavic, Eastern European and Eurasian Studies (ASEEES) 56, 158
atlas, traditional, compared to Anti-Atlas 2, 3–7
Austria, Greater 80
Austria-Hungary 147, 220–2

Balkanism 8, 30–1, 221
    positive 166n
Balkanology 29–34
Balkans, as area label 16, 29–34, 54, 59–64, 80, 148, 215–16, 222
    see also Southeastern Europe
barbarism, *see* civilisation
blackness, blacks 63, 334, 344
    black Americans 213–17
borderlessness 41, 66, 79–85, 95–101, 104–10, 137–44, 241, 252–5, 309–13
borders 133, 144, 147–52, 202, 248–9, 281–5
border zones, borderlands 67, 71–6, 79–85, 135, 147–52, 161–5, 316
Brexit 36, 76, 252, 253
Britain, UK 82, 220–2, 323
    see also England
Brookman, Olga 287–92
Bucharest 67, 115, 235
Budapest 80, 220, 221
Butler, Hubert 222–3

capitalism, 49
    late 35–8 173–7, 253, 309, 341–4, 349
    neoliberal 214
    technocapitalism 114–18
    versus socialism 40, 42, 101, 118, 151, 157, 162, 233, 316, 342
    wild 121–9
    Yugoslav 235
cartography, *see* maps
Casanova, Paschale, *The World Republic of Letters* 219–23
Central and Eastern Europe (as area label), *see* Eastern Europe
Central Asia 74, 101, 129, 132, 257, 334

centre-core/periphery relations, 15, 33, 55, 67, 75, 133, 219, 221, 227, 297, 301–7, 321–6, 336, 346
   see also peripheries
chaos, location of 35–6
Charles, Prince of Wales (now King Charles III) 47, 48–9, 50–1
children, cartography for 329–30, 336–9
   international camps for 39–45
   Romanian 42–5
China, Special Economic Zones in 173–6
cities, late capitalist 113–18, 173–7
citizen science 257–63
civilisation(s) 31, 74–5, 194
   clash of 72
   versus barbarism 67–9, 297–9
Cold War
   artistic production in 142–4
   geopolitical divisions of 40–5, 147–52, 194, 301–6, 342
   knowledge production in 118, 162, 169–70, 182–3
collaboration, academic 11–12, 53–8, 182–3, 211, 260, 302–5
communism, communists 95–6, 147–51, 248, 249, 337
continents and terrains, *see* areas; maps
Cosmism 88–91
cosmopolitanism 66–70, 210, 251–5
counterculture, Russian 265–8
   Soviet 95–101
countryside 47–51, 225–9
critical area studies, *see* area studies
criticality 9–10
   self-criticism/*samokritika* 19
Crni Srbi 213–17
Croatia 345–9

Dembińska, Zsofia 246–9
decoloniality, decolonial turn 15–17, 24n
   in service of political projects 15–16, 24n

diaspora
   black 216
   East European 253–4
   Irish 347
   Russian 239–43
digital humanities 53–8, 66, 323–4
Dimensionism 137–44
Doyle, Arthur Conan 321–5
Dreambooks, Dreamland 59–64
Dugin, Aleksandr 16, 265–6

Earth 87–92, 166, 180–4
East, *see* Global East
East–West binary 13–14, 40, 45, 54, 70, 144, 162, 208, 265, 290, 316, 342
'Eastern Europe', debates over label 8, 12, 24n, 54, 56–7
engineers, socialist 231–6
England, myth of countryside in 49
environment, natural 167–70, 211, 232–3
Eurasia, Eurasianism 16, 71–6, 91, 107, 266
Euro-Atlantic, *see* West, the
exile 258–9, 295–300

Falcon youth movement (IFM-SEI) 41
fascism 37, 147–8, 153
fashion industry, Russian 268–71
Fedorov, Nicolai 88–91
FIFA World Cup 2018 89
film, documentary, Polish 225–9
   Hollywood 241–3
folkore, and nationalism 48–50
frontier myth 89, 92, 190, 192, 194–5
frontiers, *see* borders

geology, Soviet 179–85, 260
Ghana 301–3
Global East 14–15, 17, 27, 70, 74–6, 101, 330
   queering 63–4
   and Roma 276–8
   socialist 147–52

globalisation 49–51, 118, 134, 179, 252, 281, 306, 309–13, 345–9
global–local relations 55
Global North, polarity with Global South 13, 14, 15, 70, 75, 162
  see also East–West binary; West, the
Global South 14 15, 35, 37, 40, 43, 75, 162, 216, 301–7
Gorky Colony (experimental school) 41
Greater Europe (artwork and area) 79–85
Griffith, Arthur 220–3
Gryczełowska, Krystyna 225–8

Haus der Statistik 153–8
Helsinki Accords 104, 110
Herder, Johann Gottfried von 254–5
High Line (NYC) 121–3
Hippie-land, Soviet 95–101
Holmes, Sherlock 321–6
House of Culture, Moscow 95–8
Hungary 53, 80, 84, 220–3
Huntington, Samuel, 'The Clash of Civilisations?' 72, 75

Il'f, Il'ia 239–43
Immortal Regiment 90–1
International Space Station (ISS) 87–92
internationalism 97
  socialist 39–45, 99, 101, 151, 157, 216, 247
Ireland 82, 219–23, 345–9
Irwin (art collective) 107–10
'Island Russia' 72–5
isolationism 74–6
Italy 147–52

Kant, Immanuel 254–5
Kazakhstan 131–2
Khatuntsev, Stanislav 72, 74
Khrushchev, Nikita 103, 104, 182, 193, 301
kinship, in dreambooks 62

knowledge, production of 21, 60–3
  academic 30
  vernacular 257–63, 347
Komar, Vitaly 103–7
Koolhaas, Rem 38, 123
kraeved(ka), *kraevedenie* (Russian regional studies) 257–63
Krupskaia, Nadezhda 41

laughter 3–5, 23
  ironic 317–19
Leicester 134
Lepeshinskiĭ School Commune 41
Limitrophe, Great 71–6
literature 17, 56, 66, 118, 142, 209, 219, 295–300, 321–5
Lomasko, Viktoria 332–9
low earth orbit (LEO) 87–92, 182
Luxemberg, Rosa 245–9

mail-order bride 287–92
Makarenko, Anton 41
Making Futures School, Berlin 153–8
maps 204
  in atlases 5–7
  children's 329–31, 336–9
  cognitive 37
  critical cartography 197–203
  digital humanities 55, 66
  dream-maps 60–2
  Greater Europe 79–85
  literary 323–4
  mental 31
  Republic of Letters 66–7
  Soviet countercultural 100
  Zwischeneuropa 197–203
May, Karl 188, 190, 193
mediator sanitar (health mediator) 273–8
Melamid, Alexander 103–7
migration 213, 215, 225, 254, 281–5, 288, 291, 344, 345–9
  forced 149
migration broker 281–5
Moretti, Franco 323–4
Morozov, V. 24n

Moscow 95–101, 122, 124–5, 232, 233
museums, regional 49–50, 257–63

nationalism 29, 32, 150, 220, 223, 247, 255, 278
  and folkore 47–8
  methodological 157
Native Americans 189, 193–4
New Education movement 41
Nigeria 109, 302
NSK State in Time (artwork) 107–10

orientalism, 208, 337
  demi-orientalism 165n
otherness 3–4, 10, 13, 15, 37, 69, 135, 155–6, 192, 241, 243, 259, 275–6, 278, 291
Ovid (Publius Ovidius Naso) 295–300
outer space, American 89, 91–2
  European 89
  Russian 88–92

Pangaea 180–4
pan-Slavism 201–2, 341
peripheries, peripherality 13, 33, 55, 67–9, 74–5, 107, 131–5, 162, 197–8, 223, 345–9
  peripheral encounters 213–17, 219–23, 345–8
  semi-periphery 8, 15, 16
  see also centre-core/periphery relations
Peripheristan 131–5
perspectivism 12–14
Petrov, Evgeniĭ 239–43
Pistrak, Moiseĭ 41
Poland 225–9, 245–9, 301–7
postsocialism 24n, 50, 115
post-Yugoslav space 59–64, 151–2, 213–17
precarity 214–15, 309–13
projectarians 309–13
Putin, Putinism, 15, 122–5
  anti-Putinism 268, 332

race, racism 10, 115, 129, 215–16, 273–8, 342–44
  racial stereotypes in Dreambooks, 63
raja 315–19
Red Adriatic 147–52
Republic of Letters 65–70
Roma 115, 61, 63, 217, 273–8
Romania 42–5, 47–51, 113–18, 233, 235, 295–7, 324
Rubchinskiĭ, Gosha 268–71
Russia 1–2, 13, 16, 21–2, 71–6, 87–92, 103, 121–5, 162, 175, 257–63, 265–71, 281–5, 330–9
Russian Americans 239–43, 287–92
Russian Orthodox Church 88–9
Russkiĭ mir ('Russian world') 1–2, 266–9

Šafářik, Pawel Josef, 'Slovanský zeměvid' (map) 198–203
  spelling 204n
Said, Edward, *Orientalism* (1978) 8, 208
Sanovnik, *see* Dreambook
Sarajevo 80, 315–19
School of Slavonic and East European Studies (SSEES), UCL 17–18
Second World 43, 109, 153–8, 270
Second World War, *see* World War II
semi-periphery, *see* peripheries
Serbia 214–17, 234
Seton-Watson, R.W., 'The New Europe' (map) 198–203
sex, sexuality 18, 255
  in Dreambooks 61–3
  trafficking 284–5, 343–4
  worker (Natasha) 341–4
Sharovarshchyna 161–5
Shenzhen 174–5
Siberia 74, 101, 257–8
Silicon Valley, 'Siliconisation' 54, 113–18
singularity, singularitarians 88, 91

Sinn Féin 219–22
Sirató, Károly Tamkó 137–44
Slavism, Slavs 56, 69, 148–50, 197–203, 334, 341
'social condenser' 158, 121–5
socialism, 24n
   actually existing 95–6, 100, 176
   building 157, 168–70, 232–6, 301–7
   independent 42
   in one country 99
   and technology 231–6
   world, global 151, 162
   zombie 117–18, 177
socialist realism 98, 167–9, 209, 233
Socialist World System 301–7
South-eastern Europe 29, 33
   see also Balkans
Soviet Union (USSR) 42, 88, 95–101, 167–70, 182–3, 193, 208, 239–43, 247, 261–3, 305, 333, 336–7
spacetime 90, 140–4, 225–9, 281
special economic zone (SEZ) 173–7
Spectral Aerosion (artwork) 82, 84
Spotti (chatbot) 104
Sputnik 88, 182
Südostforschung 33
Szombathy, Bálint 142–4

Third World 45, 109, 208
Thompson, Ewa 16
Tide, The (London) 121–5, 127–8
TINA (slogan) 341–4
Todorova, Maria, *Imagining the Balkans* (1997) 8
Tomis (Constanța) 295–300
translation 66, 118, 240, 322–6
transnational processes 29–31, 76, 135, 207–11, 215–17, 219–23, 240–1, 253, 271, 322, 325
TransState (artwork) 103–7
travellers/travellees 68–9

Trieste 147–52
Tsoĭ, Viktor 265–8, 271
Tsymburskiĭ, Vadim 71–6

Ukraine 1–2, 16, 21, 22–3, 129n, 132, 135n, 161–6, 246, 267, 329–30, 332, 334, 339
United Kingdom (UK), *see* Britain
United States of America (USA) 182–3, 187–8, 192–5, 215, 239–43
universalism 15, 19, 40, 42–5, 69–70, 74, 76, 118, 158, 170
urban planning 174–6
urbanisation 17, 114–16, 306
USSR, *see* Soviet Union

virtual spaces, digital 53–8
   print 65–70
visual culture 197–204
vlogs, as ethnography 287–92
Volosy (art collective) 95–7

Wasilewska, Wanda 246–9
Wegener, Alfred 180–2
West, the 10, 13, 20, 33, 35, 75, 101, 107, 117, 217, 252, 265, 271
   former 24n
whites, whiteness 13, 18, 63, 128, 193–4, 210, 213, 216–17, 258, 334, 343–4, 344n
wildness 162–5
Wild West 187–95
world literature 219, 321–6
World War II 90, 148, 168, 247

Yugoslavia 147–52, 189–94, 235
   post-Yugoslav space 59–64, 151–2, 213–17

Zaryadye Park, Moscow 121–2, 124–5, 129n
Zelens'kyĭ, Volodymyr 132
Zwischeneuropa 197–204